Between the eighth and the sixth centuries BC, the Phoenicians established the first trading system to encompass the entire length of the Mediterranean basin, from their homeland, in what is now Lebanon, to colonies in Cyprus, Tunisia, Sicily, Sardinia and southern Spain. The Phoenician state was able to maintain its independence, despite the territorial expansion of the Assyrians, in return for tribute provided by its western colonies. Archaeological research over the last two decades has changed our understanding of these colonies and their relationships to local Iron Age communities.

Dr Aubet's original synthesis of archaeological and historical data is the first modern study of the Phoenicians to be published in English. It will be of interest not only to Mediterranean historians and archaeologists, but also to scholars studying the trade systems of state and non-state societies.

THE PHOENICIANS AND THE WEST

THE PHOENICIANS
AND THE WEST
Politics, colonies and trade

MARIA EUGENIA AUBET

Universidad Autónoma of Barcelona

TRANSLATED FROM THE SPANISH BY
MARY TURTON

CAMBRIDGE
UNIVERSITY PRESS

Published by the Press Syndicate of the University of Cambridge
The Pitt Building, Trumpington Street, Cambridge CB2 1RP
40 West 20th Street, New York, NY 10011-4211, USA
10 Stamford Road, Oakleigh, Melbourne 3166, Australia

Originally published in Spanish as *Tiro y las Colonias Fenicias de Occidente*
by Ediciones Bellaterra 1987
and © 1987 Ediciones Bellaterra, S.A.
First published in English by Cambridge University Press 1993 as
The Phoenicians and the west: politics, colonies and trade
English translation © Cambridge University Press 1993
Reprinted 1994
First paperback edition published 1996

Printed and bound in Great Britain by
Woolnough Bookbinding Ltd, Irthlingborough, Northamptonshire

A catalogue record for this book is available from the British Library

Library of Congress cataloguing in publication data
Aubet, Maria Eugenia.
[Tiro y las colonias fenicias de Occidente. English]
The Phoenicians and the West: politics, colonies and trade /
Maria Eugenia Aubet: translated from the Spanish by Mary Turton.
p.   cm.
Translation of: Tiro y las colonias fenicias de Occidente.
Includes bibliographical references and index.
ISBN 0 521 41141 6
1. Phoenicians. 2. Western Mediterranean – History. 3. Tyre
(Lebanon) – History. I. Title.
DS 81.A8513 1993
909'.0974926 – dc20   92–8161   CIP

ISBN 0 521 41141 6 hardback
ISBN 0 521 56598 7 paperback

To the memory of my parents

Contents

Figures

Tables

Acknowledgements

This book would not have been possible without the generous collaboration of many people. In the first place, I should like to acknowledge the enthusiastic assistance and the patience and invaluable collaboration of María José Aubet, Josep Fontana and Vicente Lull, to whom, through interminable discussions, I am indebted for criticism, advice and suggestions that have been of inestimable value in my investigations.

I also owe a debt of gratitude to Ingrid Gamer-Wallert, Gustav Gamer, Milagros Gil-Mascarell, Juan Maluquer de Motest, Sabatino Moscati and Manuel Pellicer for their stimulation and the interest they have always shown in this work.

To Manuela Barthelemy, Anna Maria Bisit, Concha Blasco, Eric Gubel, Hans Georg Niemeyer, Rafael Puertas, Wolfgang Röllig, Diego Ruiz Mata, Javier Teixidor and Hermanfrid Schubart I owe information and material almost invariably given with no thought of self-interest and which has considerably facilitated the work of investigation.

Lastly, I should also like to express my gratitude to the German Archaeological Institute in Berlin for having given me the opportunity to work in the specialist libraries in Germany during the year 1986.

My thanks to all of them.

For permission to reproduce published material the publishers wish to thank the following:
Paul Geuthner, Paris, figures 5, 24 and 25; Dr Nina Jidejian, figure 6; Musée du Louvre, figure 9; De Boccard, figure 11; Thames and Hudson, figure 12; The British Museum, figures 17 and 21; Dr Annette Rathje, figure 19; 'L'Ermo' di Bretschneider, figure 20 (from F. Poulsen, *Der Orient und die frühgriechische Kunst*, 1968); Professor Dr Wilhelm Schüle, figure 23; Dr D. Joaquin Ruiz de Arbulo, figures 26, 27, 28, 29, 30; Professor Vincenzo Tusa, figure 31 (from the Museo Nazional di Palermo); Dr Ingrid Gamer-Wallert, figure 32; Archaeologia

Fenicio-punica-Università degli Studi di Cagliari, figure 33; Les Publications d'Art et d'Archéologie, figures 36 and 37; Editions J. Picard, figure 38; Professor Piero Bartoloni, figure 42; Professor José Luis Escacena Carrasco, figures 46, 47, 48; Deutsches Archäologisches Institut, Madrid, figures 49, 61, 63, 64, 65, 66, 68; Dr D. Jesús Fernández Jurado, figure 51; Professor Dr Juan Pedro Garrido, figure 52; Museo Arqueologico de Sevilla, figure 55; Professor Dr H. G. Niemeyer, figure 62; Dr D. Manuel Pellicer, figure 67; Direction Générale des Antiquités, Lebanon, figure 69 (from Saidah, 'Fouilles à Khaldé', *Bulletin Musée de Beyrouth*, vol. xx, 1967); Dr Patricia Bikai, figure 70.

The translation of this work has been made possible by a grant from the Dirección General del Libro y Bibliotecas del Ministerio de Cultura de España.

Introduction

Nowadays anyone intending to embark for the first time on a study of the Phoenician colonization of the Iberian Peninsula or keen to know the state of archaeological investigation in that field will come up against three types of difficulty: one of a technical nature, another of a methodological nature and a third concerning the question of subjectivity in reading the historical testimony.

Among the difficulties of a technical or instrumental nature, it is worth pointing out the lack of up-to-date reports which provide a critical assessment of the archaeological data obtained in the last fifteen years in the western Mediterranean. The vast literature that exists on the question is scattered in a multitude of articles in specialist journals or in the proceedings of meetings not always accessible to students of the ancient world. Lastly, there is the relative confusion in the way the terminology in use is handled: the words 'Phoenician', 'Punic' and 'orientalizing' are bandied about indiscriminately without establishing clear differences between them, or at times contradictory or incoherent terms are used, such as 'Iberico-orientalizing', 'Phoenicio–Punic' or 'Punico–archaic'. Obviously this does not help to make things easy for the reader, since behind this terminological confusion lie much more complex methodological and conceptual problems.

As regards the difficulties of a methodological nature, it must be emphasized that a reconstruction of the history of Phoenician trade in the West or in the Mediterranean in general must of necessity be based on two types of documentary sources or instruments of analysis, which very often disagree with each other: the written testimonies handed down to us by the classical historians, and the archaeological record proper. The divergences between these two categories of data raise a host of difficulties for investigators and these are not always easy to resolve. Thus, for example, the discrepancies that occur between the historical dates given by the classical historians and the chronology established by archaeological investigation have fuelled, among other things, the prolongation of a controversy already endemic among the orientalists, which began in the last century, concerning the dating of the first Phoenician foundations in the far west.

The classical sources are of vital importance in an analysis of the Phoenician question if they are handled prudently. It must not be forgotten that certain legendary aspects concerning Phoenician colonization in the far West were picked up by Greek and Roman historians many centuries after the events took place and the only contemporary written sources for the Phoenician diaspora – the Assyrian annals and the biblical texts – make no mention of anything that happened further away than the island of Cyprus. Even so, the classical texts contain valuable information concerning the Phoenician expansion westwards. It is on how these sources are managed that the historical reconstruction of the past depends to a large extent. Archaeology, on the other hand, provides us with information that is basically empirical, a kind of general framework that can be used as a starting point for working hypotheses. Nowadays any explanation of the Phoenician colonial phenomenon is likely to be analysed on the basis of new theories and from new methodological perspectives. Given that hypotheses cannot advance without some previously determined theoretical framework, we do not claim in this book simply to revise or update the subject of the Phoenicians in the west, but rather to raise a series of questions about the whole matter and, as far as possible, to give pertinent answers as well.

The third difficulty presented by a study of the Phoenicians in the far western Mediterranean lies in the inevitable subjectivism, not to say ideology, of those interpreting the data. The role played by the Phoenicians in the west has rarely been judged objectively. At times, they have been considered to have had very little effect on the internal cultural dynamics of the native Spanish communities, and their socio-cultural importance in the process of development that was to culminate in the realm of Tartessos in western Andalusia has been played down. Logically, this leads to an over-valuation of the part played by indigenous Iberians or of the specific influence of the later Greek colonization in nurturing the economic power of Tartessos.

At other times the Phoenicians are ascribed more importance than they had in reality and they are portrayed as the only protagonists in the cultural process which gave rise to the Tartessian cultural complex. This view undervalues the indigenous peoples in favour of the idea that the Phoenicians arrived in a territory inhabited by a few passive, receptive communities – the Tartessians – who were unaware of the immense economic potential of their territory. Thanks to the 'eastern miracle', it is thought, Tartessos set about exploiting its abundant mineral and agricultural resources.

On the other hand, the treatment meted out to the Phoenicians in the classical texts, and even today on the part of some historians, does not exactly give us an impartial and objective picture of their historical and cultural standing. In a way it is understandable that, for political reasons, the classical authors branded the Phoenicians as pirates, as cunning navigators, and held them responsible for introducing greed and luxury into Greece. It is equally acceptable that the Romans should show outright hostility towards them, speaking of 'perfidious Punica', its proverbial cunning, its disloyalty and low moral sense. What is less understandable is the reason why even today some historians insist on the poor quality of Phoenician art, its lack of originality, and that, unlike the Greeks, the Phoenicians were more interested in making profits than in producing poets, artists and historians.

However, the Phoenicians' principal legacy to the history of the west – the alphabet – is now unanimously acknowledged. The signs and names used by the Phoenicians to designate the letters of the alphabet – alef, bet, and so on – have been preserved down to our own day, thanks to the mediation of the Greek world.

The Phoenicians did not just give us a system of writing, they incorporated the Iberian Peninsula into the Mediterranean trade routes of the period, which for more than two hundred years tied many Mediterranean territories into an organizational structure and to certain institutions that were basically oriental. For a long time, the Phoenicians were the principal intermediaries between east and west and this role of mediators smoothed out to a considerable extent the socio-economic imbalances which existed previously between those states said to be 'civilized' and the 'barbarian' peoples. At the time of the Phoenician arrival in the Iberian Peninsula at the turn of the eighth century BC or a little earlier, the indigenous Andalusian communities were deeply rooted in prehistoric economic structures. When the Phoenicians left, at the beginning of the sixth century BC, the Peninsula was an integral part of that 'history' that bore their mark, and the indigenous cultural process had, by acculturation, acquired other ways of attaining more complex, in other words more 'modern', socio-economic levels.

This book will attempt to bring the reader and the student interested in the Phoenician question a synthesis of the present state of investigations and an outline of new hypotheses about the Phoenicians and their colonial enterprise in the west.

The study covers the colonial period proper, that is to say the ancient horizon of the eighth to sixth centuries BC. Consequently, we shall not deal here with the so-called Punic horizon of the sixth to third centuries BC, a period in which many of the old colonial enclaves came into the political orbit of Carthage. In reality, the Punic period corresponds to a quite distinct socio-political context, in which the geo-political circumstances of the western Mediterranean experienced considerable transformations which would demand a separate study of their own.

To enclose or define the function and category of the Phoenician settlements in the west and Andalusia within a particular macro-economic and historical model requires, logically, an analysis of those political and economic factors in Phoenicia in general, and in Tyre in particular, which would have made this diaspora to the west possible or would have fostered it. In our judgement, only a critical examination of the economic, political and social situation of the city state of Tyre – mainly responsible for the colonization – and of its mercantile policy could help us to gauge the category and economic function of the centres in the west. That is why we give priority to a study of the political and economic situation in the Phoenician cities before, during and after the period of expansion through the Mediterranean.

The question of who the Phoenicians were seems to us a good starting point if we are to place the circumstances that prompted this people to organize a commercial enterprise on such a scale at the beginning of the first millennium BC in their historical and geo-graphical context. Consequently, the first chapters are devoted to analysing the identity of the Phoenician people, starting from ethnic, linguistic, geographical and historical factors. These are followed by a section devoted to the way in which the Phoenicians organized their trade and navigation during the period of colonization, so as to be able finally to tackle the study and interpretation of the colonial enclaves in the central Mediterranean and the Iberian Peninsula, equipped with the elements appropriate to forming a judgement.

Who were the Phoenicians?

THE NAME: CANA'ANI, PHOÍNIKES, POENI

A study of the terminology used to define a community or population is a question that goes far beyond a simple exercise in historical erudition when, as in the case of the Phoenicians, not all the ethnic, linguistic, geographic or cultural implications appear with sufficient clarity. The theme of the name by which antiquity knew the Phoenicians provides a starting point of undeniable importance for determining the features that identify this eastern population.

The name by which history knows the Phoenicians is a word of Greek origin, which appears for the first time in the period of Homer and Hesiod – in the ninth to seventh centuries BC – and has no known equivalent in the eastern languages.

The original name *phoinix* and its derivatives, the feminine *phoinissa* and the plural *phoínikes*, are a Greek invention and nobody but the Greeks used the term to designate this eastern people and certain cultural features connected with them. The word used to designate the country of the phoínikes, *Phoiníke*, comes rather later, and refers to the coastal territory between Aradus (Arvad) and Mount Carmel with boundaries corresponding roughly to those of modern Lebanon (Fig. 1).

The root of *phoinix* is neither Phoenician nor Semitic, and at present the linguistic problem of the origin of the Greek word has not been solved. What does seem to have been verified is that the Phoenicians never called themselves 'Phoenicians'. Already in antiquity, the Greeks were trying to find an explanation for the origin of the name, connecting its ethnic meaning with other semantic equivalents of the same word. Among other meanings of *phoinix* we would single out that of 'red', a colour that was probably an allusion to the purple textile industry, for which the Phoenician cities were famous in Homer's time.

According to this etymology, 'Phoenician' would be derived from the Greek *phoinós*, a word of Indo-European root indicating 'red',

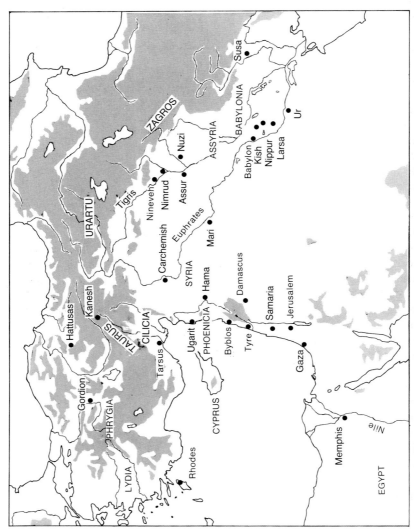

Fig. 1 Near East

'blood', 'to stain with blood', 'death' or 'crime'. Greek lexicographers linked the origin of the word with the manufacture of purple textiles and also with the dark complexion of the Asian peoples, and the majority of modern authors keep to that explanation. According to them, when maritime contacts between Greece and the Levant were renewed in the time of Homer, the Greeks would have begun to call the inhabitants of a country which was held to be the most wealthy centre for the manufacture of purple cloth in the whole Mediterranean 'reds' or phoínikes. So Phoenicia would mean 'the country of purple cloth'.

Another theory concerning the origin of the word 'Phoenician' postulates a connection between that word and the name of the eponymous hero *Phoinix*, to whom legend attributes the invention of the purple dye that was to colour wools and fabrics. This legend, picked up by Pliny, tells of the chance discovery near Tyre, by a shepherd, that his dog, by biting a mollusc – no doubt the murex – had stained himself red; the dog was brought before the king of Tyre, Phoinix, who is thought to have adopted the colour purple as a sign of royalty and emblem of the monarchy. After that, purple could only be worn by kings. That this legend is Phoenician in origin is shown by the fact that some coins from Tyre carry the image of the famous animal.

In other myths, Phoinix appears as the father of the Phoenicians and eponymous with the territory, the 'Phoiniké'. He is also frequently considered to be one of the brothers of Europa; during his travels in search of his ravished sister, he is believed to have settled in a country to which he gave his name, as did her other brothers: Cadmos in Thebes, Syros in Syria and Cilix in Cilicia.

As can be inferred from all these myths and legends, Phoinix, the eponymous hero of the country, is none other than the king of Tyre, who combines in his person all the characteristic attributes that give authentic identity to the Phoenician people: the purple, the alphabet (the *phoinikeia grammata*, also invented by the hero) and the date palm, another emblem of Tyre's coinage, called *phoinix* in Greek.

In Homer, Hesiod and Herodotus, the word *phoinix* also designates a musical instrument similar to the lyre (also invented by Phoinix), a place name frequently found in the eastern Mediterranean and, lastly, a fabulous bird with red wings, the *ave fenix*, of unknown origin. All these meanings of *phoinix* are said to be derived from their country of origin, Phoenicia, which in turn had taken this name from the Greek word used for the colour dark red. Besides, it is surprising that the name given to an industry or its colour should lie at the origin of the name of the territory and its inhabitants. Why should the opposite not be true?

That the origin of the term is confused can be seen in those same Homeric texts, where the Phoenicians are also called *sidones* or *sidonioi*, that is, Sidonians. Nor can the use by Homer of the term Sidonian as a synonym for *phoinikes* be explained since, in the days of the poet, the most powerful Phoenician city was not Sidon but Tyre. In short, all this indicates the difficulties the Greek world found in drawing up an ethno-political definition of the Phoenicians: a people without a state, without territory and without political unity.

Other theories deny any connection between 'Phoenicians' and phoinós ('red'), and claim to derive the Greek word from the Mycenaean *po-ni-ki-jo* or *po-ni-ki*. This word, which is documented in Linear B texts from Knossos and Pylos, refers to an aromatic herb or condiment of eastern origin – perhaps Pliny's 'herba phoenica' – and also to elements used in decoration, presumably red in colour, and seems to have been coined at the end of the second millennium BC, a period when contacts between the Aegean and the Levant were most intense and when the legends of Cadmos, Phoinix and the rape of Europa are likely to have emerged. However, we must point out that none of the Mycenaean texts mentioned seems to refer explicitly to a country, its inhabitants or the colour purple.

The origin of the Greek *phoinix* has been sought with equal lack of success in Ugaritic or Hebrew words like *puwwa* or *pwt* – 'dye', 'substance' – and even in the Egyptian *fnḫw* whose similarities to the Greek 'Phoenician' are purely acoustic. The word *fenkhu*, documented from the ancient Egyptian empire, has no connection whatsoever with Phoenicia, which the Egyptians in fact called 'Retenu' or 'Ḥa-rw'.

From all that has been said we deduce that the only clear evidence we have is the Greek name 'phoinikes' with which, from the times of Homer, the Greeks designated the peoples of the Levant and in particular the eastern merchants who were beginning to frequent the waters of the Aegean. The origin of the Greek term is still unclear today.

We know that the Phoenicians called themselves *can'ani*, 'Canaanites', and their land Canaan. This term is of eastern semitic origin and very probably indigenous to the country. The etymology of the word, starting with *kn'n*, however, is just as obscure and as controversial as the Greek Phoinix, if not more so.

In Genesis (9:18, 10:15) Canaan is the son of Ham and the father of Sidon, that is of the Phoenicians, like the eponymous hero Phoinix.

The biblical texts use the name *kena'anîm* or *kananaioi* to designate the inhabitants of the great coastal plain to the north of Israel, which doubtless implies a relatively uniform geographical, linguistic and cultural reality. On occasions, however, the term Canaan refers to a more restricted territory, confined to the area around Tyre (Isaiah 23:11). The Phoenicians were also frequently called by the name of their city of origin – Tyrians, Sidonians, Giblites – or simply, in biblical and Assyrian documents, *sîdonim* or *sidonioi*, as in Homer. The king of Tyre is also called 'king of the Sidonians', a very significant fact which doubtless reflects a specific geo-political situation, particularly during the tenth to eighth centuries BC, which we shall examine in the next chapter.

In Hebrew, *cana'ani* or *kina'nu* also means 'merchant', so Canaan would have been synonymous with 'land of merchants'. Yet again, a profession that made the Phoenicians so renowned would have lent its name to a territory. And so the hypothesis that the name of the territory ended by designating one of the most characteristic activities of its inhabitants, that of trade, would again be the most convincing.

Some linguists claim that the Greek *phoinix* is no more than a simple translation of the Akkadian *kinaḫḫu*, a word which appears in texts of the fifteenth to fourteenth centuries BC found at Nuzi. In these documents the term alludes indiscriminately to the country of Canaan and to its most important export, red-coloured wool or *kinaḫḫu*. According to that, the Hurrian texts of Nuzi seem to show not only the semantic parallel existing between 'canaanite' and 'purple', but also a direct association between the name of the country and the colour purplish red, both in Akkadian and in Greek. However this does not solve the problem of who gave the name to whom, whether the territory to the colour or vice versa. All the indications point to the first possibility.

Indeed, ever since the middle of the fifteenth century BC, in other Levantine and Egyptian texts and inscriptions, we meet the name of the country of Canaan without it being in any way associated with the colour red. Thus it is mentioned as *kn'ny* in texts from Ugarit, as *ki-in-a-nim* in texts from Alalakh, and as *kn'nw* in inscriptions of Amenophis II. So too, in texts from Mari, the Canaanites are mentioned with a strictly ethnic meaning, and in the famous letters of El Amarna, dated to the first half of the fourteenth century BC, the inhabitants of the land of Canaan are called the *kinaḫḫi* or *kinaḫna*. Lastly, with corroboration from the recent finds at Ebla in Syria, the name of Canaan, signifying a place – *ca-na-na-um, ca-na-na* – would probably have arisen in the middle of the third millennium BC.

All this etymological discussion brings us back to where we started. The Nuzi texts demonstrate that since the middle of the second millennium BC at least, the name 'Canaan' has a dual meaning: ethnic and toponymic on the one hand and for the colour red or purple on the other. So an obvious parallel with the etymology of the Greek 'phoinix' is established. In both cases, the purple cloth and dyeing industries would have taken the name of the country of origin. The Greeks of the Mycenean period or the beginning of the first millennium BC could have come across a place name designating the colour red and with an equivalent in their idiom, phoinix, and all they would have done is translate it.

Philo of Byblos and Hecateus of Miletus in their day reached the same conclusions. In the sixth century BC Hecateus remembered that *Phoiníke* had previously been called *Chna* and that it had been the transcription into Greek of the Semitic 'Chanaan'. Philo of Byblos argues on the same lines: he mentions a historical personage called *Chnas* or *Chanaan* who was later rebaptized with the name of 'Phoinix' and called 'father of the Phoenicians'. Consequently, the eponymous hero Phoinix would be the transcription into Greek of another eponymous Semitic hero, Canaan, the son of Ham. It is obvious, therefore, that the correct and original name of the Phoenicians was Canaanites. This is what their Asian and Egyptian neighbours called them and this is what they called themselves. In the Roman and late Roman periods, they were still known by the name of 'Canaanites'. The evangelist Matthew (15:21–22) called the Phoenician woman whose daughter was cured by Jesus of demonic possession a Canaanite; St Augustine (Ep. ad Rom. 13) mentions that in his day (fifth century AD) the North African citizens (the Carthaginians) still called themselves *chanani*.

However, we know the Phoenicians by the name the Greeks gave them and not by their original name. The Hellenic term has been definitely consecrated by usage which obliges us to make a few observations of a conceptual and chronological nature.

In modern terminology, it is customary to use the name 'Canaanite' to designate those peoples who spoke North West Semitic and lived in the territory of Syria–Palestine at least from the beginning of the second millennium BC. These same populations, who have a common historical, geographic, cultural and linguistic base are known as 'Phoenicians' from the year 1200 BC onwards, thus establishing an artificial barrier between the Bronze Age and the Iron Age and conferring different chronological implications on the two terms. According to this, the 'Phoenician' succeeded the 'Canaanite' from 1200 BC until the conquest by Alexander the Great in 333 BC. The year 1200 BC was fixed by historians as a frontier separating the Canaanite Bronze Age from the Phoenician Iron Age on the basis of the geo-political changes that took place in the zone following the political convulsions which shook the eastern Mediterranean at the end of the Bronze Age. In the next sections, we shall see that these events in no way justify a change of nomenclature in the history of the Canaanite territory.

Equally dubious is the terminology used to define the Phoenicians in the west. The contradictions arise from the name used by classical historians who use the words 'Phoenician', 'Punic' or 'Carthaginian' indiscriminately to refer to the western Phoenicians who were fighting against Rome. If the word 'Carthaginian' raises no major difficulties because it is synonymous with 'inhabitant of Carthage', analogous with Gaditanian or Tyrian, the word 'Punic' requires some clarification.

The Roman authors use the terms *poenus* and *phoenix*, which are merely a transcription into Latin of the Greek *phoinix*, changing the first consonant, to designate the Phoenicians in general and the Carthaginians in particular, without making any clearer distinction. *Poenus*, with its adjectives *punicus* and *poenicus*, generally alludes to the North African Phoenicians, because the terms 'Punic' and 'Carthaginian' tend to be used interchangeably.

It is modern historians who have magnified the distance between 'Punic' and 'Phoenician' with implications of a geographic and chronological nature very similar to those existing between the terms 'Phoenician' and 'Canaanite' in the east. In modern writings, the Phoenicians of the east are called 'Phoenician' and the Phoenicians of the west, living in the sphere of influence of Carthage, are called 'Punic'. This presents us with a new terminological and conceptual problem: what to call the Phoenicians of the west before the time when Carthage assumed political and military hegemony there. This event took place in the sixth century BC, and so the ancient period of the eighth to sixth centuries BC remains to be defined, the strictly colonial and commercial period, that is to say, precisely the one we are dealing with in this book and which embraces several generations of Phoenician colonists arriving from the east who, in a very short while, settled and prospered in the west.

Faced with the relatively late meaning attributed to the term 'Punic', covering basically the sixth to second centuries, the word 'Phoenician' or 'western Phoenician' is situated earlier in order to designate those groups and settlements established in the west before the Carthaginian empire. Exceptionally, a few historians prefer to call only the first generation of colonists arriving in the west 'Phoenician' and all the rest 'Punic', or to use the term 'paleo-Punic' to define this ancient colonial horizon.

While admitting the incongruity of fixing chronological limits to terms which, originally, were not supposed to be exclusive, we shall use the current nomenclature in this book since all these words nowadays have clearly defined cultural connotations. So we shall call the Phoenicians of the second millennium BC 'Canaanites', the Phoenicians of the first millennium BC in the east and of the eighth to sixth centuries in the west 'Phoenicians' and the western Phoenicians from the middle of the sixth century BC onwards 'Punic'.

THE TERRITORY

The territory called Phoiníke by the Greeks extends along the coastal fringe of the eastern Mediterranean and its geographical boundaries coincide roughly with those of modern Lebanon. This region which we call Phoenicia, situated between the mountains of Lebanon and the Mediterranean sea, is all that had been preserved of ancient Canaan, once the socio-political crisis that rocked the eastern Mediterranean between the years 1200 and 1100 BC had been surmounted (Fig. 2).

During the Bronze Age, the land of Canaan had included all the coastal territory of Syria–Palestine lying between the Mons Cassius in the north – near the mouth of the Orontes in Syria – and the Egyptian frontier in the south. Around the year 1200, the date that is used as a reference point to mark the transition to the Iron Age in Syria–Palestine, three decisive historical events were to prompt a general restructuring of the Canaanite territory: the Israelite conquest of the mountainous region to the south of Canaan (Modern Palestine), the military occupation of the coast of Palestine on the part of the Philistines, and the establishment of the Aramaeans in the northern and northeastern territory of Canaan – the modern Syria. These incursions, which we shall study more thoroughly in the next chapter, would considerably reduce the extent of the country of Canaan which, in a very short time, lost three quarters of its territory, almost all its 'hinterland' and more than half its coast.

At the beginning of the Iron Age, Phoenicia had shrunk from a distance of 500 km to little more than 200 km from north to south (Fig. 3). The reduction of its territory to a narrow coastal fringe, the eastern confines of which were formed by the final spurs of the

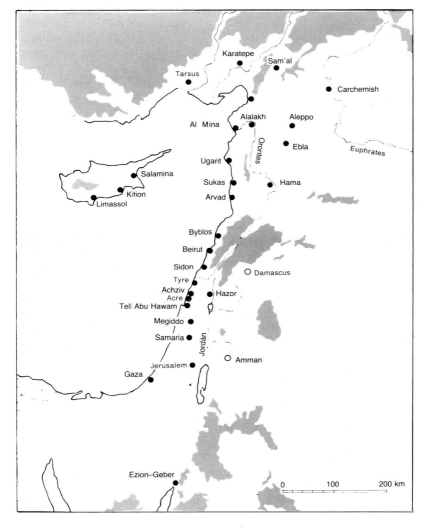

Fig. 2   Eastern Mediterranean

mountains of Lebanon, was largely instrumental in deciding on the maritime adventure of its inhabitants. There can be no doubt that the reorganization of the Canaanite territory brought inevitable political, economic and demographic repercussions, as will be seen later.

The northern limits of the country remained firmly established to

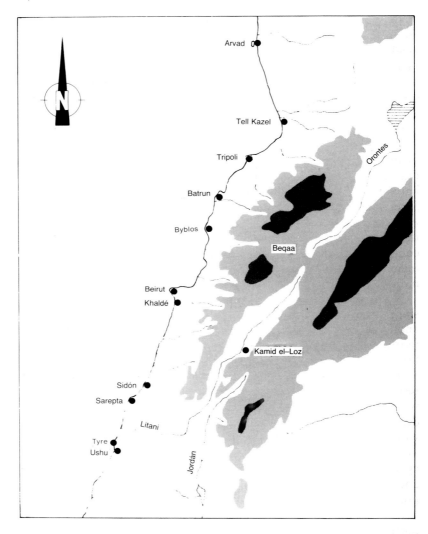

Fig. 3   Phoenicia

the north of the isle of Arvad, the ancient Aradus, near the mouth of
the Nahr-el-Kebir. The southern frontier remained at the level of Akko
(Acre) and the promontory of Mount Carmel, although occasionally,
when the kingdom of Tyre extended its limits, this southern frontier
moved a considerable distance southwards.

The eastern confines of Phoenicia were formed by the Lebanese mountains which run parallel with the coast and at some point reach a height of more than 3000 metres. The mountains of Lebanon, with their peaks and dense forests of cedars, would protect Phoenicia from incursions from the east while at the same time shaping a narrow territory crossed by little rivers and torrents which flowed through small transverse valleys, whose average length from east to west did not exceed 30 km.

The principal Phoenician cities were situated on the coast, on small mainland promontories dominating a bay or on small natural inlets that gave ships protection from winds and storms and served as harbours. This is the case, for example, at Byblos, Berytos (Beirut), Sarepta, Sidon, Akko and Akhziv. Two cities, however, Tyre and Arvad, were located on islands close to the coast, which transformed them into genuinely impregnable fortresses so long as they kept their control of the sea. Nowadays, Tyre forms a peninsula joined on to the mainland, due to the sediments that have accumulated around the mole built by Alexander the Great during his blockade of the city.

Not only could Phoenicia count on a coastal territory ideal for shipping but it also enjoyed a mild climate, not unlike that of today, and a countryside rich in valleys, watercourses and an exceedingly fertile agricultural soil. Even so, the land suitable for cultivation was nowhere near adequate to support an extremely dense population.

In addition to its agricultural potential, Phoenicia had other resources at its disposal, the most important of all being the vast forest wealth of the interior. If the landscape nowadays is considerably degraded due to the intense exploitation of the timber in its forests, with the consequent deforestation of huge areas just behind the coast, in Phoenician times the interior was covered with cedars, pines and cypresses which were exploited and contributed to the wealth, fame and prosperity of cities which, like Byblos, furnished Egypt and Meso-potamia with cedarwood for building.

Moreover, the Phoenician cities could count on plenty of game in the neighbouring mountains – bears, panthers and wolves, for example – and on important iron and lignite mines, which no doubt contributed to the development of their famous shipyards.

The Phoenicians obtained abundant material from the sea, in par-ticular the murex, a mollusc which they used to develop profitable dyeing and purple cloth industries. The salting of fish was another of the industries that benefited the port cities.

In short, we can state that, reduced to a narrow coastal territory, the

Phoenicians had no alternative but to operate within the limits of a mountainous hinterland, rich in wood and iron, suitable for the development of shipbuilding enterprises, a coast with enormous possibilities for creating fishing industries, and arable land which, in some areas, was unable to supply the demands of cities that, at times, sheltered huge concentrations of humanity.

On the other hand, the geography of the coastal plain made up of compartmentalized regions separated from each other by river valleys and mountain spurs formed a kind of internal patchwork which favoured the development of independent political units organized into city states. All this, combined with the growing competition between the main Phoenician ports, was a constant obstacle to the process of political unification and the building of a 'Phoenician nation', to which the Phoenicians never aspired, despite the fact that, for a long time, Tyre imposed its hegemony on a large part of the southern coast of Phoenicia. In spite of this, the Phoenician cities never managed to form themselves into a unified state, not even in circumstances of grave danger and pressure from the Assyrian empire.

Phoenicia, then, was a land squeezed between the mountains and the sea, with a great density of population from the tenth century BC onwards and with the Mediterranean as the only possible route for natural expansion. The marked maritime leanings of its cities and their consequent control of the sea gave them naval supremacy and, at the same time, guaranteed their political independence in the face of powerful neighbours and the independence of the main seaports from each other. In short, its maritime position was the key to the international politics of the period and to the interests of its neighbours in the interior. Proof of this is the fact that control of the Phoenician ports and their seaborne trade was at the origin of most of the power struggles, first with Egypt, and later with Assyria. Control of the Phoenician cities and their trade gave Egypt supremacy over Asia, and Assyria over the Near East in general.

THE HISTORICAL ANTECEDENTS: THE BRONZE AGE IN CANAAN

From the beginning of the third millennium BC the region of Syria–Palestine gravitated around great cities like Byblos, Tyre and Megiddo, which maintained intensive political and commercial relations with Mesopotamia and Egypt. Up until 2500 BC, the texts from Byblos call this territory *Ga-na-ne* (Canaan) or *La-ba-na-an* (Lebanon).

Table 1. *Phoenician chronologies*

	Amiran 1969		Baramki 1961	Bikai 1978
3100		I		
2980		II		
2650	Early Bronze		Early Bronze	Early Bronze
		III		
		IV		
2300				
2200		I		
1950				Middle Bronze
1900		II		
1730	Middle Bronze			
1600			Middle Bronze	
1550		III		
		I		
1400				
1300	Late Bronze	II A	Late Bronze	Late Bronze
		II B		
1200				
1150		I		
1050				
1000		II A	Early Iron	Early Iron
900	Iron			
800		II B		Middle Iron I
725			Middle Iron	
600		II C		Middle Iron II
550				
				Late Iron
			Late Iron	
330				
64			Hellenistic	Hellenistic

During the Canaanite *Early Bronze Age* (3100–2300 BC) (Table 1), the most dynamic city, developing the greatest activity in the field of international relations, was undoubtedly Biblos, or Byblos, as the Greeks called this trading port, the modern Jebeil, whose name was originally Gubla, Gubal or Gebal. As the principal Mediterranean port of the third millennium BC, Byblos was an integral part of the international political scene, thanks to its close ties with the pharaohs of Egypt, its principal customers, whom it supplied with large quantities of cedar wood for building. Some Egyptian inscriptions from around 2600 BC mention the ships of Byblos transporting wood and oil and also the acquisition of boats from Byblos by the Egyptian authorities. This is the most brilliant period of Byblos' trade and of its powerful shipbuilding industry.

For its part, Egypt's interest in Byblos takes the form of cultural and religious influence over the Canaanite city and the presence of governors and commercial agents sent by the pharaoh. In reality, Byblos would be an Egyptian colony during a large part of the Ancient Empire and Canaan a vassal of the Egyptian sovereigns.

Recent archaeological discoveries at Ebla show that between 2500 and 2300 BC the Phoenician cities became the principal intermediaries in trade between the great Syrian states and the Nile Valley. In the archives at Ebla, various Canaanite cities are mentioned, outstanding amongst them *a-ra-wa-ad* (Arvad), *sa-ra-pa-at* (Sarepta), *ak-zi-u* (Akhziv), *ba-u-ra-at-tu* (Beirut), *za-a-ru* (Tyre) and *si-du-na-a* (Sidon), although it is Gub-lu, Gubli or Gubla that is always mentioned as the chief commercial centre and described as the capital of a powerful kingdom. In exchange for products from Ebla – metal, fabrics, perfumes, wine, oil and ewes – Byblos exported linen and, in particular, precious metals – gold and silver – to the interior.

So, in the Early Bronze Age, some of the characteristic features that would define the later Phoenician world were taking shape: the important Egyptian or Egyptianizing component in its artistic, craft and religious manifestations; the role of intermediary between the Asian states of the interior and the Mediterranean and, lastly, the commercial and industrial vocation of its coastal cities.

The growing power of the monarchs of Byblos is made plain by their building activities, the most outstanding of all the monumental constructions being the great temple dedicated to Baalat-Gebal, 'the Lady of Byblos', the chief tutelary deity of the city. Built in about 2800 BC, the numerous inscriptions and Egyptian offerings found inside the temple tell us of Egypt's interest in maintaining friendly political relations with the royal house of Byblos.

Another city that is mentioned repeatedly in the diplomatic documents of the period is Tyre, even though this centre did not equal the prestige of its northern neighbour during the third millennium. The name Tyre is also a Greek transcription of the original name, Şor, mentioned in the texts of Ebla. A legend picked up by the Greek historian Herodotus places the origins of Tyre around the year 2750 BC. Herodotus tells us that when he visited Tyre in the fifth century BC, he heard the priests in the temple of Melqart say that the sanctuary had been built when the city was founded, about 2300 years previously (Herod. 2:44). This legend, that the priests of the temple may have learned from the annals of the city, had not been taken seriously by any modern historian. However, the excavations carried out in 1973–1974 made it clear that the first human occupation of the island does indeed date from the middle of the third millennium, the time when monumental buildings, possibly temples, were being erected in Tyre. The founding of Tyre is thus 'very ancient' in the words of Isaiah (23:7) or 'older than Sidon' (Strabo 16:2, 22).

At the end of the Early Bronze Age, Tyre, like Byblos, shows signs of having been abandoned or destroyed. Indeed, the period between 2300 and 1900 BC is characterized by a break in the seaborne traffic to Egypt as a consequence of the invasion of Syria–Palestine by the Amurru or Amorites, nomadic Semitic groups who, after burning and sacking the main Canaanite cities, entrenched themselves in the internal centres of the country, Aleppo and Mari. Once this crisis was over, Byblos appears once more as a prosperous city whose interests again coincide with those of Egypt.

For a good part of the Canaanite *Middle Bronze Age* (1900–1550 BC), Egypt again exercised sovereignty over the chief cities of Canaan: Byblos, Ugarit and Megiddo. The Egyptian texts now speak of an independent monarchy in Tyre, and Byblos is mentioned as a bridgehead of Egyptian domination over the Levant. The famous Egyptian-inspired Temple of the Obelisks at Byblos and the royal tombs – great hypogean or subterranean tombs hewn out of the rock, where the monarchs of Byblos are accompanied by splendid gold and alabaster vessels – date from this period. As can be inferred from certain Mesopotamian texts and from archaeological finds, Byblos and Ugarit also maintained trading relations with Crete, Mari and Ur during this period.

During the *Late Bronze Age* (1550–1200 BC) the cities of Ugarit, Byblos and Tyre came to form part of the great Mediterranean trading networks which linked Egypt, Mycenae, Syria–Palestine and

Mesopotamia. The fourteenth century BC in particular coincides with the period of greatest commercial and maritime activity by the Canaanite cities, which were an integral part of the Egyptian province of Syria–Palestine during the Eighteenth Dynasty.

A considerable part of the diplomatic correspondence kept up by the kings of Byblos and Tyre with the pharaohs Amenophis III and Akhenaton has been preserved. Discovered at the Egyptian site of El Amarna and written in Akkadian cuneiform, the letters of Abi-Milki, king of Tyre, and Rib-Addi, king of Byblos, provide us with valuable political and economic information about Canaan during the four-teenth century BC. In them, the Canaanite monarchs insist on their loyalty to Egypt while announcing the dispatch of ships loaded with cedar wood to the Nile, as an expression of tribute with, apparently, no counterpart from Egypt.

In the correspondence from El Amarna, Tyre is described for the first time as a monarchy enjoying prestige and political influence. The establishment at this date of a great satellite city on the mainland – Ushu or Paleotyre – no doubt reflects a demographic highpoint in that Canaanite state, even though its king, Abi-Milki, is already alluding in his letters to a certain political crisis in the interior of his territory and to a situation of generalized insurrection in the Syrian cities, in the face of the apparent indifference, if not impotence, of Egypt. This, then, heralds the changes that were to mark the transition to the Iron Age in Canaan; they imply loss of prestige by the Egyptian power in the region and a profound transformation of the geo-political scene in the Levant as its main repercussions.

The texts from Ugarit and other recently excavated Canaanite centres, like Kamid-el-Loz, have moreover made a valuable contri-bution to our knowledge of the Canaanite language of the second millennium and its dialectal variants, the evolution of its system of writing, and its epics and poetry.

The alphabet, which is documented in cuneiform since the fifteenth century in Ugarit, is a Canaanite invention which would have replaced the older pseudo-hieroglyphic and syllabic writing, known through the discoveries at Byblos. The consonantic writing of Ugarit, expressed by means of graphic signs taken from the Mesopotamian cuneiform and consisting of thirty letters or signs, was definitively reduced to the twenty-two letters of the conventional alphabet from the twelfth century BC.

Furthermore, the discoveries at Ebla and Ugarit demonstrate that the Canaanite language, already documented during the third millennium, forms part of a group of languages called 'Semitic of the north east', quite distinct from other more eastern groups such as Akkadian and Babylonian, which presents a host of dialects and local variants from at least the second millennium. The Phoenician language of the first millennium is nothing more than a direct descendant of this common Canaanite stem and in its turn shows a diversity of dialectal variants – Giblitic, Tyrian, and so on.

The Bronze Age in Canaan ends with generalized symptoms of violence, destruction or socio-political decline. The destruction and final abandonment of Ugarit around 1200 forms part of the succession of events in Canaan at the end of the Bronze Age, especially the Israelite invasion around 1230 BC and the general instability produced by the so-called 'Sea Peoples'. These latter, outstanding among them the Philistines of obscure origin, after laying waste the Hittite empire and destroying numerous Canaanite cities, took possession of the southern coastal territory of Canaan around 1180 BC. To these Philistines, who gave their name to that part of the country – Philistia – Palestine – is attributed the introduction of iron metallurgy into the Levant. All these events had as a consequence a cultural and political power vacuum which ultimately facilitated the incursion of the Aramaic tribes who occupied the interior of the territory – the modern Syria – towards the eleventh century BC. The crisis of the end of the Bronze Age in Canaan culminated in a general reorganization of the old land of Canaan, which was reduced to what will become Phoiniké or Phoenicia proper.

The period of transition to the Iron Age in Phoenicia, dated to 1200–1050 BC, is obscure and with scarcely any political activity, although as we shall see, there was a slow and gradual recovery in many of its coastal cities. There are references concerning Tyre itself, which suffered violent destruction. Commercial activity was likewise reduced to a minimum since the Philistine fleet blockaded the main ports and reduced the possibility of an immediate naval and mercantile recovery between the years 1050 and 975 BC. It is important to gauge this period of inactivity of the Phoenician cities carefully since some written sources of the Hellenistic period place the founding of Gadir by Tyre and the beginning of the commercial diaspora of Tyre at precisely these dates.

Phoenicia during the Iron Age

During the first millennium the principal Phoenician cities suffered a series of vicissitudes which obliged them to make successive readjustments to the direction of their commercial policy. It was in fact during one of those phases of reorientation of their economic policy that favourable conditions arose for initiating a process of maritime expansion westwards.

In this chapter, we shall not attempt an analysis of Phoenician history as such by looking at a succession of political or dynastic events; we simply hope to highlight those socio-economic factors and variables which built up throughout the Iron Age to produce at a particular point in time a situation of such tension that Tyre was left with no alternative but to expand towards the west. In this framework it is important to understand how the commercial policy of the Phoenician cities, and of Tyre in particular, evolved and was continually being readjusted, if we are to analyse the causes that impelled Tyre to undertake this long-distance commercial and colonial venture and grasp the real scope of the Phoenician settlements in the west and in the south of the Iberian Peninsula.

THE LITERARY SOURCES

The people who bequeathed the alphabet to humanity and had produced the extraordinary Canaanite literature of the second millennium have, paradoxically, left very little written documentation concerning the first millennium. In relative terms, we know much more about the Phoenicians in the west than in their own homeland; hence modern manuals devote much more space to the western Phoenicians than to those in the east. This is due principally to two factors: the dearth of direct or genuinely Phoenician historical references, and the paucity of the archaeological record concerning the great cities of the Iron Age. Consequently we are faced with a mass of empirical information out of context.

In order to reconstruct the history of the Phoenician cities we rely on three groups of written sources: the Assyrian annals, the biblical texts, and the references passed down by a few classical authors. It is a partial and, in some cases tendentious, set of documents in the sense that it consists of political propaganda – the Assyrian annals – or overtly hostile texts – in the Bible – and accounts written long after the events they are describing – the classical literature.

Even so, the importance of these literary sources is considerable, provided the reader looks critically at the facts. So, for example, the Assyrian annals, intended basically to extol the monarchs, provide valuable information about the payments and tributes imposed on the kings of the Phoenician coast and about the volume of commercial transactions and the merchandise supplied to the Assyrian Empire by the Phoenician cities.

The texts of the Old Testament contain first-hand documentation about the political pacts and trade agreements signed by the monarchs of Tyre and Israel, while at the same time reflecting the misgivings of the Israelite ideologists in the face of Tyre's excessive political and ideological power over the northern territory of Israel. This unease is made manifest, specifically in the writings of Ezekiel and Isaiah.

However, we know that the Phoenicians, like all the peoples of western Asia, had their own historical annals and their own poets and writers. Flavius Josephus mentions the existence of some Annals in Tyre. There are also allusions in Isaiah to the fame of the poets of Tyre and Sidon, and great thinkers and historians are mentioned who lived in Beirut and Tyre.

In his well-known works *Antiquitates Iudicae* and *Contra Apionem*, written in the first century AD, Flavius Josephus recalls that there existed very ancient public chronicles in Tyre, in which the names and dates of the most outstanding kings of the city were recorded. Josephus also mentions a Greek author of the Hellenistic period, Menander of Ephesus, as the translator of the chronicles of the kings of Tyre. Although he was guilty of some contradictions, it is known that Josephus copied the translation of the 'History of the Phoenicians' by Menander, based on a 'History of Tyre', which the writer from Ephesus was apparently able to consult personally among the official documents preserved in the said Phoenician city.

Flavius Josephus mentions too the existence in Tyre of a royal archive which still in his day preserved a copy of the diplomatic correspondence between Hiram I and Solomon and was kept by public officials in charge of the state archives.

From all this we can infer that royal annals existed in Tyre, containing archive material, the names of the kings of the city and the most outstanding events of each reign. These 'Annals of Tyre' must be similar to the 'Annals of the Kings of Judah', a work that has been lost but which provided considerable material to the writers of the biblical Book of Kings. We must therefore conclude that in the course of the tenth to eighth centuries BC, a literary genre developed in Phoenicia and Israel which was historiographic in character and of which only fragments or indirect reports have been preserved.

In spite of the gaps in his work, the list of the kings of Tyre handed down to us by Flavius Josephus forms one of the most important sources of historical information for the reconstruction of the history of the Phoenician city during the period of her expansion westwards.

There is mention of a second monumental work of Phoenician historiography which we know through the fragments preserved by Philo of Byblos, a Greek writer of the first to second centuries AD. Philo asserts that he translated into Greek, in eight volumes, a 'Phoenician History' by the Phoenician author Sanchuniathon or Sakkunnyaton, who is thought to have lived in Beirut or Tyre at the end of the second millennium BC.

We are indebted for all we know about Philo of Byblos to Eusebius of Caesarea, a writer of the second to third centuries AD who interpolated various extracts from the 'History' by Philo of Byblos into his work. Regarding the controversy aroused by Philo's work, and in particular because of its connections with Greek mythology, the fact should be emphasized that a Phoenician writer, Sanchunathion, considered an authority on Phoenician history and religion, was living around the year 1000 BC and that we are indebted to him for a monumental 'History of the Phoenicians' compiled from the annals preserved in the temples of the principal Phoenician cities.

Various archaeological discoveries, such as those made in the archives of Ugarit and Kamid el-Loz, bear out what we have been saying, namely that there was a long tradition of Phoenician historiography, which had developed in connection with official and state bodies.

Lastly, in the account given by the Egyptian Wen-Amon, dated to the year 1070 BC, explicit reference is made to the existence of diaries and official chronicles, written on papyrus and preserved in the Phoenician royal palaces. He also mentions that at the Phoenician court a detailed record was kept of commercial transactions and of the most outstanding facts connected with the royal house. One of these transactions – the delivery of 500 rolls of papyrus by Wen-Amon to the king of Byblos in exchange for cedar wood – gives some idea of the volume of papyrus needed by the royal house of Byblos in order to keep its official records.

THE 'DARK' PERIOD OF THE TWELFTH AND ELEVENTH CENTURIES BC

After the crisis of 1200 BC, described in the previous chapter, the activity of the Phoenician cities remains virtually unknown. Nevertheless, and although the main Bronze Age centres of Ugarit and Alalakh had been destroyed, with the consequent deterioration in international trade, there are indications that a few cities managed to recover and, in a very little while, to renew their commercial activities. This is so in the case of Byblos and Sidon, cities which were to dominate the political scene in Phoenicia in the Early Iron Age (1150–900 BC).

Taking their inspiration from local sources, various classical authors like Menander of Ephesus and Justinus (18:3, 5) announce that the city of Tyre was 'founded' by Sidonians in the year 1191 BC. This legend hints at the possibility that, after its destruction, Tyre was rebuilt under the auspices of Sidon, a city which all the evidence suggests was the most important centre in southern Phoenicia during the twelfth and eleventh centuries BC. This situation, in turn, explains the fact that at a later period Sidon would claim, at least on the coinage, that the city of Tyre was her daughter. 'Sidon, mother of Carthage, Hippo, Citium and Tyre' say the legends on the coins of the Hellenistic period.

In any case, it is worth pointing out that, before Hiram I comes to the throne (969 BC), no mention of Tyre appears in official documents of the period. Neither does the city seem to generate any significant political activity, such as can be seen in the cities of Byblos and Sidon.

In the light of this evidence, no expert on Phoenician history in the east subscribes today to the theory that Tyre was colonizing the far west of the Mediterranean at the end of the twelfth century BC. The likelihood of any international move by Tyre on the Mediterranean scene must be almost out of the question before the tenth century BC and, in our opinion, the political background that can be glimpsed in the Egyptian account by Wen-Amon and from a reading of the Book of Judges (1:31) provides a solid argument in support of this view. Indeed, from the time of Saul to David's victory over the Philistines, that is between the years 1050 and 975 BC, the Philistines and other groups of pirates issuing from the incursions of the so-called 'Sea Peoples', controlled all the coast between Gaza in the south and the territory of

Mount Carmel and Tyre in the north, from time to time hampering shipping as far as the city of Sidon itself.

Moreover, in Assyrian inscriptions from the time of Tiglatpileser I (1114–1076 BC) mention is made of the tribute received by that monarch from the chief Phoenician cities: Sidon, Gubal and Arvad. There is no mention of Tyre among them.

Undoubtedly the most important document referring to this obscure period of Phoenician history is the account given by Wen-Amon, an envoy from the Egyptian authorities of the twenty-first Dynasty to the Phoenician court with the aim of acquiring cedar wood. Wen-Amon has left us the most complete description we know of the Phoenician coast in the years 1075 to 1060 BC (Appendix II). In it Tyre yet again appears to be relegated to a secondary status, whereas Byblos, followed by Sidon, occupies a privileged place in the international relations of the period.

Byblos is described as the most powerful port and the main exporter of cedar wood to Egypt. In return, the city obtained vast quantities of papyrus. At a later period, Byblos would develop into the major distribution centre for the Egyptian papyrus trade and would for a long time supply writing material to the Greek world. Furthermore, the word used by the Greeks to designate papyrus, *byblos*, would finally give its name to the Phoenician city of Gubal and to anything connected with paper and written books, including the 'good' book, the Bible.

In Wen-Amon's account, the Phoenician coast appears to be dominated by Tjekker pirates, in spite of which Byblos managed to maintain its friendly trading links with Egypt. Nevertheless, the treatment received by the envoy of the pharaoh, Wen-Amon, indicates a change of attitude on the part of the arrogant Phoenician authorities as a result of the declining political prestige of Egypt.

The importance of Byblos declined shortly after Wen-Amon's visit. Probably the rapid growth of Tyre from the tenth century BC onwards damaged that city's commercial interests, as well as those of Sidon and Arvad.

However, we know the names of some of the kings of Byblos, such as Zakarbaal, the king who received Wen-Amon, and most notably Ahiram, who reigned in Byblos around the year 1000 BC and whose name has become famous thanks to the discovery of his sarcophagus, bearing one of the earliest known Phoenician inscriptions. Of Ahiram's successors we know little more than their names.

The city of Tyre, barely mentioned before the tenth century BC and considered as a satellite centre, dependent on Sidon at the beginning of the first millennium, came to occupy a position of hegemony in Phoenician history from the arrival on the throne of Hiram I (969–936 BC). With this monarch the Phoenicians' 'golden age' began and Tyre became the most important port in the Mediterranean. From the tenth century BC onwards, the history of Phoenicia merges into the history of Tyre.

TYRE IN ANTIQUITY

The Phoenician expansion westward was the work of the kingdom made up of Tyre and Sidon. It has occasionally been hinted that the colonization could have come from various cities on the Phoenician coast. However, the Old Testament is clear and categorical in this respect. The trading and seafaring city *par excellence* was Tyre, and even when a state of Tyre–Sidon was in existence the political and economic initiative and direction was in the hands of Tyre. It is therefore appropriate to discuss in detail here the characteristics of that city and its immediate surroundings on the basis of the literary and archaeological documentation (Appendix I).

Tyre is known nowadays by its Arab name of Ṣur. It is situated some 40 kilometres to the south of Sidon and 45 kilometres north of St John of Acre, the ancient Akko. Its original name was Ṣor, transcribed in the Assyrian annals as Sur-ri. The name by which we know it today is derived from the Greek transcription of Ṣor: Tyros.

Its present configuration is very different from that of the ancient city. Today Tyre is a peninsula joined to the mainland, the consequence of a series of silts and sediments deposited down the centuries on the mole built by Alexander the Great in the year 332 BC on the occasion of the siege of the city (Fig. 4). In antiquity, Tyre was an island 'in the midst of the sea' (Ezekiel 27:32). Legend tells that the city was founded on rocks joined together by the roots of a sacred olive tree. According to Tyrian sources, Hiram I joined the two original islands in order to enlarge the city.

The strategic position of Tyre, a safe distance from the coast and provided with reefs to the north and south (Fig. 5), met the criteria demanded by the techniques of harbour building and seafaring in the pre-Roman period. Indeed, ancient ports were not so much built as hewn out of rocks and reefs so as to be protected against the prevailing winds and tides and against possible attack from the sea. In the west, the Phoenician enclaves, set up for the most part on small islands and coastal promontories, merely reproduced on a small scale the model of

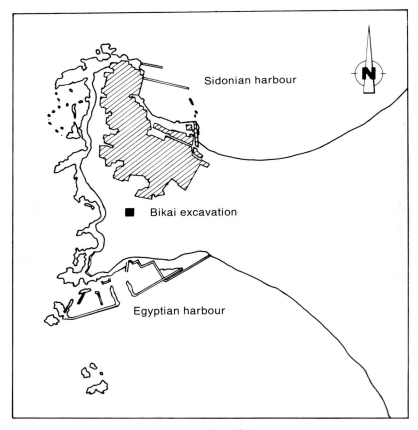

Fig. 4   Plan of Tyre

the settlement at Tyre. The example which shows the most similarities with Tyre is Cadiz.

The description of the harbours at Tyre, given by Arrianus on the eve of the conquest by Alexander (Arr. 2:20, 10) coincides in broad outline with that of other classical historians (Strabo 16:2, 23). At Tyre, according to them, there were two harbours, one natural and the other artificial. The natural harbour was situated to the north of the city and was an enclosed area inside the walls of Tyre. It was called 'Sidonian' because it was aligned northwards towards Sidon. The artificial harbour was located to the south of the city and was built in the ninth century by Ithobaal I. It was called 'Egyptian' because it faced towards

Fig. 5 Aerial view of Tyre, 1935

Africa and it was connected to the 'Sidonian harbour' by means of a canal across the city. This arrangement of the harbours and the existence of a communicating canal brings us back once more to the layout of Phoenician Cadiz, as will be seen later. The fact is that all the economic activity of Tyre was centred around its two famous harbours. 'Situated at the entry of the sea' sang Ezekiel (27:3).

We do not know the exact extent of the island of Tyre. Pliny asserts that its perimeter measured 22 stadia (*Nat. Hist.* 5:76), some 4 kms, although some recent estimates calculate that the island was 700–750 metres wide, which would give an area for the island city of roughly 53 hectares. In any case, it was a city of considerable size for the period (Fig. 6).

As for its population, the specialists agree that it was greater than that of modern Sur. It is reckoned that some 30,000 persons lived in Tyre, that is a density of some 520 inhabitants per hectare – a density that could increase in times of war, when the residents of the mainland suburbs like Ushu took refuge on the island and raised the population to a figure in the region of 40,000 persons. These calculations are based on accounts in Arrianus, who reported that some 8,000 defenders fell during the siege by Alexander the Great. Another

Fig. 6   Aerial view of Tyre, 1938

30,000 survivors, including women and children, were made slaves by
the Macedonians.

Various legendary traditions record that the most ancient temple
of Melqart was not in Tyre, but in the city known as 'ancient Tyre',
Tyrus vetus (Justinus, 11:10–11) or even *Palaeotyron* (Curcius Rufus,
4:2–4), situated on the mainland. From the city of Palaeotyre, not so far
located but which has been identified with the modern village of Tell
er-Rachidiyeh, came the supply of drinking water for Tyre. The water
was carried to the island of Tyre in small boats up until the times of
Hiram I, who built cisterns and other engineering works on the island.
It is said, moreover, that the first human settlement on the island,
during the Bronze Age, came from Palaeotyre on the mainland.

The Egyptian and Assyrian texts call Palaeotyre *Ushu* (Fig. 7). It was
considered to be a second Tyre on the mainland and lasted as a satellite
city until it was conquered by Nebuchadnezzar. The Book of Samuel is
probably referring to Ushu (II, 24:6–7) when it mentions the 'fortress'
from which Tyre was able to control all the territory as far as Akhziv
in the south that remained outside the frontiers of the kingdom of
David.

A river, the Ras el-'Ain, crossed Palaeotyre at its mouth, recalling
once again the topography of the enclaves in the south of the Iberian
Peninsula.

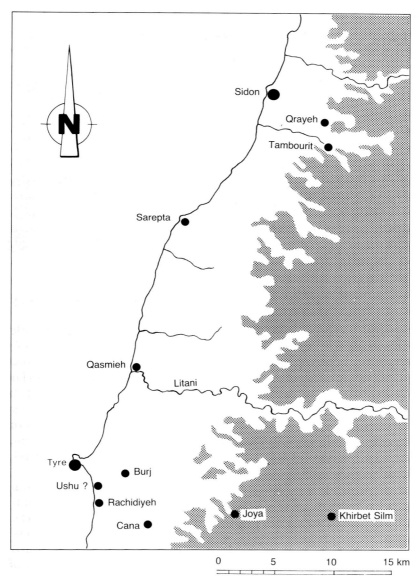

Fig. 7   Southern Phoenicia and the territory of Tyre

Fig. 8   The island of Tyre – bronze bas-relief from the gates of Balawat
(ninth century BC)

To the island of Tyre, overpopulated as it was, its mainland territory
was a vital necessity, supplying it with agricultural products, drinking
water, wood and murex. In isolation, the city was nothing.

With the help of successive descriptions of ancient Tyre that have
been preserved, and thanks to various representations of the city in
Assyrian art, it is possible to reconstruct the original appearance of the
'greatest and most glorious' city of the Levantine coast (Curcius Rufus
4:2, 2).

In the matter of its architecture and layout, we know that Hiram
built the three major temples of the city – those of Melqart, Astarte
and Baal Shamen – and that there was a big marketplace close to the
harbour. We know, too, about the royal palace, erected in the southeast corner of the city (Arrianus 2:23, 6), within whose walls the royal
treasures and archives were preserved (Ezekiel 28:4).

The most ancient representation of the city of Tyre that has been
preserved is in the form of a bas-relief on the bronze gates at Balawat,
dated to the middle of the ninth century BC, in which Tyre is shown on
its rocky island, surrounded by a wall with five towers (Fig. 8). Two
gates in the wall, with arches, might represent access respectively to the
two harbours of the city. As for the elevation of the wall of Tyre, it is
reported that, on its eastern side, it reached a height of 45 metres
(Arrianus 2:21, 4).

In another bas-relief in stone from the first quarter of the eighth
century BC, discovered in the palace of Sargon II in Khorsabad, we see
a maritime scene, in which ships are transporting stout trunks of cedar
wood against a background in which can be discerned two islands
close to the coast. The one on the right is Tyre and the one on the left
might be Arvad (Fig. 9). Here again, Tyre is represented on a rocky
island, protected by massive fortifications. Its three main temples stand
out above the walls. Once again it evokes the image of Tyre compared
to a great ship 'fortified in the midst of the sea' (Ezekiel 27:32).

Fig. 9 Bas-relief at the palace of Sargon in Khorsabad (eighth century BC), showing Phoenician ships with the islands of Tyre and Arvad in the background

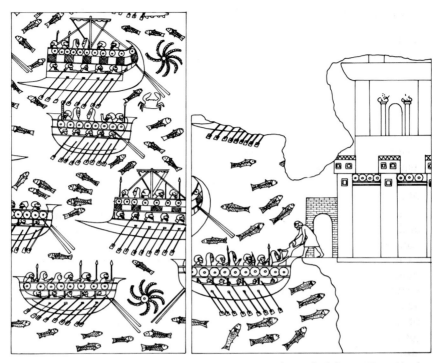

Fig. 10   Flight of King Luli of Tyre – Assyrian bas-relief from Khorsabad
(early seventh century BC)

Undoubtedly the most evocative representation known to us is in an
Assyrian bas-relief, now lost, which adorned the palace of Sennacherib
in Nineveh. Thanks to an unpublished drawing, Barnett was able to
identify and reconstruct the scene, which would be dated to around
690 BC (Fig. 10).

The bas-relief shows the flight of King Luli of Tyre in the year 701
BC before the Assyrian armies. The king is seen boarding a ship with
his family, possibly in the 'Egyptian harbour', which will carry him
safely to exile on the island of Cyprus. In front of the city, a flotilla of
bulky, rounded ships awaits the king – galleys or merchant ships –
escorted by more elongated warships. People have claimed to see in
this scene a reproduction of the famous 'ships of Tarshish'.

In the background can be seen the city of Tyre. Various buildings
can be distinguished, rising above the walls and towers of the city.
Above an arched gate on the left of the wall towers an important

building with a cornice, the main entrance of which is flanked by two great pillars or isolated columns with voluted capitals. In all probability we have here a representation of the great temple of Melqart and its twin columns of gold and emerald (Herod. 2:44).

HIRAM I AND THE FOUNDING OF TYRE'S COMMERCIAL EMPIRE

During the tenth century, a number of circumstances in the Near East would create a situation favourable to the commercial and territorial aspirations of Tyre.

Indeed the downturn in Egypt's political power, the defeat of the Philistines at the hands of David in 975, the political unification of Israel, the still precarious situation of the Aramaic kingdoms in Syria and the immobility of the Assyrian Empire in the east brought about conditions that were optimal for enabling an ambitious state like Tyre to maintain its independence of any foreign power and more particularly of Egypt. From then on, throughout almost three hundred years, the policy of Tyre would consist in exploiting to its own advantage the diverse situations offered by the geo-political landscape of western Asia. Throughout the whole of the Middle Iron Age (900–550 BC), this strategy would make Tyre the foremost naval and commercial power in Asia.

Hiram I, the founder of Tyre's commercial empire, owed his prestige above all to his politico-commercial relations with Solomon. Hiram is credited with achieving the monopoly in sea transport of the period (II Chron. 8:18), the naval power of his city and her hegemony over the Phoenician coast in the teeth of her rivals, Byblos and Sidon, which is why Hiram called himself 'king of Tyre and of Phoenicia'.

His commercial policy consisted exclusively in controlling the trade routes of the Asian continent. This enterprise was undoubtedly helped by the policy of growth and expansion of the kingdom of Israel during the reign of Solomon (960–930 BC). A first stage in Tyre's expansionist line was opened with the famous commercial treaty signed by Hiram I and Solomon, by virtue of which the two monarchs agreed to engage in large-scale commercial transactions. In return for advanced technology, building material, specialist technical assistance, services and luxury goods supplied by Hiram, Solomon provided Tyre with silver, farm products and 'food for the royal household' (I Kings 5:11). The alliance with Solomon secured access for Tyre to the routes of the interior leading to the Euphrates, Syria, Mesopotamia and Arabia, and guaranteed both a supply of cereals, so lacking in her territory and, at the same time, an outlet for her manufactured products. Territorial aspirations on the mainland were a constant preoccupation and necessity for the monarchs of Tyre.

The second stage in Hiram's expansionist policy coincides with the organization of a joint naval enterprise with Israel aimed at opening up a new market: the Orient. The biblical texts describe how, on the initiative of Tyre, Solomon and Hiram built a merchant fleet at Ezion-geber, near Elath on the Red Sea (I Kings 9:26). Their ships, manned by Phoenicians, were the 'ships of Tarshish' (I Kings 10:22 and 49), which sailed every three years to a distant country, Ophir, and brought back gold, silver, ivory and precious stones. The destination of these voyages is generally located on the west coast of the Red Sea (Sudan or Somalia), in Arabia or even in the Indian Ocean. What is certain is that the Old Testament invariably refers to the east, which is why the hypothesis that the destination of these voyages might have been the south of the Iberian peninsula has been definitively discarded nowadays. The similarity observed in the first two syllables of the words Tarshish and Tartessos does not justify for the present distorting the whole of Hiram's commercial policy, which was clearly orientated towards the continent of Asia.

The Phoenicio–Israelite incursions into the Red Sea are above all a demonstration of the fact that, during the tenth century, Tyre was already capable of organizing long-distance maritime expeditions.

Through the biblical texts and those of Flavius Josephus, we know that Hiram and Solomon made considerable profits from their naval expeditions, profits which they spent on embellishing their respective capitals, in an obvious desire to express their political power.

With the help of Tyrian architects, Solomon built the temple in Jerusalem. To Hiram, on the other hand, is attributed the rebuilding of the harbour of Tyre, with the addition of mighty shipyards, the extension of the city by joining the two islands together, the building of the royal palace and market and the reconstruction of the temples. He was responsible likewise for building the great temple of Melqart – the guardian of the city – which became famous for its two great pillars of gold and emerald. The building activities of this monarch transformed Tyre into the most splendid and envied city of the Levantine coast, 'beautiful and perfect' in the words of Ezekiel.

Various reports mention a direct intervention by Hiram in Cyprus to stifle an uprising of the 'kiti(um)'. This suggests the possibility that control of the eastern Mediterranean through its sovereignty at sea and over the east coast of the island was among Tyre's objectives. It suggests, likewise, that Tyre had certain political rights over Cyprus. In any case, this strategy would not bear fruit until the reigns of Hiram I's successors, with the foundation of the first Tyrian colony in Cyprus, Kition, in the middle of the ninth century.

At the end of the tenth century the immediate successors of Hiram I were to witness important changes in the political situation in western Asia. These changes – the division of Solomon's kingdom into two states, Judah and Israel, and the rise of the Aramaic states in the north, would oblige Tyre to reorientate her commercial policy. This first adjustment, the work of Ithobaal I, opened the way to a new Phoenician 'golden age'.

THE COMMERCIAL STRATEGY OF TYRE DURING THE NINTH CENTURY

The reign of Ethbaal or Ithobaal I (887–856 BC) marks the beginning of Tyre's genuine territorial expansion into the continent of Asia. With this monarch, too, the sovereign of Tyre began for the first time to call himself 'king of the Sidonians' as recorded in Homer and in the Old Testament (I Kings 16:31).

The new title assumed by the kings of Tyre is the result of the expansionist intentions of Ithobaal, who was to succeed in re-establishing his dominion over all the southern territory of Phoenicia. Ithobaal created a single state that embraced both Tyre and Sidon. From then until the end of the eighth century BC, this new territorial confederation with its capital in Tyre would be governed by the royal house of Tyre. Proof that there was a single state of Tyre–Sidon in the ninth and eighth centuries BC – 'the united kingdom of Canaan' mentioned by Isaiah (23:1–14) – is seen in the facts that during that time Sidon disappears from the Assyrian inscriptions and that the two cities develop one single policy under the sovereignty of a single monarch residing in Tyre.

Equally significant is the fact that during this period oriental sources mention for the first time the founding of Tyrian colonies. Indeed Ithobaal I is credited with the establishment of two colonial enclaves, at Auza in Libya and at Botrys to the north of Byblos. Although the colony at Auza has not been identified, the one at Botrys corresponds to the modern Batrun, near Byblos and right in Giblite territory, which would seem to imply that Byblos and its immediate surroundings were under the dominion of Tyre. Once again, the evidence supports the notion of clear territorial aspirations on the mainland on the part of Tyre, aspirations we shall see increasing throughout the ninth century BC.

The dominant role of Tyre in the commercial sphere in Asia prompted Ithobaal I to seek new sources of raw materials and a gradual control of the market through an ever more active and simultaneous presence on three fronts: Israel, Syria, and the east coast of Cyprus.

As regards Israel, the policy of Tyre consisted in consolidating diplomatic and trading relations with the new neighbour through marriage alliances. Thus, Ithobaal's daughter, the Jezebel of the Bible, married the king of Israel, Ahab (874–853 BC) and was held responsible by the prophets, and Elijah in particular, for introducing the abominable worship of Baal into Samaria, the new capital of the kingdom (I Kings 16:31). Undoubtedly all the diplomatic activities initiated by Ithobaal I were directed towards obtaining basic foodstuffs and acquiring access to the trade routes of the interior.

The hostility with which the Hebrew prophets received Jezebel and the apostate Ahab reflects the uneasiness produced in Israel by the growing Phoenician influence on its institutions. Archaeology confirms that that influence was not simply ideological. During the ninth century BC we can document the presence of Phoenician architects and craftsmen in Samaria, Hazor and Megiddo. In Samaria itself, the influence would persist until the destruction of the city in 721 BC. In addition, there is evidence that a Tyrian business area existed in the town centre (II Kings 3:2) and various archaeological finds (of 'Samarian pottery', for example) point to the presence of Phoenician craftsmen in the royal palace of Ahab and his successors.

In the royal palace of Samaria pieces of ivory have been discovered which were intended to ornament furniture and were carved and decorated by Phoenician craftsmen (Fig. 11). It is said that Solomon's ivory throne had been the work of artists from Tyre (I Kings 10:18). It is worth pointing out in this connection that both Homer and the biblical texts are unanimous in considering carved ivory as an article of luxury and social prestige (Ezekiel 27:6) or as synonymous with ostentation, power and corruption (*Od.* 19:565). The Old Testament refers explicitly to the 'ivory house' of Ahab in Samaria and reproaches the men of Samaria with 'lying on beds of ivory' (I Kings 22:39; Amos 3:15 and 6:4). Worked ivory is one of the products of Phoenician craftsmanship that brought the most renown to its commerce, especially in the eighth and seventh centuries BC. In archaeological terms, these pieces

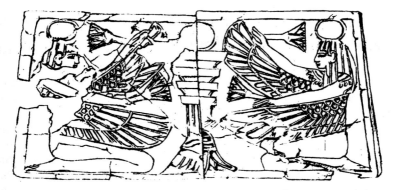

Fig. 11 Phoenician ivory from the royal palace of Samaria (eighth century BC)

appear, with rare exceptions, only in royal palaces in the Near East (Nimrud, Khorsabad), in princely tombs of the Mediterranean (Salamina, Praeneste) or in the big Hellenic sanctuaries.

The presence of such prestige objects in the royal palace in Samaria highlights one of the mechanisms of exchange most characteristic of Tyre's commercial strategy: the reciprocal exchange of gifts between princes and monarchs to mark the beginning of more widespread transactions. Included, naturally, within these norms of reciprocity was matrimonial exchange.

The second front to which the political interests of Tyre were directed during the ninth century BC consisted of the northern territories of Syria and Cilicia. In antiquity, the north of Syria, and particularly the coastal territory on the gulf of Alexandretta, was an important crossing point of communication routes and gave relatively easy access to almost the whole of western Asia. Nevertheless, for the Phoenicians, the main attraction of the gulf lay in the access routes to the rich metal deposits in southeast Anatolia by way of the marts or trading posts of Tarsus, in Cilicia, of Sam'al (Zinjirli), Karatepe, Carchemish and Aleppo.

Already in the tenth century, Solomon was acquiring horses and carriages all the way from Cappadocia and Cilicia, probably through Phoenician intermediaries. This leads us to envisage a direct interest on the part of Hiram I in supplying this market. However, it is in the ninth century BC that a real presence of Tyre in this territory is recorded.

The Assyrian annals mention a Phoenician harbour installation at

Myriandros, near the modern Iskanderun, on the gulf of Alexandretta. This installation controlled access to Cilicia and the Euphrates. Furthermore, in the time of Salmanasar III (858–824 BC), the Assyrian texts mention the presence of Tyrians, maybe a commercial agency, on the banks of the Euphrates.

The Phoenician presence in Cilicia and in the north of Syria during the ninth century BC is confirmed by archaeological and epigraphic documentation. In addition to the discovery of Phoenician pottery at, among other places, Carchemish and Tell Halaf, the most significant archaeological documents are the Phoenician inscriptions. Outstanding among them is the stele of King Kilamuwa (850–825 BC), the ruler of Zinjirli, capital of the neo-Hittite kingdom of Sam'al. The inscription, dated to 830 BC is written in the Phoenician language, which must be significant in a territory whose official language was Hittite or Aramaic.

Another stele from the vicinity of Aleppo is dated to the second half of the ninth century BC and dedicated to Melqart, the god of Tyre, by Bar-Hadad, king of Aram or the Aramaic people. Even though the inscription is in Aramaic, it is addressed to the god of Tyre by a Syrio-Hittite king, which suggests that there may have been a Phoenician sanctuary in the area. The presence of Melqart would thus imply political tutelage on the part of Tyre and her monarch over this territory.

Somewhat later and dated to the eighth century BC are the bilingual inscriptions – in Hittite hieroglyphics and in Phoenician – at Karatepe, erected by the founder of the city, Azitawadda. Situated some 30 km from Zinjirli, the fortress of Karatepe controlled the routes leading from Cilicia to northern Syria and was the capital of one of the most powerful Anatolian or neo-Hittite kingdoms of eastern Cilicia. Another strategic enclave, the neo-Hittite city of Carchemish, shows Phoenician influences in its architecture and craft work. In the time of Tiglatpileser III (745–727 BC), the Assyrian annals still mention the presence of Phoenicians there (Fig. 2).

There can be no doubt that the use of Phoenician as an official language and the invocation of Melqart of Tyre by the rulers in northern Syria and Cilicia reflect a Phoenician political and cultural influence of some importance in this territory. Before the Aramaic language had become established in this region at the end of the ninth century BC, everything seems to indicate that the commercial interests of Tyre resulted in political pressure on the princes of the Aramaic and neo-Hittite city-states. Thanks to a network of factorships and trading posts in place on the gulf of Alexandretta and the coastal region of Cyprus, Tyre was able to secure a monopoly of the trade in metals and slaves in Cilicia, the Taurus Mountains and the Euphrates and, at the same time, to control the sea routes to Cyprus and Crete.

Thus Tyre became a commercial power in the reign of Ithobaal and his successors. During the ninth century Tyre extended her mainland frontiers to limits never reached before, and this must necessarily have had repercussions on the appearance and internal organization of the city. The building of the city walls and of the second, artificial harbour in the south of the island, the so-called 'Egyptian harbour', are attributed to Ithobaal I.

In one of the bronze reliefs on the gates of Balawat, mentioned earlier, from the palace of Salmanasar III – in the mid ninth century BC – Ithobaal is represented loading tributes for the king of Assyria into his ships (Fig. 8). The ships, at anchor in the port, are carrying silver, gold, bronze and purple cloth:

> I received the tribute from the boats
> of the people of Tyre and Sidon

So says the inscription of Salmanasar III on the bronze doors of his palace. He is alluding, no doubt, to the metals, and in particular the silver, coming perhaps even then from the west.

The most outstanding of Ithobaal's direct successors is Pygmalion (820–774 BC). During his reign the city of Tyre is mentioned for the second time in the oriental sources in connection with the founding of colonies. Tradition relates that, as the result of a crisis that arose between the king and the aristocracy of Tyre, Pygmalion's sister Elissa – the Latin Dido – found herself obliged to flee to the west where she founded Carthage in the year 814/813 BC.

During the second half of the ninth century BC, the steady advance of the Assyrian armies across the territories of northern Syria suggests a setback with disastrous consequences for Tyre's trade in that region. The campaigns of Asurnasirpal II and Salmanasar III against Syria coincide, moreover, with the growing power of the Aramaic kingdoms, all of which will oblige Tyre yet again to reorganize her commercial strategy.

As a consequence of the loss of the Syrian market at the end of the ninth century BC, two decisive events occurred almost simultaneously: the establishment of Greek traders from Euboea at Al Mina, close to the mouth of the Orontes (Appendix I), and the founding of Kition by Tyre which, as we shall now see, marks a turn towards the west in the economic and commercial policy of Tyre.

THE FOUNDING OF KITION

The island of Cyprus maintained contacts with Phoenicia from the second half of the eleventh century BC. A few inscriptions found on the island suggest a possible Tyrian presence from the time of Hiram I, that is to say the tenth century BC, and perhaps some kind of protectorate in the eastern territory of the island.

These sporadic relations were transformed between the end of the ninth century and 600 BC into direct settlement of a Phoenician population in the southeast of the island, so that in practice the territory was incorporated into the kingdom of Tyre–Sidon. The territorial expansion of Tyre towards the west may quite probably date to around 820 BC, with the founding of Kition and the annexation of a part of the territory of southeast Cyprus. Moreover, Kition is the first Phoenician overseas colony confirmed by archaeology.

The founding of this colony probably arose from Tyre's need to secure at all costs the island's copper, a coveted metal at that period, which brought substantial profits to Cyprus as well as giving the island its name. On the other hand, this event reflects an obvious change in Tyre's commercial strategy: for the first time, the city finds itself obliged to develop direct control over an overseas territory. From the end of the ninth century BC, Tyre's new colony will guarantee to her monarchs the commercial exploitation of the copper of the interior of the island and, in particular, the mineral from the rich deposits at Tamassos.

Kition, close to modern Larnaka, was both a commercial port and a colony, and was to take the place of the ancient Enkomi, one of the chief Cypriot cities of the second millennium BC which enjoyed the advantages of an important natural harbour and its eminently strategic position. Not only was Kition one of the most important cities in Cyprus until the Hellenistic period, but it has the advantage today of having provided a host of archaeological finds, outstanding among them the temple of Astarte, the largest Phoenician temple known at present (Fig. 12).

In a Cypriot inscription dated to 750 and originating from Limassol, a Phoenician governor acknowledges himself to be a servant of the royal house of Tyre and offers a dediction to Ba'al Labnán, that is, to the Baal of Lebanon. The title given to the offerer is that of governor of the city of *Qart-hadasht*, which in Phoenician means 'new city', 'new capital' or neapolis. It is the same name that will be borne by the future new North African capital and will give us the word 'Carthage'. It is

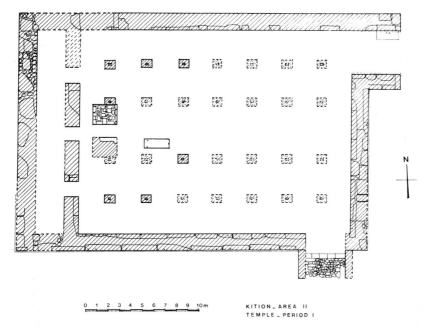

0 1 2 3 4 5 6 7 8 9 10m   KITION _ AREA II
                           TEMPLE _ PERIOD I

Fig. 12   Plan of the temple of Astarte in Kition

important to emphasize this fact because the name Qart-hadasht
frequently seems to go with the Phoenician diaspora to the west as a
synonym for the establishment of a 'new Tyre'.

We do not know where the Carthage in Cyprus was located; some
authors identify it with this same Kition–Larnaka. In any case, the
establishment of the new colony coincides with the arrival in the island
of Phoenician luxury imports which appear at Paphos, Amathunte and
Kurion. In the eighth and seventh centuries, the Phoenician influence in
Cyprus will be considerable. The chambered tombs in the royal necropolis of Salamina, near Enkomi, have yielded many silver, bronze and
ivory objects of Phoenician manufacture, which reflect the opulence
and power of the local kings at the time when the Phoenicians were
establishing themselves in the island.

Within the new direction taken by Tyre's commercial policy in the
ninth century, however, the founding of Kition is not an isolated case.
Indeed, there are archaeological indications of the presence of Phoenician ships in the Aegean from the middle of the ninth century BC. The
distribution of the first Phoenician imports in Greece indicates the

Table 2. *Kings of Tyre, Assyria and Israel*

Assyria	Israel	Tyre	Colonies
Tiglatpileser I 1114–1076	Judges 1200–1020		Gadir Utica
Asur-rabi ca. 1001	Saul		Lixus
	David	Abibaal	
Tiglatpileser II 965–933	Solomon 960–930	Hiram I 969–936	
Asurdan II 932–913	Jeroboam	Baal-eser I 935–919	
	Nadab		
Adad-Nirari II 911–891	Zimri	Abdastrato 918–910	
Tukulti-Ninurta II 889–884	Omri	Ithobaal I 887–856	
	Ahab		Botrys
Asurnasirpal II 883–859	Ahaziah	Baal-azor II 855–830	Auza
Salmanasar III 858–824	Joram		
		Mattan II	
Samsi-Adad V 824–810	Jehu	829–821	Kition
	Joacaz	Pygmalion	
Adad-Nirari III 810–783	Joash	820–774	Carthage
Salmanasar IV 782–772	Jeroboam II		
		Ithobaal II	
Asurdan III 772–754	Zechariah	750–740	
Asur-Nirari V 754–746		Hiram II	
Tiglatpileser III 745–727	Menahem	739–730	
		Mattan II	
Salmanasar V 727–722	Isaiah	730–729	

Table 2. (*cont.*)

Assyria	Israel	Tyre	Colonies
Sargon II	Hosea	Elulaios	
722–705	————	729–694	
Sennacherib			
705–681		Baal I	
		680–640	
Asarhadon			
681–670			
Asurbanipal			
668–626			
Asur-etililani			
626–612			
Sin-sar-iskun			
621–612		Ithobaal III	
Asurubalit II		Baal II	
612–609	Ezekiel	Mattan III	
		Hiram III	

sporadic presence of Phoenician merchants operating chiefly in Crete and the islands of the Aegean, rather than organized trade. But it is the kind of trade that is reflected in the Homeric epics (Od. 13:272–277).

From the second half of the ninth century, the ships of Tyre start to frequent Crete and the islands of the Dodecanese, thereby inaugurating a trade route into which they will be definitively integrated later, principally connected with Rhodes and Crete. We do not know what exactly the Phoenicians obtained in exchange for jewels and bronzes, possibly slaves or silver from Laurion or Thasos. The important thing is to stress that the founding of Kition was accompanied by a first impulse towards establishing commercial exchanges with the west by sea, and this is quite well confirmed by archaeology for the period after 850 BC.

ASSYRIAN TRIBUTARY POLICY AND PRESSURE ON TYRE IN THE EIGHTH AND SEVENTH CENTURIES BC

Asurnasirpal II reigned from 883 to 859 BC, and until around the year 879 BC, the Assyrian empire had not created major problems for the Phoenician cities. Tyre managed to remain on the fringes of the armed conflicts that brought Assyria up against the states of western Asia, and preferred to pay tribute rather than confront the powerful Assyrian war machine. What is more, Tyre occasionally took advantage of the Assyrian advance to make the Mesopotamian monarchs her prime customers (Table 2).

In order to safeguard their economic interests and guarantee free trade, the Phoenician cities frequently found themselves forced to pay tribute to the neo-Assyrian Empire. The story and the volume of the tributes paid by Tyre are recorded in the Assyrian annals of the day, allowing us to define the type of merchandise channelled by the Phoenician city and to get a rough idea of the prosperity of her port.

The tribute paid to Asurnasirpal II by Tyre consisted of gold, silver, tin, linen, monkeys, ebonite and wooden and ivory chests. Salmanasar III (858–824 BC) received silver, gold, lead, bronze, wool dyed purple, ivory and vessels. Lastly, Tyre paid Adad-Nirari III (810–783 BC) and Tiglatpileser III (745–727) huge quantities of iron, ivory and purple cloth.

The growing power of the Assyrian Empire made the Phoenician cities a key factor in the international politics of the seventh and sixth centuries. Their strategic position and their political and economic importance conditioned to a considerable extent the balance of power between Assyria and its great rival, Egypt. Hence the interest of the Assyrian monarchs in controlling the Phoenician ports and their commercial networks.

Until the middle of the eighth century BC, the Assyrian kings did nothing that might harm Phoenician commercial interests, nor did they intervene in her internal affairs. They restricted themselves to collecting tributes from the Phoenician cities or exploiting differences and any lack of solidarity between them, as Salmanasar III did.

Genuine political and military pressure on the Phoenician cities and the first direct opposition to their trade began with Tiglatpileser III, the first sovereign to wage war on Phoenicia, making part of the Phoenician coast into an Assyrian province (Fig. 13). The intervention of Assyria in the economic affairs of the Phoenician ports marks the beginning of a particularly critical period for Tyre's trade.

The chief consequences of Tiglatpileser III's campaigns against Urartu, Damascus and their allies were the deportation of hundreds of citizens to Assyria, the capture of Arvad and the surrender of Tyre and Damascus. In all this, the position taken by Tyre is more than significant. Although her ruler, Hiram II (739–730 BC), together with the king of Aram-Damascus, had headed an anti-Assyrian coalition, Tyre

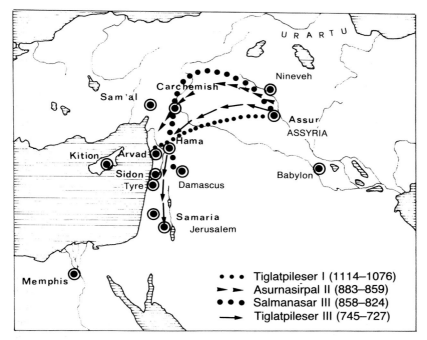

Fig. 13 The Assyrian campaigns in the Near East

was not incorporated into the Assyrian province, submitted swiftly to the king of Assyria and lost only some of her territory in the interior.

In short, Tyre not only received special treatment at the hands of Tiglatpileser III but she consolidated her trading position in Cyprus and overseas.

The favourable treatment meted out by Assyria to the king of Tyre is explained by a need to foster certain common interests. During the eighth century BC, Assyria was not in a position to take Tyre's place in maritime trade, so it was very much in her interest to enable the latter to continue her operations, as it no doubt helped to keep the imperial finances in a healthy condition. Tyre managed to safeguard her trade and her role as an intermediary, although at the cost of abandoning other Phoenician cities like Arvad and Byblos to their fate. However, Tyre paid a very heavy price. From 734 BC on, Assyria insisted on the presence of inspectors and customs officials in the port of Tyre and, shortly after, received from King Mattan II a tribute of 150 talents of gold, a sum never before equalled in any collection of tribute from Phoenicia.

The reign of Elulaios or Luli in Tyre (729–694 BC) brought a momentary lull in the conflicts that put the coastal cities at loggerheads with Assyria. At that time, Tyre possessed the most powerful navy in Asia. But Elulaios had to suppress a rebellion in the cities of Kition, Ushu, Sidon and Akko. The anti-Assyrian policy of Luli led to confrontation successively with Salmanasar V (727–722 BC), Sargon II (722–705 BC) and lastly with Sennacherib (705–681 BC). One of the consequences of all this was the siege of Tyre by Salmanasar which lasted five years, from 724 to 720 BC. During that time, the Assyrian king blockaded the port, cut the water supply and forced up the prices of basic necessities.

With Sargon II, Assyrian policy underwent a change which would have grave repercussions for Tyre. This monarch did not just pressurize or annex territories as his predecessors had done, he initiated a systematic strategy of destruction, devastation, mass deportations and repopulation of the conquered territories, chiefly in Phoenicia and Israel. Even so, Sargon always deliberately drew back from a final destruction of the island of Tyre.

This situation continued until the year 701, when King Luli, after rebelling against Sennacherib, was forced to flee to Kition, where he would die in exile. The year 701 marks the end of the powerful unified state of Tyre–Sidon. In a very short while, Tyre lost Sidon and the greater part of her mainland territory and her inhabitants were deported to Nineveh. While the throne of Tyre passed into the hands of pro-Assyrian monarchs and governors, the rivalry between Sidon and Tyre was once again being fanned from outside. This is the humiliated and beleaguered Tyre of which Isaiah sings in his famous oracle (Appendix III).

At the beginning of the seventh century, the kingdom of Tyre consisted solely of the city and its suburbs on the mainland. It was a tiny state confronting a gigantic empire in its phase of maximum territorial expansion. The treaty signed by Baal I of Tyre, Luli's successor, and Asarhadon of Assyria (681–670 BC) is particularly interesting. In it, at a date between 675 and 671 BC, Tyre is granted complete freedom to trade with the north and the west. The clauses of the treaty are, nevertheless, humiliating for a city that had been the mistress of the sea. Indeed the king's authority was considerably reduced because the treaty imposed Assyrian representatives in the affairs of the port and limited commercial shipping under threat of confiscation of the merchandise. All this undoubtedly obliged Tyre to strengthen the power and autonomy of some of her western colonies.

Successive blockades of Tyre at the hands of Asarhadon and Asurbanipal in 671–667 BC and in 663 BC left the city more isolated than ever and in the worst crisis of its entire history. Around the year 640 BC the entire mainland territory of Tyre was made into an Assyrian province. A reflection of this critical situation can be seen in the colonies of the west as well: this is the period when Carthage embarks on a policy of expansion on her own account, starting with the 'foundation' of Ibiza in the year 654 BC. In spite of everything, Tyre was not destroyed like the other Phoenician cities in the north and even preserved a certain commercial and maritime autonomy in the eastern Mediterranean for a time. The foundation of the last known Tyrian trading post, Memphis, in the capital of Egypt, dates from the years 635–610 BC.

Meanwhile, a new power was beginning to threaten from the east: the neo-Babylonian empire. The Babylonian ruler, Nebuchadnezzar, after conquering Nineveh, Jerusalem and Damascus, laid siege to Tyre for thirteen years (585–572 BC). This time the siege of Tyre had catastrophic repercussions as Ezekiel had prophesied. The king of Tyre, Ithobaal III, was deported to Babylon and with his successor, Baal II, who died in 564 BC, the institution of the monarchy disappeared. In its place was imposed a government of 'judges' under the suzerainty first of Babylon and later of the Persian Empire. The heritage of Tyre's monarchic institution will be revived, however, in the west by Carthage.

This brings the history of Tyre to an end. During the sixth and fifth centuries BC Sidon will take over her position in international trade and the ancient rival will become the most powerful and flourishing city in Phoenicia (Diodorus 16:44) until it is conquered by Alexander the Great.

=== 3 ===

The bases for the expansion in the Mediterranean

Having set the parameters of Tyre's economic policy and traced the main lines of her commercial strategy during the Iron Age, we can approach the question of the origin of Tyrian expansion in the Mediterranean. Once the causes have been established, it will be possible to fix the dates and define the character of the most ancient settlements in the west – marts, trading ports, staging posts or colonies. If the foundation dates of Cadiz, Utica and Lixus at the end of the second millennium are disregarded, given their ambiguity, and also the possible reasons for such an early expansion as being debatable and implausible, it is usual to attribute the Phoenician diaspora to the west, traditionally, to Assyrian pressure on the cities of the coast. Most authors who have dealt with the question have made pronouncements on these lines, authors such as Cintas, Garcia Bellido, Moscati and Niemeyer, among others.

According to this hypothesis, Tyre's expansion to the west would have been merely a response to the demand for raw materials imposed by Assyria and to the political and military pressure on Tyre which is supposed to have forced large masses of the population in the east to flee to the west. From the eighth century BC, Tyre is thought to have realized that she would have to cede all the initiative in the economic and commercial affairs of her maritime empire to Carthage.

If we accept this hypothesis, the economic role of Tyre in the international politics of the period would be reduced simply to a passive response in the face of the political and fiscal demands of Assyrian imperialism, one that is typical of a vassal relationship. The lethargy and the profound crisis that Tyre went through in the eighth and seventh centuries would have led in the end to an interruption in maritime trade with the west and the subsequent autonomy of the colonies. In their flight westwards, the Phoenicians would have headed for places they already knew: the small commercial staging posts founded during the twelfth century.

However, all the written references in the east state that the power of Tyre remained virtually intact until her conquest by Nebuchadnezzar in the sixth century BC and that her economic activity was curbed only occasionally. So we shall have to base our ideas on other theoretical assumptions when determining the causes and timing of Tyre's expansion to the west.

Other authors, like Albright and Röllig, from a completely different standpoint, state that the main causes of the diaspora were the internal dynamics of Phoenician society and the inexhaustible demands for raw materials – basically metals – precisely during the period at which the written sources in the east place the climax of Tyrian commerce, that is in the days of Hiram I in the tenth century BC.

But colonization of the west in the days of Hiram I is not supported by the archaeological record. Moreover, the search for access routes to the east promoted by that monarch and the establishment of Tyrian enclaves in Syria and Cilicia had no purpose other than to make good the economic deficit and supply the demands of the great powers of the interior. Consequently the factor or factors which might destabilize this complex economic and commercial network and unleash the diaspora must be sought in another period.

Other hypotheses – the vacuum left at sea by the Mycenaean might, for example, or an earthquake – have not prospered, given that they have not marshalled adequate arguments to be taken seriously.

Our hypothesis starts from the basis that there was no one causal factor but that the diaspora arose from the coming together of various interrelated factors over a long period of time, some being more important than others, depending on circumstances, until an external stimulus or one of the factors should serve to unleash or destabilize the system as a whole.

The main question is not to determine the moment or the cause of the foundation of the enclaves at Carthage and Cadiz in the west, but to clarify at what moment it became necessary or worthwhile for Tyre and other Phoenician cities to organize a naval enterprise which undoubtedly involved risk and, more particularly, considerable costs to the state.

THE VARIABLES

We must now recapitulate the information that we have been accumulating in the previous chapters and mark out the analytical bases on which to restate the question of the origin of Tyrian expansion.

The literary sources report two moments of Tyrian colonization in the west: a phase of ancient foundations in the twelfth century BC (Cadiz, Utica, Lixus) not confirmed by archaeology, as we have seen, based on western and later references; and a second phase, the beginning of which we can situate towards the end of the ninth century, documented from written references in both east and west. This second phase is contained in the policy undertaken by Ithobaal I and his successors and was to culminate in the foundation of colonies in northwest Africa – Auza, Carthage – and in Cyprus (Kition).

Our analysis will concentrate primarily on this latter phase on the basis of the existing empirical, historiographic and documentary data.

In order to determine the historical framework and identify the genuine idiosyncratic characteristics of the Mediterranean colonies and marts, it is essential for us to dwell on the factors of an internal and/or external nature that prepared the way for the commercial or colonial expansion to the west.

Concerning factors of an internal nature, a commercial or colonial enterprise directed towards distant territories is only viable in very special circumstances: either at a time of shortages or political crisis, or else in a situation of stability, prosperity and solid institutional organization, in which the need to channel or export excess production – by means of tributes, taxes or the circulation of manufactured articles – could have provoked an openly expansionist policy with the consequent search for sources of raw materials, agricultural land or trade routes. And there are factors of an external nature insofar as the prosperity of the Phoenician cities, and particularly of Tyre, was founded largely, as far as its external policy was concerned, on three axes: their role as intermediaries between the great powers of the east, their specialist production of luxury goods destined for a foreign clientele, and their preoccupation with becoming the main supplier of precious metals to the Asian empires. In this framework of international relations, the role played by Assyria was bound to be important, and perhaps even decisive, but only as a corollary to the circumstances of the internal socio-economic policy of the Phoenician cities; only the Assyrian empire could contribute to the commercial strangulation of Tyre or, on the contrary, serve as a stimulus to a naval and commercial initiative of considerable scope in that field.

Thus the ultimate causes of the expansion westwards must be sought fundamentally in the internal dynamics of Phoenician society in the east.

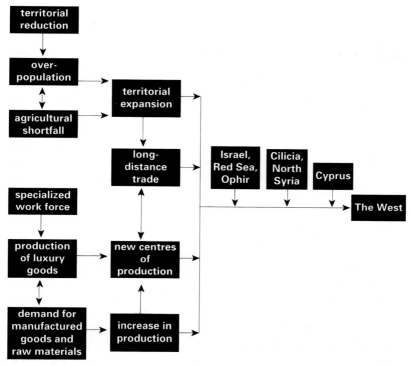

Fig. 14   Variables of the Phoenician expansion in the west

So we shall examine in the first place each of the internal factors that might play a part in this whole process, such as elements of balance or destabilizing factors in the system, and identify the moment at which a western venture might offer Tyre genuine economic rewards. In determining the causes of Phoenician colonization, we consider the following variables to be particularly significant (Fig. 14):

The geographic environment
The agricultural deficit and overpopulation
The specialized industries
The trade in metals and the silver standard
International trading circuits
Relations with Assyria
The infrastructure of long-distance trade.

The geographic environment

We lack studies reconstructing the palaeo-environment in relation to the Phoenician territory and, more concretely, the Iron Age. Even so, a few ancient references and various recent analyses carried out in peripheral regions enable us to determine the political, social and economic implications for Phoenicia of the serious reduction in her territory that occurred around 1200 BC. Without becoming involved in determinism such as assures us that the morphology of the territory predestined the Phoenicians to become the first naval power in the east, we must stress the importance of climatic and geographic factors in the course followed by the principal cities in the Iron Age.

We have already mentioned the loss of the major part of the Canaanite territory that occurred during the transition from the Late Bronze to the Early Iron Age, a reduction associated in the written tradition with the invasion of the 'Sea Peoples'.

In addition, we must point out that various studies in palaeoclimatology record important climatic changes around 1200 BC, which had serious repercussions on populations and living space.

Indeed, during the sub-boreal period (3500–750 BC), important climatic oscillations occurred in the Near East which profoundly affected the relation of man to the environment. So, for example, during the first half of this climatic period, in the years 3500 to 2000 BC approximately, a humid phase is documented in the region which will have led to the first expansion of human groups into the desert areas of Syria–Palestine and the establishment of settlements of a new type in the Negev, the Jordan valley and the Dead Sea, that is, in steppe and desert regions.

After 2000 BC, the steppe advanced northwards and there was a regression of the forest zones which became restricted to the mountainous parts of the temperate zones; lastly the sea level on the Mediterranean coast fell by up to two metres between the years 2000 and 500 BC.

This gradual rise in temperature, drought and aridity is recorded chiefly in Syria–Palestine, Egypt and southeast Europe so it seems that it was not a generalized phenomenon, since in other lands like the Zagros or Central Europe the change is hardly perceptible, or is actually accompanied by increased humidity.

About 1200 BC new climatic variations are recorded which, in a large part of Syria–Palestine, result in the Mediterranean-type vegetation being replaced by a desert-like Saharan type and in a serious degradation of the woodlands following a considerable decline in rainfall. Various pollen analyses to the west of the Taurus Mountains and in southeast Turkey indicate that until the year 1200 BC there were still cedar woods on the high plateaux and at heights over 1000 metres.

A climatic crisis of this magnitude would undoubtedly produce destabilization and the uprooting of important centres of population as well as mechanisms for reducing the rate of demographic growth and, most particularly, a concentration of people in more favourable regions like the Phoenician coast.

The hypothesis of a great drought has occasionally been put forward as the ultimate cause of the fall of Mycenae and Ugarit in 1200 BC. It is difficult to express an opinion on this question but it is worth pointing out that some written reports of the period mention epidemics of plague in the Hittite Empire and in Egypt – maybe the 'seven plagues' of the Bible – as well as drought and famine in Ugarit. Moreover, it is the period in which legend situates the displacement of groups of people who fled to the west – Ulysses, Aeneas, Herakles – or who irrupted violently into the cities of the east – the 'Sea Peoples'.

The Phoenician territory seems to have been one of those least affected by the climatic changes, having at the time a mild climate with long, warm summers, mild winters and abundant rainfall on the coasts and in the mountains, as Lebanon still has today. Towards the interior, in the Beqaa valley, however, the rainfall is much reduced, to some 500 mm, giving pronounced drought in summer.

The abundance of spring streams that could be used for irrigation is found exclusively on the coastal plain, which constitutes the real agricultural hinterland of the Phoenician cities and which is in every respect inadequate to feed the large conurbations. The profound climatic and political changes would deprive the Phoenician cities of a large part of their sources of raw materials and basic foods, since Phoenicia was never able to become a genuine agricultural power.

We know that cities like Tyre, which sheltered huge concentrations of people, succeeded, by dint of drainage works and the building of cisterns, in growing crops intensively on the coast and supplied the urban population with drinking water during the tenth century BC. Ezekiel refers to the fertility of the coastal strip near the island of Tyre: 'thou hast been in Eden, the garden of God' (28:13 and 16).

Even so, Phoenicia had a grain deficit. The cereals grown on the high mountainsides could not meet the needs of a population that had been constantly growing since the beginning of the Middle Iron Age. So the loss of the agricultural hinterland and the climatic deterioration of

1200 BC brought with them a concentration of population in the coastal plain and, with that, two new destabilizing factors: agricultural deficit and overpopulation, two sides of the same coin.

Agricultural deficit and overpopulation

From the tenth century onwards, there are clear allusions to a deficit in foodstuffs in the territory of Tyre, a city that imported huge quantities of oil and cereals from abroad. The pact agreed between Hiram and Solomon envisages, basically, an exchange of Phoenician materials and technical assistance against Israelite silver and agricultural products. Hiram I demanded food for the royal household (I Kings 5:23) and insisted that the amount of grain paid by Solomon be considerable, which seems to reflect a substantial dependence on the part of Tyre in the matter of foodstuffs at that time.

Various classical authors of a later period mention problems of overpopulation in Phoenicia just before the period of colonization began – Justinus (*Epitome* 18:3,50); Curcius Rufus (6:4.20); Tertullian (*De anima* 30). In his history of the war against Jugurtha, written in the year 40 BC, Sallust is still more explicit: the arrival of the Phoenicians in North Africa (Carthage) is explained by the need to relieve the country of an excess of population and by a spirit of conquest (*Jug.* 19:1–2). The reference is not without interest, in that it is the first and only time that overpopulation and territorial conquest and not commercial objectives are mentioned as causes of the colonization of the west.

Both the archaeological record and various studies in palaeo-demography confirm a vigorous demographic growth in Phoenicia and, in particular, in Tyre at the beginning of the first millennium BC. Between the twelfth and eighth centuries BC a considerable increase in settlements is in fact on record all along the coast. In some regions, like the Beqaa valley, the population growth gave rise around the tenth century BC to genuine demographic pressure on resources. The demographic theme has attracted hardly any attention from modern authors working on Phoenician colonization. This is due principally to the fact that the question of imbalance between population and resources has always been a variable associated with Greek colonization, whereas the Phoenician expansion westward has long been interpreted from one point of view only, that of trade.

And yet, excessive population must have been a serious problem for the Phoenician cities, especially during the tenth to eighth centuries

BC; that is, before the massive deportations of thousands of Phoenicians to Nineveh in the time of Sennacherib. The engineering works begun in Tyre by Hiram I – including the invention of the cistern and extensions to the city – undoubtedly reflect a need to adapt the urban space to an increasing population.

The problem of overpopulation and of a shortfall in food supplies explains, among other things, Tyre's preoccupation with extending her territory in the tenth to eighth centuries BC. This is the time when Tyre acquired dominance over Sidon and all the southern lands as far as the bay of Acre and Mount Carmel. With her policy of annexation, it is obvious that Tyre is seeking access to the agricultural lands of northern Israel.

A few biblical references (II Sam. 8; I Kings 5:15) show that, as early as the end of David's reign, Hiram I was seeking an economic pact with the new Israelite monarchy, so we must consider the treaty signed later with Solomon as a renewal of earlier agreements (I Kings 5:16).

It cannot be a coincidence that Hiram I should send an ambassador to King David immediately after that monarch's victory over the Philistines in the year 975 BC, that is to say, when Israel had for the first time achieved dominance over the trade routes leading to Egypt and Arabia. All this reflects the importance Tyre attached to her southern frontier, in other words, the agricultural lands of the plain of Asdralon, the natural granary *par excellence* of Israel for the production of wheat and oil.

Solomon committed himself to delivering considerable quantities of wheat and olive oil annually to Tyre (I Kings 5:25) in exchange, as we know, for technical assistance (architects, craftsmen), cedar and cypress wood and 120 talents of gold (I Kings 5:24; I Kings 9:11–14).

One clause in the treaty between Hiram and Solomon, however, usually passes unnoticed, even by specialists, because its content is so strange. In fact, mention is made in the pact of the cession to Tyre by Israel of '20 cities' in the lands of Galilee (I Kings 9:11–14) as a guarantee of the agreements. This, of necessity, implies that Tyre was in a dominant position in the 'land of Cabul', that is, over vast territories of the plain of Asdralon.

Archaeology appears to confirm this clause in the treaty. Indeed, it affirms that there were Tyrian enclaves in Akhziv, Akko, Tell Keisan and Tell Abu Hawam, dominating the bay of Akko and, consequently the whole of the plain of Asdralon lying between the hills of lower Galilee and the dunes bordering the bay of Haifa (Fig. 15). In two of these settlements – Tell Abu Hawam and Tell Keisan – the

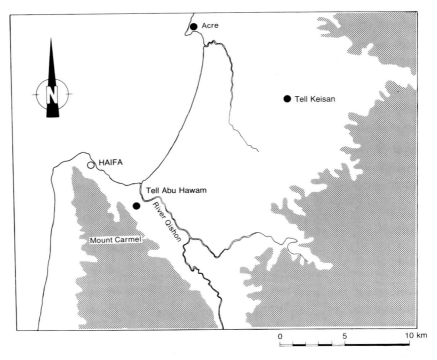

Fig. 15   The colonies of Tyre in the Bay of Haifa

establishment of a Phoenician population seems to start as early as the beginning of the tenth century BC, that is to say in the time of David (Appendix I).

In Tell Keisan, the archaeological record has shown a prosperous trade in olive oil and large-scale wheat cultivation in the area from the beginning of the Iron Age. (Of more than 5,200 samples of grain from this site, 70% proved to be of wheat and the remaining 30% of barley and other cereals.)

The plain of Acre, formed by alluvial soils and subject to a Mediterranean climate, was suitable for growing winter wheat. In this context, the interest shown by Hiram in these agricultural lands as soon as the Philistines were driven out of the region, the pacts with David and with his son Solomon and the cession to Tyre of lands in the plain of Asdralon acquire a new politico-economic dimension.

In any case, the political treaties signed with Solomon, the expansion of the kingdom of Tyre southwards, the progressive control over routes leading to the agricultural hinterland through agreements with Israel or, later, by means of Tyrian installations in the north of Syria, the whole of Tyre's political strategy, in short, is dictated by territorial ambitions arising largely from the three factors we have referred to: limited space for agriculture, overpopulation and a shortfall in food supplies.

The specialized industries

The Phoenician cities consisted of large centres specializing in the manufacture of luxury and prestige articles destined for international trade and to satisfy the needs of a very restricted social elite in the east for prestige, authority and dominion. For their intrinsic value, the luxury goods required raw materials not readily available, and therefore valuable, and highly specialized techniques of craftsmanship.

The Phoenician workshops became famous for the production of sumptuous articles of carved ivory, of gold, silver and bronze receptacles and of golden jewellery with filigree and granular decoration, which we find mainly outside Phoenicia, in royal or princely tombs and in the palaces of the east. Consequently, this production implied the need for exotic materials and, above all, for precious metals.

During the ninth century BC, Tyre and other Phoenician cities became the only suppliers of manufactured goods to the neighbouring states which, like Assyria and Israel, could not procure them for themselves without increasing the costs of their military or political expansion. By absorbing the Phoenician production, whether by way of tributes and taxes or by trade and reciprocal arrangements, the Assyrian and Israelite economic systems helped consolidate the Phoenician economy.

At first sight, the provision of luxury products to the Assyrian Empire might seem irrelevant to its economy. However, it should not be forgotten that the dignity of the Assyrian monarchy required its palaces, temples and capital city to display its power and wealth, at a time when those institutions were channelling these luxury goods from the coast to other Mesopotamian sectors or trading circuits.

As Byblos and Ugarit had done before, Tyre now became the principal purveyor of luxury merchandise within a trading circuit that stretched from Mesopotamia to Anatolia and the Aegean. In the long run, the distribution of this merchandise led to a greater specialization of the workforce and to an increase in production when circumstances favoured such exchanges. This circulation of luxury goods was carried on by means of two exchange mechanisms that are not always easy to differentiate: impost and trade.

A large number of luxury objects of Phoenician manufacture found in the Assyrian palaces – silver and bronze vases, for example, and decorated ivories – are not exclusively forms of tribute but are the product of trade. In practice, tributary relations would stimulate commercial exchanges between Assur and Tyre, which explains the commercial advantages, the protection and the autonomy that Assyria granted the Phoenician cities during a very long period, as will be seen later.

It will be inferred from all this that Tyre's whole policy was directed towards securing her supplies of metals and exotic materials for her specialized workforce. It was vital, therefore, to control the trade routes by sea and land which guaranteed the supply of raw materials and the distribution of her merchandise. Thus would be born in the tenth century a commercial empire which would be built up into a bond uniting the Mediterranean with the great Asian states of the interior.

The trade in metals and the silver standard

From the lists of tributes paid by Tyre to Assyria, we may infer that within the scale of exchange values, the fundamental system of payment used by Tyre consisted of silver, iron, tin and lead (Ezekiel 27:1–26).

In the ancient world, metal was indispensable to guarantee economic self-sufficiency. Metal meant having at one's disposal raw material for agriculture, for the military industry or for craftsmen, and a prestige element which was hoarded in the form of cups, vases or tripods, among other things. This is why it is very often difficult to differentiate between economic factors and prestige elements.

In the period in which we are interested, the great mineral reserves were located in Anatolia (silver, copper, lead, tin and iron), in Sinai and Cyprus (copper), in Etruria and the island of Elba (tin, copper and iron) and in Tartessos (silver, gold and tin).

The enormous quantities of silver that Tyre needed and had at her disposal – 'Tyre heaped up silver' (Zechariah 9:2–3) – could only come from Anatolia via Cilicia or else from the south of Spain.

During the first millennium, before the tenth to ninth centuries BC, there are no indications that metal was circulating on a large scale in western Asia. Neither the Assyrian economy nor the situation in the

Aramaic kingdoms or in Israel relied on an organization capable of moving considerable quantities of metal. This is the role that Tyre would assume from the reign of Hiram I.

The biblical references concerning trade with Ophir and various archaeological finds in Ezion-geber, where the existence of a Phoenician copper refinery from the tenth to ninth centuries BC has been recorded, show that Tyre was channelling the supply of metals to the interior of the Asian continent in the tenth century, and in particular of gold from Ophir and copper from Sinai.

Hiram I restricted himself to renewing a trading pattern that had brought prosperity to Ugarit as early as the Late Bronze Age. Indeed, during the fourteenth and thirteenth centuries BC Ugarit, which had specialized in the transport of metals between Anatolia, Cyprus, Egypt, the Aegean and Canaan, moved huge quantities of tin and copper and speculated on the prices of gold and silver. The city bought gold from Egypt at a low price and sold it at a higher price to the Hittite Empire. The role of Ugarit, the first centre of the metal trade in all western Asia, implied an organized system of sea transport.

The generalized crisis of the twelfth century led to a decline in the demand for luxury goods and in the supply of ivory and precious metals, the distribution of which in the Near East had been in the hands of Ugarit and Byblos, fundamentally. With the reduction in the volume of commercial exchanges in Syria–Palestine and the consequent interruption in the economic activities of Canaan–Phoenicia, the role of intermediary that had brought such profits to the Canaanite cities came to an end.

Once the crisis was over, around the tenth century BC, thanks to the initiative and recovery of Tyre, the Phoenician cities found they needed to seek new sources of metal supplies and new customers for their luxury products. Moreover, Phoenicia had a guaranteed sale or outlet for metals that were so necessary to the ancient economy and vital for industry, agriculture and the production of arms.

Metal, like any heavy merchandise, is easier to transport in boats than on land, as the Greeks would realize during the first millennium BC (Aristotle, *Politica*, 1257 ff.). Ugarit had at its disposal merchant ships of some 20 metres in length and with a loading capacity of up to 200 tons.

During the first millennium, iron was the most important strategic material for the great states of the interior – Assyria, Babylonia – which needed vast quantities to equip their armies. The Assyrian annals and the records of private merchants name Phoenicia, Damascus and Cilicia as the regions from which metal was obtained and they, in turn, obtained the iron ore probably from the mines in the Taurus Mountains.

The 160 tons of iron discovered in the ruins of the palace of Sargon II give some idea of the quantity of metal reaching Assyria from 'the countries on the coast'.

In the Assyrian lists, Tyre, Carchemish and Damascus again figure at the head of the centres supplying the largest quantities of gold and silver to the states of the interior at that period.

During the Assyrian era, the value of gold and silver was again very high. Trade in silver, both as ingots and in the form of manufactured articles was desirable, not only for profit or for hoarding but also for acquiring social status and rank, proof of the existence of a system of reciprocity – gifts, rewards – and a system of equivalency very close to that of an actual pre-monetal circulation.

In western Asia, because of their high value, gold and silver offered enormous advantages for business dealings and the value of things came to be determined according to a metal standard. Thus, the Akkadian word *Kaspu* meant both the metal itself and the value or form of payment for a piece of merchandise. We would find a modern equivalent in the French 'argent' or the Argentinian Spanish 'plata'.

In Ugarit, the general system of payment was stipulated in silver. 'Price' in Ugaritic was synonymous with 'weight' in Akkadian and the value of products and the volume of payments and wages was frequently fixed through the medium of a specific weight of gold or silver. Even so, the exchange metal *par excellence* was always silver, which was cast in ingots, disks, bars and rings which circulated at a set weight, stipulated in shekels.

During the first millennium, silver finally came to fulfil the function of a standard rate for commercial transactions. Its weight and quality were stabilized through 'hallmarks', a process for which the temples were sometimes responsible.

The normal unit of weight was the mina (0.5 kg) which was equal to 60 shekels. A shekel of silver was equivalent to some 200 shekels of copper and 277 shekels of tin.

A talent of silver (some 30 kg) was equivalent to 50 minas and 3000 shekels. In relation to gold, the equivalency was 1:4, that is to say that two shekels of gold were equal to 8 shekels of silver.

This makes it very difficult to say exactly when the circulation of metals ended and a monetary circulation began. In the days of the neo-Assyrian Empire, silver already functioned as a standard of value and exchange. This means that it was already circulating with a standard value, in short, as 'money'. The circulation of metals or metallic objects, such as gold and silver cups, with possible pre-monetary connotations is one of the most controversial questions of ancient economic history.

In the lists of merchandise at Ugarit and in the lists of tributes paid by Phoenicia to Assyria, the weight of the metal cups seems to be homogeneous. Thus a gold cup corresponds to 1 mina (of gold), to 4 minas of silver and to 60 shekels of gold. This means that it has a precise standard value, it is a unit of value.

Wen-Amon was robbed by pirates in Dor of a number of silver ingots intended as payment for wood in Byblos and with a total weight of almost 3 kg. Egypt had to replace them with an equivalent value in gold and silver cups.

All this leads us to assume that both Tyre and Assyria had evolved towards an economic system in which there are references or units of value which operate as equivalent exchange values in silver or gold, in other words, 'money'. We are faced then with an economic system with units of value (coinage and money), exchange values (prices), defined standards of weight, that is ponderal units and speculation on the value of gold, all features of a market economy with its laws of supply and demand.

In this new system, the pre-monetary standard of reference had replaced the simple barter system, typical of a primitive economy, where the value of the merchandise is determined basically by the value of its usefulness (use value).

If we accept all this, that is to say, if we subscribe to the idea of a mercantile-type economy, the role of Tyre in this whole mechanism acquires another dimension and her colonies in the west, too, take on another dimension in the framework of the circulation of metals.

Between the end of the ninth and the end of the eighth centuries, Assyria experienced a shortage of silver. This can be inferred from the loan of a mina of silver at the extraordinary interest rate of 400%. Some authors, like Winter, have interpreted this fact as the consequence of a drastic reduction in the supply of precious metals, and especially silver, to the Assyrian Empire. All this must undoubtedly be seen as an immediate repercussion of the Syrio–Urartian alliance which, in the event, deprived Tyrian merchants of access to the Anatolian metals.

By way of contrast, in the days of Sargon II, at the end of the eighth century BC, Assyria experienced an economic growth and an increase in the circulation of money which caused the shekel of silver at one stage to be divided into smaller units. The presence of a large number of silver ingots and disks with guarantee marks throughout the Assyrian empire, moreover, indicates that silver is beginning to be accumulated or hoarded. Sargon boasted of 'having accumulated silver in his palace' and of having succeeded in 'making the buying price of copper comparable with that of silver in Assyria'. No doubt Tyre and other centres were introducing that metal into Assyria from new sources of supply in the west.

The abundance of silver and its increased circulation in Assyria finally brought about a fall in the price of the metal in the days of Asurbanipal, in the middle of the seventh century BC, together with its counterpart, a general increase in prices. Logically, gold increased considerably in value relative to silver. So here we are in the eighth century BC looking at a typically inflationary process, as we should call it in modern terms, and a feature of a monetary economy.

The general rise in prices and the depreciation of the unit of value used in exchanges was bound to lead in the long run to conflicts and social tensions. The immediate consequence for Tyre was a decline in external, chiefly Assyrian, demand. For Assur, it entailed the end of her dependence as far as Tyrian sources of supply were concerned. It is no coincidence that this is precisely the moment, in the middle of the seventh century BC, when Assyria decides on a final and definitive assault against Tyre.

So the introduction of large quantities of silver into western Asia by Tyre, roughly between the years 720 and 650 BC, when the access routes to Cilicia, Anatolia and the Red Sea had been closed to Tyre's trade, can be explained only if the Phoenicians had already initiated large-scale exploitation of new metal-bearing strata. Such an abundance of silver could only come from the Rio Tinto mines in Huelva which had just started to be exploited.

Trading circuits

Each of the Phoenician cities controlled a small area of land which made them into sovereign states, called *Uru* (city) or *Kur* (territory, country, region) by Assyrian sources. Of these independent political entities, Tyre–Ushu was undoubtedly the most densely populated.

The hypothesis that Tyre never had territorial ambitions on the Asian continent has always been defended. We have already seen how the policy pursued by the city from Hiram I to Ithobaal I shows the exact opposite. The position of the Phoenician cities made them preeminently suited to become intermediaries between Mesopotamia and Egypt. This role depended logically on control of the trade routes to Syria and Mesopotamia along a few natural highways.

The mountains of Amanus and of the Lebanon and the hills of Samaria and Judea formed a genuine natural barrier for the Phoenician cities, a barrier that protected them from the great currents of invasion coming from Mesopotamia. The mountains of the Lebanon are difficult of access in the eastern direction. In the centre, the depression formed by the Orontes, the Litani and the Jordan and the Beqaa valley, which is difficult to negotiate, lie in front of a second mountain chain, the Anti-Lebanon, which marks the limit of the great desert tableland of Syria.

The most prosperous Phoenician city, Tyre, did not enjoy a position that favoured communications with the interior. From the Phoenician coast, the only access routes to the east consisted of the valley of the Orontes and the plain of Amuq, the pass leading from Arvad to the lake of Homs and the Akko depression which led to the Jordan valley. Consequently, Tyre faced the dilemma of either signing political or commercial pacts with Israel and the Aramaic kingdoms of Syria or else extending her frontiers by annexing the territory of Akko or by establishing colonies on the mouth of the Orontes. Otherwise Tyre was left with nothing but the sea. In other words, the economy of Tyre was safe provided that enclaves like Akko, Tell Keisan, Akhziv or Myriandros were in her sphere of territorial influence.

The first circuit: Israel, the Red Sea and Ophir

The commercial and territorial expansion of Tyre began after the rout of the Philistines in 975 BC. This event opened up for the first time all kinds of possibilities for a state needing to find an outlet for its products and afflicted with a deficit in foodstuffs and an excess of population.

The joint enterprise organized by Hiram and Solomon guaranteed that Tyre would obtain supplies of food, that her manufactured products would gain entry into Israel and that she would obtain precious metals originating in Ophir. In this way, the alliance with Solomon met all the economic needs of Tyre and implied the first step in the policy of growth engaged in by her monarchy.

The Red Sea project, financed by Hiram and Solomon, set out, above all, to satisfy the demand for gold which arose at that time in the

Asian Near East. Up till then, Egypt had been the main supplier of gold to those regions and, in fact, flaunted its monopoly of the distribution of precious metals to the east. The building of a merchant fleet at Ezion-geber and the trade with Ophir must be seen as a hostile act against Egypt's enfeebled trade and as a first attempt on Tyre's part to break the Egyptian monopoly over the distribution of precious metals in Asia.

However, the trading circuit in the Red Sea came to an end with the accession of Sheshonq – the Shishak of the Bible – to the Egyptian throne; once Solomon was dead, Sheshonq attacked Palestine and took Jerusalem in about 930 BC. From then on, Egypt was once again a threat to the growth of Tyre and Israel. The partition of the kingdom of Israel and the rivalry between the two, skilfully exploited by Egypt, led in the end to the loss of Tyre's most important customer for luxury goods – Israel – and the disappearance of a vital source of wealth for her economy – Ophir. Moreover Tyre's relations with the northern kingdom, Israel, would get progressively worse until the Phoenician city found itself on the verge of establishing a new circuit to compensate for its losses in the south.

Peaceful coexistence between Israel and Tyre lasted, in effect, until the middle of the ninth century BC with Solomon's successors – Omri and Ahab – thanks to the periodic renewal of the old treaties of alliance at the instigation of the new capital, Samaria. The move to the new capital of the kingdom, right on the trade route linking it to southern Phoenicia, and the marriage pacts between the royal houses of Tyre and Samaria, are an expression of the wish to maintain good relations between the two kingdoms.

However, after the reign of Ahab (874–853 BC) a spirit of enmity grew up in Israel, resentment and annoyance with the old ally in the north who was blamed for unilateral violation of the treaty of alliance (Psalm 83:7; Isaiah 23; Ezekiel 26–28; Zechariah 9:2–3; Amos 1:9). It is possible that this crisis stemmed from the distinctly pro-Assyrian turn taken by the house of Omri around 841 BC. In the middle of the ninth century BC, Jehosaphat attempted vainly to reopen the Red Sea trade (I Kings 22:48–49), when Tyre had already consolidated a new trading axis: that of Cilicia and northern Syria.

The second circuit: northern Syria and Cilicia
Both the Assyrian annals and the archaeological record bear witness to the presence of Tyrian traders in the north of Syria from the beginning

of the ninth century BC. The establishment of permanent settlements on the gulf of Alexandretta assured Tyre of access to the fertile alluvial plains of the region, a certain monopoly in the provision of silver, iron and tin from Cilicia and Anatolia and an outlet for her manufactured products towards Aleppo, Zinjirli, Karatepe, Carchemish and Til Barsip (Fig. 18).

From her establishments on the Gulf and on the Euphrates, Tyre controlled the movement of goods towards Mesopotamia and southeast Anatolia, supplying these with gold, silver and bronze. By way of tributes and commercial transactions, this new economic axis led directly to Assur at a time when the Assyrian empire was about to undertake military incursions into Syria.

But this trading circuit was to be interrupted between the end of the ninth century and the beginning of the eighth century BC. Indeed, around 800 BC an alliance was concluded between Urartu and the kingdoms of northern Syria, which culminated in a very little while in Syria–Urartu having an iron control over the trade routes linking the Mediterranean with the east, which gave them direct access to Cilicia, Anatolia and the Aegean, that is to say, to the main metal-bearing deposits of western Asia. This situation is reflected in a severe reduction in the supply of metals to Assur, especially silver, the distribution of which had been mainly in the hands of Tyre until then.

Very soon, the territorial restructuring of Cilicia, the consolidation of the Aramaic states and the progressive Greek competition in the region, combined with the military campaigns of Salmanasar III on the Orontes, meant that after 800 BC Tyre lost her preeminent position in Syria and her commercial monopoly in that territory.

Furthermore, at the end of the ninth century and as a consequence of the unification of the Aramaic tribes, the kingdom of Aram–Damascus was consolidated. The main caravan routes between east and west and between north and south passed through Damascus and from then until the Assyrian conquest of Damascus in 732 BC they were under the control of the king of Damascus. Taking advantage of a temporary Assyrian decline in the years 824–811 BC, Hazael of Damascus started to expand southwards, towards Israel and Judah, in order to obtain possession of the trade routes to Egypt and Arabia. With this dangerous neighbour, Tyre finally lost a large part of her land trade and her activities were reduced to exchanges of luxury goods with the powerful rulers of Damascus.

The third circuit: the Mediterranean
From now on, only one trading circuit was left to Tyre for her ultimate monopoly: Cyprus and the west. This is the period when Pygmalion, whose name is associated with the founding of Carthage, was ruling in Tyre. It is also at the end of the ninth century that Kition was founded in Cyprus.

From the beginning of the eighth century, the production and distribution of luxury goods for consumption by elites suffered a harsh reverse when the Assyrian empire revised its requirements, which now were slanted more towards raw materials, especially silver, iron and copper. Faced with this new demand, Tyre was obliged to widen her trading orbit and, consequently, to increase production of goods for exchange or else create new centres of production on the basis of a new trading axis.

The political resurgence of Assyria following the accession of Tiglat-pileser III to the throne in the middle of the eighth century, was made possible by the conquest and control of central and northern Syria which was helped by the breakdown of the Syrio–Urartian alliance. From the conquest of the lands of Syria and Urartu, only Carchemish was saved and this gave Assur access to the Anatolian metals. With the conquest of Damascus in 732 BC, Phoenician territory was surrounded by Assyrian provinces on her eastern, southern and northern flanks. This policy culminated in the campaigns of Sargon II, who seized Cilicia and the gulf of Alexandretta in 715, severing Tyre's last commercial links with the region. However, by then the Tyrians were already established in North Africa and Andalusia, as the archaeological record shows.

Relations with Assyria

There are very few detailed studies in existence concerning the Assyrian economy as a whole and undoubtedly the best are the works of Diakonoff, Jankowska, Oppenheim and Postgate.

The dominant hypothesis assumes iron control on the part of the Assyrian rulers over Phoenician territory and the commerce of Tyre. Trade would have been reduced to a mere compulsory exchange and the only alternative to this kind of 'war economy' for Tyre would have been expansion into the western Mediterranean.

The Soviet researchers maintain that Assyrian economic and commercial supremacy was supported on two basic factors: its considerable agricultural production and its success in controlling international trade through non-economic coercion and 'forcible exchange', based in turn on two political expedients: booty and tribute.

Forcible exchange would have come about as a result of the different levels of economic development in western Asia. This imbalance would have forced Assyria to replace the free exchange of products with this exchange based on coercion, in order to unify the various economies in favour of the centre. As a developed state, Assyria needed metals and other products, demand for which increased with the increasing luxury of the dominant elite. Given the conditions existing in the international market at the beginning of the first millennium BC, with peripheral economies incapable of investing or channelling these products, Assyria, with her favoured strategic position controlling the great trade routes of the Euphrates, the Tigris and the Zagros, would have found herself compelled to force international trade and, in the long run, political unity.

As the result of massive deportations of the inhabitants of the conquered territories, the Assyrian kings came to dominate a huge, ruined and depopulated territory in the eighth century BC.

In Diakonoff's opinion, the main problem of the Assyrian kings stemmed from the treatment meted out to the great international trading centres like Tyre and hence his doubts as to whether the autonomous city should be considered as a threat to the stability of the empire or as one of the pillars of its economy.

Postgate (1979) contradicts some of Diakonoff's theories by claiming that Assyria never practised a policy of intervention in the affairs of other kingdoms and that there was never any Assyrian government monopoly over international trade. On the contrary, this author thinks that contact with Mediterranean trade helped the Assyrian rulers, who even went so far as to encourage private commerce. Assyria's whole economic policy would have been one of '*laissez faire*', refraining from manipulating the economies of annexed regions or controlling market prices. On the other hand, he defends the hypothesis that the royal reserves of gold and silver were a vital component in the Assyrian economy, which made it very vulnerable to changes in provision from outside: any interruption or increase in the supply of silver could have disastrous effects on its economy and create serious administrative problems.

In short, Postgate, with other authors like Oppenheim, considers that the exchange relationships between Assur and Tyre were based on mechanisms other than booty and tribute, peaceful trade being one of them. In view of this controversy, it may be as well to look again at a series of the most significant events in the relations between Tyre and Assyria.

The Assyrians were the first to initiate a colonialist and militarist strategy in the Near East during the first millennium. They appeared on the Mediterranean coast during the ninth century BC and demanded payment of tributes by the principal states and cities of the Levantine coast. The Assyrian tribute lists almost always start with metals, followed in importance by ivory, cloth, wooden furniture and perfumes.

The first report of payment of tributes is recorded in the case of Asurnasirpal II, who received tribute from Tyre, Sidon, Byblos and Arvad in the year 876 BC at the mouth of the Orontes. This first Assyrian intervention does not at any time imply a real danger of conquest but rather an opportunity for Tyre to obtain important concessions in the matter of trade. At those dates, Ithobaal I was governing Tyre.

In an Assyrian relief of the time (Fig. 16) we see some envoys from the king of Tyre bringing presents on the occasion of the formal opening of Asurnasirpal II's palace. Rather than as an act of vassalage, Ithobaal was probably happy to pay tribute as a toll for transit towards the routes to the interior of Syria, with the aim of gaining access to new sources of raw materials.

Like his predecessor, Salmanasar III (858–824) saw the coast as nothing more than a hunting ground and a region from which to receive tribute. There was no systematic plan of conquest and Phoenicia had no place in the main objectives of this Assyrian ruler. Crossing the Euphrates and reaching the mouth of the Orontes, Salmanasar obtained gold, silver, copper, iron, purple cloth, cedar wood and ivory from the Phoenician kings.

With the accession of Adad-Ninari III (810–783 BC), a qualitative and quantitative change can be seen for the first time in the tribute material from Tyre. Once northern Syria had been subdued, this monarch installed himself in Damascus, where he received ambassadors from the king of Tyre and substantial quantities of gold, silver and ivory. The volume of these tributes shows clearly a considerable increase in the wealth of the region at the end of the ninth century BC.

Adad-Ninari received twenty times more than Salmanasar III from the Phoenician cities, which no doubt reflects greater pressure for tribute on the part of Assur or else the prosperity of the Phoenician ports which were then in a position to import and pass on a greater volume of precious metals.

Fig. 16   Phoenicians bringing tribute to the king of Assyria – bas-relief from
the palace of Asurnasirpal II in Nimrud (859–839 BC)

Another novelty can be seen in the lists of Assyrian tributes at the
end of the ninth and beginning of the eighth centuries. Cedar wood is
no longer mentioned and the number of luxury goods and finished
products – metal vases, carved ivory objects – and above all precious
metals has increased. We do not know whether the decline in wood is
the result of the ecological crisis in Phoenicia or whether the
woodlands were laid bare by human activity, but what is interesting to
note is the change implied in the direction of Tyre's commercial
strategy: the appearance of new sources of raw materials and silver.

It can be said, then, that until the eighth century BC, payment of tributes to Assyria was more or less a matter of routine and had little repercussion on the Tyrian economy. However, with the accession of Tiglatpileser III (745–727 BC) to the throne of Assyria, things changed. Although Phoenicia did not figure in his plans of conquest, the military policy of Assyria was to create a political and economic ring round Tyre and Sidon. But an independent and autonomous Tyre, once Hama, Damascus and northern Phoenicia were subdued, could be very beneficial. It is not without significance that the reign of one of the most aggressive Assyrian monarchs with regard to the Levantine coast coincided with one of the most prosperous periods for Tyre's commerce, between 790 and 738 BC.

As Isaiah rightly comments (23:2–8), by paying tribute Tyre remained safe from a power on which, in reality, the prosperity of her trade depended.

The exchange relations between Tyre and Assur were not based only on the imposition of tributes, there was, in fact, genuine trade between the two. There is evidence, too, of free trade and even of private trade on the part of Tyre during the Assyrian period.

Indeed, in a letter from an Assyrian governor to Tiglatpileser III, dated in Nimrud to 738–734 BC, the importance conceded to private trade by the Assyrian monarchy is demonstrated. In that letter there is talk of 'buying and selling', that is of commercial transactions and not of tribute, in the ambit of the Phoenician cities. This Assyrian official writes that 'he has allowed the people of Sidon to fell the wood [of the Lebanese mountains] and to work with it but not to sell it to the Israelites or the Egyptians'. Assyria imposes certain restrictions but allows trade to develop.

Oppenheim (1969) has shown, moreover, that there was regular overland trade through which products and raw materials originating from many different places (Cypriot copper, iron from Cilicia, wine from Syria, tin from Armenia, perfumes and textiles from Phoenicia, slaves, horses, linen, honey) reached the Mesopotamian cities; Tyre had the monopoly for supplying these through her agents and subsidiaries in Babylonia, Uruk and Ur.

Yet again, the facts endorse the hypothesis of preferential trading relations with Tyre and of a clear desire on the part of Assyria to open her market to products arriving from Tyre and Sidon. Just as his successors would do, Tiglatpileser III was able to subdue a territory politically but without breaking up its trading circuits if that redounded to his own benefit, since military annexation of the kingdom of Tyre would have shifted its economic axis towards Cyprus and the west, which was not part of Assyrian political plans.

Nevertheless, in exchange for freedom of trade and getting back into the Syrian market after the fall of Damascus in 732 BC, Tyre and her king, Mattan II, had to pay exorbitant amounts of gold. The 150 talents of gold paid by Tyre to Tiglatpileser III are equivalent to some 4,300 kg of precious metal.

We can say that from the middle of the eighth century BC relations between Assur and Tyre ceased to be a prestige activity and a matter of collecting tributes for Assyria and came to be based on the key position occupied by Tyre as a centre of economic power. Assur obtained tribute and was assured of preferential treatment in trade so she had no reason to intervene in Tyrian economic affairs or to compete with her trade.

Even in difficult times of open conflict between the two states, of all the cities on the coast as far as Gaza, the only one that was not incorporated into the empire in 734–732 BC was Tyre. So Tyre received favoured treatment in return for just one condition: not trading with Egypt, Assyria's great rival. In conclusion, we can say that the commercial ties with Tyre were vital to Assyria's economy and for the balancing of its finances. So the idea of a profound crisis in Tyre from the eighth century BC and of a major decline in her economy and trade is far from the truth. On the contrary, the Assyrian era was beneficial for Tyre and for the whole of southern Phoenicia until its fall at the beginning of the sixth century BC. It is the flourishing city described by Ezekiel (26, 27) on the eve of the siege by Nebuchadnezzar. From all this we can infer that the Phoenician cities played an essential part in the stability and growth of the Assyrian empire. The empire at its height in fact fostered exchange relations of benefit to both states. Assyria needed raw materials, especially wood and metals for her agriculture, her craftsmen and her military industry. Faced with an obvious imbalance in the economic counterparts, there was no other solution for Assur but to force such exchanges through tributes and tolls.

That Assur controlled the trading circuits of the coastal cities is shown by the fact that as each Assyrian monarch came to the throne, rebellion broke out in the Phoenician cities. The importance attached by Assur to controlling the trade routes of Cilicia, Urartu, Damascus and Israel proves yet again that there was Assyrian trade in the west.

The collection of tolls and tributes from Tyre, measured in terms of a silver standard or its equivalent in luxury goods, must be interpreted as a way of controlling a trading partner while at the same time respecting his autonomy. This kind of impost was aimed at reorientating the economic and commercial activity of the Phoenician cities towards Assyria and not towards other dangerous competitors like Egypt. To satisfy Assyrian demands, Tyre needed to obtain and channel huge quantities of silver.

Assyria demanded from Tyre things it could not obtain easily in other territories: at first iron for its war machine and later silver, gold and bronze. From the end of the eighth century BC Phoenicia was to be the main supplier of raw materials in the east, implying that Assyrian demand now determined the expansionist tendency that was Tyre's habitual policy, turned this time towards the western Mediterranean.

Tiglatpileser III's successors, Salmanasar V and Sargon II, did not modify that monarch's economic strategy. They attacked Israel and even conquered Cyprus from the Syrian coast, but they did not touch Tyre. It was only because of the general insurrection led by Luli and Hoseas that Phoenicia became, for the first time, the main object of Assyrian repression at a time, it must not be forgotten, when Phoenicia had lost her economic importance for Assyria. Thus Sennacherib, established near Tyre, would take Sidon and Akko and force the king of Tyre, Luli, to flee into exile in 701 BC (Isaiah 23:1–14). The decline of Tyre started at the beginning of the seventh century BC and culminated in the blockade by Asurbanipal in 668 BC. Assyria had broken Tyre's political organization in 701 BC but still took a long time to modify her commercial system.

It can be said, then, that the whole history of Assyrian expansion to the west followed a plan: to control the southern road of Syria–Palestine, with the aim of attacking Egypt, which Asarhadon finally did. This strategy involved domination of Hama, Damascus and Israel, but not Phoenicia. Tyre succeeded in sustaining a policy of compromise, reorientated her trade toward Assur and preserved her autonomy to the end, all this with substantial economic rewards.

Infrastructure of long-distance trade

It is natural that booming trade should move those involved to widen their sources of supply. Tyre's western adventure must be placed in such a context: one of a commercial and colonial enterprise, with all its complex implications.

As we have said, the two great problems for the rulers of Tyre were a shortage of food and the supply of metals. The first could be solved by means of trading agreements (for example, with Israel), or colonization of agricultural territory (Botrys, Miryandros, Kition, Carthage). Both ways required state intervention. Procurement of metals depended instead on importing them from far-off lands. The founding of colonies in the west could meet this twofold requirement: production of surplus food and procurement of silver, gold, copper and tin.

For an undertaking of this nature to be profitable, the transport of ore or processed metal must be done in large quantities. The production of metals demands a whole series of complex processes from the phase of extraction in the mine, through transport, smelting, making alloys, finishing and marketing. Consequently, an undertaking of this nature demands an administration governing all these facets. The organization, moreover, has two major constraints: its production capacity and distance, which is why it is rarely undertaken by an individual or a commercial firm.

Long-distance trade must be based on solid and solvent organization, since it involves many professions: producers, craftsmen, brokers, transporters, miners, merchants, technicians, shippers and so on. The greater the distance, the greater must be the trading value of the product, to justify the scope of the commercial network. Only if the merchandise has real value will it compensate for the enormous costs of transport.

In short: an enterprise on this scale will not be embarked on at a time of crisis or economic decline but rather in circumstances that create new demands for raw materials and offer outlets for surplus manufactured products. The expansion to the west and the founding of the colonies in southern Spain could only be undertaken by Tyre when she was sure of attaining her objectives: guaranteed silver ore and plentiful food resources, and the certainty of real economic rewards. In this sense, the western adventure can only be described as genuine expansion with all its implications: territorial, agricultural, colonial, commercial, demographic and interventionist.

As for the dates of the expansion to the west, these must be restricted to a very definite time span: between the end of the ninth century and 720 BC, the point when the Assyrian market was flooded with silver obtained from new sources of supply. We have the starting point in two historical dates in the second half of the ninth century BC, the founding of Kition, around 820 BC and the founding of Carthage in 814 BC. Consequently, the establishment of the Phoenician centres in

Spain and the earliest exploitation of the silver in the mines of Rio Tinto and Aznalcollar in Huelva must fall between these dates and the end of the eighth century BC. This time scale seems to coincide, as well, with the one drawn up in Book I of Eusebius' *Cronica*, a work containing the inventory of the 'thalassocracies' or naval powers that dominated the Mediterranean after the fall of Troy. In this list, originally attributed to Diodorus, the Phoenician thalassocracy lies in eighth place, after the Lydians, the Meonians, the Pelasgians, the Thracians, the Rhodians, the Phrygians and the Cypriots (Diodorus 5:84) and is said to have lasted 45 years, roughly between 850 and 810 BC.

This raises the question anew of when it was profitable for Tyre to take on such huge expense in a western enterprise that involved an enormous deployment of means of transport, human material, equipment and personnel.

4

Phoenician trade: exchange mechanisms and organization

Insofar as we are dealing with a people who were traders first and foremost, it is right to ascribe to commercial exchange and all the political and social institutions connected with it the importance they deserve in the unfolding of the Mediterranean expansion. This means defining the part played by the state, the palace, the religious institutions, the temple and private initiative as driving forces in the commercial enterprise in the west.

The Phoenician commercial network in the Mediterranean is one of the best-known diasporas of its kind and one of the most fully described in classical texts and in studies of ancient trade. But it has rarely been studied in depth. For the most part, the tendency is to consider the main features of this maritime enterprise to be piracy, barter, improvisation or colonial adventure. It has often been the custom, too, to lay down a linear succession of stages in the evolution of trade – 'silent' trade, barter, mart, colony – without taking account of the fact that when the Phoenicians embarked on their expansion westward, they had centuries of mercantile experience behind them.

We shall now proceed to a general appraisal of the part played by trade, traders and the Phoenician commercial and political institutions in the light of the various economic theories that have dealt with the question, although, unfortunately, they refer largely to the second millennium, and of the classical and eastern sources most closely connected with the Phoenician world; but we shall always start from the hypothesis that the Phoenician establishments in the west are, basically, a long-distance projection of Phoenician society and its institutions.

THE STATE AND PRIVATE INITIATIVE IN THE TRADE OF THE NEAR EAST DURING THE SECOND MILLENNIUM

No society can fail to consume, nor, by the same token, can it fail to produce and distribute. It follows, then, that economic activity as a whole, centring on the production, distribution and consumption of goods, is a dynamic and circular process. Within that circulation of products, distribution provides the fundamental link. What is more, all the enduring relationships in a society involve transactions, exchanges and, when things become more complex, trade.

Students of ancient societies are not well versed in questions of economics and so we tend at times to situate economic activity within the parameters of modern economic analysis – money, markets, profit, the accumulation of earnings, price mechanisms. Logically this fosters the compartmentalization of types and somewhat abstract economic categories and a tendency towards explanatory reductionism, in which the concepts are too rigid to bring all the variables into play. So, for example, it is usual to treat private enterprise and state enterprise as mutually exclusive, or mercantile exchange may be ruled out when other systems of exchange, such as reciprocity and redistribution, predominate.

When adequate written documentation is not available, it is extremely difficult to reconstruct the exchange mechanisms of the ancient world. Trade in the Near East in the second millennium BC has been only partially reconstructed and that is thanks to the discoveries of important archives of written documentation, such as those at El Amarna, Babylonia, Ugarit or Kanesh. Even so, all this information is insufficient to enable us fully to grasp how trade worked and evolved during that period. In the words of a specialist, it is 'like trying to reconstruct the organization of the tramways using nothing but the information printed on the ticket'.

For the first millennium BC, the written documentation concerning trade is much sparser and it is almost non-existent in the Phoenician world. However, a few written references concerning Tyre or the Tyrian enclaves in the west allow us to glimpse the characteristic feature of its trade. For the west, and in particular for the Phoenician establishments in southern Spain, reconstruction of trade should preferably be based on the archaeological record. But this entails serious difficulties when it comes to an economic reading of the data.

The distribution and characteristics of objects, which are studied in archaeology, are merely the end products of complex systems of production and exchange and in assessing them it is very often an 'impressionist' view of the spread of trade that predominates. Moreover, some of the methods of archaeology have carried little conviction when it came to interpreting the archaeological record. Not very long ago, mechanisms of commercial exchange in the Aegean were still being inferred from the curve of the fall or growth in the spatial distribution of commodities of trade. Acts of exchange arise in reality from much more complex relations than can be implied by a spatial distribution of this kind. Recently, a few specialists – McC. Adams, Hodder and Orton – have shown clearly the inability of the so-called 'New Archaeology' to reconstruct fairly large-scale socio-economic mechanisms such as trade.

In spite of everything, it is possible to attempt a partial reconstruction of the organization of Phoenician trade from the scant documentation in existence and on the basis of the solid mercantile experience of the Asian Near East, about which we have abundant documentation and whose traditions were undoubtedly inherited by Tyre.

An acquaintance with the theories of economic history on the subject of ancient trade in the Near East, then, seems a good reference point from which to start our discussion.

Economic theories of the Substantivist School

Forms of exchange

As a specific institution, the exchange of products is an expression of the social context in general since it involves all the elements in society. So it can be said that trade is an aspect of social relations and that there exist as many systems of exchange as there are types of society. The more complex the social structure, the more complex will be the trade.

As for the economists of the so-called 'substantivist' school of Polanyi and his followers – Dalton, Oppenheim, Renfrew, Zaccagnini and Liverani – they accept three main models nowadays for the way exchange works in primitive and archaic societies, in order of complexity:

(a) Reciprocity: this system lies at the root of movements between symmetrical social groups (Polanyi) and is characteristic of tribal societies (Sahlins). It involves qualitatively homologous or quantitatively superior counterparts. One aspect of reciprocity consists in the exchange of gifts and it is their social or prestige value that is all-important. We find an example of reciprocity in Homer, when he describes aspects of Phoenician and Greek trade in the Aegean; we shall look at this in detail later.

(b) Redistribution: a feature of state or archaic societies (Polanyi) and also of chiefdoms (Sahlins). It involves collecting commodities in a centre and subsequently sending them out again. It requires a centre of social and economic power and is characteristic of highly centralized societies, such as Egypt or Mari. Redistribution takes place through huge systems of central storage – palaces or the like – and there are no counterparts. One aspect of redistribution is a tribute or vassal relationship.

(c) Commercial exchange: this coexists with or is superimposed on the previous two models in primitive chiefdoms and states (Polanyi). It involves equivalent counterparts, the economic function is dominant and it is a relatively peaceful method of obtaining goods in short supply. It is precisely its two-sidedness that ensures peaceful development. There were two basic types of commercial exchange, according to Polanyi:

– Treaty trade, also known as 'administered trade', a feature of economies which, as in Phoenicia, make ample use of 'money' and carry on huge exchange activities but in which there is no clear notion of gain or economic benefit nor of a market proper. This is because prices are fixed beforehand by treaty or prior agreement between the two parties. The institution that administers and regulates the commercial activity and at the same time determines the agreements with the native population in distant lands is the port of trade, also defined as the place where treaty trade develops.

– Market trade, in which the mechanisms of supply and demand and the concept of price are in operation. This type of trade does not appear before the fourth century BC, according to Polanyi's theory, so that, in principle, it would not be relevant to Phoenician society.

The concept of market

In Polanyi's opinion, the market arises when there are at least a certain number of buyers and sellers, and when the unit price on offer is affected by the decision of all of them. So it is the market that determines the form trade takes, the use of coinage, the prices, the dealings, the losses and profits.

Elements typical of a market would be private enterprise, risk, profits and earnings, and the fluctuation of prices following changes in supply and demand. The function of market prices would be to regulate the supply of products in relation to the demand and to channel the demand for goods towards the available supply. For all this, the substantivists define the market as a supply–demand–price mechanism. If the conditions of supply (scarcity) or demand change, that change is reflected in the prices and so on, which means that the market is a relatively recent self-balancing and self-regulating mechanism.

The concept of trade without a market or trade administered by the state is especially interesting to us, because it was proposed by Polanyi and his school with the so-called 'trading peoples' – Ugarit, Tyre, Carthage – particularly in mind, that is, the peoples who were noted for their almost exclusive dependence on trade, in which the entire population was involved directly or indirectly.

Polanyi was the first to work out a series of categories and theoretical schemes applicable to ancient societies, which is why his work had such repercussions amongst archaeologists, prehistorians and historians of the ancient world. Even today, the principal specialists in ancient trade follow the theories propounded by Polanyi in the fifties. It is the existence or not of a market that in the last resort has been the hallmark of the polemics between those called 'substantivists' – Polanyi and his school – and the formalists, as we shall see.

For the substantivists, a large part of contemporary economic theory is not applicable to primitive and ancient economic systems because the categories used by modern economists have been constructed basically to analyse enormously complex market economies. On the contrary, societies are thought to have existed in which the economy was not regulated by market mechanisms – supply, demand, price – but by other types of institution. If market rules did not exist in the period that directly concerns us, there would have been no system of competitive markets or prices.

The substantivists defend the hypothesis that neither Babylonia nor Tyre, two of the greatest international trading centres of the Near East, was the cradle of the price-making market. The Tyrians would have developed their trade basically through operations fixed by legal arrangements (pacts, treaties) and consequently with no thought of gain. This type of pre-mercantile trade is what Polanyi defines as 'treaty trade'.

Particularly typical of this type of trade was the organizing of expeditions to distant places to obtain raw materials. Since this trade was very costly, costs had to be reduced by means of compensatory measures, such as, for example, restricting trade to materials of high value produced in very limited areas. In this sense, trade could constitute a formidable economic enterprise in which a privileged sector of the population took part. For that reason, in a situation of pre-mercantile economy, long-distance trade would have to be controlled by the state and subordinated to its interests, according to Polanyi. It was the state that laid down the terms of the exchange and fixed prices. In order to guarantee the mutual security of both parties, this trade needed institutional agreements or previously covenanted treaties.

This type of trade allowed the occasional intervention of merchants who obtained benefits, not in the form of profit on the 'price' of the merchandise but rather as a revenue granted by the state or the monarch.

Ports of trade

The port of trade is the main axis of administered trade and the chief institution of long-distance trade before the appearance of the market. The concept of a *port of trade* was introduced by Revere, Arnold and Chapman into Polanyi's work and later extended by Dalton to designate the place reserved for professional organizations of merchants who developed their activities under the authority of the state. There was no competition between them because prices were fixed in advance for very long periods of time. Thus the merchants are more like state officials receiving commission than independent traders risking capital and seeking profits.

The port of trade came to be constituted in the long run like a small state located on foreign territory and recognized internationally as neutral. With the advantage of being neutral territory, its importance for international trade was considerable; hence the great political powers always avoided annexing these free cities or free ports and practised a policy of non-intervention so as to enable them to continue functioning as ports of trade. Al Mina, Ugarit, Tyre, Carthage, Danzig, Hong Kong and Dahomey are considered to be classic examples.

During the first millennium BC, a few ports of trade, like Tyre, were able to attain the rank of genuine powers on an international scale. At first, however, the port of trade was a great commercial depository with warehouses and subsidiaries, in which merchants were protected, sometimes under the auspices of a sanctuary. The presence of warehouses, some kind of sanctuary, the existence of few burials – that is to say, few residents – and the absence of control of the territory are indications that enable the archaeologist to identify a port of trade. They are the typical features that we find, for example, in Ugarit and Al Mina.

For a port of trade to fulfil all its functions, it had to be established on the coast or the banks of a river and it required a prior understanding with the indigenous population, based on treaties regulating facilities for the transport, unloading and storage of merchandise.

These treaties fixed the equivalencies so that metal or silver were not needed as a medium of exchange. This would explain, moreover, the resistance of the Phoenicians and Carthaginians to using and adopting a coinage, given that, as 'ports of trade', their cities were never organized as price-making markets. Polanyi thinks that where no market existed, neither coinage nor money could exist.

In the absence of a market, another institution characteristic of long-distance cross-cultural trade would have been a special district outside the walls of the great cities devoted to commercial transactions. In the Near East, this commercial enclave, of which more later, was called *kārum* (port, wharf). The substantivists see this kind of 'market' as a physical location or meeting-place for the exchange of products and it could have existed in Mesopotamia without necessarily adopting the mechanisms of a price-making market.

Only after the fourth century BC would the Greeks have incorporated the idea of profit as an objective, together with a competitive element in the market. Aristotle would have been a direct witness of the birth of the system of price-making markets governed by their own laws: the laws of supply and demand.

Polanyi's theory has undoubtedly served to fill a gap in the study of ancient trade and to re-open discussion about the economic systems present in the Near East, which apparently do not seem to fit into the categories of a modern economy.

The economic theory of the Formalist School

Those known as 'formalists' – Burling, Leclair, Belshaw, among others – opposed these theories; for them every primitive or archaic society has competitive procedures, or markets, if you will, and so the categories of modern political economics would be in every way applicable to them. In other words, the concepts and propositions of 'formal' economics, created to explain the phenomena of the market economy, would be applicable in whole or in part to analysis of ancient economies.

Recently, too, other anthropologists and specialists in economic history, like Leemans, Meillassoux, McC. Adams, Barceló and Renger, have criticized, from other standpoints, the analytical separation postulated by Polanyi between treaty trade and market trade. These authors consider the division to be overly rigid and the resulting ancient economic activity too compartmentalized. Elements of mercantile trade and treaty trade overlapped and would not necessarily

have constituted exclusive, consecutive and ineluctable stages. The
distance between one and the other would not have been so well
defined nor would it have been so clear that the market generates
prices or is the nerve centre of economic activity.

There are discrepancies, too, about the significance of money and a
minted coinage, which at times confound the substantivists. So, for
example, in Babylonia detailed accounts of transactions are expressed
in monetary terms on the basis of an accounting system that preceded
money as a general medium of exchange. Money, which is not the
same as minted coinage, can, in the sense the economists give it, be an
abstract entity, a form of credit. In other words, the absence of metal
coinage in Babylonia and in Tyre does not necessarily mean that there
was not a market system. There would always have been price fluctuations, according to the formalists, and state control of the economy
had to be a late phenomenon. What is more, it is now on record that,
in Mesopotamia, market and price fluctuations coexisted with systems
of redistribution and reciprocity from the end of the fourth millennium
BC.

The formalists and other critics of Polanyi's thesis maintain, furthermore, that a very early, inter-regional trade existed in Mesopotamia
carried on by merchants who obtained profits from it, that the *kārum*
could function as a market, with all that that implied, and that silver
served as an indirect medium of exchange. These authors likewise
postulate that there are market elements in redistributive societies,
with demand and speculation on prices; in short, that the state did not
always channel goods from the institutional sphere to the private, that
there was a need to create a system of equivalencies, that prices,
equivalencies and tariffs were expressed in silver and lastly that there
were regulation, speculation and fluctuation in prices. All these
elements inherent in the notion of market appeared very early in the
Near East.

Other recent contributions to the problem of trade in the ancient East

The study of trade cannot be restricted to analysis of a single feature,
isolated and extrapolated from the overall social and political structure
(Meillassoux). Still less can it be studied as a timeless phenomenon,
given that it forms a continuous, dynamic and complex process, in
which a host of socio-political and economic factors must be considered. Various recent studies of the social function of the trader, or

tamkārum, and of the specific role of the oriental *kārum* as a market-place have ultimately opened up new channels for research into ancient trade.

The *tamkārum* – *a cornerstone of trading relations*

In the ancient Near East, commercial trafficking was in the hands of traders, the so-called *tamkāru* (singular: *tamkārum*), an Akkadian word for the businessman *par excellence*. The *tamkārum* was the person charged with commercial exchange, who travelled with his merchandise from place to place and who occasionally operated through commercial representatives or financed the trade of others.

It is known that since the middle of the third millennium, private commercial transactions took place in Mesopotamia, in which a very advanced system of accounting in terms of gold and silver was developed, particularly in long-distance trade. At the same time, there is clear evidence that the temple and the palace devoted themselves very early on to making profits by practising usury or acting as bankers. All this means that much of the trade in Mesopotamia was organized by and for the state, coexisting with private traders.

During the second millennium BC, this 'capitalist' economy appears to be closely linked to long-distance trade, for which we have documents showing strong governmental control yet again – for example, in Ur – or else private initiative – for example, in Sippar.

Very early on, the primitive *tamkārum* became a powerful merchant with a fixed abode and agents abroad; he financed commercial enterprises or granted credit to third parties.

The code of Hammurabi (1792–1750 BC) shows us the Babylonian government and palace participating in trade and using the *tamkāru* as agents. The palace imposes taxes on commerce, grants credit and maintains mechanisms for controlling trade. In spite of this, it tolerates and stimulates private trade. Contrary to the general opinion of Polanyi and the substantivists, private initiative can be considered as one of the pillars of the economic power of Hammurabi in Babylonia. In the days of this monarch, powerful, independent merchants, financed by private capital, came to dominate the overland trading networks of Mesopotamia.

Many business letters from the *kārum* of Nineveh, Sippar, Ur, Larsa or Babylonia are known. Leemans has studied the official and private archives of the palaeo-Babylonian period in this connection, the royal archives of Mari, the correspondence of Hammurabi with officials in the south, letters from merchants to their agents in Ur, Larsa and

Sippar and, lastly, commercial letters from the city of Larsa to enclaves in northern Mesopotamia. With the help of all this correspondence, it has been shown that most of the trade of the period came within the orbit of government. The state provided the capital through a high official, the *wakil tamkāri*, who not only was director of the king's department of trade but also organized the movement of government merchants. Alongside these, a few merchants supplemented government business with private dealings.

Oppenheim puts forward the theory that in the palaeo-Babylonian period, since a market economy did not exist, merchants were grouped in associations of a guild or professional type. These associations came within the sphere of the temple or the palace, which contributed the capital to finance such mercantile organizations. It was only from the second millennium BC on that the decline of the temple would have favoured the development of private initiative in international trade.

From the fourteenth century BC in Ugarit and other cities of the east, commerce and diplomacy are intermingled. The trader, integrated into the public sector, not only took part in public administration but was entrusted by the state with starting up commercial agencies and was commissioned to buy and sell in his capacity as emissary or consul. As a last instance, in Ugarit, much of the responsibility for trade concerned the state, to which taxes were paid by traders on merchandise and by franchises on commercial transactions. In exchange for supplying the royal household, the trader operating in the sphere of the palace was exempted from paying ordinary taxes.

The great Ugaritic merchants had agents or correspondents abroad or trading partners with whom they kept up a correspondence about dealings, loans, cases of debt or insolvency. The legal texts found in Ugarit demonstrate that the Ugaritic businessman always moved in the circles of a few privileged families in the city.

But the merchant of Ugarit is not just a commercial agent in the service of the palace, on whose account he performs all his activities. Yet again it is recorded that state trade did not preclude his developing activities on his own account. The *tamkārum*, on his departure on a trading excursion, received a grant from the palace consisting of a quantity of silver, or of merchandise calculated in silver, for which he had to account on his return. It is precisely this grant that distinguishes the commercial agent of the palace from the private merchant.

In conclusion, we can say that in the Near East a merging of the institutional and public sphere with private activity was usual in any mercantile activity. The balance between the two always depended on the socio-political conditions of the moment, although we might point out that the private space won by the merchants was much more extensive than can be glimpsed through Polanyi's theories. Very often, private initiative was stimulated by the palace itself.

In western Asia, moreover, the merchant enjoyed enormous social prestige. In government circles, the merchant always had a high social status, shared in the profits of the palace and occasionally formed part of the royal family. Only thus can we appreciate the significance of the hymn to Enlil, the chief god of the Sumerian pantheon, who is addressed as 'merchant (*dam-gar*) of the vast land'. So the rank of merchant is comparable with that of a god, which would be unthinkable if the merchant had been a subordinate or had not belonged to a dominant class, as will be the case in Greece.

Neither in the east nor in Greece is a 'trading middle class' known; that will be a later and typically European institution. On the contrary, we find ourselves faced with the two extremes of the social scale. Thus the trader of low social background will be typical of the Greek world, while he is unknown in the Near East. Very soon the contrast will be seen between the eastern concept of the *tamkārum*, a trader by status and closely linked with the governing class and the institutions of the temple and the palace, and the *naukleros* and outsider of ancient Greece, a merchant from a humble background, out of place and linked with the lower classes from which he comes. The first is a qualified professional and specialist, devoting himself to business and diplomacy, offering credit, owning land and inheriting his position. The second develops trade on a small scale and is undervalued for his work.

The kārum *of Kanesh: an example of a market*

One of the best-known systems for organizing international trade is that of the Assyrian commercial enclaves in Asia Minor during the twentieth to nineteenth centuries BC. This type of commercial enclave, called a *kārum*, has been found in the Hittite capital itself, Hattusas, as well as in Alishar and other Anatolian centres. The best known, however, is the *kārum* at Kültepe, the ancient Kanesh in the region of Cappadocia.

These palaeo-Assyrian colonies in Anatolia have always served as an essential point of reference when analysing the organization of ancient trade in general and are a key element in the polemics that even today divide the economists and historians who support Polanyi's thesis from those who oppose it.

In many Mesopotamian cities there was a port area or suburb outside the walls which functioned as a centre for commercial activity. This zone, the equivalent of an *emporion* or a mediaeval *portus*, which was called *kārum*, was organized like a marketplace. In the suburbs of the ancient Anatolian city of Kanesh at the beginning of the second millennium, there was an Assyrian enclave inhabited by businessmen who, over several generations, grew rich by buying and selling, forming partnerships and lending or investing money. These *tamkāru* acted as intermediaries between the distant *kārum* of Assur and the subjects of an Anatolian prince, the prince of Kanesh, who ruled over a region rich in copper. This Assyrian commercial diaspora into Cappadocia was due to Assur's need to obtain gold, silver and copper from Anatolia to complement the supply of tin reaching her from Iran.

The Assyrian colonists who settled in Kanesh formed a kind of family enterprise, passed on from father to son and dependent on the *kārum* in Assur. Assur supplied the products, lent the money and invested large sums in return for interest. The thousands of written tablets discovered in Kanesh, which Garelli began studying and transcribing some time ago, support the notion of a corporate and hierarchical organization of highly specialized traders.

Of more than 15,000 written tablets from Kültepe, only some 3,000 have been published so far. And a good part of the theories of Polanyi and his school in favour of treaty trade or marketless trading rests on the first discoveries made in this 'colony' of Assyrian merchants in which an important documentary archive had been discovered, belonging to three generations of merchants. When Polanyi published his conclusions in 1957, only a tiny part of the archives of Kültepe was known, the part published by Garelli.

Polanyi asserts that the Assyrian merchants in Kanesh were not traders in the sense of people who earn their living from the profits obtained by buying and selling, thanks to the price differential in those transactions, but had merchant status, by virtue of birth or by royal appointment. Their incomes were derived from commission or interest. The extraction of copper, which was in Anatolian hands, went on in accordance with equivalencies, and prices were fixed in advance according to those equivalencies.

In short, this was treaty trade, in which the public authorities guarantee all the operations and the merchants are therefore immune from risk. The Assyrian trader restricted himself to stimulating copper extraction by the natives through loans and investments, paying future suppliers in advance. Although the *tamkārum* is an independent agent, the whole operation is a public service and an integral part of state trade. This model of a permanent settlement of traders on foreign territory is directly related to another type of organization of eastern trade: the 'port of trade', which will be associated later with the cities of Ugarit, Sidon, Tyre and Carthage, still in keeping with Polanyi's model.

Recent work undertaken on the *kārum* at Kanesh and the study of fresh written documents from the archives of that Anatolian city have made it clear that the Assyrian commercial enclave was a much more complex centre than Garelli or Polanyi could have imagined some time ago. The *kārum*, situated at the foot of the city, included houses and residential districts, not only for Assyrian merchants but also for natives and other foreign traders. One great commercial house (*bit kārum*) was outstanding, along with several firms or branches (*bitum*) controlled by powerful merchant families.

At first it was a male Assyrian population that settled in Kanesh, made up of merchants and their employees, whose families continued to live in Assur. Gradually itinerant traders and commercial agents began buying land in the area, all bringing their families, so that the commercial enclave became a genuine colony.

The exact relationship that existed between the metropolis of Assur and the various Anatolian *kāru* is not known. From the correspondence carried on between the Assyrian merchants of Kanesh and their representatives in Assur we can infer the presence in Cappadocia of veritable merchant dynasties controlling powerful commercial firms. One of these merchants, Imdi-ilum, is a typical businessman with his own archive and agents in Assur who receive commission in return for buying and investing for him. He is a *tamkārum* of high social rank, who travels constantly and from Kanesh controls the caravans and activities of his many agents. Imdi-ilum owns a kind of family firm, probably inherited from his father, he has properties in Assur and keeps his own agents in Konya, a land rich in metals. It is estimated that this typical businessman succeeded in accumulating a veritable fortune in talents of silver.

The new documentation from Kanesh concerning, it should not be forgotten, the second millennium, shows that, alongside certain elements of 'treaty' trade, the vast majority of commercial activities rested on private initiative. There are orders to 'sell at any price', which means that there is risk, there is weighing up of costs, margins of gain and profits. Various allusions to the poor demand for tin, to a fall in prices, to emergency situations at certain times of the year, to the fluctuation of prices and to changes in supply and demand lend credence to the hypothesis of a quite well developed market trade. Silver did indeed function as money, that is to say, as an indirect medium of exchange and it is clear that the merchants of Kanesh were not state employees.

Other recent data also invalidate many of Polanyi's hypotheses about the mutual exclusiveness of state trade and private initiative. We now know, too, that the main objective of the Assyrian enclave in Kanesh was to obtain not copper but gold and silver. The gold and silver were not destined for the Assyrian state but for the pockets of the merchants themselves who, although they paid taxes to the 'city' (Assur), formed a genuine private or 'capitalist' enterprise. In any case, the Assyrians of Cappadocia did not devote themselves to trading in copper and wool because Assyria needed them but because that trade was a means of obtaining more gold and silver. All this activity appears to be financed by great bankers and private investments. Lastly, all the indications point to a dense network of trading posts controlled from Kanesh, which succeeded in linking the Arabian Gulf with Anatolia and Iran through complicated ramifications, and middlemen operating between producers and consumers.

But all this mass of archaeological and literary information, relating chiefly to the second millennium, is interrupted almost completely after 1200 BC. This means that to reconstruct the mechanisms of trade in the first millennium, we must rely almost exclusively on the archaeological record and a less exact literary documentation. This lack of documents poses serious difficulties when it comes to analysing the organization of Phoenician trade in general and discussing the interrelation that existed between the political power and commercial activity in particular. The question once again is to determine which sectors of society ran the Phoenician enterprise in the Mediterranean, whether it was the state or private initiative.

PHOENICIAN TRADE AND ITS FORMS OF ORGANIZATION

The political collapse of 1200 BC in the Near East and the disappearance of the great palatine institutions of the Late Bronze Age gave rise to new models of commercial organization although the solid mercantile traditions of the second millennium were preserved at the same time. A good part of those traditions will be gathered up by Tyre.

Some authors are of the opinion that, unlike the second millennium, trade in the first millennium was primarily in private hands and that the strategy of Phoenician mercantile activity consisted basically in making profits and creating a demand in the quest for gain. At first the palace would have stimulated commercial activity, holding a monopoly over international trade, only to give way later to individual initiative in matters of commerce.

In the view of some authors, a mercantile oligarchy, inevitably associated with private activity, would have gradually taken over the management of long-distance trade from the palace. In Tyre, the rise of this oligarchy would have shifted the epicentre of trade towards the Mediterranean and would be responsible for the institutionalization of the colonies. The many divergencies observed in the Phoenician enclaves in the west would be due precisely to separate trading circuits, that is to say, to the activity of a multiplicity of centres directing the organization of trade. Moreover, only private initiative would have been capable of seeking new incentives for trade and opening up new metal routes in the west, all of which would be unthinkable on the part of the state.

The reality, however, is much more complex than appears at first sight. Firstly, there is no evidence in the first millennium for such a clear evolution in trading systems in Phoenicia from a state controlled stage to private mercantile enterprise. As we shall see later, the mercantile oligarchy of Tyre or Byblos was not only present from the beginning in all the commercial initiatives of the Phoenician cities, but the mere fact that the written sources hardly mention the private sector in the commercial transactions of the Phoenician world in the first half of the first millennium does not authorize us to assert that there was no independent trade. From the available documents, which we shall go on to discuss, we can infer a strong role for the monarchy in the organization of trade (Wen-Amon's account, the prophecies of Ezekiel), the presence of solidly organized oligarchic elites (Wen-Amon, the treaty of Baal and Asarhadon) and a private trade more akin to piracy than to mercantile activity proper (Homer).

Merchants, princes and shipowners

Wen-Amon's story

All the indications are that in the twelfth to tenth centuries BC the organization of Phoenician trade was subject to the political power and in this respect it was closer to the Late Bronze Age structures – Ugarit – that to those of the Iron Age. This hypothesis seems to be supported by the account given by Wen-Amon, in which, among other things, the Egyptian envoy attempts to obtain supplies direct from the royal palace of Byblos. Furthermore, King Zakarbaal possessed a strong administrative organization, held a monopoly in the exploitation of wood and controlled the port and the territorial waters. In short, at the beginning of the Iron Age the palace seemed to constitute an institution capable of managing commercial activity, the supply of raw materials and the trade routes by means of legal and fiscal prerogatives over the coastal ports (Appendix II).

The king of Byblos, Zakarbaal or Sicharbas, boasts to Wen-Amon that he possesses fifty coastal vessels (*br*) anchored in the port of Sidon and another twenty passenger or cargo (*mnš*) ships in the port of Byblos. So the complement of Byblos' merchant fleet is considerable if we remember that the account refers to the first half of the eleventh century BC.

Of particular interest, however, is what this account tells us about the way trade was organized. Zakarbaal explains to Wen-Amon that the twenty ships in Byblos trade in *ḫbr* or *ḫubŭr* with Smendes of Egypt and that the fifty ships lying in Sidon are in *ḫubŭr* with one Wrktr, or Urkatel, a resident of Tanis (Fig. 17).

In Wen-Amon's account the term *ḫubŭr* thus occurs twice, once in relation to a Phoenician prince or merchant living in Egypt. The term, which has equivalents in Ugaritic and in Hebrew (II Chronicles 20:35–37) has been translated as community, guild, syndicate, commercial chain, firm, company, association or consortium. For the majority of the authors who have studied the etymology of the word, the exact meaning would be syndicate, company or trading partnership, similar to the Hebrew *ḥ-b-r* or *ḥabbar*, used to designate an association or guild of merchants (Job 40:25). Consequently, the twenty ships of the king of Byblos would have been in trading partnership with King Smendes, in the manner of the joint enterprises of Hiram and Solomon or, later, like the *ḫubŭr* of Jehosaphat and Ahaziah. Indeed, the kings Ahaziah of Israel and Jehosaphat of Judah set up a *ḫubŭr* in the ninth century BC with the object of resuming the voyages to Ophir, initiated by their forebear Solomon (I Kings 22:48; II Chronicles 20:35). All Jehosaphat was doing was to adopt a Phoenician model of a merchants' consortium traditionally used for joint large-scale shipping enterprises under the protection of the monarchy. The profits or losses in an enterprise of this kind could be so high that it was necessary to join forces under state management.

In Wen-Amon's story, the fifty coastal vessels lying in Sidon were not in partnership with another monarch but with Urkatel or Werket-el. The fact that he had a fleet of fifty merchant ships could only mean

Fig. 17   Phoenician ship – bas-relief from the palace of Sennacherib in Nineveh (c. 700 BC)

that Urkatel was a powerful merchant very close to the royal house of Byblos and wielding, perhaps, more economic power than the king himself.

The presence of the powerful Urkatel suggests that there may have existed in Phoenicia from earliest times a highly developed private commerce, operating in circles very close to the palace or directly subordinate to the royal house. In that case, the *ḥubŭr* might be organized corporations or shipping consortia running a regular trade between the Phoenician coast and Egypt and operating with complete autonomy under the protection of a wealthy man.

To judge by other biblical references, these merchant companies must have come into being in response to the need for protection against piracy and their function must have consisted in providing the necessary capital to build and equip merchant ships and ensure their protection against pirates, risks and losses. Various allusions in the Old Testament confirm these examples of maritime consortia, for example, between the king of Tyre and the 'kings of the islands' (Ezekiel 27:35).

Wen-Amon's account makes it quite clear that during the eleventh century BC the international trade developed by the Phoenician cities possessed several mercantile organizations operating under the protection of powerful 'princes' – Smendes of Egypt, Urkatel, the king of Byblos himself – who possessed important merchant fleets and who, on occasions, lived in distant lands or kept permanent representatives in foreign ports. The existence of these shipping consortia or commercial firms, run by powerful shipowners, like Urkatel, who provided capital and had commercial agents or partners and branches abroad, is already recorded in Ugarit, where these personages normally appear attached to the palace.

Even when these merchants appear to operate independently and organize their own voyages, the words of Zakarbaal suggest a trade very close to the orbit of the king and coexisting with the merchant fleet of the king of Byblos. The idea, therefore, of private trade invading the domain of state trade from the tenth century BC on, that is after the reign of Hiram I, does not fit in with the interpretation of Wen-Amon's story. At first the two spheres of trade were complementary and, in one way or another, came within the protective orbit of the palace.

We are undoubtedly dealing with a mercantile elite on whose successes and enterprises the wealth of Tyre depended. They are certainly the great 'men of the city', as described in the Ugaritic texts of the fourteenth century BC and whom we always find very close to power. From the biblical and Ugaritic references we can infer that these commercial firms pivoted, in the manner of the *kārum* at Kanesh, around family clans, guilds of merchants and 'houses', as the Old Testament calls them, including the most powerful, 'the house of the king'.

This can be deduced from the famous verse in Isaiah (23:8): 'Tyre, the crowning city, whose merchants are princes, whose traffickers are the honourable of the earth'.

Zakarbaal mentions a Council of State in the city of Byblos, which may have acted, among other functions, as a board of commercial management, presided over by the king and by the 'princes of the sea' (Ezekiel 26:16). In any case, we know that later, during the seventh to third centuries BC, the power of the king centred round a Council of Elders, the 'suffetes', who, in both Tyre and Carthage, formed part of the city oligarchy.

We do not know how this advisory council of the king's worked nor what exactly were its powers. In this respect, the treaty signed by Asarhadon and King Baal of Tyre in the seventh century BC is significant, in that the merchant fleet of Tyre was the property partly of the king and partly of the 'elders of the country', that is, of the shipowners and merchant princes.

In the tenth century BC, the written sources concerning the times of Hiram and Solomon refer to an exclusively state trade. The palace of Hiram I managed international exchanges, had rights of ownership over timber and sent its own specialist workforce to the king of Israel (I Kings 5:6–10; I Kings 7:13). In return, the oil and grain supplied by Solomon went directly into the possession of the palace of Tyre. Everything seems to indicate that the royal palace was then the vital axis of the Tyrian economy. The state dimension in the joint shipping enterprise of Tyre and Israel shows clearly to what extent the state was behind the great international undertakings of Tyrian trade. It must, however, be borne in mind that there is no information in existence about other forms of commercial organization in this period. The agreement signed by Hiram and Solomon is a formula typical of commercial treaties between royal houses and envisages the exchange of gifts and ambassadors such as we know in the Near East from the days of Amarna. It would be ingenuous to suppose that the enterprise in the Red Sea and Ophir embraces all the trade carried on in the tenth century BC.

From the ninth to eighth centuries on, this whole scenario under-went substantial changes. Stemming from the Assyrian expansion, we witness the massive arrival in western Asia of the private element in the sphere of commerce, coinciding, in the opinion of some authors, with a considerable decline in the part played by the Phoenician palace and monarchy in economic activity. Still according to this hypothesis, the development of private initiative would explain why, in the west, the original trading posts began changing into genuine colonies in the eighth and seventh centuries BC. In Israel, too, the private sector would have invaded trade after the reign of Solomon, at the expense of the traditional part played by the monarchy.

The available written information does not at present allow us to subscribe to a change of this nature in Phoenicia from the ninth century. Even in Assyria, where the written sources are much more explicit, the question of whether or not there was private trade and, if so, whether it was more important than the public sector remains highly controversial.

In our view, the essential question is not whether Phoenician trade in the ninth to seventh centuries was basically a private or a state undertaking. In the Near East in general, and in Phoenicia in particular, public trade and private initiative, almost always associated with the search for profits and the desire for gain, were perfectly complementary. It was a synchronous process in which both the private sector and the palace were looking for profits and in which the palace needed the private merchant as much as the trader needed the protection of the palace.

But we also know that from the ninth century BC till the neo-Babylonian period, a large part of long-distance overland trade was in the hands of independent Tyrian merchants operating on a large scale through agents and branches in Babylonia, Ur and Uruk and supplying textiles, perfumes, copper and iron to the chief Mesopotamian cities.

We also find hints of private trade in Phoenicia in the correspondence of an official of Tiglatpileser in charge of the Phoenician coast who, at the end of the eighth century BC, tells the Assyrian king that he has allowed the 'people of Sidon' to trade and work the wood of the Lebanon in exchange for not selling it to the Palestinians and Egyptians, potential enemies of Assyria.

In the seventh to sixth centuries BC, merchants and craftsmen are again known to be circulating freely in the east and they sometimes appear organized into professional associations rather like guilds. Even in the days of Nebuchadnezzar II, in Babylonia, the leader of the palace merchants is a high functionary (*rab tamkāri*) called Hanunu or Hanon, a typical name of Phoenician derivation.

The only diplomatic document we know from later than the tenth century BC referring to Tyre shows yet again that the organization of Phoenician trade at the beginning of the seventh century BC does not differ substantially from that described in Wen-Amon's story in the eleventh century BC. Indeed, the treaty signed between Asarhadon and King Baal of Tyre, dated around 670 BC, refers explicitly to the 'ships of Baal' and to the ships of 'the people of Tyre', on which sailing restrictions were imposed. So there are two categories of merchant ships, those of the royal house and those of the great merchants of Tyre. It is not difficult to imagine that these 'people of Tyre', like the 'people of Sidon, Arvad and Byblos' who take part in the Tyrian commercial enterprises (Ezekiel 27:8–24), are the 'merchant princes' of Isaiah, that mercantile oligarchy close to the palace from which Urkatel and other 'great Phoenician traders' came.

The commercial orbit of Tyre in the texts of the Hebrew prophets
The maritime power and international importance of Tyre made that city the object of many prophecies and oracles from the prophets of Israel, who, rather than announcing it, seem to be wishing for its final destruction.

Outstanding among the texts most rich in information and, at the

same time, most disturbing, are the famous laments for Tyre, the work
of Isaiah and Ezekiel.

Of the oracles against Tyre, the most ancient is that of Isaiah, a
prophet who lived between the late eighth and early seventh centuries
BC. The oracle against Tyre, which, it must not be forgotten, contains
later interpolations into the text, occupies the whole of Chapter 23 of
the book of Isaiah (Appendix III).

Isaiah

Isaiah's prophecy falls into two quite distinct parts: the first (vv. 1–14),
which evokes past days of glory and decline in the city, and the last
(vv. 15–17), which is notable for the messianic announcement according to which, after seventy years of silence, Tyre will be restored and
will resume the commercial traffic of yore.

Verses 1–14 are particularly interesting in that they announce the
destruction of Tyre by the will of Yahweh and contain one of the most
ancient references to the 'ships of Tarshish', famous for transporting
riches, as they did in the days of Hiram I.

In Isaiah's prophecy, Tyre is synonymous with arrogance, beauty,
luxury and pride and her past greatness is compared with her present
condition: the ports closed, the court abandoned, the coast devastated
and Sidon no longer dominant but oppressed; and all this by divine
punishment.

Some authors relate the destruction thus announced to the conquest
by Asarhadon in 677 BC, although most experts prefer to connect the
oracle of Isaiah with the campaigns of Sennacherib against the coast
and with his victory over King Luli of Tyre in the year 701 BC, or with
Asurbanipal's offensive (668–626 BC). The fact is that the disaster
foretold by the prophet did not happen. Isaiah would probably have
been writing in unsettled times and in a period when Tyre was
seriously threatened with destruction during the reigns of Salmanasar
V, Sargon II and Sennacherib: Isaiah himself would have been a
witness and a contemporary of these threats.

The prophecy is presented in the form of a lament by the ships of
Tarshish when, returning from Chittim, they find Tyre destroyed by
the will of Yahweh in order to humble her pride (vv. 6–9). The
prophet's description speaks of a city, Tyre, controlling the trade of all
the nations, the market of the nations (v. 2) and whose ships cross all
the seas. Her merchants form an aristocracy, since they are princes
(*šarim*) and are the greatest of the earth (v. 8). These merchants arrive
in distant lands where they settle for a while (v. 7). Distant lands must

not be taken to mean the colonies in the west, since the geographic orbit of Tyre's trade in Isaiah is restricted to the eastern Mediterranean: Egypt, Chittim and Tarshish.

To the prophet it is obvious that trade was the main motive for Phoenician activity at sea and that Tyre was famous among her neighbours and contemporaries for her extraordinary riches and economic power.

Ezekiel

The second great prophetic text about Tyre, that of Ezekiel, presents us with information of incalculable value about Tyre's trade and zones of economic influence, so much so that it is considered to be one of the most relevant sources of information for reconstructing the Phoenician economy in the days of the Mediterranean expansion (Appendix III).

Ezekiel was a prophet deported to Babylon by Nebuchadnezzar in 597 BC. It is thought that he wrote his oracles around 586 BC, that is at the beginning of the Exile, so that his prophecies against Tyre would reflect a political situation from the beginning of the sixth century BC.

In fact, Ezekiel was describing the destruction of Tyre and formulating his oracle at the precise moment when Tyre was being besieged by the troops of Nebuchadnezzar. Nevertheless, reasonable doubts exist about the authenticity of the work and whether this prophet was really deported to Babylon. Various experts are of the opinion that Ezekiel lived in reality at the end of the seventh century BC and that his work was not compiled in the form we know today until the fifth to fourth centuries BC. In the opinion of other authors the prophecy of the destruction of Tyre refers to events that took place before the year 732 BC so that it would reflect a situation more relevant to the ninth to eighth centuries BC. The controversies around the authenticity of Ezekiel's work arise from the very text itself, contained in Chapters 26–27, in which unity of composition is strikingly lacking.

In effect the central poem about Tyre appears to be divided into two parts by a passage in prose (Chap. 27, vv. 12–24), in which an account is given of all the nations trading with Tyre and a list of the principal merchandise arriving in her port. This passage contrasts with the rest of the prophecy, which seems to be written in verse and in which Tyre is compared allegorically to a ship.

It is thought that whoever was responsible for writing these verses, it was not Ezekiel, and that the anonymous author did no more than transcribe and copy an old poem describing a situation which, moreover, is wrong for the beginning of the sixth century BC. The passage is in effect extraneous to the general context of Chapter 27 and there are also linguistic arguments which invalidate the supposed unity and suggest that it does not belong to the original book.

This passage in prose, which Ezekiel himself may perhaps have heard in Babylonia, gathers together the fragments of an ancient Tyrian poem, rediscovered in the neo-Babylonian period. In these verses that include the catalogue of the nations trading with Tyre, mention is made, among others, of Judah, Damascus and Israel, states which, at the time of Ezekiel, had long been under Assyrian domination, so that it is unlikely that they could provide Tyre with the many luxury products the prophet describes. To sum up, the prose part of Chapter 27 would refer to a period before Assyrian domination over Judah, Israel and Damascus, perhaps corresponding to the period of Ithobaal's reign and so to the period of the greatest expansion of Tyre's trade in the east, during the ninth to eighth centuries BC.

In general it can be said that the description Ezekiel gives of Tyre on the eve of the Babylonian siege is today a unique document for the economic history of the period. So it is worthwhile analysing the two parts of the prophecy separately, the part in verse, describing the commercial greatness of the city shortly before its fall and in which Tyre appears in metaphoric form as a great ship about to be wrecked; and the passage in prose which includes a roll call of the nations maintaining trading relations with Tyre and the imports arriving periodically at her port.

The prophecy concerning Tyre begins in Chapter 26, where the city appears to be impregnable, built on a rocky island with its port open to the ships and merchandise of all the nations. Tyre is the chief commercial intermediary between the Asian continent and the Mediterranean, a bridge between the nations and so coveted by the great powers of the interior. In the poem, Tyre stands majestic, regal, almost mythical and a gigantic chorus of islands and shores appears on the stage, summoned by the voice of the prophet. The greatness of her splendour will be matched by the greatness of her fall.

At the sound of Tyre's fall, the islands and shores will tremble, all the princes of the sea will descend from their thrones and the cities which had glorified her name will shake with the terror inspired by her (26:15–18). This general mourning no doubt reflects Tyre's hegemony over the sea and over the territories governed by princes and the renown of her trade on an international level.

The best-known text of Ezekiel is Chapter 27, to which we have already alluded and which contains his second prophecy against Tyre.

The city is represented as a ship, commanded by expert sailors and protected by brave warriors, to the equipping of which all the nations of the earth had contributed (27:3–11). We should point out that the comparison with a great ship which finally founders at sea in the midst of a political storm is a well-known literary device in the form of a metaphor, intended to reinforce the devastating image of a city engulfed in a violent tidal wave.

The prophecy begins by detailing the commercial links possessed by Tyre, situated at the entrance to the sea and enthroned on her two ports (vv. 1–3). Her market, in which innumerable peoples of the coast converge, is what gives her international status. Tyre is a ship loaded with riches, built of cedar and fir trees from Senir (Mount Hermon) and from Lebanon, decorated with purple, blue and red from Alishah (Cyprus) and Yawan (Greece) and bearing linen sails brought from Egypt (vv. 4–7). The ship is manned by oarsmen from Sidon and Arvad and experts from Byblos repair any damage (vv. 8–9). In short, the chief Phoenician cities work for Tyre and the most important cities on earth trade with her.

The end of the lament expresses all the economic and political weight of Tyre at that period, linked to every nation through trade and her power redounding to the ends of the earth (vv. 25–36).

The celebrated passage in prose, contained in verses 12–24, is still more eloquent. Once more the geographic horizon reflected by the prophet or his interpolator is restricted to Anatolia, Arabia, Egypt and Cyprus. In it the chief nations trading with Tyre are made known with the type of commodities that are exchanged commercially, giving their origin and content. The value of this information lies not just in the minute description of the products imported by Tyre but in the reconstruction of a number of commercial networks which should probably be situated at a time very close to that of the Tyrian expansion to the west.

Tarshish is mentioned as holding a monopoly in the metal trade – silver, iron, tin and lead – in the eastern Mediterranean, referring probably to some unspecified territory in Asia Minor. It is followed by Yawan, Tubal and Meshek, which supply mainly horses and slaves. Yawan designates the Greek islands of Cyprus and the Cilician coast, that is to say Ionia, and Tubal would correspond to Akkadian Tabalu in Asia Minor, perhaps in the central Taurus area. Meshek is usually associated with the Akkadian Mušku, the country of Muṣri, between Armenia and Cilicia, which would correspond to the biblical Miṣraim, where as early as the tenth century BC Solomon obtained horses

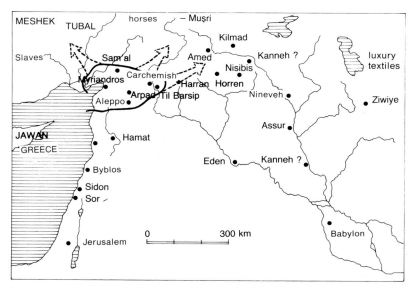

Fig. 18   Tyrian trade in the Near East (in Ezekiel)

(I Kings 10:28–29). Lastly the text mentions Bet Togarma, which supplies Tyre with horses, bloodstock and mules.

It can be said that the first part of the list of nations trading with Tyre (vv. 1–3) reflects a commercial network embracing Cilicia, Armenia and the Ionian isles and coincides exactly with the trading circuit of North Syria, Cappadocia and the Gulf of Alexandretta, which, as we know, Tyre controlled during the ninth century BC (Fig. 18).

There follows a mention of the sons of Rodon (Rhodes), who provide Tyre with ivory and ebonite, Edom or Aram, who supply garnet, purple cloth and rubies, Judah and Israel who export oil and grain and, lastly, Damascus which sends Tyre wine and wool (vv. 15–18). After mentioning Uzal, Sheba (probably Saba in Arabia) and Rama, who trade in spices and precious stones, the text ends by citing Harran, Kanneh, Eden, Assur and Kilmad (v. 13), countries producing luxury cloth and which we should situate to the east of the Euphrates – Harran, Kanneh, Eden – and on the Armenian Tigris – Kullimeri.

Tyre, then, operates worldwide and her products enjoy universal demand, while at the same time the whole known world furnishes her with every kind of commodity. It is trade on a grand scale by sea and by land, using routes that head basically eastwards and had been opened up by Hiram I. In short, it is international trade of great scope in which the political institutions had inevitably to intervene as the ultimate guarantors of its success.

Allusion is made, moreover, to the great market in Tyre (v. 18) which may perhaps be a reference to a place of exchange near the port, in the Eurychoros (big place), the building of which tradition ascribes to Hiram (Fl. Josephus, *Ant.* 8:145).

A number of recent studies on the text of Ezekiel appear to indicate that all these far-flung powers who traded with Tyre acted as her 'agents', that is to say as part of a vast mercantile organization in which commercial agents under the direct tutelage of Tyre would be working for her in their own countries of origin. Indeed, in the original text, the nations are called *sohar* or *rokel*, equivalent to the *tamkārum* of the second millennium, and in this case they seem to be directly dependent on the king of Tyre. This means that Ezekiel's text is not referring to nations as such, but to agents of Tyre acting as intermediaries with those nations.

The list of commodities given in Ezekiel's text is a mixture of luxury products and subsistence goods, although, surprisingly, there is no mention of copper. Maybe the supply of copper for the Tyrian workshops was not a matter of preferential trading. Surprising, too, is the absence of Cyprus, the great copper producer and ally of Tyre in this international trade, an absence that some people interpret as indicating that there were problems on the copper trade route in the first half of the first millennium.

Pirates and traders: Phoenician trade in Homer

Professional trade
An exceptionally important source in evaluating other aspects of Phoenician trade is Homer, whose texts confine themselves to describing a situation in the Aegean, without being greatly concerned to seek the causes or institutional background of this seafaring trade.

Homer's texts and his Trojan cycle reflect Greek society in contact with these eastern navigators for the first time and describe geopolitical conditions in a state of constant flux. Thus, for example, in the Iliad, the Phoenicians are expert craftsmen in metal and in luxury textiles, their exceptional talents as sailors are appreciated and they appear in the Aegean on very rare occasions. The Odyssey, composed two or three generations after the Iliad, describes the Phoenicians as already dominant at sea in conflict with the Greeks and sees them as traders and pirates who appear much more frequently in Greek waters.

Phoenician trade in Homer is not organized trade but individual enterprise, attempting to open up markets in Greece, offering wares to the highest bidder and, above all, seeking profits. The trade is small in volume, carried on by merchant ships that pursue other complementary activities, such as carrying passengers and trafficking in slaves. We see these merchants frequenting the ports of Lemnos, Pilos, Ithaca, Syros, Crete, Libya and Egypt.

The situation described by Homer is more akin to casual trade than to a regular commerce with colonies or trading posts throughout the Mediterranean. There is no mention of colonies or permanent Phoenician settlements, nor, indeed, of the Greek city-state. On the contrary, Phoenician trade frequently appears associated with management by her monarchs and with the practice of gifts and hospitality. Hence, it all reflects an atmosphere very close to the start of Tyrian expansion westwards, that is, a situation more appropriate to the ninth century than to the eighth to seventh centuries BC, which is the period when the epics of Homer were being written.

Another aspect to be borne in mind is the Homeric attitude to trade and traders or, in other words, the Phoenicians. Unlike the Near East or mediaeval Europe, ancient Greece considered trade to be incompatible with the Greek concept of aristocracy and ethics. The ethics of Homer forbid the practice of commerce as a profession, for social rather than economic reasons. In the Greek world, the professional trader had a very low social status and belonged to a despised social class. The Homeric noble ideal assumes that goods are acquired through looting and piracy, hence the completely negative attitude seen in the Iliad and the Odyssey to trade and traders and, by extension, to the Phoenicians. Their unpopularity would persist in Greece until the classical period. In the Athens of the fifth to fourth centuries BC mercantile activity is dishonourable, both for the merchant trafficking on his own account, the *emporós*, and for the owner of a merchant ship, the *nauklerós*, and also for the exporter engaged in seafaring expeditions, or *endokós*.

In Homer, trade is left to foreigners. In reality, the external trade of the Greek cities appears to be in the hands of the Phoenicians – the 'Sidonians' – the foreigners who are not always well received and, as such, are untrustworthy. The words addressed to Odysseus suffice to give an idea of the negative image of the trader in general: 'You seem to be a skipper of a merchant crew rather than a trained athlete'

(*Od.* 8:145–164). And before the court of Antinous, Ulysses had to defend himself against the suspicion of being still worse, namely 'a merchant seeking to snatch profits'.

Homer's contempt for the merchant and his homonym, the Phoenician merchant, has deep roots of a social and ideological nature which must be linked with the great political crisis of the Greek aristocracy, of which Homer and Hesiod were witnesses. Trade in general, and Phoenician trade in particular, apparently played an important part in the way the crisis was managed. Let us look briefly at the way this process unfolded.

In Greece, the crisis in ancient trade implies the end of trade by aristocratic exchange, linked to the landowning oligarchy, called *prexis* trade by Homer or *ergon* trade by Hesiod. The aristocratic trade was essentially private and evolved as a complementary activity to agriculture, tending toward trade in slaves, wine, oil and metals. This trade, conditioned by the agricultural cycle, was confined to the summer season, that is, to the dead season for agriculture. Hesiod, in the seventh century BC, dubs the period from 25 October to 5 May an unsuitable time for seafaring and observes in his book 'The labours of the day' that it is desirable to set out on a voyage in the fifty days following the summer solstice.

As true mouthpieces of the aristocracy, Homer and Hesiod claim that piracy is an honourable activity, especially as an alternative to trade (*Iliad* 11:328–331), a defence that would be taken up later by Aristotle and Thucydides (1:5, 2). This activity, also performed by the Phoenicians and the Euboeans (*Il.* 23:744; *Od.* 13:272), appears in Homer to be directly related to trafficking in slaves. This piratical *prexis* trade was occasionally indulged in by warships for commercial purposes and lasted on in the Mediterranean until the end of the seventh century BC. One known example of the aristocratic merchant is Colaios of Samos, who visited Tartessos at the end of that century.

The crisis in this type of trade is attributed to the gradual development of a non-aristocratic, specialized trade in the hands of professionals – the *emporós* – which burst on Greece in the form of foreign, that is, Phoenician trade. At first, the Greek word *emporós* designated a traveller or passenger in a ship belonging to another person, or else a Greek merchant who had no ship of his own. In the days of Hesiod, the word became the name for a specialized activity, the *emporie* trade which breaks with the self-sufficiency of aristocratic trade by making commercial activity autonomous with respect to shipping activity in general. Very soon, *emporós*, severely criticized by

Hesiod, came to designate the trader *par excellence* who ventures forth to sea even in spring.

In Homer, *emporie* trade is still something alien to the aristocratic world and appears for the first time associated with an external factor: the Phoenicians.

These latter appear haunting the ports of the Aegean, where they trade in slaves and wine and reserve special honours for the local lord. Their craftwork and their finest and most delicate ornaments, such as the multi-coloured cloth, the work of 'Sidonian' women, are admired. Paris himself is said to have acquired a piece of this cloth in Sidon to give as a present to Helen before carrying her off to Troy (*Il.* 6:289). Their technical skill and their mastery as workers in gold and bronze are likewise admired.

But, above all, the Phoenicians are the trading people *par excellence* sailing from one end of the known world to the other and spending a whole year in selling their cargo (*Od.* 15:455). The Phoenicians are pirates and ravishers of women and they monopolize seaborne trade. Homer does not attach too much importance to these commercial activities, nor is he interested in the profit, since they are not Greeks. 'They are fine sailors, but rogues' (*Od.* 15:415–416).

Of special interest for the study of the Phoenicians' commercial organization is the episode narrated to Ulysses on his arrival in Ithaca by the swineherd, Eumaeus. Aristocratic by birth, Eumaeus had been kidnapped and subsequently sold as a child by Phoenician merchants at the instigation of a slave woman from Sidon, 'a city rich in bronze' (*Od.* 15:415–428). This episode takes place on the island of Syrie, perhaps Syros, where a group of Phoenicians had arrived bearing articles of adornment, necklaces, jewels and gewgaws, articles that Homer calls *athyrmata* (*Od.* 15:459). The Phoenicians remained for a whole year in the port of Syrie in order to reload their ship with other merchandise, taking advantage of the delay to kidnap the king's son, Eumaeus.

In the same way, Ulysses tells that in Egypt he fell in with a rascally, thieving Phoenician, who prevailed on him to journey with him to Phoenicia, where he had property and a house (*Od.* 14:287–300). When the fine season came round, he put him aboard his ship with the intention of selling him as a slave in Libya. As they passed Crete, Ulysses had managed to escape.

So we see the Phoenicians travelling freely through Greek waters and we know of prolonged calls in Syros or in Egypt and of a regular trade with Libya. And we have a Phoenician merchant, who owns his own ship and a house and property in his country, who deals in slaves in the springtime, gets good returns and plies the route from Phoenicia via Crete and Egypt to Libya.

The episode in the port in Lemnos, included in the Iliad, is of the utmost interest to us since it allows us to guess at Phoenician trading practices, which are very similar to exceedingly ancient forms of exchange (*Il.* 23:740–745). This episode tells how, on the occasion of the funeral of Patroclus, Achilles offered a large silver crater, a 'master-piece of Sidonian craftsmanship', as a prize. The vessel, 'The loveliest thing in the world', was 'shipped by Phoenician traders across the misty seas' and displayed in various ports until it finally arrived in the port of Lemnos, and was offered as a gift to the king, Thoas. Later the same silver vase served as a ransom for one of Priam's daughters, captured by Achilles, and thus finally came into his hands.

It is thus a Phoenician crater with a 'history': displayed for sale at first, it is then presented as a gift to the king of Lemnos, subsequently used as a ransom and finally offered by Achilles as a prize in the funeral games of Patroclus, a prize which is won by Odysseus. It was not by chance that the crater ended up on the island of Ithaca.

The episode undoubtedly gives food for thought. Imagine an archae-ologist discovering a silver vessel with these features which are typical of many examples from tombs in Cyprus and Italy (Fig. 19). With a discovery of this nature, only one firm fact is known: the Phoenician origin of the vessel. How can a 'commercial history' be reconstructed from that isolated piece of information? It is obvious that it is virtually impossible to reconstruct such a complex series of commercial trans-actions from a limited archaeological record.

The episode of Achilles' crater, moreover, is clear evidence of an itinerant Phoenician trade in which merchants transported their goods and objects of great value from one port to another. These luxury products, consisting generally of craters, cauldrons and tripods, passed from hand to hand as prizes, ransoms or ceremonial gifts to local kings or lords. At the end of all their wanderings, these products finished up as symbols of social status. This circulation of valuable objects among social elites must be fitted into the model of gift exchanges. These goods always have a high social and economic value and occasionally they figure in genuine operations of buying and selling, but always in the closed circle of the Greek aristocracy – Achilles, the king of Lemnos, Priam, Ulysses. The Phoenician crater, the cauldrons and the tripods that appear in this context in the Homeric epics, are called *keimélia* (*Il.* 17:292).

Fig. 19 Phoenician silver bowl from Idalion, Cyprus (eighth century BC)

On the subject of the circulation of reciprocal gifts among social elites, another episode should be mentioned in which, once again, the Phoenicians are involved. Reference is made to another chased silver crater with a rim of gold, held to be the work of Hephaestus, a crater that the king of Sidon had offered as a gift to Menelaus when he was a guest in his house (*Od.* 4:615–619). In this case, the practice of gifts seems to be associated with that of hospitality.

This episode appears to have surprised historians of ancient Greek trade, inasmuch as the practices of gifts and hospitality are considered an essentially Greek form of reciprocity. Maybe the Phoenicians adopted an eminently aristocratic system, that of exchanging gifts, through Greek influence. The Phoenicians confined themselves to practising what they saw in the Aegean. Furthermore, it is thought that, in the period described by Homer and Hesiod, this system of exchange was coming to an end. The practice of the gift, as a form of rank and power relationships, would constitute an institution linked with the *prexis* or aristocratic trade. When specialist, professional commerce reached Greece, it would have entailed the end of a system of reciprocity between princes, and profit, economic considerations and financial interest would have replaced the old aristocratic practices.

And yet, the evidence shows that the exchange of gifts between social elites, with participants ranging from the king of Sidon to the king of Lemnos, far from being an institution that the Phoenicians happened to adopt in the Aegean, was a practice with a long tradition in the Near East and particularly characteristic of the Late Bronze Age in Mesopotamia, Canaan and Egypt. The Phoenicians inherited this exchange mechanism from their predecessors, the Canaanites, and practised it at all times and in all places. It will be one of the formulae, moreover, which the Phoenicians will use in the west as a means of opening up new markets.

Gift exchange

In his well-known 'Essai sur le don', Marcel Mauss showed that in ancient and primitive societies, exchange occasionally took the form of an exchange of gifts. So we are dealing with a form of trade in which social condition and wealth are directly involved. This type of reciprocal exchange would be, like any other activity, a 'total social phenomenon', as well as having a clear economic significance, since it has implications that are at once social, religious, magical, economic, utilitarian, moral and legal. In the opinion of Malinowski, in many, if not all, primitive peoples, economic acts belong in some chain of reciprocal present-giving.

Within the process of presents and counter-presents, the grades or relationships of equivalency vary from a balanced and equitable exchange between equals to an asymmetrical reciprocity that conceals relationships of power or gain. During the sequence of donation or presentation, these presents are exchanged for equivalent goods or else are received on the condition that counter-presentations will be offered later on, which, in turn, give the right to receive fresh presents. So the gift comes into circulation and creates social obligations. This is what happened with the crater of Achilles.

According to the principles of reciprocity, the exchange of gifts implies recognition of the right of one social sector to a prerogative, or else seeks to outdo a rival in opulence, privilege, rank and power. In this sense, the reciprocal exchange of gifts has a supra-economic character, to the extent that it is not the possession of riches that confers privilege and status but their transmission and distribution. In the case of Achilles' Phoenician crater, the article has value as long as it is offered as a gift but not as an article that is acquired, and it passes from one court to another until, perhaps, it returns to its starting point.

In the sphere of reciprocal obligations, the exchange of gifts creates expectations of reciprocal conduct and, in the long run, rights, obligations and the recognition of continuing transactions. In special circumstances that call for a formula to initiate ties of solidarity or of trade, the mutual exchange of gifts may help strengthen bonds of friendship and at the same time open up a continuing circuit of exchanges. It is one of the practices that usually follow the installation of traders in a foreign country and which the Phoenicians will use throughout the Mediterranean.

It is to the credit above all of Finley and Zaccagnini that they showed that the mechanisms of reciprocity, identified by Mauss and Malinowski among primitive peoples, were broadly similar to the exchange of gifts in Homeric Greece and the Asian Near East during the second and first millennia BC.

Reciprocity, gift and aristocratic trade are categories in which social rather than economic considerations would predominate, according to the model proposed by Polanyi's school when discussing primitive forms of exchange.

When Telemachus visited Menelaus in his palace in Sparta, seeking news of his father, his host offered him as a parting gift three horses, a carved chariot and a magnificent cup, to which the youth replied: 'Please make the gift you offer me a keepsake I can carry' (*Od.* 4:590–605). The Greek word used for it is *keimélion*, that is to say, something that can be kept, a treasure, a non-utilitarian article which is not used but is kept safe, since its function is to be owned or to be given as a present.

Just as in Italy in the eighth and seventh centuries BC, in Homer's Greece this circulation of 'treasures' is the prerogative primarily of the aristocracy and seems to be closely linked to the norms of hospitality and friendship. 'Let us honour him like a god with gifts' says Homer. The giving of presents thus forms part of a network of honorific activities – it is as honourable to give as to receive – in which the use or display of treasure for its own intrinsic value becomes a symbol of prestige and status. And the more genealogy or 'story' these articles have, the greater their value since those articles with a history of which Homer's heroes boast cover both the donor and the recipient with honour. In other words, it is the social context that determines the value of these articles and value means power, first and foremost.

In the Near East, this system of exchange is recorded particularly from the time of El Amarna, and it is generally concerned with political and commercial relations between royal houses, given that it is the usual formula by which two kings or princes initiate or renew diplomatic and trading relations. We have examples of this in Phoenicia itself.

In the correspondence of El Amarna, reciprocity is chiefly an expression of the ideals of fraternity and parity between political elites, where it is not always easy to distinguish between gifts, tribute and trade. It has been suggested in this connection that tribute is merely a gift that has become obligatory.

In Amarnian trade of the fourteenth to thirteenth centuries BC, the commercial transactions between the monarchies of Egypt, Babylonia, Assyria, Cyprus and Canaan carry with them a series of factors that lie outside economics – the exchange of gifts – and tend to establish personal and diplomatic relations. We have a case, for example, of Cyprus sending ivory to Egypt in exchange for ivory. This cannot properly be called trade, since no profits or economic advantages are being sought in rational economic terms, but it is an 'irrational' and anti-economic act in which what counts is not the merchandise itself – the ivory – but the sending of ivory for ivory, that is to say, a balanced reciprocity in the form of a social act through which it is hoped to establish diplomatic relations that, in the long run, will indeed produce economic advantages. The economic 'irrationality' consequently produces economic rationality, according to Godelier's terminology.

The story of Wen-Amon constitutes a good example of reciprocity from the beginning of the first millennium. In it can be perceived a twofold level of exchange: the mercantile proper and the ideological or prestigious. On the mercantile plane, the business consists of a request for wood on the part of Wen-Amon to which Zakarbaal replies demanding an equivalent counterpart in the form of gifts. It is the same procedure as in Amarnian trade, in which the haggling and bargaining are no more than attempts to delay the business transaction in expectation of an anticipated payment (Appendix II).

But in Wen-Amon's account we can already perceive a deterioration in the classic ceremonial of Late Bronze Age transactions. Wen-Amon flings an ideological discourse at the king of Byblos, in which he reminds him of the obligation to supply wood for the god Amon, as his predecessors had done. But Zakarbaal, protesting independence, invokes the ancient friendship between the kings of Egypt and Byblos in order to demand counterpart in gold and silver from Wen-Amon. The prestige of the king of Byblos is at stake, since the absence of reciprocity would amount to a breach of contract, of friendship and of hospitality.

Wen-Amon does not come to buy or to sell but to renew a trading relationship that had linked Byblos with Egypt during the second millennium, through uninterrupted exchanges of gifts. The economic background to this reciprocal exchange rests in reality on Byblos' obligation to provide cedar for building Amon's barque. Zakarbaal's negative response is therefore due to an absence of balanced reciprocity or of return gifts, which the Giblite king expects as a gesture of good will and recognition of his social status.

From all that has been said, we can infer that during the eleventh century BC Byblos is still making use of the international diplomatic norms through the exchange of gifts, the prerogative of the monarchies of the Late Bronze Age. The practice of gift exchange acquires a distinctly ceremonial or prestige character between royal houses, and will be seen again in Tyre during the reign of Hiram I.

When Solomon succeeds his father David on the throne of Israel, Hiram sends him messengers and gifts, or what amounts to the same thing, makes a gesture of good will with the object of renewing relations with the new monarch (I Kings 5:15). Moreover, the agreement on friendship and commercial cooperation signed by the two monarchs contains a vocabulary of fraternity and friendship very close to that used in Amarnian trade. The starting point is a gift as a greeting, to which the new king replies with other gifts or counterparts, which, in turn, evoke a response. This begins a sequence of exchanges of gifts which still does not constitute trade because no immediate counterparts are demanded – so it is 'irrational' – but which in the long run will lead to trade in the true sense, that of Ophir and the Red Sea.

Gift exchange is a deeply rooted exchange system in the Phoenician world which is not documented solely in the days of Zakarbaal of Byblos, in the reign of Hiram or in the epics of Homer but which was practised in a pre-commercial, ceremonial and diplomatic manner by the Phoenicians in the initial stages of their expansion into the Mediterranean. We can document it in the island of Cyprus, in Sardinia, in central Italy and also in Tartessos, that is, in those territories where the indigenous society maintained a hierarchical social structure endowed with chiefs, princes or petty local rulers.

Many luxury articles of the eighth and seventh centuries BC discovered in the Mediterranean have an acknowledged attribution to Phoenician workshops probably rooted in Tyre itself. We are thinking particularly of a group of metal cups made of silver and bronze, some of them with gold leaf at the rim, like the crater of Hephaestus described by Homer, which have been found in the Assyrian royal palaces or in tombs belonging to native princes in Cyprus, Etruria and Latium (Fig. 20). Before finally becoming part of princely burials, all

Fig. 20   Phoenician silver bowl from Praeneste, Italy (seventh century BC)

these cups would probably have had their 'history' like Achilles' Phoenician crater.

The Phoenician silver cups, like other Phoenician luxury articles found in the west, are therefore prestige goods, in that their circulation is due to a sequence of successive exchanges, of a ceremonial and diplomatic type between social elites and within very restricted circles. So we must speak of a 'prestige economy' insofar as the wealth circulated only amongst kings and leaders.

And the prestige factor possesses its own exclusive symbolism: wealth and the ostentatious hoarding of it. It is thus one of the most important factors in the creation of a surplus, since it stimulates the movement of persons and goods and mobilizes large quantities of luxury goods. In this process of reciprocity and trade, in which, it must be said, economics come before social considerations, we may say that the Phoenicians were past masters.

In Cyprus, as well as in Italy and the Iberian peninsula, the Phoenicians knew how to use and exploit the absence of organized trade between the indigenous populations, introducing prestige goods into those territories, aimed basically at their princes. In so doing, the Phoenicians aspired not only to create a demand in areas where there was none but also to initiate friendly relations with those sectors of society that controlled regions with plentiful resources. This action implied recognizing the social rank of the local leaders. So it is not by chance that we find the greatest concentrations of prestige goods in native burials situated in the territories that were richest in metal ores: southern Etruria, the lower Guadalquivir and Huelva.

Once again we must stress the difficulties facing the archaeologist when it comes to distinguishing between an exchange of gifts and commercial exchange on the basis solely of the archaeological record.

In Etruria and Latium, some of these prestige objects have the name of the owner inscribed on them or contain inscriptions alluding explicitly to donations, give the name of the donor or contain donation formulae. The presence and distribution of such objects in princely tombs at Cerveteri, Vetulonia or Praeneste have made it possible to reconstruct in part the circuits in which sumptuous gifts were exchanged between Etruscan or Latin chiefs, on the basis of silver cups and Phoenician ivories, pitchers and oriental gold gems. This system lasted in Etruria until the middle of the sixth century BC, when a gradual transition to a monetary economy took place in the region.

Something similar can be seen amongst the 'barbarian' societies of Hallstattian Europe, where it started with the intervention of a Greek colonial element rather than a Phoenician one. The discovery of large bronze craters, tripods and chariots in princely tombs of the Celtic chiefs on the upper Danube or in Burgundy – the tumuli of, for example, Hohenasperg, Hochdorf, Grächwyl and Vix – argues in favour of a system of gifts of a ceremonial and prestige type very similar to that used by the Phoenicians; they have the character of a 'donum' or *keimélion* and tend to open up markets to Greek trade in the interior of Europe.

It is thought that some elements typical of primitive currency can be seen in the system of reciprocal gifts, in the sense that certain metal objects in the form of cups, tripods or cauldrons could have a pre-monetary value as a means of exchange, for hoarding or as an expression of value.

Pre-monetary circulation

A question that is still a subject of debate today is that of whether valuable and prestige objects constituted 'money' or not, that is, pre-coinage symbols before the appearance of minted coins. Moreover, this debate must be seen in conjunction with the very small part played by Phoenicia in the origin of coinage. This is still surprising, even today, dealing as we are with the archetypal trading people, whose sway in this field, at the very moment when the first minted coinages appeared, was considerable. Contrary to the assertions of Polanyi and

Malinowski, namely that there could have been no money in primitive and ancient societies because there was no price fluctuation, we now know that a system of price adjustment existed in Mesopotamia, Anatolia and the Levant and that 'money' was used before the minting of coins. In reality, any negotiation concerning valuations and equivalencies implies prices. It is said, too, that anything given in order to obtain something else is money. Furthermore, let us remember that price is the expression in money of the value of a commodity.

In Sumer and Babylonia there was price regulation and wages were stipulated in silver or cereals, which acted as equivalents. We have already seen in the previous chapter that, from the second millennium BC, silver was not used as a metal in commercial transactions but as 'money' or a unit of exchange.

Some authors talk of 'primitive money' – shells, metal bars, ingots – or the expression and units of value used in primitive and ancient societies. So, for example, in Africa or in the epics of Homer himself, livestock functioned as a measurement of value. Laertes, the father of Ulysses, bought Eurycleia for the price of twenty oxen (*Od.* 1:430–431) and in that sense, livestock was 'money'.

In the Near East researchers have managed to identify 'pre-coinages' in Ur, Susa, Mari and Kanesh, on the basis of calculating the measurements and analysing the weight of metal rings. These rings fulfil the function traditionally ascribed to coinage: measurement of value, a medium of exchange and ease of transport. Similarly the possibility of an Aegean ponderal unit has been suggested in connection with certain copper ingots found in the wreck at Cape Gelidonya.

However, it is not enough to make calculations of the weight of metal artefacts in order to infer monetary circulation. It is necessary to define the characteristics of this metal standard within the economic context in which it circulates. So, for example, an article may be a form of coinage or a medium of exchange without having a pattern of defined weight, that is, without a ponderal value. Hence the importance of the circulation of gold and silver cups and craters that appears in the east in relationships of tribute and interregional trade and, lastly, in the exchange circuits of prestige goods.

In the texts from Mari, the majority of the silver cups mentioned in commercial transactions or reciprocal exchanges have a specific weight, which suggests the existence of a precise unit of accountability, that is a homogeneous weight. Consequently they could serve as metal standards. Ugarit, too, in the fourteenth to thirteenth centuries BC, developed specific weight systems, based on a shekel weighing 9 to

9.9 grams. As in Mari, the silver cups mentioned in the Ugaritic texts are homogeneous in weight. Their unit of ponderal value would reside, however, not in their weight of approximately 1 mina (50 shekels), but in their character as a unit in commercial and ceremonial exchange.

Mauss had already linked the exchange of gifts and reciprocity with the origin of the notion of 'money' as a measure of value. Faced with the view that articles of value were simply external signs of wealth, Mauss defended the idea that precious gifts came to serve as use values and as media of exchange, given that possessing them brought power of acquisition. Other modern experts support this hypothesis, holding, like Parise, that precious metals and valuable articles functioned like 'money'. In other words, the reciprocity, prestation and counterprestation of presents would be an organized form of trade in which the external signs of wealth could easily be converted into pre-coinage symbols. These precious and prestige goods are the *agalmata* and *keimélia* of Homer's day, that is, the craters, cauldrons and tripods. In the well-known Achilles episode, a bronze tripod was worth twelve oxen and a woman was worth four oxen. On the other hand, the Phoenician silver crater was worth one hundred oxen. Strictly speaking we should be talking of a metal circulation with units of value.

The circulation of these *agalmata*, or values in circulation, was very extensive, given that in the days of Homer it stretched from the palace of Sidon to the kings of Cyprus, the Aegean and Etruria. With time, as they passed from hand to hand, their value increased until they gradually became pre-coinage symbols, that is to say, genuine ponderal and monetary units, before minted coins appeared.

In reality, in the east it is as difficult to define the transition from gift exchange to commercial exchange as it is to define the transition from this metal circulation to the circulation of coinage. The most ancient monetary circulation had to be restricted to assuming the same functions of prestige and hoarding as the *agalmata* or prestige goods. But with one difference: the most ancient coinage, in its function as a measurement and repository of value, cannot stray too far in its initial circulation from the centre that issues it. That is to say, the earliest known circulation of coins is much more restricted than that of the *agalmata*. If we accept that the origin of coinage must be a continuation of previous experiments, its appearance in any case implies a backward step in the ambit of metal circulation.

Coinage is defined as the circulation of money in the form of an equivalent piece of metal. The minting and issuing of the coinage are in the hands of the state and it constitutes a fungible possession that serves as a common measure of value and as an instrument of exchange.

It has been said that the Assyrians already knew a kind of minted coinage at the end of the eighth century BC: the so-called 'heads of Ishtar', equivalent to half a shekel, which were a kind of small copper coin of unknown characteristics. The temple of Ishtar would have been responsible for issuing it and the kingdom of Lydia could have taken up the idea, thanks to its close connections with the Assyrian kings.

Nevertheless, the invention of the first minted metal coinage is attributed to King Gyges of Lydia, at the beginning of the seventh century BC (*Herod.* 1:94). The most ancient coins were of electrum, an alloy of gold and silver, deriving value as a noble article in circulation from the *agalma*. The difference was in the imprint or die, which guaranteed the face value and weight of the little disc of precious metal that had been issued. It was the state or a similar authority that had the power to lay down a system of equivalencies.

The study of the first known systems of coinage indicates unequivocally that they were preceded by various pre-monetary experiments. The fact that the area of Lydia and the Greek cities of Asia Minor – Ephesus, Aegina – were among the earliest to mint coins shows that the first coinage did not arise precisely in the centres of international trade but in *poleis* which required rapid transactions at a local level. In other words, it is almost certain that the coinage did not spring from the needs of international commercial strategy but from internal needs and socio-ideological exigencies.

It has been observed, moreover, that in the first Greek states to monopolize the minting of coins, the economic repercussions were very few. No state at that period could guarantee the value of its coinage outside its own frontiers or had very clear equivalencies with silver, the monetary standard *par excellence*. Coinage originates, therefore, from political needs and for reasons of local prestige, that is to say from non-economic considerations.

From this standpoint we can look afresh at the question of the Phoenicians' much debated 'backwardness' in minting coins. The fact that the great trading peoples like Tyre and Carthage joined so belatedly in the minting of coins raises questions about the relationship between organized trade and a minted coinage. We already know the position of Polanyi and Dalton on this matter: the Phoenicians were reluctant to adopt coinage because they did not have a market economy.

The most plausible hypothesis, however, is the one that suggests that the Phoenicians shunned coinage precisely in order to safeguard their international trade which was much more far reaching and heterogeneous than the purely territorial and local trade in which the electrum coins were circulating with conventional values based on local silver, so that their value and equivalencies were perforce restricted to the ambit of the *polis* or states in which they were circulating. In their place, until well into the sixth century BC, market necessities ensured that in the orbit of Phoenician trade a circulation of sumptuary goods predominated, following the norms of reciprocity, the equivalencies of which were stipulated by the aristocratic elites of the Mediterranean. Thus, the Phoenicians will maintain forms of exchange more typical of the Late Bronze Age than of a monetary economy. The latter will gradually replace the old aristocratic formulae of yesteryear in the Mediterranean. It is no accident that as the new systems of exchange and trade were gaining ground successively in Greece, Italy and the Iberian peninsula from the sixth century BC onwards, the forms of organization of ancient Phoenician trade were gradually disappearing from the scene.

SUMMARY

On the question of the organization of Phoenician or eastern trade, alternative hypotheses have arisen which contradict the empirical propositions of Polanyi and are more in accordance with the archaeological record. So, for example, in place of the traditional and substantivist interpretation of 'gift trade', considered under the preconceived heading of reciprocity and characteristic of an 'irrational' or 'ceremonial' economy, in which social rank and status would prevail, a more appropriate explanation is now put forward which considers reciprocity as an exchange in which profits are sought and mutual trust between princes and merchants plays a part. In any case, this exchange marks genuine trade between royal houses, in which the gift would be no more than a form of payment in advance.

The opposition between state and private trade in the ancient east has proved equally unworkable. The two spheres merge and we need only point out that private commercial activity always increased in periods of weakening state power.

For example, in Cappadocia, the Assyrian king was a participant in the trade in Anatolian metals in direct competition with the great, private commercial 'houses' or firms and both of them acted in accordance with the mechanisms of a competitive market. From the middle of the third millennium until the Roman period, there is ample evidence of private trade in the Near East in which the king or the palace behaves like any other consortium. Monarchs do indeed take part in international trade, not in order to fix prices by treaty but to make their own profits, as Hiram and Solomon did.

A characteristic feature of this organization of trade was the pronounced family orientation of the great firms or mercantile consortia, which behaved like family brotherhoods. Thus private merchants used to operate within great families whose members inherited the business from each other. Today, we should call this 'nepotism', but it was merely a formula to ensure loyalty between the members of a merchant company.

Furthermore, the epigraphic evidence from both Kanesh and Ugarit demonstrates that in the ancient east and in Phoenicia there were price fluctuations, market operations, changes in supply and demand, profits and private speculation. The accumulation of huge stores of grain and metal in Babylonia and Assyria in the second to first millennia BC clearly indicates the existence of a market.

Lastly, we see the temple functioning as a financial body, lending gold and silver for interest and giving credit for trade. Even in Ugarit we see merchants paying vast sums to obtain trading concessions and competing directly with the palace. The circulation of money in the form of rings, bars and ingots merely bears witness to a wholly mercantile activity.

Many of the ideas expounded by Polanyi and Finley some time ago seem ingenuous now: for example, the assertion that long-distance trade carried no risks but was rewarded by payments of commission by the state; or the idea that in the ancient economy generally, exchange was governed more by considerations of status and social solidarity than by economic motives. There is no business without risks, and commercial exchange with no thought of profit would be very strange. The statement that 'the market implies a desire for gain, that is far removed from Homeric exchange, which was not seeking profits' gives an excessively idyllic picture of the mechanisms of exchange in the ancient world, to say the least.

5

The great political institutions: the palace and the temple

The so-called 'great institutions' arose originally with the production of surpluses and it is the production and distribution of surpluses that underlies commercial exchange. Therefore the relationship between the great political institutions and the rest of society depended to a large extent on trade, and external trade in particular.

Religion and government can be as important for the structure and functioning of the economy as are monetary institutions. The differences between the two are minimal in the ancient Near East and their functions are complementary to the point of being indistinguishable. In Tyre, the two great political institutions, the palace and the temple, were respectively the house of the king and the house of the god, and sheltered the same symbolic entity: the king of the city or Melqart.

THE PHOENICIAN MONARCHY

The monarchic institution is very ancient in the Phoenician cities. In Tyre, it is present from the first half of the nineteenth century BC until the conquest by Alexander. In the time of El Amarna, Tyre was known as the capital of a kingdom (URU), which included a fringe of territory on the mainland (KUR), centred on Ushu.

Information about the structure and importance of the monarchic institution in the Phoenician cities is very scarce. Unlike other Asian monarchies, the Phoenician kings did not, as far as is known, indulge in recounting their exploits and political enterprises in commemorative inscriptions or reliefs in which the monarchs generally occupy the foreground. There is therefore no political propaganda, either internal or external, and the only commemorative epigraphs that we have appear in a few royal tombs in Byblos and Sidon.

All this has been interpreted as an unusual way of envisaging the figure and function of the king in Phoenicia. The sovereign could not act with full political autonomy or invoke the figure of a national or dynastic god, given that his powers were limited by those of a powerful merchant oligarchy which would have placed substantial restrictions on the power of the sovereign.

In reality, we have at our disposal very little information about the power of the Phoenician kings. Everything, however, makes us think that, until the seventh century BC at least, their power was more or less absolute, as can be inferred from the behaviour of Hiram I, Ithobaal or Luli of Tyre.

Following the oriental model, the power of the great Phoenician monarchs like Hiram I found expression in the building of a new royal palace. The palace was a reflection of the aspirations of the king and of the power of the monarchy in every period.

In political and commercial affairs, the kings of Tyre and of Byblos were advised, as has already been indicated, by a Council of Elders, or representatives of the most renowned and powerful families in the city, whose power probably lay in their mercantile interests. As far as we can tell from the correspondence of the kings of Tyre and Byblos with the pharaohs of El Amarna, this institution goes back at least to the middle of the second millennium BC. King Ribaddi of Byblos mentions in his letters a social group endowed with great power and relative importance in his city, whom he calls 'the city' or 'them'. At somewhat more recent dates allusion is made to this group as a governing body acting alongside the king and appearing as his equal; they are given the names of 'lords of the city' in Byblos, 'the great of the city' in Sumur and 'the men of Arvad'.

All this obviously reminds us of the words of Isaiah and Ezekiel when they mention the 'merchant princes' of Tyre (Isaiah 23:8) or the 'princes of the sea' (Ezekiel 26:16). No doubt this is a reference to the merchant oligarchy of the city which, in much more recent times, Arrianus called 'the important Tyrians' (2:24,5) and Polibius 'the lords of Carthage' in the treaty signed by Hannibal and Philip II of Macedon. This last reference is certainly to the Council of the Ten, which was the basis of political power in Carthage, power which, in special circumstances, was assumed by two of its members, who were known as suffetes in Carthage and Cadiz.

In tablets from El Amarna, there is already explicit reference to a Council of Elders – in Akkadian *šibutu* or *shibūti* – in central Phoenicia, which we meet again in Wen-Amon's story (passage II, 71). Indeed, in Wen-Amon King Zakarbaal seeks the advice of a Council of State to consider the extradition demand by the Tjekker, which is hanging over the Egyptian envoy. This Council is called *mw'd*, a word that has been linked with the Hebrew *môᵉd* or assembly. This seems, then, to be an allusion to the senate of the city, made up of the elders or the great of the community, the suffetes.

The Assyrian, Hebrew and Greek written sources so far analysed show that this Council of State went on functioning in Tyre, Byblos and Carthage throughout the seventh to third centuries BC. Among other matters assigned to it were questions concerning religion and taxes. Moreover, an inscription discovered in Sarepta suggests the possibility that a college or committee of ten may have existed in that city charged with governing the territory.

Still more explicit is the text of the treaty between Asarhadon and King Baal of Tyre, dated to the middle of the seventh century BC. In it, Asarhadon nominates an Assyrian governor in the court of the king of Tyre who is to assist in governing the city: 'in conjunction with you, in conjunction with the elders of your country', says the text, referring to the said governor. It calls these 'elders' *parshāmutu*.

Although we do not know exactly how this Council of Elders or of princes worked or what its political responsibilities were, everything seems to indicate that this kind of senate advised the Phoenician king on questions of state, but we do not know whether its function was purely consultative or whether it formed a direct part of the government. We are told, however, that it was made up of nobles and high officials, as in some Mesopotamian cities of the neo-Babylonian period, where we also find a Council of Elders assisting the king and resolving matters of a judicial, fiscal and religious nature. In some cases, the greatest hierarchies of the state worked in conjunction with this institution; according to the inscription on the sarcophagus of Ahiram of Byblos, these hierarchies consisted of the king, the governor and the commander of the armies.

Those who belonged to the Council of Elders or Council of State in each of the Phoenician cities were called *špt* in Phoenician, equivalent to the Akkadian *šapitum* and to the Hebrew *šophêt*. In Israel, for example, these suffetes or 'judges' governed the territory in exceptional circumstances in the years 1200–1030 BC. There, they were leaders of clans and tribes, magistrates by divine right, who would be the fore-runners of the monarchy. The best-known of the judges of Israel was Saul.

Something similar happened subsequently in Tyre in the neo-Babylonian period, when Tyre was governed by suffetes – the *dikastai* – who represented the king of Babylonia or the king of Tyre itself, then a captive in Mesopotamia.

There is a possibility that some of the commercial settlements in the west, like Carthage, were administered in principle by suffetes, that is by civil magistrates or judges who, as in Tyre or Babylonia, governed in the name of the king of Tyre. For some authors, however, the presence of these *sóftim* in Carthage would go back no further than the fifth or even the third century BC. Be that as it may, the charge of suffete or governor, assigned to Tyrian colonial establishments, is intended simply to reproduce an oriental institution that goes back at least to the second millennium BC. Furthermore, this institution guaranteed the administrative ties between the colony and the metropolis.

From the Limassol inscriptions in Cyprus we may infer that in the Cypriot Carthage there was a governor or prefect, 'a servant of Hiram', in the middle of the eighth century BC, who took to himself the title of *sokhen*, equivalent to the Akkadian *zu-ki-ni*. The charge corresponds to that of a prince or local governor and his function was to channel copper to Tyre in the time of Hiram II, to administer the Tyrian colony and to ensure political links with the metropolis. In spite of that, the suzerainty of the king of Tyre over the colony, probably Kition, is virtually absolute.

As for the Phoenician monarchy, it was a hereditary and strongly endogamous institution, judging by the history of the kings of Tyre. Inherent in the charge of king were its priestly functions, which imparted one of their most characteristic features to the kings of Tyre.

The priestly connotations of the monarchy can be deduced from the titles paraded by the Phoenician kings at different periods. Thus the king of Sidon called himself 'priest of Astarte', and the king of Byblos 'priest of the Lady'.

The Phoenician monarchy used religion to create a favourable image for itself and to win the favour of the people. Hence the significant political role played by the priesthood. In Tyre and other cities, the priestly cast wielded much power, was in the service of the city and, in fact, sanctioned the official character of the monarchy. Temple and palace retained an almost absolute power in this sense, especially if we bear in mind that the function of chief priest was in the hands of the king himself or of members of the royal family.

The Annals of Tyre mention monarchs with priestly duties. Some kings, like Ithobaal, 'priest of Astarte', made much of the charge before coming to the throne. This sacred and priestly nature of the Phoenician monarchy may have had very remote origins, since it is known in Canaan from the second millennium BC. We have an example of this in the legendary king of Salem, Melchizadek (Gen. 14:18), who was chief priest of the Canaanite god Elyon and, as such, blessed Abraham in the Canaanite city of Salem, a city which, from the first millennium BC, came to be called Jerusalem.

If one of the main functions of the Phoenician sovereign was that of chief priest, it is logical to suppose that religious activity would form one of the characteristic features of the Phoenician monarchy. The piety in which the kings of Tyre gloried is well known through their successive reconstructions of the temples in the city.

The Phoenician kings were not priests of just any divinity but of the chief divinity in the metropolitan pantheon, which conferred on the local god the title of the authentic lord of the city. In this theocratic concept of the state, in which the king governed in the name of the god, the functions became merged. This is true of Tyre, where the king and the god Melqart are at once the incarnation of the same institution: the state.

In the treaty of Baal and Asarhadon, the gods Melqart and Eshmún are invoked, the chief god of Tyre and of Sidon respectively. By annexing the Sidonian territory, Tyre had taken on new religious obligations.

There is significance too in the divine element that appears in royal names. So, for example, the sons of Hiram are called Balbazer and Abdastratus, which amounts to saying, respectively 'servant of Baal', or of Melqart, and 'servant of Astarte', the two principal divinities of the Tyrian pantheon.

Sometimes, the king of Tyre, in addition to his priestly qualities, claimed to be divine, making himself equal to the very god of the city. This, not unreasonably, provoked the wrath of the Hebrew prophets, as is demonstrated in the third prophecy of Ezekiel (Ez. 28), devoted entirely to the king of Tyre. This oracle is somewhat difficult to read and interpret (Appendix III). The prophet here launches a violent attack against the monarch: 'Being swollen with pride, you have said: I am a god. I am sitting on the throne of God, surrounded by the seas' (28:2). Ezekiel accuses him with these words: 'you are a man and not a god and you consider yourself the equal of God. [You think] you are wiser now than Daniel' (28:3).

The king of Tyre is seen here as a god in every sense, as in Phoenician sources which call the king simply Ba'al, meaning 'God'.

Ezekiel's accusations contain a somewhat ironic tone which is difficult to interpret. The allusion to Daniel is more intelligible today, thanks to the texts from Ugarit. Daniel is a mythological figure and, as such, forms part of a Canaanite myth in which this character is notable for his very great wisdom. Once again, the verses in Chapter 28 of

Ezekiel are alluding to Canaanite, not Hebrew myths, and in form they resemble a very ancient poem. The power, beauty and splendour of the Tyrian monarchy match the framework of the ninth century BC better than the times of the prophet.

Ezekiel's lament for the king of Tyre continues with these words (28:12–15): 'You were once an exemplar of perfection, full of wisdom and perfect in beauty; you were in Eden, in the garden of God. A thousand gems formed your mantle ... I had provided you with a guardian cherub; you were on the holy mountain of God; you walked amidst red-hot coals.'

Again we have a reference here to a very ancient Canaanite myth, that of the birth of the perfect 'cherub' out of the fire. The king, therefore, is identified with the masculine form of a 'cherub', a cherubim or winged sphinx who walks on the holy mountain.

Thanks to Phoenician figurative art we know that their pantheon was wont to be represented on mountains (Fig. 21). The allusion to the cherubim walking on fire suggests immortality. In oriental myths, fire, or the rite of cremation, symbolizes purity and immortality. In this connection, let us remember Moses' burning bush, which was not consumed, or the myth collected by Plutarch about Isis burning the son of the king of Byblos every night to make him immortal.

It is obvious that Ezekiel is ridiculing the king of Tyre for making himself a god and identifying himself with the emblem of the god of the city, its winged creature, the masculine sphinx. Like the cherub and like Melqart, the king considers himself to be immortal and revitalized by fire. Like the gods, he walks over the sacred mountain, the Eden.

This elegy against the king of Tyre closes Ezekiel's trilogy against Tyre. For the prophet the Tyrian monarchy is the embodiment of pride, presumption, blasphemy, arrogance and a repudiation of the divinity in order to supplant it. The exaltation of the king will be followed by his fall. In Tyre, the priesthood of the sovereign and the sacred nature of the monarchy seem to have been more pronounced than in other Phoenician cities, perhaps because of the very singularity of the god of the city, Melqart. The power of Melqart and of his temple were enormous, particularly in connection with the commercial policy in which the kings of Tyre were engaged.

But the deep resentment of some of the Hebrew prophets and, in particular, their anti-monarchist posture, are not due to the institution itself. What they cannot tolerate in the monarchs of Tyre is that they have set themselves up as priests and cherubs, that is to say, as the sole intermediaries between man and the deity. And as we know, it is

Fig. 21   Cherubim – Phoenician ivory from Nimrud

precisely this function of intermediaries before Yahweh that the prophets of Israel claim for themselves.

THE PHOENICIAN TEMPLE AND MELQART OF TYRE

The Phoenicians made their religion into one of the best instruments of their commercial and colonial policy. Like all ancient peoples, the Phoenicians felt closely bound to their gods. The god was the lord of the city and, as such, exercised his authority over the community organized around his temple.

The view of the Phoenician religion that has come down to us is very incomplete and negative since we are indebted for the available information chiefly to their neighbours, the Israelites, and their political enemies in the west, the Romans. Even today, some authors stress the baseness of the Phoenician religion, its amoral rites, its religious brutality, the human sacrifice and sacred prostitution, all of them features that mark many of the religions of antiquity.

Phoenician religion, however, was one of the main instruments of the state and the monarchy. Moreover, the Phoenician religious cults appear to be very much conditioned by the economic and social interests of each city and by the political exigencies of the moment. In the case of Tyre, the cult of Melqart is a direct reflection of the policy and aspirations of her monarchs.

With respect to the ancient Canaanite religion, the Phoenician religion of the Iron Age presupposes an ideological break, which implies profound religious, ideological and socio-political changes at the end of the second millennium. The Phoenician pantheon seems to reflect cities shut in on themselves at the beginning of the first millennium, which must have favoured a gradual move towards strictly local religious variants. So it is not correct to speak of the Phoenician pantheon or the Phoenician religion because each city, shut in around its king and its god, had its own local pantheon.

The most significant changes that took place in the Phoenician religion after the crisis of 1200 BC appear not to have their origin in the preceding Canaanite context. Indeed, in a very short time the great deities of the Ugaritic–Canaanite pantheon, like El, Dagan or Anat, disappear, and deities that had been marginal until then, like Ashtart – Astarte – come to the fore. Nevertheless, the most important novelty is the appearance of human sacrifice, unknown, apparently, in the second millennium, and the birth of 'national' gods with no known predecents, like Melqart, Eshmún and Reshef.

Another important novelty in the Iron Age cults is animal sacrifice, so well described by Leviticus, as well as human sacrifice. This latter, also known by the biblical name of 'Moloch sacrifice', would develop in a special way in the Phoenician enclaves in the west, where it appears linked with fertility rites and the monarchy. In Phoenicia, human sacrifice was very sporadic and disappeared in the middle of the first millennium.

From the beginning of the first millennium, we are struck by the very limited number of gods in the public pantheons. There are no triads and Canaanite polytheism disappears. In its place, pairs of deities arise and concentrate the power and the functions of the old Canaanite pantheon in themselves. Each Phoenician city has its own pantheon made up of a pair of gods. This phenomenon makes very clear, among other things, how strongly individualist the Phoenician cities of the Iron Age were.

In Byblos, the central position was occupied by Baalat Gebal, the 'Lady of Byblos', of very ancient local tradition, who not only protected the city and the royal dynasty, but reigned over the city jointly with her partner, the god Baal Shamem. In Sidon we find the same divine pairing, but in this city it is Astarte and Eshmún who dominate. In Berytos, the chief divinity was also female: Baalat. Apart from the goddess of Byblos, none of these gods have important predecessors in the second millennium.

In the city of Tyre, by contrast, the chief divinity was masculine: Melqart, the protector of the city, symbol of the monarchic institution and founder of colonies. Astarte, Baal Shamem and Baal Hammon play a supporting part.

About the seventh century BC the Phoenician pantheon is becoming increasingly complex and the sway and influence of some of the gods increases, gods who, like Tanit and Baal Hammon, will be enormously popular in the west. Particularly interesting for us is the figure of Melqart, so closely linked with Phoenician trade and expansion through the Mediterranean. Melqart has no known antecedents in the second millennium and his personality and religious cult are documented only from the time when Tyre gained sway over the other Phoenician cities. His figure takes shape, then, from the tenth century BC and has its roots in the reign of Hiram I. He was god both of fertility and of the sea and the Tyrians called him 'Lord of Tyre', that is, Ba'al de Ṣor. His name itself, Melqart, means 'king of the city' (melek-qart), showing that the origin of his cult has eminently urban roots. However, this does not rule out other attributes peculiar to this god, as we shall see. Consequently, the god represents the power of the monarchy and also possesses certain human characteristics, since the foundation of cities and colonies is attributed to him. Furthermore, some myths refer to Melqart as a hunter.

According to the testimony of Herodotus, who visited Tyre in the middle of the fifth century BC, the worship and the temple of Melqart had arisen at the same time as the city, so around 2300 (*Herod.* 2:43–44). So in Tyre itself, Melqart already appears to be associated with a foundation myth (Arrianus 2:15,7–16,7).

The Greek historian saw the temple in Tyre with his own eyes and describes it flanked by the two famous columns of gold and emerald and, inside it, the tomb of the god. Some authors have hinted at a direct link between the two pillars of the temple in Tyre and the Pillars of Hercules at the other end of the Phoenician world, in the city of Gadir (Arrianus 2:17,1–4).

The consecration or 'invention' of Melqart is ascribed to Hiram I, according to the testimony of Menander of Ephesus (*Ant. Iud.* 8:5,3:146; *C. Ap.* 1:118). That monarch built the new temple of

Melqart, demolishing the ancient temple of Tyre, dedicated perhaps to Baal Hadad. Yet again, the building of a temple to Melqart symbolized the founding, refounding, rebuilding or reorganization of a Phoenician city (Isaiah 23:4).

The initiative for the first celebration of an annual festival dedicated to Melqart is also attributed to Hiram I; it commemorates the resurrection or awakening of the god. This annual feast day, the *egersis*, was very similar to that of other eastern gods who died and rose again, like Adonis. The festival was celebrated in the month of the Peritia (February–March) and consisted of a genuine immolation of the god through ritual cremation. The intention was, logically, to revive him and make him immortal by virtue of fire. The belief in resurrection by fire, already known in Ugaritic myths, explains the fact that Melqart is also called 'fire of heaven'.

The *egersis* or resurrection of Melqart took place, then, every spring, when the rains stopped, which gives the personality of the god a solar and especially an agrarian character. Probably the god was burned in effigy on a pyre and the myth assures us that he revived at the smell of fire. Then he was buried and subsequently came the resurrection and manifestation of the god. During the festival, hymns were sung and foreigners were expelled from the city.

The agricultural nature of Melqart, a god who dies and is reborn each year in accordance with the natural cycles, was eclipsed by his great maritime prowess. On the coins from Tyre, Melqart appears as a sea god, mounted on a hippocampus. As god of the sea, he was the patron of shipping and trade.

During the Phoenician expansion into the Mediterranean, all these myths found their way to the west. A version of the legend locates the death of the god in Spain. Some classical authors, like Sallust and Pausanias, mention the tomb of the god in Iberia and the celebration of his death and resurrection in Gades (Paus. 9:4,6).

In the annual awakening of the god, the king of Tyre seems to have played a very active role. The monarch not only took part in the ceremonies, but intervened directly in the festival through a ritual marriage with a priestess or the queen herself, as was customary in oriental religions. This rite, the *hieros gamos*, had the royal couple playing the role of stand-in for the divine couple, Melqart and Astarte. No doubt this festival, combined with the deification of the king of Tyre, provoked the wrath of the Hebrew prophets.

At first, the Melqart of Tyre could have been a deification of the king of the city himself, the *mlk-qrt*. If that were so, Melqart, the

Tyrian national god, would be a theological exaltation of the king and, as such, the ancestor of the city, the hypostasis of the king and, in short, the king himself. This type of idealization and deification of the monarchy, which so disturbed Ezekiel, has no precedents in the Canaanite world, nor is it recorded in other Phoenician cities. As far as Ugarit is concerned, for example, it implies a qualitative leap regarding the figure of the king, whose ancestor, moreover, is that same Melqart.

A legend that shows in its origins the influence of the religious nationalism of the Tyrians associates the origin and invention of the 'purple' with the 'Lord of the City', Melqart. In this way, Melqart is not only the god and ancestor of Tyre, but is responsible for its wealth and prosperity. This makes him its chief benefactor and protector.

The history and fate of Melqart is the history and fate of Tyre and her daughters, the western colonies. In Hannibal's famous oath of 215 BC, the Tyrian pantheon is still mentioned, consisting of Heracles (Melqart) and Astarte, as well as Iolaos or Eshmún, all of them symbols of the monarchy.

In the history of Cyprus, Melqart–Eshmún, that is, the royal family of Tyre, appear as founders of the kingdom of Kition. In the fifth century BC, Kition is still minting coins with the effigy of Melqart.

When Alexander the Great besieged Tyre, the Macedonian, who claimed to be descended from Heracles, expressed a wish to offer a sacrifice in the temple of Melqart for ends that were clearly political (Arrianus 2:15,7–16,7). The Tyrians were categorically opposed to this, considering the place to be sacred. Melqart was the symbol of their autonomy and independence, but above all he was the symbol of their national identity.

If the king of Tyre used religion for political ends and for propaganda, it is logical to suppose that the priests involved in the worship of Melqart must have played a decisive political role in the history of Tyre.

We know that a priestly college was responsible for the worship and administration of the temple. These clergy were recruited, moreover, from among the most influential families in the city; the most influential offices such as that of high priest were held by members of the royal family. Let us remind ourselves that the sister of Pygmalion, Elissa or Dido, foundress of Carthage, was married to the high priest of the temple of Melqart, and that the kings Tabnit and Eshmunazar of Sidon were high priests of Astarte. On ascending the throne of Tyre after a coup d'état in 887 BC, Ithobaal made great play of the office of priest of Astarte.

On the occasion of the founding of a colony or commercial enclave, Tyrian custom demanded that a temple be built in honour of Melqart. This created a religious bond between the colony and the metropolis, and the presence of the god in distant lands ensured the tutelage of the temple of Tyre in the enterprise. In other words, the presence of Melqart guaranteed or drew attention to the intervention of the monarchy in every distant commercial activity.

The most ancient Tyrian foundations in the Mediterranean appear to be linked to a temple which, in most cases, was dedicated to Melqart. In fact, Tyrian expansion to the west coincides with the gradual introduction of the worship of Melqart in Cyprus, Thasos, Malta, Carthage, Gadir and perhaps even in Rome.

In Gadir and Carthage, the figure of Melqart finds its way even into the story of the foundation. This is probably a reflection of the firm intention to associate the origins of these western settlements with the city of Tyre and, by extension, with its temple and its king. Not only did the god appear in association with the oldest settlements in the west, but, occasionally, the building of a temple preceded the founding of the city. This seems to have been the case at Cadiz. Moreover, in certain foundations, the figure of Melqart had considerable weight, as, again, in Gadir. Only in Gadir and Tyre were the god and his relics worshipped and his resurrection commemorated annually (Silius Italicus 3:22).

Two other very ancient temples were established in the west at the same time as the founding of the Tyrian colony: in Utica (Pliny *N. Hist.* 16:40) and in Lixus in Atlantic Morocco (Pliny 19:63). In Paphos and Cythera, the only trace of the passage of the Phoenicians in the early period consists of the temples of Aphrodite or Astarte (Herod. 1:105), and in Thasos the presence of Phoenician navigators exploiting its gold mines is attested by the founding of a temple to Heracles or Melqart (Herod. 2:44). Lastly, in Memphis the Phoenicians formed a settlement around a sanctuary dedicated to the 'foreign Aphrodite', that is, Astarte (Herod. 2:112).

The building of a sanctuary to Melqart in any relatively important Tyrian foundation reflects a constant preoccupation on the part of the first colonists arriving in the west: to legitimize the foundation. The presence of the god automatically converted the settlement into a prolongation of the country of origin, the kingdom of Tyre, at the same time as it ensured peaceful trading relations with the natives, since it offered sacred protection to the transactions. Phoenician trade in the west, then, began under the aegis of the god Melqart, that is to say, of the king of Tyre.

In addition to becoming the tutelary deity of the great Tyrian maritime enterprises, the figure of Melqart was linked with exceedingly complex political and economic interests. In Carthage, for example, the cult of Melqart was introduced at the very origin of the city. Elissa, the foundress, had brought objects sacred to the god with her to northwest Africa. Her husband, Acherbas or Zakarbaal, had been the chief priest in the temple at Tyre, so he had ranked immediately after the king on the social scale. So, in one way or another, the royal family and the temple of Tyre are behind the myth of the founding of Carthage (see Chapter 8).

The story goes that ever after, the Carthaginians sent an offering or tribute each year to the god Melqart of Tyre; this consisted of a tenth part of the public treasury. This custom persisted until the Hellenistic period (Diodorus 20:14,2; Polybius 31,12; Arrianus 2:24,5).

This annual embassy indicates that Carthage, the 'new Tyre' or Qart-hadasht, remained under the tutelage of Tyre for a long time. There seems to have been only one reason for this: the tutelage of the king of Tyre over the Carthaginian maritime enterprise and the financial participation of the temple of Tyre in western trade. The annual tribute conscientiously sent by Carthage was nothing other than the profits from the western enterprise, reverting to the temple of Melqart and consequently to the royal palace in Tyre. In this way, it can be said that the function of the sanctuaries to Melqart in the west consisted in serving as a bond uniting Tyre with the Mediterranean trading centres. In exchange for seeing that all was well with shipping and trade, Melqart received a tenth part of the profits made. So his function was not exclusively religious, but basically political: to ensure the dependent relationship of Cadiz or Carthage to Tyre. This link still existed in the Hellenistic period. Thus, at the time of the siege of Tyre by Alexander, it is said that the city kept hoping till the last moment for help from its brothers, the Carthaginians (Diodorus 17:40,3; 20:14,1–2).

Equally significant is the fact that in Carthage the cult of Melqart almost always arose in association with the monarchic ideal. Before Tanit and Baal Hammon became popular, Melqart wielded considerable power in Carthage and his cult declined only in the period of government by the suffetes. As a dynastic god, Melqart symbolized the monarchy, while Tanit and Baal symbolized the oligarchy, represented by the family of the Magonidas. His cult won renewed popularity only with the arrival of the Barcidas, known for their monarchic aspirations in Carthage. On the coins of the Barcidas in Spain, Hamilcar, Hannibal and Hasdrubal deified themselves, adopting the appearance and effigy of Melqart. Significant, too, is the presence of a great many god-like names in Carthage, formed from the name of the god of Tyre (A-mlkr). For the rest, the episode of the other Carthaginian general, Hamilcar, is well known; like the foundress, Elissa, he committed suicide by throwing himself into the fire. Suicide by fire is an integral part of the ritual of the god, that is to say, of resurrection and immortality through sacrifice.

6

The routes of Phoenician expansion into the Mediterranean

The distribution and location of the principal Phoenician settlements in the Mediterranean make it clear that the ancient foundations met a twofold requirement: trade and shipping (Fig. 22).

From the very moment at which the first commercial enclaves were established on the western coasts, the Phoenicians had control in practice of the main trade routes, from Cyprus and Crete in the east to Gibraltar in the west. If we accept the dates for the founding of Cadiz, Lixus and Utica as round 1100 BC, as some authors claim, we are speaking of a maritime monopoly lasting some 500 years.

The organization of such a vast commercial network was obviously a response to equally important objectives in the eyes of Tyre, in essence the precious metal that made the costs of an enterprise on such a scale worth while. Possibly Tyre and other cities on the Levantine coast had heard from sailors and ships' captains of the abundance of gold, silver and tin in the far west of the Mediterranean. A few centuries earlier, at the end of the second millennium, ships from Cyprus and the Aegean had forged a way through the waters of the central Mediterranean and along the coasts of Sicily, Italy and Sardinia, so the west was not totally unknown to the peoples of the eastern Mediterranean.

However, if the initial and most important objective of the Phoenician diaspora to the west was to obtain metals, as all the written references of the period unanimously agree, the siting of some of the settlements like Carthage, Utica, Ibiza or the trading posts on the Mediterranean coast of Andalusia, located in areas not particularly rich in metal resources, is not so easy to explain.

The Phoenicians' superiority as seafarers was clear to the peoples of antiquity. The reputation of being expert pilots, enjoyed by the people of Tyre and Sidon, combined with the seafaring conditions at the time, lead us to think that shipping played an important part in the organization and form of the Phoenician diaspora to the west and in the way in which it developed.

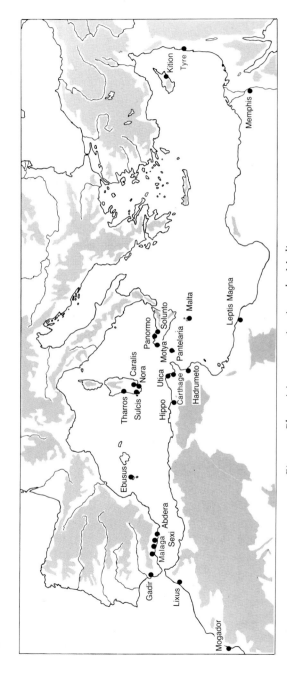

Fig. 22 Phoenician expansion into the Mediterranean

We know that, on their travels through the Mediterranean, the Phoenicians established themselves on islands and islets, coastal promontories with good natural anchorages, bays and inlets sheltered from the winds and currents, easy to defend against possible dangers from the sea or the mainland and situated at the mouths of rivers or natural access routes to the interior of the territory.

Although shipping systems and techniques were not the only factors that helped to shape the Phoenician commercial network in the west, they certainly determined, to a large extent, the general topography of the Phoenician colonies and their later evolution and provide us with an approach to the analysis, in later chapters, of other questions of an economic and geo-political nature concerning the geographic distribution of the Phoenician diaspora.

THE PHOENICIAN SETTLEMENTS: THEIR DISTRIBUTION

The Phoenician centres in the western Mediterranean should be seen as links in a commercial chain; their location allows us to reconstruct the Phoenician shipping routes before Carthage irrupted onto the geopolitical scene in the west in the sixth century BC. Insofar as we are engaged in reconstructing Phoenician sea routes in the Mediterranean, we shall omit all the secondary colonial or commercial foundations, that is, those that are offshoots of existing Phoenician centres in the west.

From the written tradition and the archaeological record, it is possible to distinguish three groups of Phoenician or Tyrian settlements in the western Mediterranean. The order in which these groups are presented is random in principle, since we are basing ourselves solely on the classical authors.

In order of antiquity, the first Phoenician establishments in the west were the colonies of Lixus, Cadiz and Utica. From this information it is obvious that, in their Mediterranean diaspora, the Phoenicians opted for the most westerly territories and those port enclaves situated on the direct route of access to the Straits of Gibraltar and the Atlantic.

According to the testimony of Velleius Paterculus (1:2,3; 1:8,4) the Phoenician fleet, which was already in control of the seas, founded Gadir some eighty years after the fall of Troy, and Utica a little later. According to the chronology attributed to the Trojan war (1190 or 1184 BC), the date for the founding of Gadir or Gadeira lies round about 1110 or 1104 BC and that of Utica, in North Africa, around 1100 BC. The colony at Cadiz was founded on a small island, now attached to the mainland, facing the estuary of the Guadalete and the kingdom of Tartessos. Other classical authors place the founding of Cadiz 'shortly after' the fall of Troy, without being more precise: Strabo (1:3,2), Pliny (*Nat. Hist.* 19:216) and Pomponius Mela (3:6,46).

This same Pliny adds that in Lixus, in Atlantic Morocco, there was a sanctuary to Heracles (Melqart) that was older than the one in Gadir and he places the mythical Garden of the Hesperides in this area (Pliny, *N.H.* 19:63). Ancient Lixus, situated on the mouth of the modern Loukkos, and in a well-sheltered bay, is close to the modern El Araich or Larache. According to the classical texts, it was apparently the most ancient Phoenician colony in the west, although, like Cadiz, it has not so far yielded any archaeological material earlier than the seventh century BC.

A third foundation, Utica, on the coast of Tunis, seems to consolidate the access route to the Atlantic. Concerning its origins, Pliny reports that in his day – that is, in the year 77 AD – the cedarwood beams placed there 1178 years earlier at the foundation of the city were still preserved in the temple of Apollo. That would place the foundation date around the year 1101 BC. Silius Italicus says that Utica was a 'Sidonian' foundation (3:241–242) and the Pseudo-Aristotle dates its Phoenician origins to 287 years before the founding of Carthage (*De mirabilis auscultationibus*, 134) in the year 814, which again gives us the date of 1101 BC. Such a dating coincidence makes us suspect a single common source of information for all these classical authors. To conclude, let us say that, up till now, the archaeology of Utica does not allow us to speak of Phoenicians frequenting this stretch of the Tunisian coast earlier than the eighth and seventh centuries BC.

After this first batch of distant foundations, of debatable chronology, we find no new historical references until the ninth century BC, the period in which two new colonies are founded in North Africa: Auza and Carthage. Auza, founded by Ithobaal of Tyre (887–856 BC), on the coast of Libya, has still not been identified. By contrast, we have a plentiful supply of written information at our disposal for the founding of Carthage. All the classical historians, inspired apparently by the writings of Timaeus, a historian of the fourth to third centuries BC whose work has been lost, agree in fixing the origins of Carthage in the year 814 or 813 BC. Thus, supported by Timaeus, Dionysius of Halicarnassus states that Carthage was founded 38 years before the first Olympiad (*Ant. Rom.* 1:74,1) in the year 776 BC, which places the origin of Carthage in 814 BC. This coincides with the testimony of Velleius Paterculus (1:12,5), who attributes a duration of 667 years to the history of Carthage. As we know, Carthage fell under the power of Rome in the year 146 BC (667 + 146 = 813).

In Justinus' account (18:4–6), Carthage was, like Auza, Utica and Gadir, a Tyrian foundation and the work of Elissa, the sister of the king of Tyre, Pygmalion or Pumayyaton. Elissa is said to have fled to the west because of the assassination of her husband, Acherbas or Zakarbaal, at the hands of the king. In founding the city, Elissa and the Tyrian refugees were helped by the men of Utica and, with a clearly political intention, called the place 'Qart-hadasht' (= new city or capital).

The earliest archaeological finds so far recorded in Carthage come from the sanctuary of Salammbô and go back no further than the eighth century BC.

If, by their early chronology and remote geographical location, the foundations of Lixus, Gadir and Utica form a separate block, the origin of Carthage seems to mark a second milestone in the process of Phoenician expansion into the Mediterranean, in the sense that access to the Atlantic route was still definitively controlled by naval traffic. It can be said, borrowing the words of Strabo, that during the ninth and eighth centuries BC 'the Phoenicians were already established in Iberia and Libya' (Strabo 3:2,14). By those dates 'they arrived far beyond the Columns of Hercules [Gibraltar] and founded cities in those parts and also in the middle of the coast of Libya, shortly after the fall of Troy' (Strabo 1:3,2).

We do not know at what precise moment the Phoenicians settled on the east coast of Andalusia. We are merely told that between the coast of Almeria and that of Malaga there were in former times 'a multitude of Phoenicians' (Avienus, *Ora Maritima* v. 440 and 459–460). There is concrete mention of three cities, Malaka, Sexi and Abdera (a distinctly oriental name) (Strabo III 4; 2–3), identified respectively as the present-day cities of Malaga, Almuñécar and Adra (on the coast of Almeria) and it is precisely on that stretch of coast that one of the largest concentrations of ancient Phoenician population in the whole of the western Mediterranean has been confirmed by archaeology; furthermore, their chronology provides the oldest known dates for Phoenicians frequenting the west, from at least the beginning of the eighth century BC.

Another group of Phoenician colonies, the exact date of whose foundation is unknown to us, is situated in the island of Sicily. We are indebted for the most significant piece of information to Thucydides, who writes:

The Phoenicians also inhabited the whole of Sicily, after having occupied promontories on the sea and the islands close to the coast in order to facilitate trading relations with the Sicilians. When the Greeks arrived in large numbers from beyond the sea, they left the greater part of the country and congregated in Motya, Solunto and Panormo, where they lived in safety alongside the Elimians, thanks to an alliance with the latter and to the fact that that part of the island was not very far from Carthage. (Thuc. 6:2,6)

So we understand that the Phoenicians occupied a large part of the island until, at the end of the eighth century BC, the arrival of the Greek colonizers forced them to settle in Motya, Solunto and Palermo, that is in the far west of Sicily. In spite of that, the new situation was favourable from the strategic point of view since from Motya they dominated the Carthage Straits. Motya was the main Phoenician settlement on the island (Diodorus 16:48,2 and 51,1). It is a small isle, close to the coast and its archaeological record does indeed place its origins at the end of the eighth century BC. This is not the case in Palermo, where the necropolis shows no evidence of Phoenician occupation before the seventh century BC, and Solunto has not so far been identified.

Diodorus tells us that the Phoenicians, already masters of the west, also took possession of Malta, a good refuge, provided with good harbours (Diod. 5:12,3). Archaeological discoveries in the necropolis in the Rabat region and in sanctuaries in the interior of the island (Tas Silg) confirm the presence of Phoenician sailors from the end of the eighth century BC at least. It is thought that the Phoenician colony might have been centred on Melite, the modern Medina-Rabat.

The Phoenicians also occupied Gozo and Pantelleria and, perhaps, Lampedusa as well (Diod. 5:12; Pseudo Scylax 111). The original name of the island of Gozo, *Gaulos*, of Phoenician origin meaning a type of merchant ship, and the old name of Pantelleria, *Iranim*, likewise suggest links with ancient Phoenicia.

Leptis Magna, Hippo and Hadrumetum, on the North African coast, form another group of colonies believed to have been founded by Tyre or Sidon (Sallust, *Bell. Iug.* 77:1; Silius Italicus, *Punica* 3:256; Pliny, *N.H.* 5:76). So far, however, these settlements have not yielded archaeological evidence from the early period, except, apparently, Leptis Magna.

Lastly, mention must be made of the island of Sardinia, where archaeology records the presence of Phoenician colonists from the seventh century BC at Nora, Sulcis, Tharros, Bithia and Caralis (Cagliari). In the case of Sulcis and Tharros, archaeological documentation goes right back to the eighth century BC. From the distribution of these cities, we can deduce that Tyre was interested in controlling the whole of the southwest of the island.

The written sources relating to the Sardinian foundations say very little about their origins. Some references, however, are especially interesting in that they appear to associate the Phoenician occupation of Sardinia with elements arriving from the Iberian peninsula. Pausanias (9:17) states that the first to anchor their ships in the island of Ichnusa were Africans (Carthaginians) under the command of their chief, Sardo, who gave his name to Sardinia. Later, the Iberians passed through the island with their admiral Norax, and founded Nora, the first city on the island (Solinus 4:1). Thus Phoenicians, Carthaginians and perhaps Phoenicians from Gadir all had a hand in colonizing Sardinia.

Through this overall picture we can confirm that almost all the southern coasts and islands of the western Mediterranean were under Phoenician dominion, a dominion that seems to have been consolidated during the eighth and seventh centuries. The density of the Phoenician enclaves in the west, moreover, shows that the diaspora into the Mediterranean was no simple expedition like the one in the Red Sea, nor a local colonization, as in the gulf of Alexandretta, but that it involved the displacement of major contingents of the Phoenician population, especially in the eighth century BC.

In this whole process of expansion westward, Kition acted as a genuine bridgehead. Maybe on the return trip some Phoenician enclave in Egypt fulfilled an identical function. Herodotus (2:112) mentions a last Phoenician colony at Memphis, where the Tyrians occupied part of the town and built a temple to Astarte.

Various naval-technical circumstances undoubtedly combined in shaping this network of Phoenician enclaves in the Mediterranean. We shall now discuss to what extent this was so.

TECHNIQUES AND SYSTEMS OF NAVIGATION

We are assured that the Phoenicians invented the art of navigation and learnt the rudiments of astronomy, which they applied to navigation, from the Chaldeans (Pliny, *Nat. Hist.* 7:57). These navigational techniques hardly evolved at all until the Middle Ages and it is quite possible that the information included by Ptolemy in his famous Mapa Mundi was based on Phoenician navigational charts.

Underwater archaeology has so far not succeeded in recovering any

Phoenician ship from the period of expansion into the Mediterranean. Even so, it is possible to reconstruct the Phoenician systems of navigation from the historical references of the period and from pictures of Phoenician ships that appear in Assyrian reliefs. Thus we know that the Phoenician boats used sails which were square and that the handling of the vessels was heavy, cumbersome and dangerous. We know too, that they resorted to oars when there was no wind and that they practised coastal navigation and sailed the high seas, that is to say, sailed at night in the open sea.

The Phoenicians undertook naval expeditions to the Indian Ocean and the Red Sea and succeeded in circumnavigating Africa. They were sufficiently familiar with the Mediterranean to know which were the most advantageous places to establish their staging posts and colonies. They adapted their system of navigation to fit any circumstances. Thus, they faced no serious difficulties when it came to embarking on regular sailings from one end of the Mediterranean to the other. So we can dispense with the traditional idea that ships in such a remote period were of such shallow draught that they were incapable of facing the dangers of the open sea.

Coastal navigation

It is generally thought that captains in antiquity were accustomed to sticking close to the coast so as to avoid the dangers of the open sea. At night, they beached their ship or dropped anchor in some well-sheltered and shallow inlet. According to this theory, the Phoenicians, without adequate navigational instruments, would have sailed by day and at a prudent distance from the coast, like all their contemporaries.

For a very long time people insisted that the Phoenicians sailed exclusively by day in short stretches of 20 or 30 miles a day. This theoretical model, worked out by Cintas years ago (1949), rules out any possibility of sailing by night. The daily stages would, according to this author, coincide with the average distance of some 19 to 25 miles observed between the Phoenician or Punic settlements along the African coast. These coastal staging posts, moreover, all followed the same settlement pattern: a small island close to the coast or a headland on the mouth of a river, with harbours protected against the wind. Cintas called it the 'Punic landscape'.

This theory is relevant if we accept that there was only one system of navigation. But the system of coastal sailing off the shores of islands, bays and headlands is slow and dangerous because it forces sailors to hug the coast by day and anchor at night, with all the disadvantages that that involves. So it is suitable for small fishing boats and local traffic but not for long-distance trade.

What is more, not all the Phoenician enclaves in the west fit the model of coastal staging posts. If all Phoenician navigation had been of this type it would not explain, among other things, the presence of enclaves in Sardinia or the Balearics. Ibiza, for example, is more than 25 miles from the nearest staging post. As the crow flies, it is more than 65 miles from Ibiza to the southeast of Iberia. From Abdera to Oran the distance is over 130 miles and from Oran to the mouth of the Guadalhorce, in Malaga, is more than 200 miles. The shortest stretch between the Algerian coast and Cape Gata, for example, is a distance of 100 miles in a straight line, which would be equivalent to some three days' sailing without sight of a single Phoenician port. Moreover there is not one single Phoenician enclave on the Moroccan coast from Oran to Gibraltar (235 miles as the crow flies) before the fifth century BC.

The theory of a chain of staging posts or naval bases for taking on stores or seeking refuge at night does not fit in either with the distances between the Phoenician settlements on the Mediterranean coast of Andalusia. In this region, the average distance between one colony and the next as the crow flies is only 3.75 miles. Consequently we must ask ourselves whether, alongside the obvious existence of Phoenician coastal sailing, we should not be looking for other factors or practices to explain the location of a good many of the ancient Phoenician enclaves whose arrangement does not fit in with the mathematical distances of 20 to 25 miles for coastal navigation.

Sailing the high seas

The siting of the Phoenician foundations in Sicily, Sardinia and Ibiza makes it quite clear that the Tyrians sailed the open sea and that not only could they face the hardships of the high seas but they must necessarily have travelled by night.

At certain periods of the year, it was very hazardous to embark on regular voyages of thousands of miles on the high sea, due to the strength of the winds and currents in the Mediterranean. This is why the open sea was very often 'no man's land'.

During the eighth and seventh centuries BC, however, both navigation on the open sea and systems of lighting at night are fully documented. Thus, when Hesiod speaks of *ergon* trade, he seems to be describing commercial operations lasting an estimated fifty days and not small-scale or coastal navigation. In the Odyssey, trips lasting more than six days and nights are mentioned and a four-day voyage from Crete to Egypt with no intermediate ports of call is described (*Od.* 14:257–258). Later, in the Hellenistic period, Strabo refers explicitly to sailing the high seas in the Mediterranean (3:2,5).

Sailing the high seas necessarily involves sailing by night and therefore the existence of some system of orientation. Night sailing, in common with sailing out of sight of land, uses the stars to steer by and, more especially, the Pole star which forms part of the constellation of Ursa Minor. Knowledge of astronomy, which allowed the ancients to sail the open sea without risk of losing their bearings, is fully reported in Homer's epic (*Od.* 2:434; 10:28; 15:476). However the discovery of the importance of Ursa Minor for sailing by night is attributed to the Phoenicians and it is significant that the classical world called the constellation 'Phoiniké'.

The Phoenicians, then, had an excellent knowledge of astronomy many years before Homer, even though the true position of the Pole star was not determined mathematically until the fourth century BC.

The Mediterranean was and still is good for sailing the open sea, except in winter when fog and storms make it difficult to see the coast and the stars. In those conditions, there was no other solution, right down to the Middle Ages, but to tie up in port and await better days. But in normal conditions, boats were guided by the Pole star or else by reference to land, since it has been proved that in favourable weather conditions, with very few exceptions, the coast or the mainland is visible from any point in the Mediterranean. From a map of theoretical visibility, taking in all the coasts of the Mediterranean, it is clear that there are very few parts of the sea from which at least a mountain or a high coastal range cannot be seen (Fig. 23). This is especially true along the whole northern coastline of the Mediterranean and along the African coast in the west.

According to mathematical calculations, a rock rising 30 feet above sea level disappears from sight of a boat 8 miles away. The summit of a mountain 7,500 feet high disappears at a distance of 125 miles. The Mulhacen or the Canigo in Spain are landmarks that present no problems in this respect. Visibility is excellent along the whole of the Iberian peninsula, the Straits, the coasts of Morocco and Algeria and a large part of Tunisia. On the other hand, there is a large area of the sea where land visibility is much reduced: the African coast from southern Tunisia to Sinai and also between the Balearics and the islands of Corsica and Sardinia.

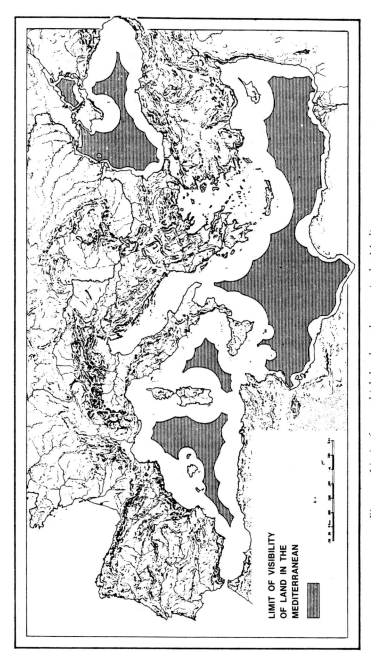

LIMIT OF VISIBILITY
OF LAND IN THE
MEDITERRANEAN

Fig. 23   Limits from which land can be seen in the Mediterranean

We can affirm, then, that the days in the Mediterranean when, in good weather, sailors cannot see land or reference points on the coast are very few. On the whole in winter, visibility does not exceed 65 miles on foggy days, although a lookout posted on a mast 30 feet high gains some 7.5 miles in visibility. But in antiquity mariners did not sail in winter, other than in exceptional circumstances.

Fishermen today still navigate by a limited number of high-altitude points and have no need of maps or navigational instruments. A ship leaving Tyre for Gadir could do the voyage in a more or less straight line on the open sea without losing sight of land by making one slight detour northwards between the Ionian isles and Sicily.

Distances travelled, sailing periods and duration of the voyages

Throughout antiquity, sailing was restricted to periods of good weather. Except in case of war, the ships weighed anchor at the beginning of spring and returned to port in October. The period reserved for sailing was thus fairly brief, judging by the limits spoken of by Hesiod in his 'Works and days' (vv. 663–665 and 678–684): '50 days from the moment when the sun turns in the heart of drowsy summer' (the end of June till the middle of September). Nevertheless, the possibility of going to sea between March and the end of October was envisaged. Winter sailing was not widespread in the Mediterranean until the sixteenth century.

This limited number of sailing days is confirmed by other classical authors, like Herodotus. This latter, describing the circumnavigation of Africa by the Phoenicians carried out on behalf of the pharaoh Nechao (609–594 BC), reports that when autumn arrived, the Phoenicians landed and grew wheat while they awaited a favourable period, so that the voyage lasted two years (Herod. 4:42).

We do not know the exact speed of the ships, which would depend on the type of craft and the winds and currents. Various circumstances might prolong a voyage: the type of trade; limited days suitable for sailing, which could mean that a Phoenician vessel might remain at anchor for a whole year in the same port – bad weather, lack of wind, and so on. Yet, even so, it is possible to calculate the average speed of boats from the information known for the classical period. And it is possible in turn to determine the duration of a voyage working from the average speed of the boat and the number of hours sailed daily, not forgetting days of bad weather and those spent taking on food or resting.

In the classical period, a ship took 9 days from Corinth to Leucas,

9 hours from Corfu to Brindisi and 15 days from Greece to Sicily, or even less (Thucyd. 6:1). To calculate the duration of a voyage and the speed of a boat, it is necessary to take into account not only the sailing days but the system used: oars or sail. In the sixteenth century a rowed galley, very like the Phoenician and Greek warships, needed 206 hours to cover the distance from Venice to Corfu, some 1000 miles. For a distance of 2000 miles it would need 883 hours, including the time when the boats were delayed, estimated at 60% of the total time. No doubt this percentage was higher in antiquity.

Herodotus calculates an average speed for day and night sailing of 600 to 700 stadia, that is, 68 to 82 miles per day (Herod. 4:86,1). This agrees with the average speed attributed to merchant ships by Thucydides (Thucyd. 2:97,1; 3:3,5; 6:1) and would give an average speed of some 54 stadia (6 miles) per hour, indicating that the distance between Carthage and Gadir could be covered in 7 days, from Sicily to Crete would take a good 3 days and from Gibraltar to Pirene some 7 days (Avienus, O.M. 560).

For long-range sailings, the known voyage of Colaios from Samos to Gadir at the end of the seventh century BC has been estimated at some 1440 sailing hours, equivalent to 60 days, to cover a distance of 2000 miles. So Colaios took two months to get to Tartessos and therefore had perforce to stay in Gadir or some other port all winter, awaiting the next sailing season.

It has been calculated that the Phocean Greeks in the sixth century took some 240 hours, equivalent to 45 days' sailing, to cover the distance of some 1360 miles in a straight line between Phocea and Ampurias. This estimate is based on the average speed of Phocean warships – the pentaconters – of some 6 miles per hour. It means that the Phoceans, taking a month and a half to reach Spain, could do the return voyage in one summer. Leaving Phocea at the end of May, they could be back in September, with only 15 days for loading and unloading merchandise in Ampurias. Such a brief stay could hardly compensate for three long months at sea.

From all these calculations it is possible to work out how long the crossing from Tyre to Gadir took; the distance as the crow flies is more than 2600 miles, and would take 80 or 90 days, that is to say some three months. Given the limited sailing season at that period, it is obvious that ships had to remain at anchor in ports on the Straits of Gibraltar for a very long time, so a Tyrian seaborne expedition to the western Mediterranean would frequently last more than a year between the outward and return voyages.

The Phoenician ships

The first explicit mention of Phoenician ships refers to a fleet of forty merchant ships carrying cedar, which left a Phoenician port bound for Egypt around the year 3000 BC. From at least the middle of the third millennium we have evidence of large merchant ships – the 'ships of Byblos' – on the open sea trading with Egypt. It is partly to this long experience that the reputation of the Phoenician pilots as experts in the arts of navigation is due, also that of the naval engineers of Tyre, highly valued as shipbuilders and sought after by other eastern monarchies like Israel. Byblos, Tyre and Sidon had learnt all these techniques from Egypt, a country with a long shipping tradition that had grown out of travel on the Nile, principally by sail but using oars for auxiliary propulsion.

Outstandingly important were the boats of Hatshepsut, called 'ships of the Punt'; we know their shape from the eighteenth Dynasty reliefs at Deir el-Bahari. These ships were very capacious and capable of sailing long distances without tying up. The space normally reserved for oarsmen was used for carrying cargo so the boats travelled under sail and were generally slow and bulky. The 'ships of the Punt' constitute the direct prototype of the Phoenician merchant ships.

This type of boat, which was so practical for commercial voyages, was very soon adopted in the Levant and the Aegean where its round, big-bellied shape would be characteristic. In the Aegean, the crossings are shorter because of the large number of islands and the strong winds, which are more dangerous than in the Red Sea, and so oars would become more important in Cretan and Mycenaean shipping. The space intended for cargo was now reserved to accommodate an ever-increasing number of oarsmen, which meant that the ships gradually became faster and lighter. Later, the Greek world would use this type of boat equally for both commercial and warlike purposes.

In spite of the disadvantage of its lack of speed, the slower, more roomy merchant ship under sail continued to be the most suitable for long journeys in the Mediterranean. The Phoenicians were able to take advantage of all these innovations and very soon the merchant navy of the coast of Canaan was sharing the waters of the eastern Mediterranean with Egyptians and Mycenaeans, as is shown by the discovery of the ship at Cape Gelidonya, among others. The pictures in the Egyptian tomb at Kenamon, moreover, dated to the days of Amenophis II (eighteenth Dynasty), show us merchant ships manned by Phoenician, or if you will, Canaanite sailors. These are big ships fitted with solid decks and high sides, which could undoubtedly transport plenty of freight in the holds and on deck. They are big-bellied freighters with rounded ends, driven by large square sails in the style of Hatshepsut's ships.

During the first millennium Phoenicia inherits the paunchy freighter and the Aegean type of boat, manned with more and more oarsmen and so capable of ever greater speed. Furthermore the Phoenicians are credited with inventing the keel and the ram and with caulking the joints in the planks with bitumen. They knew the adjustable sail and the double steering oar which enabled them to turn and manoeuvre very rapidly.

The Phoenicians used three main types of ship.

Local shipping

The earliest Phoenician boat is known from the bronze friezes on the gates of Balawat (ninth century BC; Fig. 8). They are small craft rowed by one or two men, and have rounded ends and figureheads in the form of horses' heads. These are the same boats that are carrying wood in a relief at Khorsabad (Fig. 9).

It is more than likely that this type of craft with the prow in the form of a horse's head is the origin of the legend that Hippos the Tyrian was the inventor of cargo ships (Pliny, *N.H.* 5:206). The geographer, Strabo, also says that in the Hellenistic period the sailors of Gadir were still using these boats, known as *hippoi* or 'horses', so called from the figure decorating the prow (Strabo 3:3,4). The Gaditanians used these craft for fishing in the region of Lixus. Occasionally one of these fishing boats would stray too far and vanish at sea.

The *hippoi* of Gadir are consequently the direct descendants of the little Phoenician cargo boats of Balawat and Khorsabad. As lightweight craft, they seem to have been used solely for local transport and for fishing. This type of boat was still in use until very recently on the island of Malta.

Merchant ships

The cargo-carrying merchant ship is heir to the great Syrio–Canaanite ships of the second millennium. Propelled by a huge square sail, the ship had the capacity to transport victuals, provisions and merchandise. Consequently it was ideal for long voyages on the open sea. In order to gain cargo room, these ships tended to be very wide and spacious, hence their Latin name: *naves rotundae*. It was their round shape, too, that inspired the Greeks to call them *gaulos* – bathtub – equivalent to the Phoenician *gôlah*.

The *gaulos* is thought to be the Phoenician merchant ship by antono-
masia and was, no doubt, the main instrument of the Phoenician
diaspora westwards. Maybe the island of Gozo, near Malta, owes its
name to these voluminous freighters.

In the oft-quoted Assyrian relief in the palace at Nineveh, showing
the flight of King Luli of Tyre to Cyprus, these big-bellied freighters can
be seen, escorted by a flotilla of warships (Fig. 10). They are boats with
a high prow and stern, dependent for their motive power almost
entirely on sail. Nevertheless they have places for oarsmen, judging by
the Assyrian relief, and there could be as many as eighteen or twenty of
them, used exclusively for manoeuvring, since it was necessary to
reserve all the remaining space for the cargo.

We do not know the maximum capacity that a Phoenician or
Greek merchant ship could attain. Some of the texts from Ugarit lead
us to think that, around 1200 BC, a Canaanite merchantman could
have a cargo capacity of up to 450 tons. During the first millennium
BC, the normal capacity of the freighters fluctuated between 100 and
500 tons.

The speed and stability of these ships depended on their capacity.
With a favourable wind, they could reach some 5 knots, so they were
able to cover a distance of 400 miles in 4 days (*Od.* 14:257–258).

Thanks to Wen-Amon's story, we have evidence of the existence of
Phoenician merchant fleets, consisting of up to fifty ships, from the
eleventh century BC. The king of Byblos and the shipowner Urkatel
possessed a fleet of that kind. In the time of Hiram I, during the tenth
century BC, the Tyrian merchant ships are the 'ships of Tarshish',
according to the biblical texts. Originally, these were the ships that
carried precious merchandise from distant lands, from the east at first
and later from the Mediterranean. But we know little about what they
were really like.

The power and monopoly of the royal house of Tyre in matters of
sea transport rested on its ships, the *ôniyât taršiś* (II Chronicles 8:18).
This is the time of the greatest activity in the shipyards of Tyre, which
specialized in building these great ships. There is a possibility that the
name 'ships of Tarshish' was derived not from the type of boat but
from the cargo and destination of these commercial voyages, as happened in the third millennium with the celebrated 'ships of Byblos'. At a
period later than that of Hiram I, the same name could have come to
designate the Tarsos of Cilicia and even the far west of the Mediterranean. It has also been suggested that the name 'tarsos' might have
referred to their having a bank of oarsmen and that the word *ôniját*

might be not of Semitic but of Indo-European origin and simply designate a ship: *anaji – naus – navis*.

The warships

The third and last type of Phoenician ship was the redoubtable fighting galley, propelled by oars and fitted with a ram. In contrast to the merchant ships, this type of much lighter ship was called *navis lunga*.

In the relief of King Luli of Tyre, from the end of the eighth century BC, these galleys, which served as escort to the tubby freighters, are seen at anchor in the south harbour at Tyre. One of these ships appears with the prow facing the city and has two superimposed banks of oarsmen, five in each lower bank and four others above (Fig. 10). Both sides of the ships are hung with shields identical to those that can be seen on the walls of Tyre, which means that they might well be transporting soldiers. We remember the words of Ezekiel (27:8 and 10) stating that the Tyrian fleet had soldiers and sailors coming from various countries. The fact is that their complement, counting soldiers and oarsmen, amounted to some fifty men like the famous Phocean penteconters. The Greeks called these warships, equipped with a double bank of oars, one above the other, 'biremes'.

Another characteristic of the Phoenician warships in the aforesaid Assyrian relief is the top of the prow, armed with a sharp-pointed ram, a distinctive feature of the fighting ship. This invention is attributed to the Phoenicians and would date from at least 800 BC. The ram made it possible to build more robust hulls but its force of impact depended above all on the speed of the boat, or what amounts to the same thing, on the number of oarsmen, which could be as high as thirty six. This would validate the hypothesis concerning the existence of a large Phoenician fleet equipped with genuine biremes of fifty oarsmen, or penteconters.

The penteconters usually had two officers on board and sailed in fleets of up to sixty fighting galleys, organized like genuine combat squadrons which would sail close to the coast in order to take on victuals at night, since their loading capacity was of necessity very restricted.

Thanks to Greek pottery and classical historical references, we know a good deal about how these ships evolved in Greece, where they gradually advanced from a crew of twenty oarsmen in Homer's time to a total of thirty (triconters) or even fifty oarsmen (penteconters) later, and from a single bank of oars each side to two (bireme) and even three banks (trireme). The arrangement of two banks, one above the other on each side, in the bireme in the second half of the eighth century BC considerably increased the power of these ships. The invention of the trireme, around the year 670 BC, attributed to Sidonians and Corinthians, enabled them to house a crew of 170 oarsmen; this warship was in general use from the sixth century BC (Herod. 2:158; Thucyd. 1:13).

The warships were long, narrow boats and so rather unstable, although they could make long sea crossings in spite of the lack of space for provisions, which forced them to put in to shore from time to time. From 800 BC onwards, naval fighting units had sufficient capacity to blockade the Mediterranean ports or disrupt commercial traffic. Low and narrow, with a length of 30 or 32 metres, the penteconter could manoeuvre swiftly and it was easy to hide behind a headland or small island. But it was above all a very swift ship and easy to bring alongside in shallow waters, because of its shallow draught.

The presence of oars made these ships less dependent on winds and currents and all that was required was intelligent coordination from the pilot. In addition to the crew, these ships could carry passengers in special circumstances. We know, for example, that when Cyrene was founded, two penteconters carrying a total of 200 to 300 colonists played a part (Herod. 7:184). Likewise, their loading capacity could be raised, judging by the account of the voyage of the Samian Colaios to Tartessos; on the return journey his ship took on board 60 talents (some 1500 to 2000 kg) of silver.

Unlike the merchant ship, with a small crew and cheap to run, the warship was very expensive and difficult to equip. The example of the battle of Salamina in 480 BC is revealing in this respect: it took a total of 34,000 men to equip the 200 ships of the Athenian squadron. It is obvious that very few states could meet expenses of that magnitude. It is improbable, therefore, that the Phoenicians, unlike the Greeks, systematically used these galleys for their western enterprise.

The oldest known representation of a bireme fitted with a ram on the prow is in the eighth century Assyrian relief from the palace of Sennacherib in Nineveh. It is thought that the Greeks adapted it from a Phoenician model. From the eighth century BC, this powerful offensive weapon inaugurated a new era in the tactics of naval warfare, which was to last some 1000 years. A naval battle ceased to be a confrontation between archers and lancers and became a series of successive assaults in which the first ship to strike a blow at a vital point of the enemy ship won the victory. This depended in the last resort on the coordination and manoeuvring capacity of the oarsmen.

The Phoenician penteconter attained maximum performance in the middle of the eighth century BC. An item from Menander of Ephesus, picked up by Flavius Josephus (*Ant. Jud.* 9:14), states that Salmanasar V sent an armada against Tyre composed of sixty warships with a total of 800 oarsmen and fitted out by other Phoenician cities allied to the Assyrian king. The city of Tyre, with only twelve ships, succeeded in dispersing the enemy and taking 500 prisoners. It is more probable, however, that there were sixteen, not sixty ships attacking Tyre.

The battle may have been similar to the one at Alalia (535 BC), off the coast of Corsica, or at Salamina (480 BC). The percentage of prisoners taken shows the magnitude of the Assyrian disaster, because only a battle using rams could have saved so many enemy lives, since the prisoners must have thrown themselves into the water to avoid going down with their ships. Tyre did not in actual fact disperse the Assyrian squadron, she destroyed it. This success is of the utmost interest in that it shows the existence in the eighth century BC of a Tyrian fighting squadron made up of penteconters.

The ports

Phoenician power depended to a large extent on her maritime communications and on the good condition of her ports. Unfortunately documentation earlier than the Hellenistic and Roman period concerning the Mediterranean ports is scanty, virtually nonexistent.

The texts and archaeological discoveries made in Ugarit reveal that the ships of the second millennium were much bigger than usually thought, requiring harbour installations of considerable dimensions. The texts refer to Canaanite ships colliding with wharves or harbours and the Egyptian paintings and reliefs of the eighteenth Dynasty suggest the existence of structures and footbridges in the Mediterranean ports.

Before the fourth to third centuries BC the techniques of building walls and laying foundations under water had not been discovered. Consequently we cannot strictly speak of the existence of wharves or genuine harbour constructions before the Hellenistic period. Studies of ancient ports show that before the fourth century the conditions of the site were exploited to form harbours, either carving out the natural rock or adapting reefs or rocky islands to form moles or breakwaters for protection against the winds and currents (Fig. 24). These harbour works were at least consolidated by building walls on top of them, giving rise to some enclosed harbour structures or lagoons up to

Fig. 24   Aerial view of Sidon, 1934

several kilometres wide. In the absence of this kind of shelter, ships simply ran up on the beach. All along the Mediterranean coast, the Phoenicians chose the most suitable anchorages – bays and river mouths sheltered from the winds.

On the island of Tyre there were two harbours, one artificial and situated to the south of the city, perhaps carved out of the rock, and the other, in the north, a natural one, that is, making use of the configuration of the reefs. The southern harbour, looking towards Cyprus and Egypt, was better protected against winds and tides. In the Assyrian reliefs depicting the island of Tyre, the two gates in the wall of the city seem to have formed the only access to the two harbours from inside the town itself. As we saw before, the building of the southern, so-called 'Egyptian' harbour at Tyre, in the approaches to the city, is attributed to Ithobaal I. In one of Tyre's harbours were the famous shipyards where old ships were broken up and new ones built (Diod. 17:46,1). Sidon and Memphis had their own shipyards as well.

A great many of the Phoenician port establishments reproduced the

Tyrian model and had twin harbours, one relatively open or external, reserved for merchant ships, and the other more protected, enclosed or internal, situated close to the walls of the city and intended for local traffic or warships. It seems that this was the case at Arvad, Sidon and Tell Sukas, among others. But the best known example is Carthage, a city which, according to the literary tradition, possessed two harbours, one commercial and the other military, in the vicinity of the sanctuary of Salammbô (Fig. 25). Unlike the commercial harbour, which was rectangular or polygonal in shape, the more enclosed military harbour was shaped like an artificial lake or *cothon*, a feature peculiar to the Phoenician inner harbours. Nevertheless, the exact position of the most ancient harbour at Carthage is not known; some people site it in the bay of the Kram. Recent British excavations have established that the two harbours close to Salammbô were built during the Punic wars and are consequently no earlier than the fourth century BC.

The Phoenician fleet, considered to this day to be the first naval power in history, is the product of an exceedingly steep and rugged coast which, given the lack of technical development of the day, was precisely the most likely place to provide excellent harbours.

Thanks to various surveys carried out in the ancient harbours at Tyre, we know that the island of Tyre lay at the centre of a line of reefs running parallel to the coast, which protected the city from the assault of the sea and the winds and which the Tyrians were able to adapt to make a harbour. Erosion, human intervention and a rise in the sea level in the past three hundred years have submerged the ancient reefs close to the island. Moreover, the mole built by Alexander the Great not only converted the island into a peninsula but disturbed the balance of the marine currents, which attacked the reef or southern harbour of the city with particular force (Fig. 4). The few mole constructions that have been preserved under water are from the Roman period. The line of reefs around ancient Tyre made the site into an ideal anchorage with the help of simple works of adaptation, converting the rocky barriers into roadsteads or breakwaters sheltered from the winds.

The same criteria were followed in the harbours of Sidon, Arvad and Byblos. In the west, too, the small islands of Motya and Gadir, separated from the mainland by a channel protected from the winds and currents, made excellent natural harbours and reproduced more or less faithfully the model of Tyre.

The island at Arvad also had two harbours, one enclosed or internal and the other open or external. These very favourable conditions were due to its sandstone reefs, deliberately carved and adapted on the north

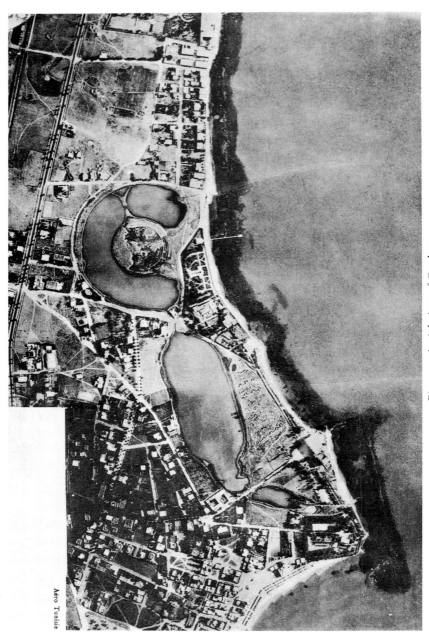

Fig. 25   Aerial view of Carthage

side so as to form a harbour structure or barrier joining the island to a tiny islet, Bint el-Arwad, a few kilometres away. This northern mole gave rise to a double harbour or channel between islands very similar to the one we shall see at Gadir. All the harbour constructions and buttresses built in ancient Arvad date from the Hellenistic period.

Ships could lie at anchor in the open sea if conditions were unfavourable, but this meant that the cargo had to be brought to the shore or to the city in small boats. In favourable conditions, ships could moor in these rocky harbours with their sails furled and their gangplanks running from the prow of the ship directly to the coast or rocky platform.

In the west, the Phoenicians had few natural harbours combining all the conditions of Tyre or Arvad, except in the cases of Gadir, Motya and Malta. On coasts with a steep, cliff-like structure, they had to moor most of the time right up against the rocky jetty, to which they could get quite close. Where the coastline was gentler and sloped more gradually to the sea, the only option was to keep a prudent distance from the coast.

Some places, however, offered unrivalled conditions for allowing ships easy access to the beach, out of reach of the winds and out of sight of other ships. This was the case in the natural bays and inlets around a river mouth, which we find on much of the coast of eastern Andalusia.

Winds and currents

Marine currents and more especially winds were the main obstacles to ancient seafaring. Currents and winds not only conditioned to a great extent the Phoenician commercial seaways, but they had important repercussions on the choice of harbour enclaves in the west, when other criteria of an economic or political nature did not intervene.

We will start from the assumption that currents in the Mediterranean have undergone no outstanding changes in the last 3000 years. As for the winds, these have remained unchanged in the last 2000 years.

The wind was the main force for ancient seafarers and was particularly important when sailing the high seas. The techniques of the day made sailing against the wind extremely difficult and only possible by using oars or else by tacking. But it can be said that big ships avoided this method of sailing in antiquity.

Currents, on the other hand, are not such a determining factor in a

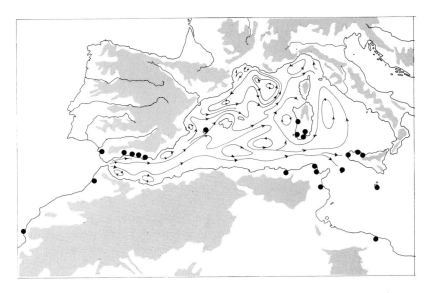

Fig. 26   Marine currents in the western Mediterranean (Ruiz Arbolo)

landlocked sea like the Mediterranean, although they are particularly
dangerous in the Straits of Gibraltar, in Syrtis Major and where the
Ionian Sea meets the Adriatic. In antiquity, however, currents were
generally taken advantage of to help a ship's progress.

Currents
In the Mediterranean the currents are wont to be superficial, seasonal
and caused by the prevailing winds. So they are variable and eminently
coastal. For merchant ships loaded with metal travelling from the
Iberian peninsula, it was essential to sail with these currents, since the
ships were mostly heavy freighters that were extremely slow and
difficult to handle.

There is, in addition in the Mediterranean, a general current running
anti-clockwise (Fig. 26). It is the result of differences in temperature,
evaporation and input of river waters into the Mediterranean, producing a difference of level between it and the Atlantic. This imbalance
means that water is constantly coming in through the Straits of Gibraltar and the Dardanelles.

So from Gadir to the Lebanon a west–east current predominates,
starting from Gibraltar and running along the African coast to Port

Said, where it turns northwards, keeping close to the coast of Palestine, Syria, Asia Minor and the north of the Aegean where it then makes contact with the strong current from the Black Sea and the Dardanelles. The two combine to form a new current heading west across from the Greek coast and islands, north of Crete, past the Peloponnese and finally arriving in the Adriatic. From there the current goes up northwards along the Dalmatian coast and then comes back down the Italian coast, runs round the south of Italy, the Tyrrhenian coast and the gulf of Genoa from where it once more heads southwards along the Spanish coast to Gibraltar. Until a few centuries ago, this general current and its ramifications, combined with the wind system, conditioned the navigation charts for the open sea.

In the Straits of Gibraltar, the current from the Atlantic reaches a speed of up to 5 or 6 knots and only begins to slacken when level with Cape Gata. Except when an east wind was blowing, which to some extent counteracts the current, the passage of the Straits of Gibraltar for a ship going from Tyre towards Gadir must have been extremely difficult. On the other hand, the reverse passage, in the direction of Oran and Algeria, for a ship coming from Gadir, poses no great problems if the vessel keeps close to the African coast, following the direction of the general current.

The wind system
In the Mediterranean, the weather is fairly good for sailing in summer, and indeed once March and April are over.

In the Straits of Gibraltar, there are only west and east winds, and according to which one predominates, it is customary to speak of westerly years or easterly years. The east winds are usually dominant in the months of March, July, August, September and December while in the other months of the year they alternate with winds from the west, that is, the westerlies (Fig. 27).

In westerly years, that is to say when the west winds blow hard, it is particularly dangerous to go through the Straits towards the Atlantic or Gadir. We must suppose that during the eighth and seventh centuries BC, access to Gadir in these conditions cannot have been exactly easy. Even today, when a westerly is blowing, vessels heave to in Algeciras Bay waiting for breezes from the east, which sometimes take two months to arrive. In winter, the westerlies can be particularly violent in the region of Tarifa.

The east winds, on the other hand, can dominate in the eastern approaches to the Straits and can be particularly violent in the region

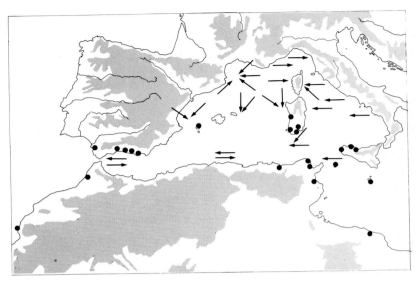

Fig. 27   Prevailing winds in the western Mediterranean (Ruiz Arbolo)

of Tarifa. When westerlies and easterlies coincide in winter, it is impossible to go through the Straits.

The east winds are also dominant along the coasts of Morocco and Algeria in summer and they often blow for days on end. In the gulf of Valencia, the winds blow from the northeast and the north and these also prevail in the Balearics. In the Tyrrhenian Sea, because of the barrier formed by Corsica and Sardinia, there are breezes from the east, while in Corsica, off Bonifacio, the westerlies prevail. On the island of Sardinia, winds usually blow from the west or north on the west coast and from the east on the east coast.

To conclude, we can state that the ancient Mediterranean sea routes, understood as the courses recommended for sailing ships on the basis of information collected over the centuries by captains and pilots, pay particular attention to the system of winds and currents. The plan of these itineraries is practically identical with that of the ancient Greek and Phoenician voyages and they provide us with an obligatory reference point when attempting to reconstruct the routes followed by the Phoenician ships in their expansion westward.

THE SEA ROUTES

It is generally thought that the sea routes taken by the Phoenicians on their voyages to the west ran along North Africa and that the return journey passed by the islands of the west-central Mediterranean.

But it is quite obvious that the Phoenicians were well able to select the most suitable places to underpin a great commercial axis, which, if we stick to the written sources, was based initially on the Tyre–Utica–Gadir route. We do not know exactly what happened at the start, that is to say, which places were destined to be staging posts for ships – to spend the winter or repair damage or take on water and food – and which coastal stations were occupied as permanent enclaves for commercial and economic purposes.

It must, moreover, be borne in mind that the voyage of a ship loaded with ore or silver ingots would of necessity have been of a different type from that of a ship carrying amphorae or luxury ceramics. Nor is slow and dangerous coastal navigation, allowing the development of dynamic and continuous trading, the same thing as sailing the open sea, which is swifter and safer but can accomplish very little on the way. It can definitely be said that the techniques, systems and sea routes entail clearly defined trading mechanisms and, vice versa, the type of trade governs the routes or systems of navigation.

If we stick to the system of winds and currents in the Mediterranean that we have described, and above all to the recommendations of the ancient routes, it is possible to trace in broad outline the sea routes followed by the Phoenician ships in their voyages to and from the west.

The Tyre–Gadir route

For a voyage to the west, a ship leaving Tyre had two possible routes: to the south via Egypt–Cyrenaica–Gulf of Syrtes–Northwest Africa, which involved sailing against the general current all the way, or else the northern route of Cyprus–Asia Minor–Ionian Sea–Sicily–Spanish Levant–Straits of Gibraltar, which in fact is the only sea route documented by archaeological finds from the Late Bronze Age and the one which links the Mediterranean with the Atlantic metallurgy of the second millennium BC.

Furthermore, along the whole North African coastline between Cape Bon and Cyrenaica and Tripolitania, no signs of ancient Phoenician shipping have been reported and this is the route that all the ancient navigators would try to avoid because of the adverse current and the dangerous passage of Syrtis Major. On the other hand, this was the most suitable route for the return voyage to Tyre, because it meant sailing with the general current.

It may be inferred from all this that the route to the west must have been the northern, island one, including Motya and Ibiza in the itinerary as nerve centres on the way to Gadir. That would explain, among other things, the vitality of centres like the island of Motya from the eighth century on. The northern route is also the only one attested by the sources, which mention Cyprus, Asia Minor or Crete as obligatory ports of call for Phoenician trade (*Od.* 15:455–458).

So this east–west route would take in the following stages: the first stop must have been Cyprus, with its chief supporting enclave at Kition, controlled by the Phoenicians since the ninth century BC. Rounding the island to the south, the ships would have had to reach the coasts of Asia Minor from there and, leaving Cape Gelidonya behind, they would arrive at the ports of Phoinike – the modern Finike – and Phoinix, in Caria or Lydia, facing the island of Rhodes (Thucyd. 2:69,1). The second stage could consist of Rhodes itself, the point at which the route must have turned to the northwest, perhaps to the island of Cythera, where we can document yet another place name 'Phoinikous'. Finally the Ionian Sea was reached, and Malta, the region where the western Phoenician settlements start (Fig. 28).

As the ancient seaways suggest, the most favourable route from the Ionian Sea would pass through the channels of Malta and Sicily, bearing towards the south coast of the latter which provides shelter from the prevailing north winds. Then the route would have to cross to the south coast of Sardinia to avoid adverse currents and headwinds; from there it could make directly for the south of the Balearics.

Arriving in the western Mediterranean the chief obstacle consists of the general current from the west as well as the westerly winds, which force ships to follow the Spanish coast from Cape San Antonio and Cape Gata to the Straits. For ships travelling from Oran and western Algeria, it is advisable to sail very close to the coast as far as Cape Negro and from there make straight for the Straits of Gibraltar (Fig. 29).

In westerly years, two forces combine in the Straits against the line of travel: the wind and the general current. The westerly winds can blow for a whole month on end, making it necessary to lie up along the coast of Malaga. Ships coming from Algiers are indeed recommended to go up as far as Ibiza in these conditions; then, making a huge detour, to look for the current running down to Gibraltar. For ships coming

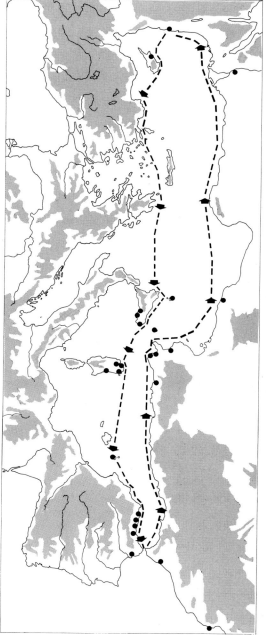

Fig. 28 Shipping routes in the Mediterranean

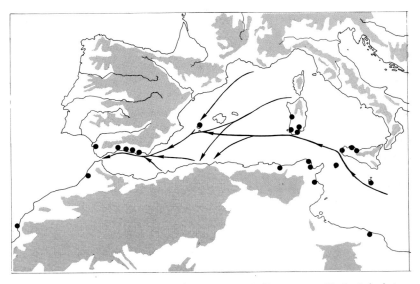

Fig. 29   East–west routes in the western Mediterranean (Ruiz Arbolo)

direct from Carthage or Utica, the Straits remained closed to traffic under sail for many weeks.

To find the Straits when going east–west, ships had to avoid the African coast as far as possible after leaving Oran and choose the itinerary south of Sardinia to Ibiza and the east coast of Andalusia, that is to say, the stretches along the coast and among the islands where we in fact document the greatest density of ancient Phoenician settlements.

The passage of the Straits of Gibraltar

Sailing logbooks advise mariners not to go through the Straits in the central channel, because of the general current, and to make the passage in summer, with an easterly wind. They likewise recommend approaching the Spanish coast from the Cape of Palos and keeping very close to it from Gata to the Mountains of Estrepona from where the Peñón divides. In the case of a persistent west wind, the only thing to do is to take refuge in the harbours of Malaga and Fuengirola. Thus the last part of the route to Gadir runs a very short distance from the coast of Almeria, Granada and Malaga, where classical tradition places a 'multitude' of Phoenicians in Abdera, Sexi and Malaka.

It is not always possible to choose the moment to approach a passage of the Straits towards Gadir. For ships and freighters kept waiting for days or months for a favourable wind, the coast of Malaga is a good support base and permanent refuge. In antiquity, the passage must have been difficult, especially if heavy merchant ships had to be manoeuvred in a headwind. It is reported that such an eventuality might even make it necessary to disembark in order to go and sacrifice to Melqart (Avieno, *O.M.* 365). To avoid going through the Straits, an overland route was sometimes advisable, starting from Malaka (Avieno, *O.M.* 178–182). The overland passage from Malaga to Tartessos entailed some four days to get there and another five days back and offered a possible alternative to anyone wanting to avoid waiting a whole month in Malaga for the west winds to abate. A wait like that might prejudice an important commercial transaction and, worse still, definitively delay the return trip to the east if winter arrived. A delay of a month could be decisive for a ship coming from Tyre and would leave the crew stranded for a whole year at the entrance to the Straits.

The Gadir–Tyre route

Sailing from west to east did not present such difficulties in summer and with westerly winds. Even so, access from Gadir to the Mediterranean is not always easy and even less so in the region of Tarifa and Trafalgar. Once again, the seaways and navigation charts are unanimous in considering the stretch of coast from Malaga to Motril, and in particular the anchorages at Vélez-Malaga and Almuñécar, as places of easy access.

The general recommendation is to go through the Straits in the central channel, making use of the general current to head easily and directly for Sardinia or Algeria. Only a strong east wind could make this last stretch difficult to get through. With a west wind it is advisable to sail down the centre of the channel from Malaga–Almeria to the Balearics, thus making use of the current. With east winds, on the other hand, the course plans recommend getting to windward on the coast of Algeria and from there to make for the Balearics or Bonifacio (Fig. 30). This detour is in response to the persistent north winds in the gulf of Valencia and the channel between Catalonia and the Balearics. From Alicante and Cartagena, too, the route passing to the south of the Balearics to head for Sardinia is better. In short, the route from Gadir to Sardinia had perforce to take in Ibiza.

In favourable conditions and especially in summer, however, the most suitable route to the east is the one running close to the African

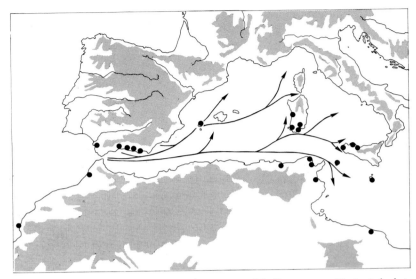

Fig. 30   The west–east routes in the western Mediterranean (Ruiz Arbolo)

coast, which keeps the ship in the general current and enables it to sail to Carthage, Pantelleria, Malta and Tyre without difficulty. To head for Sicily, it is necessary to manoeuvre along the south coast of Sardinia, an itinerary that should be avoided, however, in easterly winds.

The Atlantic route

The Phoenicians used secondary and, of course, Atlantic routes, like the one from Gadir to Lixus. It is acknowledged that there could have been coastal navigation on the Atlantic route, judging by the siting of the Phoenician emplacements on the Moroccan coast. But the beaches and inlets along the Moroccan coast are less sheltered than those on the Mediterranean, and east winds and frequent storms from the northwest are prevalent there. Once past the point of Monte Abyla and before reaching the Atlantic, there are no more natural harbours other than the bay of Tangier, ancient Tingis, a Carthaginian foundation of the sixth century BC. After Tingis, the coast is inhospitable until the fertile valleys of the Gharb and the Loukkos are reached. Lixus, on the mouth of the Loukkos, forms the main focus of ancient Phoenician trade in the region. To the south lies the great Phoenician trading establishment on the island of Mogador, frequented in the seventh century BC by Phoenician or Gaditanian ships.

It has been further conjectured that Gaditanian navigators may possibly have travelled as far as the Canaries or the Azores in pursuit of the fishery resources of the area, but nothing has so far been found to confirm this.

The circumnavigation of Africa associated with Phoenician navigators suggests that they attempted to engage in carefully planned seafaring expeditions. An expedition of this type is mentioned in connection with the pharaoh Nechao who, around the year 596 BC, financed a Phoenician voyage which took three years to accomplish its objectives (Herod. 4:42). There is a report of another similar periplus, organized this time as a Carthaginian state expedition which, under the command of Hannon, aspired to found colonies on the Atlantic coast of Africa and consolidate existing trading posts. Hannon's expedition got as far as Lixus at the end of the sixth century BC and, further south, founded the colony of Cerne, which some authorities situate in Senegal or the Cameroon. We know that Hannon sailed along the coast and made good profits, acquiring ivory, gold and skins.

Conclusions

The most advisable route for sailing from Tyre to Gadir had of necessity to go via Sardinia, Ibiza and the Mediterranean coast of Andalusia. The return voyage had to follow the African coast via Carthage and Utica and thence to Egypt and the Levant, or else it had to make a detour via Ibiza and Sardinia. In the west it was important to avoid at all costs crossing the Syrtis and, in westerly winds, going through the centre of the Straits of Gibraltar. In adverse conditions, the route from Africa to Gadir went right up to Ibiza. Interesting conclusions can be drawn from all this.

In the first place, merchant ships sailing to Gadir from the east rarely had to drop anchor at Carthage, since that city was an obligatory port of call on the return voyage to Tyre. Thus the sea routes to Gadir did not usually go via Carthage; this would explain the relative independence of the great North African metropolis shown by the Phoenician colonies in Andalusia in the eighth and seventh centuries BC.

In the second place, in the shipping circuits, the islands of Motya and Ibiza were obligatory ports of call on both the outward and return voyages. Ibiza, in particular, stands out as an important goal for sailors in the western Mediterranean, both on the routes to the south and on

journeys to the Strait of Bonifacio or on the routes heading for
Gibraltar. Consequently it must have been a strategic point of vital
importance on all the Tyre–Gadir–Tyre routes, since all the conditions
of an ancient settlement came together there. Even when Ibiza is
deemed to be a Carthaginian foundation of the seventh century BC
(Diod. 5:16,2–3), everything leads us to think that Ebusus could have
been in existence as an enclave from the eighth century BC. What is
more, the morphology of the little archipelago conforms to the preferred model of a site for the Tyrians in the west.

In the third place, the density of ancient Phoenician population
along the coasts of Almeria, Granada and Malaga could very well be
explained in terms of a more or less obligatory coastal shipping route
for all ships travelling to Gadir. In adverse conditions, Phoenician ships
could find themselves forced to remain a whole year at anchor in the
mouths of the Adra, the Seco, the Vélez or the Guadalhorce. All this is
in contrast to the depopulation characteristic of the Mediterranean
coast of Morocco and part of Algeria during the eighth and seventh
centuries BC, for reasons we need not reiterate here.

And lastly, the evidence shows that, with the colonial foundations in
Malta, western Sicily, southwest Sardinia, Ibiza, Carthage and Gadir,
the Phoenicians built up a kind of 'Phoenician triangle' in the west that
was practically impregnable and provided its naval and commercial
traffic with a solid support point and a monopoly of all the access
routes to the southwest Mediterranean. This triangle virtually closed
the Straits of Gibraltar to Greek competition and would be the foundation of the future Carthaginian maritime strength, when Carthage
converted this efficient trading network into an instrument of political
power.

The most westerly apex of the triangle was Gadir, which controlled
access to the Straits of Gibraltar and conditioned a large part of this
Mediterranean circuit. Control of the Gaditanian archipelago meant,
among other things, direct access to a territory that was one of the
richest in metal resources in the west. The establishment of a Phoenician enclave at Gadir, so difficult of access to shipping, could only have
been envisaged because of its privileged position *vis-à-vis* Tartessos; so
its original function must be deemed to have been that of a place of
transit for merchandise and a way into the Atlantic ores.

7

The Phoenicians in the west: chronology and historiography

The hypotheses so far formulated about the origins and chronology of the first Phoenician foundations in the west are almost infinite in number. The profound divergences between the archaeological record and the dates attributed by classical historians to the founding of Gadir, Lixus and Utica have long fostered a search for compromise solutions to reconcile two almost irreconcilable types of dates. These have moved from exaggerated defence of a horizon of pre-colonial activity in the west during the twelfth to eighth centuries BC, characterized by 'silent' trade or simple barter, which would have left hardly any archaeological traces, to claiming an ancient chronology for certain archaeological materials, most of them isolated and out of context, which would demonstrate the presence of Phoenician peoples in the western Mediterranean from the beginning of the first millennium.

The polemics are not over, far from it. Nevertheless, it is worth emphasizing here the fragility of many of the arguments urged today by those who postulate Phoenician pre-colonization, and situating the ideological and socio-political context in which some of the historical analyses of the question, both classical and modern, belong.

Nowadays, none of the criteria formerly used to vindicate the historical truth of the statements of a Velleius Paterculus or a Diodorus enjoy much credit among the experts. In spite of that, any more or less isolated or sporadic archaeological find can revive the polemics initiated among us in the middle of the nineteenth century, and will doubtless continue to do so in the future.

All this means that there is an underlying question of methodology behind this problem which inevitably boils down to a more or less subjective reading of the historico-archaeological data.

In this book we cannot dodge the question of chronology. On it depends the objectivity or otherwise of the analysis of the meaning and character of the Phoenician settlements in the west. In this sense, to consider the western establishments as the end result of a more or less long-term process of trial and error and barter, like the one described by Herodotus on the Atlantic coasts of Africa (Herod. 4:96), is not the same as to interpret the Phoenician expansion as a socio-economic phenomenon arising from needs that are of an equally economic nature, but are concrete and set within a defined time space.

It is therefore a matter of priority to identify the existence or otherwise of a pre-colonial stage in the west and to discuss the interpretation, more widespread among present-day specialists, that defends the existence of a series of trading posts in the west which developed during the eighth and seventh centuries into urban colonies.

CLASSICAL HISTORIOGRAPHY: GADIR, HERACLES AND THE PHOENICIANS

The majority of the myths, traditions and legends concerning the arrival of the Phoenicians in the west begin to take shape in the Hellenistic period, that is to say a little more than 500 years after the events they relate took place. So these are late sources, far removed from the facts, necessarily subjective and, as we shall see, with scant guarantees of reliability.

The question revolves around the famous reference by the Roman historian Velleius Paterculus (*Hist. Rom.* 1:2,1–3), which placed the founding of Gadir eighty years after the Trojan War, that is around the year 1104 or 1103 BC. All the classical authors who allude to the origins of Gadir–Gades (Strabo, Mela, Pliny) confine themselves to reproducing the Velleius version, with hardly any variations, which cannot but be significant.

It is possible that Velleius' source of information in turn was Timeus, or Tauromenius, who was writing at the end of the fourth or the beginning of the third century BC and is not exactly distinguished for the accuracy of his knowledge of Iberia, and this illustrates in principle the poor reliability of the original sources of information.

It is therefore particularly interesting to know the intellectual environment in which the first accounts concerning the founding of Gadir, and consequently the chronology of the origins of the Phoenician expansion to the west, were produced.

In the first place, the Hellenistic period is characterized by the great confusion that prevailed about the date and place of arrival of the first Phoenicians in the west. Furthermore, the other constant that we find among the historians of the period is the tendency, which may have arisen in an Alexandrian or Athenian environment, to consider the poems of Homer as historical. Within this Hellenistic and Roman current and especially in pseudo-historicist intellectual contexts there is another feature, closely connected with the previous one: manipulation of etymologies in the face of the enormous quantity of data associated with the Trojan War, particularly the accounts by Homer of the return of the heroes – the *nostoi*. So phantasy, imagination and ingenuity combine in an attempt to transfer the main heroes of the Trojan War to the west. This is how the legendary journeys of Aeneas to Latium and of Ulysses, Anfilocus, Antenor and Theucros to Iberia (Strabo 3:2,13; Pausanias 1:28,11) arose. None of these legends, which arose in the fourth century BC, has any historical foundation.

The Hellenistic tendency to ennoble the origin of some western cities, the obsession with fixed dates (like that of the fall of Troy) and the exaggerated respect for Homer as a historical source mean that various traditions relative to the far west have been amalgamated and chronologies adjusted to the period of the Homeric heroes. Thus, mingling historical reality, fiction and pseudo-erudition, the desire to exalt the voyages to the far west in mythology means that Hellenistic historiography will seek eponymous heroes as founders of colonies. Very soon the voyages of Heracles are linked with Gadir and Spain and, with them, the legend of the return of the Heraclides after the Trojan War (Strabo 1:1,4; 3:2,13). Hence the idea that the Greek hero–god had died in Spain (Sallust, *Bell. Jug.* 1:8,3; Mela 3:46).

The assimilation of Gadir to the Phoenicians, to the Trojan War and to Heracles is a typical Hellenistic arrangement. Significantly, this legend arose in the period (second to first centuries BC) in which the grandeur and prosperity of Cadiz and the prestige of its sanctuary to Hercules, visited by illustrious figures from the political and intellectual life of the day like Hannibal, Polibius, Fabius Maximus and Julius Caesar, exercised an enormous influence on Hellenistic thought. No doubt all this helped to forge a legend in which Heracles–Hercules (Melqart) finally became mixed up in the Phoenician founding of Gadir.

The myth of Heracles in Iberia seems to have arisen in fourth-century Athens, when the god–hero began to be identified with the Tyrian Melqart. At that time it was already known that the temple of Heracles in Gadir was 'very ancient' (Diod. 5:20,1–4), so that Heracles–Melqart came to be confused automatically with any voyages to the far west and so linked with Gadir, that is to say, the Phoenicians, its founders. And so Heracles became transformed into the father of the Phoenicians.

In order to be able to transfer the travels of Heracles to Spain and associate them with the founding of the temple in Cadiz – the Gaditanian Heracleion of the Hellenistic period – it was necessary to situate the events in the myth of the return of the Heraclides to Greece after the Trojan war. The only solution was to move the chronologies of the founding of the colonies in the west closer to the dates associated with the Trojan War, an event moreover that supplied the first historical date known to the Greeks.

Gadir, the Phoenicians, Heracles and Melqart and, indirectly the founding of Lixus and Utica were mixed up in one and the same block of legends, into which other myths connected with the far west were gradually incorporated: the Garden of the Hesperides and the Columns of Hercules. The Garden of the Hesperides (Hesiod, *Teog.* 215–216; 274–275) came to symbolize the end of the Ocean and – how could it be otherwise? – one of the goals of the travels of Heracles; and the Columns, which perhaps at first designated pillars or altars marking the limit of the travels to Greeks and Phoenicians, came in the end to symbolize the Straits of Gibraltar themselves (Pindar, *Nem.* 3:20; Strabo 4:5,5–6).

In any case, only the Hellenistic incorporation of the myth of Heracles into Iberia, assimilated to the report of far-off Phoenician foundations in the west, and the equally Hellenistic tendency to ennoble the origin of cities as prestigious as Gades, could have justified setting a date in the twelfth century BC for the founding of the temple in Gadir, that is to say, for the arrival of the Phoenicians in the west.

The inconsistency of the classical sources dealing with the founding of Gadir and the belated and pseudo-erudite context in which they were produced will not in our opinion stand up to rigorous historical analysis.

MODERN HISTORIOGRAPHY

The first important epigraphic discoveries in the west in the eighteenth and nineteenth centuries and the birth of oriental studies in the middle of the last century produced a resurgence of the legends about the first Phoenician foundations and their mythical mastery of the sea. All this meant that their history in the ambit of the Mediterranean was exaggerated.

Within this Phoeniciophile current, two monumental and all-embracing studies stand out, that of de Movers (1841–1856) and, later, that of Bérard (1902–1903), both of whom came to regard the

Mediterranean as a genuine 'Phoenician lake'. With a glaring exaggeration of the role played by the Phoenicians in the Mediterranean, these two authors maintained that they had reached the west before the twelfth century BC, that during the tenth century BC, in the days of Hiram I, they already possessed flourishing colonies in northwest Africa and in Spain and that from Gadir they had sailed into the Atlantic from Brittany to the Niger. In cultural and intellectual matters, Greece and Rome were indebted to the Phoenician civilization.

But at the end of the nineteenth century, as a result of the spectacular discoveries made by Heinrich Schliemann, and by Evans in Crete and Mycenae, and with the discovery of traces of the Greeks throughout the Mediterranean, the roles began to be reversed. With no more than a few Phoenician epigraphs in the west, the reaction was inevitable and in a very short time produced an anti-Phoenician current fundamentally opposed to the early chronologies for the founding of Gadir and Utica. This current of thought is part of the movement making Eurocentrist claims, opposed to the traditional diffusionism that saw the east as the cradle of European civilization, and convinced that not everything in the Mediterranean was Phoenician. Historians like Salomon Reinach (1893) and Julius Beloch (1894) ended by driving the Phoenicians definitively out of the Aegean and the Mediterranean, dismissing Phoenician colonization as a myth. This pro-Greek tendency in the colonization of the Mediterranean is not out of keeping with the anti-Semitic and European colonialist sentiments of the day, of which Leonard Woolley would be the chief exponent.

Reinach and Beloch defended the greater antiquity of the Greek element throughout the Mediterranean and denied the existence of major Phoenician activity in the west before the eighth century BC. In short, they denied any historical accuracy to the classical sources, going so far as to suggest that authors like Herodotus and Thucydides – the latter being charged with ineptitude – had been 'victims of the illusion of believing that Homer had been a historian'. The followers of this hyper-critical current, which lasted until 1940, men like Carpenter (1933, 1958) and Bosch Gimpera (1928–1929), had strong arguments to hand, since no trace of the Phoenicians was recorded in the west before the eighth to seventh centuries BC. At that time the polemics had developed into a fight between those who defended the priority of the Greeks (Europeanists) and supporters of the Phoenicians (Orientalists) in the discovery of the west.

Although, between 1920 and 1930, the discoveries at Byblos and

Ugarit were already taking place and the necropolis of Carthage and that of Cadiz were being routinely excavated, the Phoenician question received no new impetus until 1941, with the works of Albright. In Spain, García Bellido was at that time initiating a critical analysis of the classical texts, basing the arguments for the first time on the archaeological record. Positions were reconciled and the polemics gradually relaxed until, in our own day, we have reached the point of accepting a degree of contemporaneity in the dates. Even so, differences are being established between Greek and Phoenician colonization and distances maintained: the Greek enterprise appears to have derived from colonialist ideas and the Phoenician enterprise to have been content with founding trading establishments close to indigenous communities.

At present, there is no known indication earlier than the eighth century which would allow us to speak of Phoenician colonization in the west before that date. However, certain archaeological discoveries and the still considerable weight of classical historiography have given rise to a variety of stances in relation to the question of chronology, ranging from those who place Phoenician expansion in the eighth and seventh centuries BC, based on archaeological evidence (Carpenter, Cintas, Culican, Forrer) through those who date it to the ninth century BC on the basis of epigraphic finds (Garcia Bellido, Harden), to those who push the colonization back as far as the twelfth century BC.

The boom in Phoenician archaeology in the last ten years and, in particular, the work done in the Iberian peninsula, have enabled us to get away from extremes in the historical interpretation of the Phoenician question and to ease the antagonistic positions by means of a compromise solution. This establishes two stages in the Phoenician colonization of the west, a pre-colonial stage (twelfth to eighth centuries BC) and a colonial stage proper (eighth to sixth centuries BC).

We shall now enumerate the chief characteristics of what is understood by the 'pre-colonial horizon' followed by a critical assessment of the main arguments in its favour.

PRE-COLONIZATION?

The idea of proposing some pre-colonial seafaring activity by the Phoenicians in the west springs from a new attempt to establish a bridge-hypothesis between the historical dates for the first foundations in the west in the twelfth century BC and the archaeological evidence which does not record any permanent settlements before the eighth century BC. It is hoped thereby to fill an awkward gap of something more than three hundred years and incorporate a theoretical model used successfully for Greek colonization.

Modern criticism rejects the idea of genuine colonization in the twelfth century BC even though it suggests that archaeological documentation might not always coincide exactly with a real Phoenician presence in a settlement, at least in its early days. In other words, even when the archaeological record affirms the presence of colonists in a site from, say, the year 750 BC, that does not mean that they had not arrived in that place earlier. Quite simply, archaeology is unable to detect it. It is stated likewise that archaeology is also incapable of identifying semi-permanent or pre-colonial settlements during the first three hundred years of a Phoenician presence in the west. Obviously, we cannot subscribe to this claim which, at bottom, contains a profound lack of confidence in modern techniques of field archaeology.

By pre-colonization is meant a movement of maritime and commercial expansion with a view to seeking raw materials and without permanent settlements; this would usually reveal itself in the archaeological record through an oriental influence on the indigenous societies involved, like the Sardinians, the Sicilians and the Tartessians. Contingently, this phenomenon would be accompanied by the establishment in due course of small groups of craftsmen, ceramists or metallurgists. As a general rule, a pre-colonization, characterized by the circulation of luxury articles and prestige gifts, would imply a very simple trade by barter, which would leave hardly any archaeological traces and would directly precede colonial settlements proper. In Italy and in the Iberian peninsula, this pre-colonial stage would be dated roughly between the end of the tenth and the beginning of the eighth centuries BC.

Generally speaking this would be Phoenician shipping activity for exclusively commercial ends, setting up ports of call here and there and reproducing the model of Hiram and Solomon's ships which sailed every three years in search of noble metals. With the founding of Carthage at the end of the ninth century BC, one western enterprise would be completed and then would begin the count back or, if you like, the start of a new stage.

This pre-colonial model has allowed us above all definitively to invalidate certain extreme positions, like those supporting the climax of Phoenician expansion in the days of Hiram I, that is to say, in the tenth century BC, or those that hinted at an early Phoenician presence in the exploitation of silver mines in southeastern Iberia in the days of the El Argar culture.

The criteria used by the defenders of this model of Phoenician pre-colonization are not easy to ascertain. They often mix critical analysis with a desire or hope to see the dates handed down by the classical authors for the founding of Gadir or Utica one day confirmed.

It is vitally important, when we are weighing up the significance of the first Phoenician installations in the west, to know whether or not a more or less prolonged period of trade by barter existed before the first permanent establishments. The analysis we make of the expansion will vary according to whether we opt for this hypothesis or not: seeing it either as a complex process of internal socio-economic development from a stage of initial trading posts to genuine urban colonies, or, on the other hand, as a genuine population strategy, with no previous stages, with all the consequent demographic and colonial implications.

The arguments in favour of the existence of Phoenician pre-colonization (twelfth to tenth centuries BC) rest exclusively on various archaeological materials from Italy and the Iberian peninsula. Let us see what these materials are, on which the hypothesis of pre-colonization is based.

'Canaanite' elements in the west

For a long time, various archaeological materials have served as a basis for claiming that Phoenicians were present in the west even during the thirteenth to twelfth centuries BC. A case in point is a group of decorated ivories from the Carmona region, in the province of Seville; the incision technique was linked with that of the Canaanite ivories of the second millennium BC. Nowadays, this hypothesis has been discounted as it was based exclusively on features of technique, without taking account of the decorative style and the iconography of the Carmona pieces, which match that of Phoenician craft work of the eighth and seventh centuries in every way.

A bronze statuette, 35.2 cm tall, discovered in 1955 32 km from Selinunte (Sicily) and considered to be of an Ugaritic or Canaanite type, was dated to the fourteenth to thirteenth centuries BC, on the basis of its eastern parallels, although the date was brought forward to the thirteenth to twelfth centuries BC so as to bring it closer to the chronology of the earliest Phoenician foundations in the west (Fig. 31). The figure represents a Syrio–Canaanite deity, apparently Reshef, and probably travelled in a ship that sank off the south coast of Sicily. Its presence in this area would to a certain extent support the remarks of

Fig. 31　Bronze statuette of Reshef from Selinunte

Diodorus and Thucydides, who report the arrival of the Phoenicians on the island 'before' the end of the eighth century BC (Diodorus 5:35,5; Thucyd. 6:2,6).

More convincing hypotheses connect the statuette with the late second millennium trade that linked the Aegean and Mycenaean world with Italy and the islands of the central Mediterranean. In any case it is an isolated find and outside any archaeological context and is obviously in every way inadequate for formulating a hypothesis about pre-colonization. As an example, various Egyptian objects discovered in the Phoenician necropolis at Almuñécar are dated, strictly speaking, to the sixteenth to ninth centuries BC, judging by the hieroglyphic inscriptions. But, unlike Selinunte, we know the actual context of their provenance: a necropolis in use from the end of the eighth to the middle of the seventh centuries BC. The correct reading of the find is that the Phoenicians used genuine Egyptian 'antiquities' from the plundering of Egyptian royal tombs, as funeral urns.

Moreover we must point out that bronze statuettes very similar to the one from Selinunte have been discovered recently in Huelva and Cadiz (Fig. 32). A rigorous analysis of the pieces has shown clearly that production of this type of bronze went on in the eastern Mediterranean until the seventh century BC, preserving all its archaizing features.

Fig. 32   Phoenician deities – bronze statuettes found in the sea at Huelva

Strictly speaking, then, an isolated piece is consequently of little significance when it comes to inferring a historical reading.

Tarshish–Gadir–Tartessos

Another argument that has been used repeatedly to support the hypothesis of Phoenician pre-colonizing activity refers to the biblical

Tarshish, of which the presumed syllabic relationship with Tartessos is deemed sufficient to demonstrate the existence of Phoenician shipping in the west from the tenth century. Thus the identification of Tarshish with Tartessos, defended by certain specialists, would not only imply regular shipping traffic between Tyre and the lower Guadalquivir, but would situate the goal of the voyages promoted by Solomon and Hiram I in the Atlantic. This explains why this hypothesis has long been the most controversial, in spite of being more reasonable in chronological terms, since it visibly distances itself from the remote and compromised dates of the twelfth century BC.

Furthermore, as we shall see shortly, the question of Tarshish–Tartessos, in addition to having provided a compromise solution to fill the gap from the twelfth to eighth centuries, starts from a false premise: the supposition that the biblical term designated the name of a place when, in reality, it was not used as a place name in the Old Testament before the sixth to fifth centuries BC. The biblical texts mention the term Tarshish over a period of 400 years and its meaning varies according to the period, the author or the translation. Even today, we still do not know the exact meaning in Hebrew of the word Tarshish.

The oldest known biblical references are found in the chronicles of the reigns of Solomon and Jehosaphat, in the first Book of Kings, where the famous 'Tarshish ships' are mentioned as leaving Ezion-geber bound for Ophir in search of gold, silver, ivory, apes and peacocks (I Kings 9:26–28). Every three years, the ships returned with their tropical cargo to some vague place on the Red Sea. If at the beginning the term Tarshish perhaps indicates a port of destination, in the days of Jehosaphat the term alludes to a class of ship which again sails to Ophir (I Kings 22:49). The goal of the voyage is still Ophir and not the west.

It has been mooted that the root of the word, ršš, might mean precious stone, perhaps topaz or jasper, from the Red Sea – Egypt or the Sudan – or maybe smelting or metal refining. In any case the Book of Kings refers to merchant ships making long voyages, but not to the Mediterranean or the west, which the biblical texts consider to be 'terra incognita'. In the period when the biblical word emerges, the geographical horizon of the Hebrews was very restricted and did not extend beyond Cyprus and the Aegean. So it could hardly designate an Atlantic territory.

The Book of Kings is followed in chronological order by the text of Isaiah (2:16), in which the 'Tarshish ships' are synonymous with the wealth, luxury and arrogance of Tyre, in contrast with other biblical references in which Tarshish clearly designates a precious stone (Exodus 28:20; Ezekiel 1:16; 10:9).

Only after the sixth to fifth centuries BC is the term Tarshish used as a place-name in the Mediterranean (Genesis 10:4). Indeed, in Genesis, which was compiled much later, Tarshish appears as a daughter of Yawan (Greece), or, in late translations of the third to second centuries, it indicates the sea, Carthage itself or even Gadir. From this Mediterranean Tarshish, silver, iron, tin and lead arrive in Tyre. So the tropical cargo of former times has disappeared and at this time the classical authors are already claiming to situate the toponym in Tarsus in Cilicia, an identification to which modern authors also subscribe.

Those who advocate situating Tarshish in Spain place equal weight on an Assyrian inscription of Asarhadon, dated to the year 671 BC, which alludes to the capture of Tyre and to Assyrian conquests in the 'West', where that king was master of the sea as far as Tar-si-si. In addition to being a classic epigraph of political propaganda, Asarhadon's text shows complete ignorance of Mediterranean geography beyond Iadnana (Cyprus). What is more, if we accept that Tarsisi was Tartessos, we should have to allow that the frontiers of the Assyrian Empire extended to the Iberian peninsula, which would be ridiculous.

The idea of placing Tarshish in Spain surfaces in post-biblical historiography and above all in the mediaeval lexicons to the Bible. But the Tarshish–Tartessos equation does not gather strength until the seventeenth century. The Rio Tinto copper mines were baptized with the name of Tharsis when they were rediscovered in the nineteenth century.

In conclusion, let us say that the term Tarshish evolved with time – a destination on the Red Sea, a type of merchant ship, a precious stone – and its original meaning was lost as the centuries passed until it met up with another equally vague term – Tartessos – in the Hellenistic–Roman period.

Indeed, in the classical period confusion already reigned on the subject of Tartessos, which first designated a river flowing down full of silver (Estesicorus, in Strabo 3:2,11) and, later, a fabulous realm, rich in silver, whose kings lived for 150 years (Herod. 1:163; 4:152). The idea of identifying Tartessos with a *polis* came very late indeed.

During the first century BC, the legend of this western Eldorado faded from memory until it became confused with Gadir–Gades. This Gadir–Tartessos muddle gave rise to legends of mythical founders like Norax, the founder of Nora, and the idea of a city was born because such a rich, cultured and advanced indigenous society could be nothing other, to the Greek mind, than an urban society (Strabo 3:1,6).

The fact is that the whole legend of the fabulous Tartessos arose when Tartessos had already disappeared (Diodorus 5:35,4; Strabo 3:2,14). The only reality is the existence of a Phoenician colony – Gadir – located close to Tartessos, a territory rich in silver on the lower Guadalquivir.

The Nora stele

It is generally accepted that the inscribed stele from Nora is the most ancient Phoenician find in the west. It was found in 1773 near Pula, the ancient Nora, and contains one of the most discussed epigraphs that has appeared in the western Mediterranean (Fig. 33). Since it was published (1835), the inscription on the stele, like other Sardinian epigraphs from the same region of Nora, has been used to establish a very ancient chronology for the first colonial foundations on the island of Sardinia. On purely epigraphic criteria, the Phoenician inscription on the Nora stele is placed almost unanimously at the end of the ninth century BC.

The inscription, carved on a stele of a monumental type, seems to commemorate the building of a temple (*lbt*) dedicated to the god *Pmy* on the island of Sardinia (*b šrdn*). It probably recalls the arrival of a few Phoenicians in Nora; it was customary to commemorate such an arrival by building a temple, as happened in Gadir, Lixus or Utica. The deity, in this case Pumay, sanctioned the choice and appropriation of a territory rich in iron and argentiferous lead. In addition, the monumental inscription served as a message to sailors arriving on the Sardinian coasts, as did the god Melqart in Cadiz. Lastly, the chronology attributed to the Nora stele would confirm the quotation from Pausanias (10:17,5), according to which Nora would have been the most ancient city in Sardinia.

The significance of the presence of the god Pumay in Sardinia is not known. This is a deity usually connected with Cyprus, particularly with Kition, where kings' names of Phoenician stock have been confirmed from the fourth century BC, in the form Pumaijaton or Pumjaton, similar to that of Pygmalion, king of Tyre, whose name may have been derived from the assimilation of the names of two deities: Pumai and Elyon. In some way, this king of Tyre appears also to be connected with Phoenician foundations in the west and, in one concrete case, with Carthage.

Fig. 33   The Nora stele

Yet again, historical figures, deities, heroes and myths are mingled in the origin of the colonies in the west, just as we have observed in Cadiz. In the North African case, a god–king (Pumai–Pygmalion) is indirectly responsible for the founding of Carthage in the year 814/813 BC, and his sister Elissa came to personify the island of Cyprus, so called in the eastern texts (Alashiya). In Melqart's sanctuary in Gadir, moreover, there existed the 'sacred olive of Pygmalion' which bore fruit in the form of emeralds.

So we see the god Pumai, coming from a Cypriot environment, being directly or indirectly linked with the Phoenician colonization of the west: the Nora stele, the founding of Carthage, the temple at Gadir. Furthermore, the chronology attributed to the Nora inscription fits into a period, the second half of the ninth century BC, in which a series of historical references come together and are sufficiently convincing to allow us to think that we are getting close to the real dates of the Phoenician diaspora to the west.

Indeed, it is the period in which King Ethbaal of Tyre founded the colony of Auza in Libya (*c.* 878–856 BC) (F. Josephus, *Ant.* 8:324) and that of the arrival of Tyrians in Kition (*c.* 850 BC), considered to be the starting point of Tyre's commercial expansion to the west. Lastly, it is the moment at which Timeus places the founding of Carthage (814/813 BC) and Thucydides that of the first commercial enclaves in Sicily.

In Nora, however, no traces of a Phoenician population have been verified before the seventh century BC. Consequently, we must ask ourselves whether strictly speaking, an isolated inscription constitutes a solid argument in favour of a Phoenician presence in Sardinia during the ninth century BC. Again we find ourselves faced with a question of objectivity and method in reading the data. For the present, this is still an unchallenged hypothesis.

On an epigraphic level, the monumental inscription at Nora has direct parallels in Cypriot and Phoenician inscriptions from the years 830–825 BC. But what is seldom said is that its parallels in the east define a much broader chronological framework which even extends until the end of the eighth century BC. In other words, the chronology attributable to the Nora stele stretches from 830 to 730 BC. And that is without considering the possibility of archaisms in the graphic forms of the epigraphs in the west.

As someone has rightly suggested, the Sardinian inscriptions will never be valid as long as they cannot be integrated into a broad context and therefore they should not affect our view of the chronology of Phoenician colonization in the west.

Other pre-colonial material in Italy and the Iberian Peninsula

It has recently been suggested that material traces of Phoenician pre-colonial shipping activity (tenth to eleventh centuries) were to be found in Sicilian water. Certain types of scarab, fibula and ceramic vessels from indigenous settlements at Cassibile, Syracuse, Caltagirone and Megara seemed to argue in favour of a relatively early oriental influence in the interior of the island. This hypothesis has still not been adequately tested and has been connected with the so-called Tartessian 'proto-orientalizing' of the ninth to eighth centuries BC.

Indeed, in the past few years various authors have again been defending the possibility of pre-colonization, basing their arguments on the prosperity of the Tartessian settlements at Huelva and Seville during the Late Bronze Age (ninth to eighth centuries BC). This prosperity would be the expression of an indigenous response to a very early stimulus from the east.

Within this 'proto-orientalizing' horizon, with no permanent colonial enclaves, certain material showing eastern influence, such as the painted pottery from El Carambolo (Seville), the elbow fibulae, the Extremaduran decorated stelae, the shields with a 'V'-shaped armhole, a bronze bowl found at Berzocana (Cáceres) and a metal helmet from the Huelva estuary, must have a place.

The eastern influence in some of these pieces – pottery from El Carambolo, shields and decorated stelae – is more than dubious and still mere hypothesis. The rest of the material mentioned, as we shall see, poses problems of interpretation.

The piece thought to be the most ancient is the bowl from Berzocana, which has been related to Egyptian or Levantine workshops of the fourteenth to thirteenth centuries BC, although, in consideration of the dates for the founding of Gadir and Lixus, its chronology has been brought forward to the twelfth to tenth centuries BC. The bronze helmet from the Huelva estuary, thought to have originated in Assyria or Ur in the ninth century BC, would confirm this early oriental influence.

Again we find ourselves faced with a few isolated items, although, in this case, deliberately removed from their cultural context, which is that of the Atlantic circulation of metals during the Late Bronze Age. In effect, both the bowl from Berzocana, found together with gold torques of an Atlantic type, and the bronzes deposited in the Huelva estuary, fall well within the so-called 'carp's tongue sword complex' (900–700 BC), a name by which the period of most intensive trade in metals of the Late Atlantic Bronze Age is known, very familiar to European prehistorians. At these dates, Atlantic Europe, from Ireland to southwestern Andalusia, formed an enormous market in which manufactured articles and ingots of gold, copper and tin were circulating on a grand scale. The most dynamic centres of metal distribution were Brittany, the Loire and Seine basins, the mouth of the Tagus and Huelva.

It is in this Atlantic environment that we must situate the stelae, helmets and shields characteristic of Late Bronze II (1050–900 BC). During the ninth to eighth centuries BC (Late Bronze III), the south of the Iberian Peninsula gradually formed a bridgehead between the Atlantic trade and the islands of Sardinia and Sicily.

Iberian metals found in Sardinia (Sa Idda), and Sicilian bronzes like the elbow fibula, located in the Iberian peninsula, circulate through this secondary Atlantic circuit. At the beginning of the eighth century BC this current, aimed at obtaining metals on a grand scale, which linked Portugal and Huelva with Sardinia, Sicily and Cyprus, reaches its climax and coincides with the first real indications of a Phoenician population in the west, whose commercial strategy was very well able to interrupt, intervene in and make use of this existing trading circuit.

In conclusion, we can say that in the Tartessian area, the first Phoenician influences are not felt until the eighth century BC, judging by the results obtained in recent excavations in the indigenous hinterland – Torre de Doña Blanca, Carambolo, Setefilla, Carmona, Cerro de los Infantes. On the basis of the present archaeological record, this invalidates the idea of 'proto-orientalizing' during the Late Bronze Age.

A critical review of the arguments normally used to support Phoenician pre-colonization in the west obliges us to question a theoretical model based exclusively on a few isolated archaeological finds, assessed by means of traditional descriptive methods which do no more than establish comparisons and morphological parallels in terms of a distinctly dubious chronological framework – that of the classical sources.

None of the elements that might define the pre-colonization has a basis of rigorous and methodical checking against the archaeological context. Moreover they all correspond to a model in current use, constructed on the grounds of recent Mycenaean finds in Italy. These have served as the basis for the hypothesis of a Greek pre-colonization in the west and it is on the basis of this model that they claim to explain Phoenician pre-colonization.

Insistence on reconciling the archaeological documentation with the written classical sources leads today, as in former years, up a blind alley, because of a narrowly empiricist attitude in which, rather than objectivity and methodological rigour, it is chronology, dating, morphological descriptions and the mere anarchic accumulation of artefacts in a vacuum that prevail. Simple analogical inference and pure inductivism lead to a pseudo-historical reading of the data which are at present decontextualized. In this framework, it must not be forgotten that the Phoenician question in the west is entirely dependent on the value we give to the very rich and complex archaeological evidence from the eighth to seventh centuries, relegating the accumulated myths and legends that accompany the first colonial foundations in the western Mediterranean to second place.

As far as the east is concerned, the roles are reversed, since nowadays it is the archaeological information and not the written texts that must help us interpret ancient settlements. In the last instance, it is this archaeological evidence above all that allows us to formulate hypotheses for a historical reconstruction of the colonization.

8

The Phoenician colonies in the central Mediterranean

Analysis and interpretation of the most significant data concerning the main areas affected by Phoenician expansion during the eighth and seventh centuries BC will give us a frame of reference by which to differentiate groups, stages and even independent evolutionary processes in the west. During the initial development of Tyrian colonization in the Mediterranean, the evidence favours rather heterogeneous economic and commercial strategies in terms of different adaptations to a diversified set of economic, strategic and political circumstances; hence the interest for us in analysing the pattern of Phoenician settlement in its process of expansion, since it shows clearly the category and function of the individual colonies.

We shall start by discussing a group of colonies which share a common geographical and cultural proximity to Carthage, since that North African colony undoubtedly constituted the most important Phoenician establishment in the whole of the central Mediterranean. Its influence in political, economic and ideological matters was such that it eventually shaped a vast cultural area, formed chiefly by the Phoenician enclaves of Sardinia and Sicily. In spite of having an identity of their own and enjoying autonomy in commercial and economic matters, these islands were very soon an integral part of the Carthaginian socio-political sphere, adopting an urban model similar to that of Carthage and so presenting from a very early stage certain cultural constants that we do not observe in the more westerly Phoenician settlements of Gadir, Ibiza, eastern Andalusia and Atlantic Morocco, and which are probably to be explained in terms of certain links of a very complex nature which they maintained with the North African metropolis.

The regional – or insular – divergences to be seen in this zone will disappear from the sixth century BC onward, when Carthage bursts onto the scene as a Mediterranean political power, in response first to the advance of Greek trade and later to the nascent power of Rome. The gradual process of political domination exercised by Carthage over the old Phoenician centres in the central Mediterranean will lead to the 'Punic' period, implying the cultural and political unification of the whole zone.

In order to grasp the differential features existing between the chief colonies in the west, we have resorted to analysing a series of variables which in our opinion seem to be the most significant when it comes to defining economic objectives and so reconstructing the historical process: the institutional or political background to the colonial foundation, the socio-ideological factors involved, topography and settlement patterns and the territory encompassed by the economic activity. For this, we shall turn to the written references, when there are any, and use the data of the archaeological record which enable us to reconstruct the origin and stages of the process.

Starting from an initial hypothesis, we shall go on to compare it with the archaeological documentation: the group of Phoenician colonies set up in the central Mediterranean very soon adopted cultural and ideological features allied to the model established in Carthage. These features could be summed up in a single phrase: determination to stay in the west and consequently the early adoption of the status of colonies, a status that would find expression in a series of manifestations such as the appearance of sanctuaries, sacred precincts, territorial conquest and, lastly, defensive systems.

All this enables us to differentiate this group from the more western block in which a smaller size of necropolis, the limited extent of the settlements, the presence of warehouses, the absence of sacred precincts and other elements seem to indicate, at least initially, a certain provisional or transitory aspect of the original Phoenician population. In this respect, the Phoenician 'colony' in Malta, a stopover and port of call for ships in the ancient period, is closer to the western model than to the group of Phoenician colonies in the central Mediterranean.

The choice of a few colonial settlements will enable us to focus the analysis on those sites where the historical or archaeological information is relevant, such as the colonies of Carthage, Motya and Sulcis. If we have opted for these three centres, it is because they seem to us significant in the context of the Phoenician expansion into the centre of the Mediterranean, since they allow the colonial model in the area to be defined in its three aspects: political, strategic and territorial. These criteria cannot be considered definitive, far from it, given the state of archaeological investigation in this field. Archaeology, indeed, may provide much that is new and surprising, obliging us to modify and give a new slant to what we expound here.

For a detailed description of the archaeological finds and of the sites not dealt with here, we refer the reader to Appendix IV and to the end of the book, where can be found a detailed and recent bibliography on the subject.

CARTHAGE, THE 'NEW CAPITAL'

Although the characteristics of the only recently identified early colony are not known, both the story of the founding of Carthage in the year 814, in which the Tyrian royal family had a hand, and the number and category of the sanctuaries and necropolises in the early settlement make it clear that, from the beginning, Carthage was the authentic 'new capital' in the west. Contrary to what has long been asserted, namely that ancient Carthage differed hardly at all from other modest centres in the Mediterranean, the finds relating to the eighth to seventh centuries BC show that the new Tyrian colony very swiftly attained the status of a genuine colonial city, endowed with certain institutions that other Phoenician settlements would be slow to adopt.

The archaeological record enables us to complete the fragmentary and subjective picture given by the classical historians. Besides, nothing has been preserved of the annals or historical writings of Carthage so that we are dependent on written documentation which is the work of the North African city's principal enemies.

The story of the foundation and its socio-political background

Sceptics consider that any historical reference to Carthage that pre-dates the fifth century BC is a myth, as, too, are the story of its foundation and the figure of Elissa–Dido. The names of some Carthaginian personages, like Malco, which means 'king', also have little basis in history.

And yet there are too many coincidences between the eastern and the classical sources to allow us to think that the story of Elissa had no historical basis, unlike other myths invented at a later period such as those attributing the founding of Carthage to two personages, Azoros and Karchedon, which are none other than the Greek names for Tyre and Carthage respectively.

From the Annals of Tyre it appears that around the year 820 BC Mattan I left the throne of Tyre in the hands of his son Pygmalion, who was only eleven years old at the time. In the seventh year of his reign (814 BC), his sister Elissa had fled from Tyre and founded

Carthage (Menander, in F. Josephus, *C. Ap.* (1:125). The circumstances that gave rise to the founding of Carthage follow various chronological stages:

(1) Elissa or Elisha was married to her uncle Acherbas or Zakarbaal, high priest of Heracles (Melqart) and, as such, occupying the second position in rank after the king of Tyre. Thus, Acherbas was a powerful personage, rich and apparently a direct rival to the king. Indeed it is related that Mattan had sought to leave the throne to his two children but the people of Tyre had objected, choosing Pygmalion, who endeavoured to seize his brother-in-law's riches and ordered his assassination. His widow, Elissa, together with a group of Tyrians loyal to her husband, who were known as 'princes', fled secretly to Cyprus after paying homage to Melqart (Justinus 18:4, 3–9). The Tyrian diaspora was thus the immediate consequence of political tension in Tyre, which had brought a young monarch, supported by the people, face to face with part of the city aristocracy, led by the king's own uncle, Acherbas. (2) Bitias, the commander of the Tyrian fleet (Virgil, *Aen.* 1:738) and Barcas, the ancestor of the Barcidas (Sil. Italicus, *Punica* 1:72–75), figured among the princes who accompanied Elissa in her flight.

The first stopping place in the expansion to the west was thus Cyprus. In Cyprus (Kition?), the party of Tyrian aristocrats was joined by the high priest of Juno (Astarte), who imposed the condition that, in the land they were going to colonize, the priesthood should be hereditary among the members of his own family (Justinus 18:4–6). In this way we see both the Tyrian aristocracy and the temple involved in founding Carthage. Before setting out, the Tyrians collected eighty young girls in Cyprus who were destined for sacred prostitution and to ensure the continuation of the Phoenician religion in the west.

(3) Elissa's expedition headed straight to the site of Carthage, where it received presents and greetings from the men of Utica (Justinus 18:5, 8–17). This happened during the seventh year of the reign of Pygmalion and thirty eight years before the first Olympiad (Timeus, in Dionysius Halicarnassus, *Ant. Rom.* 1:74, 1), which, as we have already seen, shows a very tight chronology: the years 814–813 BC.

(4) The colonists were well received by the indigenous Libyans, whose king, Hiarbas, gave them free entry into his territory: they were permitted to buy as much land as could be covered by an oxhide. The astute Elissa, whom the natives called Deido or Dido (the 'wandering one'), resorted to the stratagem of cutting the oxhide into very fine strips with which she was able to mark out the perimeter of the whole

of the hill called Byrsa, where Carthage was sited. After that they founded the city and called it *Qart-hadasht*, or 'new city'. The most ancient name for the hill or acropolis at Carthage, Byrsa, is a Greek word meaning 'oxhide', which was probably assimilated by the Greeks on hearing the pronunciation of the Semitic word *brt*, which means 'fortified citadel' or 'fortress'.

(5) The native king demanded with threats to marry Elissa. Faithful to her husband, she threw herself onto a fire in order to escape this marriage. After this sacrifice by fire, her subjects deified her and preserved her cult until the last days of the history of Carthage.

In the story of the founding of Carthage, then, we find strong legendary elements and 'arrangements' typical of Greek and Hellenistic historiography, like the very name of Byrsa or the legend of the oxhide.

Nevertheless, Timeus and Flavius Josephus, who consulted eastern sources of information, agree on the date of the founding of Carthage. In reality there are no proofs that the dates are reliable, nor yet that they are a later invention.

Moreover, features can be found in the story that are clearly oriental, extraneous to the classical world and which could hardly have been invented by a Greco–Roman historian. Thus, for example, the names of the protagonists are totally Phoenician – Pygmalion (Pumayyaton), Elissa (Elisha or Alashiya) and Acherbas (Zakarbaal). Sacred prostitution and the hereditary nature of the priesthood are other Semitic traits. Lastly, the ritual of Elissa's self-immolation, totally foreign to the classical world, is well known in Phoenicia and Canaan.

Besides, the Tyrian origin of the city is confirmed by other, later facts. Thus, after its foundation, Carthage sent an embassy annually to Tyre, charged with making offerings to the temple of Melqart (Quintus Curcius Rufus 4:2, 10). These offerings or tributes consisted of the tenth part of the profits made each year by the city (Diodorus 20:14). This yearly rent indicates that Carthage very soon restored its bonds with Tyre under circumstances unknown to us. It must not be forgotten that the founding of Carthage was to some extent an act of rupture, the colony being set up by political fugitives who probably remained out of touch with the central Tyrian power during the first generations and were firmly determined to stay in the west. In this respect, it must be defined as a colony right from the outset.

Moreover, it can apparently be inferred from the story that there was a significant Cypriot embassy among the contingent of Tyrian people who accompanied Elissa. The high priest of Astarte, perhaps of the temple in Kition, joined the group of colonists and the very name of the protagonists suggests a component of Cypriot origin. It will be remembered that Elissa's name has a direct connection with the ancient name for the island of Cyprus (Alashiya) and that the name of the king of Tyre contains the Cypriot form of the god Pmy. Kition, then, might have been part of the founding institutions of Carthage and the names of the protagonists could have been created artificially to emphasize that mixed nature of the founding population of Carthage, personifying a social sector from Tyre and also from the island of Cyprus.

In any case, from all that has been said it is important to retain certain data which seem significant as we embark on a critical discussion of the meaning of the colonization:

(a) The founding of Carthage, taking place in a region already known by Tyre (Utica), is the consequence of a political crisis in the metropolis.
(b) On the institutional level, the origin of Carthage appears associated with families of the Tyrian aristocracy and the upper hierarchy of the religious institutions.
(c) The founding of the colony implicates the appropriation and marking out of a territory by dint of fortifying the inhabited area.
(d) The origin of the city is linked to a rite of human sacrifice in the form of immolation by fire.
(e) In every respect, Carthage was born with the rank of a Tyrian colony.

Geography of Carthage and the archaeological record

Of the archaeology of early Carthage we know only some necropolises, an enigmatic deposit of religious offerings – the so-called Cintas 'chapel' – and the *tophet* situated in Salammbô. There are doubts, too, about the exact site of the city, of which no traces are known prior to the fourth century BC. The conquest and destruction of Carthage in the year 146 BC and the subsequent Roman occupation are thought to be the main reason for the absence of archaeological data related to the ancient location.

The distribution and spatial organization of the chief urban and religious elements in Carthage form a model of early Phoenician settlement which, compared with that of other Mediterranean centres,

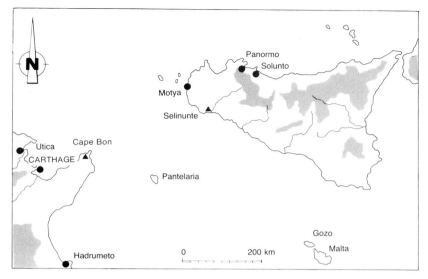

Fig. 34   The Phoenician colonies of the central Mediterranean

plainly shows a distinct hierarchical order among the Phoenician colonies, based on different territorial, economic and social rules. For its category, early Carthage offers an obligatory point of reference for distinguishing between the forms and initial organization of the Phoenician colonies in the west.

Carthage was sited on a peninsula in the Gulf of Tunis and consequently controlled a strategic passage on the shipping routes to the central Mediterranean (Fig. 34). The location of the primitive settlement founded by Elissa has been, and continues to be, problematical in that it is situated variously in Le Kram, Marsa, Sidi Bou Said or on the hill of Saint Louis, the present name for Byrsa. The German excavations of 1983 and 1986 might be able to put an end to the debate by confirming the existence of remains of dwellings and walls of the eighth century BC on the eastern slopes of the hill of Byrsa (Fig. 35).

Of eighth to sixth century Carthage, we know three great necropolises, which show that the volume of burials alone in the North African city already exceeds the usual average in other western enclaves. This argues in favour of a greater population density than in the rest of the Phoenician colonies. The areas set aside for burials surround the acropolis of Byrsa on the south, on the north (Junon necropolis), and on the northeast (Dermech–Douimes necropolis); in all of them the rite

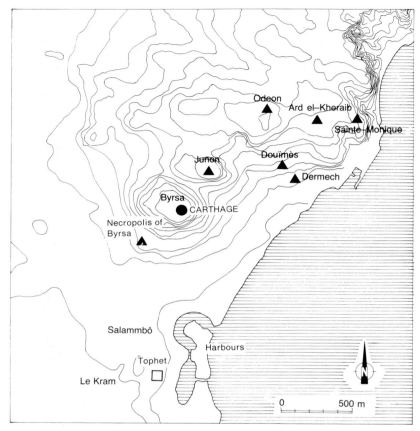

Fig. 35   Plan of Carthage

of inhumation predominates, with the exception of Junon, where we find very early cremations (Fig. 36).

The Junon necropolis is thought to be the most ancient in Carthage and came into use around the years 730–720 BC, whereas those of Byrsa and Dermech–Douimes began to be used around 700–680 BC (Fig. 37). This would mean that Carthage was not consolidated as a colony before the second half of the eighth century BC, when the urban area was being planned to meet the needs of a growing population.

The situation is similar with the *tophet* in Carthage, situated in Salammbô, to the south of the Byrsa hill and reserved for human sacrifice. This precinct was in uninterrupted use from the last quarter

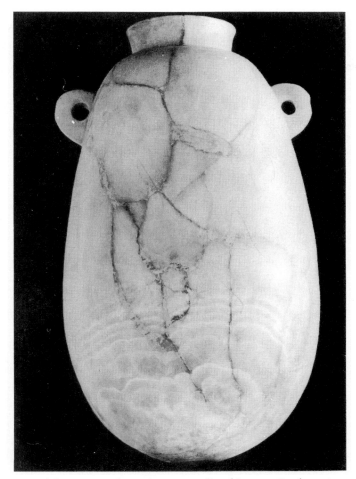

Fig. 36   Alabaster vase from the necropolis of Junon, Carthage (seventh century BC)

of the eighth century BC, judging by the chronology attributed to the most ancient level of urn burials – the Tanit I level – formed around 700 BC.

In short, it can be said that the first burials or sacrifices on Carthaginian soil date to the years 730–700 BC. This leaves a gap of about a century in the archaeological information, if we stick to the date for the founding of Carthage and to the first traces of permanent use of the territory. A strange find made in the sanctuary at Salammbô, however,

Fig. 37   Early pottery from Carthage

brings us closer to the historical time scale of the late ninth century BC.
In 1947, under the first levels of urns in the *tophet* in Carthage, Cintas
discovered a small enclosure or chamber which was catalogued at the
time as a deposit of religious offerings made at the foundation and
which contained, among other things, several pieces of Greek pottery,
apparently deposited at two consecutive times (Fig. 38). This 'chapel'

Fig. 38   Pottery from the deposit in the *tophet* at Carthage (eighth century BC)

yielded Euboic–Cycladic and Corinthian pottery, possibly from the
Euboic colony of Pitecusas (Ischia), now dated to between 760 and 680
BC. This archaeological material is, for the time being, the most ancient
known from Carthage.

Despite the antiquity of the deposit at Salammbô, Carthage did not
develop as an urban entity until the middle of the eighth century BC. It
was at this period that the *tophet* began to be used as a place of
sacrifice, with all the accompanying ideological and civic implications,
which we shall examine later, and it was also from the end of the eighth
century BC that spaces were set aside for burials and the boundaries of
the acropolis were marked by fortifications. Although almost a century
had passed since its foundation, the process of urban transformation
was still relatively rapid in Carthage in comparison with other colonies
in the west.

The first political initiatives

The first piece of historical information that we have, after the foundation in the year 814/813 BC, refers to activity abroad by Carthage,
which took concrete form in the founding of its first colony or offshoot
in Ibiza in the year 654/653 BC (Diodorus 5:16, 2–3). We know,
however, that the island had been occupied previously by a Phoenician
population.

Around the year 600 BC, Carthage was already in a position to
confront the Phoceans of Massalia (Marseilles) at sea with the probable
aim of preventing the founding of that Greek colony (Thucydides 1:13,
6). Around the year 550 BC, Carthage laid the foundations of her
mastery of the sea and the dynasty founded by Magon obtained
political control of Sardinia and part of Sicily (Justinus 18:7) and
confronted the Phocean squadron in the waters of Alalia (Corsica)
(Herodotus 1:166). Lastly, in the year 509, a treaty signed by Carthage
and Rome sanctioned for the first time in the west an allocation of areas
of political influence (Polibius 3:23). Carthage consolidated her hegemony at sea and embarked on the road that would convert her
inevitably into a naval and military power.

This would all have been unimaginable had not considerable demographic, economic and urban growth taken place in Carthage between
the years 730 and 600 BC, that is, in the period in which other Tyrian
foundations in the west had not yet progressed beyond the rank of
ports of call or trading posts. This fact has led some authors to think
that Carthage was the only Tyrian colony in the western Mediterranean.

Both the story of its foundation and Carthaginian onomastic and epigraphic evidence indicate that the 'new Tyre' played a key role from the start in welding together a few commercial interests over a vast geographical radius. Rather than reflecting a colonial, peripheral and retarded environment relative to the metropolis, Carthage from the outset developed its own, almost 'Punic' socio-cultural dynamic, which finds expression in a series of cultural and ideological traits that are missing in the east, like its militarism and the *tophet*. In the matter of industrial production, even the early pottery of Carthage has unique features.

The rapid growth of the North African colony can only be explained by the rise, after the founding of Qart-hadasht, of a strong determination to create a genuine 'new capital' in the west, destined later to watch over the interests of Tyre and to take over from it in the sixth century after the metropolis fell into the hands of Nebuchadnezzar. Significantly, the inhabitants of Carthage always considered themselves *bn Ṣr*, sons of Tyre, as can be deduced from their epigraphs.

If, during the first hundred years of its life, Carthage probably differed little from other early settlements in the west, from the second half of the eighth century BC onward the change that occurred is both qualitative and quantitative. Three alternative hypotheses become entangled around the subject: causes of a commercial, a social or a political type.

For some, the economic growth of Carthage is due to its position as an obligatory port of call for ships from Gadir carrying wealth to Tyre. And yet archaeological proofs of regular contact between Carthage and Gadir in the early period are scarce.

Another argument that stands out as a factor behind the power of Carthage is the different social origins of the Phoenician population in the west. In Carthage, the social structure reveals marked imbalances between a sector linked with the foundress, Elissa, and another sector composed of colonists and people who arrived in North Africa seeking their fortune. These differences would have favoured a rapid transition to urban and state institutions. Lastly, the possibility must be considered that, from the outset, Carthage was founded in obedience to different political objectives from those of other Phoenician enclaves which were created originally for a very definite function: that of staging posts or harbours. Carthage would correspond to a new type of Phoenician foundation, intended as a refuge for fugitives from Tyre and Cyprus and above all as an obstruction to the advance of Greek trade in the west. This would explain, among other things, the foundation in Ibiza, which closed the passage to the Straits of Gibraltar to any enemy ship coming from the Mediterranean. And it is precisely the Greek threat that would have provided the impetus to develop a military policy, to the detriment of strictly commercial aims, and to lay the foundations of the Carthaginian naval empire. It would have accelerated the transition of Carthage to a great urban centre outside the control of Tyre. In other words, Carthage owed her growth to defensive and political rather than to commercial criteria.

All the same, we should point out that the threat of Greek trade was not felt in the west before the Phoceans founded Massalia and Ampurias. The Greeks who came into the Mediterranean before that, the Euboeans, far from being commercial competitors, were the best trading partners of the western Phoenicians (see Appendix IV). Consequently, the change that took place in Carthage at the end of the eighth century was a response to other than strictly strategic, social or political causes. Analysis of the process in the remaining Phoenician centres in the Mediterranean will tell us if it was an isolated case or if, on the other hand, we are looking at a more widespread development.

Economic activity

We have little information about the economy of Carthage before the sixth century BC. But there is no reason to suppose that its economic activity was not governed by strategic and territorial factors.

The early settlement, situated on a hill, no doubt dominated rich agricultural plains which, to judge by the data, constituted one of the pillars of Carthaginian prosperity. Two great cereal-growing regions – the central area of the territory, and the hinterland of Carthage and the valley of the river Bagradas, dominated at its mouth by Utica – were still producing grain in abundance in the Roman period. In the environs of Carthage and the Cape Bon area there were fields full of crops (Diodorus 20:8, 3–4) and Carthage developed sophisticated and well-organized systems of agricultural practice to which even Rome acknowledged herself to be indebted.

An idea of the importance given to agriculture in Carthage can be obtained from the famous Carthaginian treatises on agronomy. The most famous of all, the treatise of Magon, constituted a compendium of knowledge of such scope that the Roman senate elected to translate it into Greek and Latin (Pliny, *Nat. Hist.*, 18:22). It was edited around the fifth century BC and gave instructions for growing cereals, vines and olives, which suggests plenty of experience in these techniques in North Africa.

Carthage filled North Africa with olives and succeeded in producing tons of oil for local use and for export. Cultivated fields covered the environs of the city and were worked by slave labour. The rearing of cattle, goats and horses was left to the native Libyans of the interior (Polibius 12, 3:3–4).

The most powerful citizens of Carthage had extensive lands and farms in which slaves and prisoners of war from the period of the Punic wars worked (Diodorus 20:13, 2; 20:69, 5; Appian, *Pun.* 15). References to wealthy Carthaginians owning vines, olives, orchards and pastures and to a very powerful rural nobility are numerous. Beyond this fertile zone close to Carthage, stretched the fields cultivated by the Libyans who kept ownership of their land in exchange for heavy tributes and for supplying a large percentage of grain to the city (Livy 31:48, 1; Justinus 31:3; Diodorus 20:8, 3–4).

Strictly speaking, then, we must envisage a peripheral territory in Carthage that was devoted to producing food for the urban population and was the property of eminent citizens from at least the sixth century BC. We do not know if the state kept part of the agricultural land, that is to say the *chora*, for itself. In reality the available documentation supports the existence of private rather than public ownership of land, in the hands of nobles and landowners. Perhaps the state confined itself to planning and legislating for agricultural activity, or else this minimal intervention by the public institutions should be seen as a consequence of total assimilation between the state and the landowning nobility, who were probably one and the same.

Nevertheless it should not be forgotten that all these economic data refer to Punic Carthage, that is to the sixth to fifth centuries BC. There are no known indications that Carthage controlled the agricultural hinterland during the eighth to seventh centuries BC. Previously, on the contrary, the Carthaginian economy was restricted in principle to exploiting a limited territory and the city paid an annual royalty to the Libyans in return for working the land ceded to Elissa. This tribute went on until the sixth to fifth centuries BC (Justinus 17:5, 14; 19:2, 4).

Nor did the systematic occupation of the coast begin until the sixth to fifth centuries BC, the time when Carthage seized military control of the territory through the building of imposing fortifications on the Gulf of Tunis and Cape Bon, like Ras Fortas, Kelibia and Ras ed-Drek.

MOTYA: A MODEL OF THE STRATEGIC ENCLAVE

The geographic situation of the island of Sicily confers an undeniable strategic value on its colonies. It was not an idle choice by the Phoenicians of an island which, because of its situation, had been vital to Mediterranean and Aegean shipping during the second millennium, a fact to which the Mycenean pottery found on its shores bears witness. Consequently we must assume that the settling of Phoenicians in Sicily was initially a response to certain basically strategic imperatives.

With the arrival of the Greeks on the island, the Phoenicians, who were already occupying coastal promontories and islets, found themselves obliged to withdraw to the western part, where they founded their three main colonies – Motya, Panormo and Solunto – of which Motya was undoubtedly the most important (Thucydides 6:2, 6; Diodorus 20:58, 2; 51, 1). Given that the foundation of the first Greek colonies in Sicily – Naxos and Syracuse – dates from the years 734–733 BC, we must situate the withdrawal at the end of the eighth century BC. This second phase of Phoenician expansion in Sicily is the only one documented archaeologically.

We have hardly any information about the Phoenician staging posts at Panormo and Solunto. With Motya, or Mozia, situated on an island facing the mainland city of Marsala (Fig. 39), quite the opposite is true. Thus the Phoenician establishment is in line with a typically Phoenician settlement pattern: an island site, close to the coast and well protected from winds and tides, a pattern we see repeated at Gadir and Cerro del Villar in the Guadalhorce (Malaga). We have here a settlement model quite clearly derived from the country of origin, where we already know the classic examples of Arvad and Tyre itself.

In Motya, the Phoenicians enjoyed a twofold geopolitical advantage: their alliance and good relations with the Elimians of western Sicily and the proximity to Carthage, on the other side of the Sicilian straits (Thucyd. 6:2, 6).

The fact that it was occupied without interruption from the end of the eighth to the fourth century BC makes Motya one of the best-known Phoenician nuclei and one of the few in which it has been possible to analyse the whole Phoenicio–Punic cultural sequence. Consequently it provides a model of a Phoenician settlement and must be considered as representative of the central group in the Mediterranean, since its urban topography and the spatial distribution of its most significant finds are relatively well known.

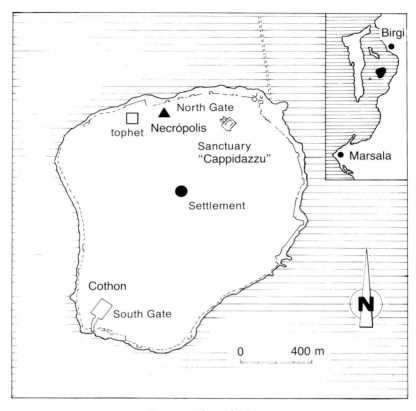

Fig. 39 Plan of Motya

The Motya site, some 40 hectares in area, has a walled perimeter of 2500 metres. Until 650 BC, the area assigned to dwellings was relatively small, as was the resident population to judge by the volume of burials in the necropolis. However, from the middle of the seventh century BC on, the funerary data indicate a considerable increase in population, with a maximum in the sixth century BC, when it was estimated at some 15,800 inhabitants.

The ancient necropolis began to be used at the end of the eighth century BC and is the archaeological complex that has yielded the earliest material so far. The grave goods indicate that we are dealing with an eastern society in its main cultural manifestations and a relatively egalitarian one.

From the seventh century BC onward, the Phoenicians in Motya established a number of mercantile and harbour installations round the periphery of the island. Thus for example, in the northern zone and around the South Gate, large industrial complexes and warehouses in use during the seventh to sixth centuries BC suggest the early appearance of specialized industries – iron and purple – in the vicinity of the gates in the wall and of the wharves.

In the seventh century BC the Phoenicians erected two major sacred precincts in Motya. One of them, 'Cappidazzu', in the northeast of the island, was a rudimentary temple at first and later acquired almost monumental proportions. The other, in the north, was the *tophet* where the urns of infant sacrifices were deposited throughout the history of the colony. The *tophet* began functioning during the first half of the seventh century BC and reveals a marked increase in sacrifices from 650 BC on.

Motya was consolidated as an urban centre during the sixth century BC, when public buildings on a considerable scale were constructed: the walls, the temenos of the sanctuary of Cappidazzu, an enclosed harbour or *cothon* to the south, and a mole at the North Gate, linking Motya with Birgi, across in Sicily. This is the period, moreover, when centres like Motya came to depend progressively on Carthage.

To sum up, we can detect in Motya three clearly differentiated stages of development in the Phoenician population: an initial stage (end of the eighth century BC), corresponding to the arrival of a contingent of Phoenician population; a second stage (seventh century BC), in which the Phoenician settlement experienced notable growth and acquired industrial and mercantile installations, as well as precincts intended for worship and sacrifice; and a third stage (sixth century BC), coinciding with great public works worthy of a genuine urban centre.

To judge by the finds on the mainland, it seems unlikely that Motya fostered a policy of territorial expansion into the interior of Sicily in the early period. The presence of native pottery in the early settlement is interpreted as proof of rapid and early acculturation and assimilation between the two populations. Furthermore, in Motya during the Phoenician stage, we do not find the features traditionally attributed to an urban colony, such as defensive structures, religious, civil and administrative institutions, division into classes or a specialized community. Nor are major public buildings known before the sixth century, nor a central temple dominating the harbour, as in Kition or Sarepta.

However, the construction of a sacred area in the Cappidazzu and of a *tophet* in the first half of the seventh century BC is indicative of a

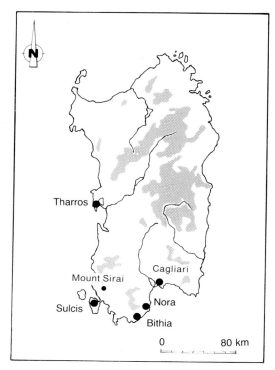

Fig. 40   The Phoenician colonies in Sardinia

qualitative change in the civic bodies of the Phoenician settlement, which seem for the first time to weld together the religious activities of the community. The population increase observed around 650 BC and the process of centralization of religious activity would, in the opinion of some authors, be an expression of the transition from a Phoenician merchant port to an urban colony in the style of those of Magna Graecia.

SULCIS AND ITS TERRITORIAL STRATEGY

The Phoenician establishment on the island of Sardinia shows a settlement on very similar lines to the ones recorded in eastern Andalusia: systematic occupation of a coastal stretch and the creation of ports with very little distance between them. Indeed, the extraordinary concentration of Phoenician settlements on the southwestern coast of

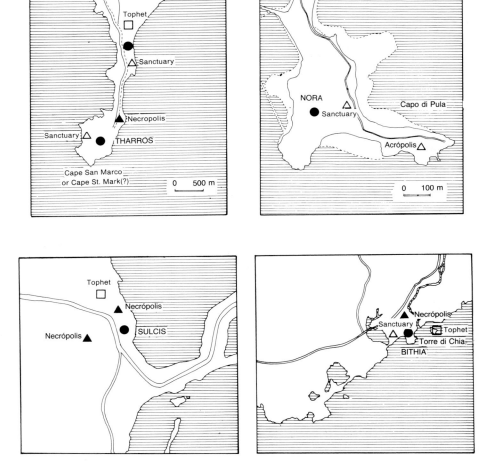

Fig. 41   Plans of Tharros, Nora, Sulcis and Bithia

the island, from Cagliari to Tharros (Fig. 40), is comparable in the
eighth to seventh centuries BC only with that along the coast of
Malaga, Granada and Almeria. However, in Sardinia this phenomenon
is the outcome of a genuine territorial strategy, that of controlling the
hinterland.

The Sardinian colonies follow a definite settlement pattern: the early enclave is located on a promontory on a cape, joined to the mainland by a narrow isthmus (Fig. 41) (Appendix IV).

Of all the Phoenician establishments in Sardinia, it is the one at Sulcis that yields the most information concerning the context of an early Phoenician settlement. The enclave at Sulcis is situated on an islet close to the cape of Sant' Antioco, which today is joined to the mainland by an isthmus resulting from the accumulation of sediments washed down by the river Palmas; it used to dominate an excellent sheltered natural harbour and apparently possessed a fortified enclosure and an extensive necropolis on the slopes of the Monte de Cresia. To the north of the settlement and outside the defensive enclosure is the site of the *tophet* which has yielded the earliest traces known so far of the Phoenician presence in Sardinia (Fig. 42). Insofar as the *tophet* is deemed to be an urban feature, as we shall see later, and usually appears in the west at a stage that comes later than the founding of a Phoenician colonial enclave, we must place the origin of Sulcis in the middle of the eighth century BC, if not earlier.

From the seventh century onward, Sulcis created an extensive network of fortified installations, aimed at ensuring direct territorial control of a hinterland rich in lead and silver. Outstandingly important amongst all these fortifications marking out a vast defensive belt behind the Phoenician colony were those of Monte Sirai, Pani Loriga (Santadi), Monte Crobu, Corona Arrubia, Sa Turrita de Seruci and Porto Pino.

The best-known fortification is the one on Monte Sirai, built on top of a destroyed or abandoned native village (*nuragha*). This installation model suggests, rather than a phenomenon of deliberate destruction, a determination on the part of Sulcis to show its territorial sovereignty in regions previously dominated by an indigenous population.

In spite of this, the military enclave of Monte Sirai seems to have maintained peaceful relations from the start with the natives of the interior, since there are no traces of belligerency. An early cremation necropolis (seventh to sixth centuries BC) in the vicinity of the fortress shows that the Phoenician population, drawn from Sulcis and perhaps formed by military personnel and soldiers, was considerable.

But the *tophet* of Monte Sirai was not built until the fourth century BC. This fact is significant because the establishment of this type of sacred enclosure always reflects the urban character of the corresponding centre. In other words, it means that Monte Sirai was an offshoot of Sulcis until the Hellenistic period, when it won independence from

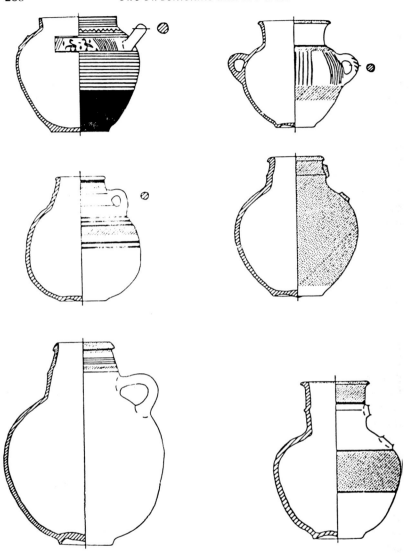

Fig. 42　　Early pottery from the *tophet* at Sulcis

the overlordship of Sulcis and acquired an autonomous urban identity. Until then, the *tophet* in Sulcis fulfilled the function of central urban sanctuary for all the rural and military communities of the interior.

The archaeology of Sulcis and the territory under its influence shows us, then, that the founding of the Phoenician colony in the eighth century BC was a genuinely strategic operation directed firstly towards ensuring control of a vast inland territory and then to defending it.

Sulcis is important insofar as it bears witness to the complex and heterogeneous nature of the objectives of Phoenician expansion in the west. In this case, the founding of the colony led to a need to bring the coast and the coastal valleys swiftly under its sway, that is, to establish economic and territorial autonomy in relation to the interior and to guarantee peaceful exploitation of the agricultural land and metal deposits.

THE *TOPHET*

The *tophet* undoubtedly constitutes the most characteristic cultural manifestation in the Phoenician settlements of the central Mediterranean and the one that has furnished the most archaeological information for a study of the ceramic and epigraphic material relating to the Phoenicio–Punic world. *Tophet* is the name of a sacred enclosure lying on the edge of the colonial centres, in which human sacrifice was practised and children were immolated in honour of the deity. The burning of children, called 'molk' sacrifice, persisted in the Punic centres of the west until the Roman period. The theme of the *tophet* in the west attracted the attention of scholars some time ago; it is considered to be a 'barbarous' rite, difficult to grasp in its full meaning, and we still do not know the reasons for its popularity in the west. As such, it surprised the Greek historians and the Hebrew prophets.

The *tophet* is particularly interesting to us because it constitutes in the west the socio-religious entity most representative of the Phoenician establishments in Tunis, Sicily and Sardinia and because, in our opinion, it is an expression of the institutional and social factors that can help us define and distinguish between categories of early colonial settlements.

The origin and the antecedents of this type of human sacrifice must be sought in the east and, in particular, in Phoenicia, since it is logical to think that the Phoenician colonists inherited from the metropolis the custom of sacrificing their offspring in situations of emergency, war or epidemic.

In the Phoenician west today there is more archaeological than written information about a rite that has been called a holocaust in that the victim is sacrificed to the deity by fire. Undoubtedly the most spectacular *tophet* in the west was the one in Carthage, at Salammbô, which was in uninterrupted use for 600 years and for the period between the years 400 and 200 BC yielded more than 20,000 cremation urns.

The name used to designate these enclosures or sanctuaries in the Phoenician colonies in the west is derived from the word *tophet*, the name of a place which the Old Testament situates in the valley of Ben Hinnom, near Jerusalem, where children were sacrificed in honour of Baal (II Kings 23:10; Jeremiah 7:30–31). The name Hinnom or *tophet* was used for an installation, perhaps an altar, and was synonymous with 'hell' and 'slaughter'.

A review, brief though it be, of the antecedents of the rite in the east will enable us to determine the social and political context in which the sacrifice developed and its ideological significance.

The antecedents: Phoenicia and Israel

The sacrifice of a child or a firstborn is exceedingly rare in the east before the Iron Age. Even so, the practice is recorded in Canaan in the age of the Patriarchs, or the Middle Bronze Age in Palestine (2000–1550 BC). The classic example is that of Abraham, prepared to sacrifice his firstborn son who was replaced in the end by a sheep (Genesis 22:1–2). So Yahweh too demanded human sacrifices.

The classic evolutionist theories, inspired by the example of Abraham, make the case for an evolution of human sacrifice in the Semitic world by the gradual substitution of a slave, an animal and, lastly, bread and wine, for the firstborn. The finds in the west, however, discredit this hypothesis.

In the texts from Ugarit there are allusions to the *mlk* sacrifice of a firstborn in times of danger or war and to the myth of Baal in which sacrifice by fire appears in association with fertility rites, rain and the annual renewal of the vegetation. In both cases the sacrifice is made for the good of the community. Melqart and Elissa also immolated themselves in the fire for the good of the community.

In Phoenicia and Israel, as in Carthage, this kind of human sacrifice was called 'molk sacrifice', a name which, in the *tophet* at Jerusalem, designated the holocaust of a child, of newborn babies or of 'sons and daughters', with the aim of restoring the forces of nature or the power of the state. In the east, the molk sacrifice was linked with Baal and with Yahweh. On the other hand, in the east not a single archaeological trace has been found relating to the place of sacrifice – the *tophet*, or to its mechanics of worship – the *molk* sacrifice. Concerning its existence, all we have is written references.

For Phoenicia, the most important source of information is Philo of Byblos (third century BC) who, as you remember, translated a 'History of Phoenicia' into Greek: it was the work of Sanchuniathon who lived in Beirut around the year 1000 BC. In this work he records at the time of the Trojan War the Phoenician custom by which, in circumstances of grave danger, disasters, plagues or wars, the 'princes of the city' sacrificed the most cherished of their sons, whom they beheaded in mysterious ceremonies in honour of Cronos (Baal Hammon), whom the Phoenicians called El. Originally, the god El had sacrificed his only son, Ieud, before the imminence of a danger threatening the country. For that he dressed him 'like a king', prepared an altar and sacrificed him (Eusebius, *Praep. evang.* I, 10, 44).

It is admitted today that Philo's sources may have been ancient, which means that in Phoenicia firstborn sons and children were sacrificed, but only in exceptional circumstances. The problem arises because this is the only testimony we know to the practice of human sacrifice in Phoenicia. Unlike its colonies in the west, in Phoenicia it was an exceptional rite, dedicated without distinction to Baal or El, and probably fell into disuse around the seventh to sixth centuries BC, according to what the Greeks heard tell on the occasion of Alexander's siege of the city of Tyre in the fourth century BC (Quintus Curcius Rufus 4:3).

In any case, we need to bear in mind here the most significant feature of the '*molk*' sacrifice described by Philo: it was a ritual reserved exclusively to the monarchy or the aristocratic families of Canaan.

The *molk* sacrifice passed from Phoenicia to Israel and Syria, where it was practised in honour of Hadad, Baal and Yahweh during the twelfth to seventh centuries BC. Because of the hostility with which the Hebrew prophets regarded this practice, we have a considerable amount of information about it in Israel. In Israel it was considered to be a foreign rite and of Canaanite origin, assimilated to the worship of the Greek Cronos or Roman Saturn, who is none other than Baal Hammon (Jeremiah 19:5). The presence of a priestly body at the sacrifice (Leviticus 18:21; 20:1–5) is interesting. The protests and indignation provoked by the practice (Jeremiah 7:31; Ezekiel 16:18; 23:37) indicate that it had become a real danger in Israel and that it was very widespread in pagan circles. The earliest legal text known concerning this (Exodus 22:29–30: 'the firstborn of thy sons shalt thou give to me') and the successive legal prohibitions against the *molk* sacrifice in the lawgiving of the Pentateuch indicate that it had taken root early in Israel, where the rite revolved around the sacred figure of the firstborn, typical of the Semitic world.

Various known examples serve to illustrate the range and meaning of human sacrifice in Palestine. Thus, in the period of the Judges (c. 1200–1000 BC), Jephtha offers to burn his daughter as a sacrifice in honour of Yahweh, in exchange for victory over his enemies (Judges 11:30–31). The sacrifice of sons to Yahweh before a battle was customary (I Samuel 7:9; 13:9; 31:10). In the ninth century BC, King Mesha of Moab sacrificed his firstborn, burning him on the walls of the city on the occasion of the siege by Jehoram of Israel (II Kings 3:26–30). King Ahaz of Judah (735–715 BC) also made his son a burnt offering in the valley of Hinnom (II Kings 16:3), a sacrifice that was repeated by his grandson Manasseh (II Kings 21:6; Jeremiah 32:31–35). Lastly, it was Josiah, in the seventh century BC, who, on the occasion of religious reforms initiated in his reign, succeeded in dismantling the *tophet* in Jerusalem, declaring the valley of Ben Hinnom to be impure and prohibiting the rite (II Kings 23:10; Jeremiah 7:30–32).

From all we have set down so far it can be inferred that the *tophet* of the Phoenician centres in the west and the practice of human sacrifice have direct antecedents in Syria–Palestine where practices of this type appear to have been exclusive to patriarchs, chiefs and kings and linked to interests of state. With human sacrifice, burning or ritual death, the rulers hoped to calm the wrath of Yahweh or of Baal. However, nowhere does it appear to have attained the magnitude and the proportions that these practices attained in the ambit of Carthage.

While being foreign to classical thought and considered to be idolatry by the Hebrew and Graeco–Roman writers, human sacrifice appears to have been much more widespread than its detractors would have us believe. The world of Homer provides examples in three well-known cases: Iphigenia, sacrificed by her father Agamemnon; the Cretan Idomeneo, who, on his return from Troy, sacrificed his son; and Achilles, who sacrificed twelve valiant Trojans on Patroclus' funeral pyre (*Il.* 23:175–176). Yet again the practice is reserved for kings and heroes.

Carthage and the historical tradition

The classical sources attribute frequent holocausts of children to the Carthaginians in order to emphasize the harsh and cruel nature of these people and their Phoenician forefathers. 'The Phoenicians, and more especially the Carthaginians, when they want some important project to succeed, promise to sacrifice a child to Cronos if their wish is fulfilled' (Clitarch, *Schol.*, Plato, *Rep.* 337A). The Carthaginians living in Sardinia also sacrificed to Cronos on certain prescribed days (Clitarch, *Schol.*, Homer, *Od.* 20:302). Clitarch and Diodorus (20:14, 4–6) also tell us that the sacrifice took place in front of a bronze statue of the god, with arms outstretched over a blazing hearth; the child slid down over the arms and fell. It seems that the victims were covered with a grinning mask and that is why, according to Clitarch, they died laughing and hence the term 'sardonic' (Sardinian) for a sarcastic smile.

Justinus reports that the *molk* sacrifice was introduced in the west by Elissa in order to save Carthage and remain faithful to her dead husband. Elissa's suicide in the fire, which automatically conferred divine status on her, is a foundation myth, involving class, and it is in her honour that children would have been sacrificed in Salammbô.

Other sacrifices and self-immolations by kings and generals of Carthage have a place in this class tradition. Thus we are told that in the fifth century BC, during the siege of Agrigentum, a terrible pestilence fell upon the troops of Hamilcar and Hannibal; Hamilcar, the surviving general, then sacrificed a child to Baal in order to obtain help from the gods (Diod. 18:86). The Carthaginian general Malco, defeated in battle and condemned to exile, had his son killed in front of the city (Justinus 13:7). Lastly, the general Hamilcar committed suicide by throwing himself on to a fire during the battle of Himera (Herod. 7:165–167).

Another tradition refers to collective holocausts within the Carthaginian aristocracy. Thus, in the year 310 BC, the Carthaginians were besieged by Agatocles of Syracuse and thought that Cronos–Baal had abandoned them, displeased because the custom of sacrificing the most noble children in his honour had declined and it was usual to buy children of the poor instead. The citizenry then decided to revive the old custom and Carthage organized a gigantic holocaust in which 500 children were sacrificed; as in former days, they were the sons of the noble and the powerful (Diodorus 20:14; Plutarch, *De Superstitione* 13).

Molk sacrifice in Carthage only ceased when the city fell under the power of Rome in the year 146 BC (Quintus Curcius Rufus 4:3). Even so, and in spite of express prohibition by the Roman authorities, it continued to be practised in secret until the second century AD, which gives us an indication of how deeply rooted it was among the Carthaginians (Tertullian, *Apolog.* 9:2–3).

Human sacrifice in Carthage, whether individual or collective, seems to have been a privilege of kings, military men and dignitaries, suggesting that it was a practice linked with the interests of the state and of the community, represented by the ruling class. In any case, we are not primarily interested in determining the reasons why a refined and cosmopolitan people reached such a degree of 'barbarity' nor in taking part in the polemic as to whether it was a regular or exceptional practice; we would rather touch on the sociological aspect of the question through an institutional and social reading of the archaeological record. Indeed, the *tophets* of Carthage, Motya and Sardinia provide us today with enough information to attempt to penetrate the social and economic significance of human sacrifice and its direct relationship with specified categories of Phoenician settlement in the west.

Archaeology of the tophet

In the west, the *tophet* is an open-air enclosure clearly marked out and surrounded by walls which define a space reserved for sacrifice, on the periphery and generally to the north of the inhabited centre (Fig. 43). Inside were deposited cinerary urns, sealed at the top with a stone baetyl or pilaster; they are replaced by stelae with an inscription dedicated to Baal or Tanit from the sixth to fifth centuries onward.

The most spectacular *tophet* in the west is, of course, the one at Carthage, known as the 'precinct of Tanit'. In uninterrupted use from the year 700 BC until the fall of Carthage in 146 BC, it has so far yielded more than 20,000 cinerary urns. It is surrounded by a stout wall, covered an area of 6000 square metres in the fourth century BC and in it up to nine superimposed levels of urns have been identified, corresponding to three great phases of use: Tanit I (725–600 BC), II (600 to late fourth century BC) and III (third century to 146 BC) (Fig. 44).

Recent excavations at Salammbô have revealed the following significant aspects:

Fig. 43 The *tophet* at Sulcis

Fig. 44 The *tophet* of Salammbô, Carthage

(a) Regular and individual, not massive, deposits were practised, predominantly of newborn babies in the seventh to sixth centuries BC and of three-year-old children in the fourth century BC. So it is not necessarily a matter of firstborns.

(b) From the seventh century BC on, remains of goats and sheep appear inside the urns; so the substitution of animals was not gradual, since it took place from the beginning.

(c) In the most ancient urns (seventh to sixth centuries BC), 62.5% of the contents consist of human remains; only 30% are animals and 7.5% contain both a child and an animal. In the more recent urns, from the fourth century BC on, 88% are human as against 10% animals and 2% both together. These analyses show that in Carthage human sacrifice, far from declining, increased to reach its highest levels in the fourth to third centuries BC. Between the years 400 and 200 BC, some 20,000 urns containing infant cremations were deposited in Salammbô, so there is no question of the sacrifices being casual or sporadic.

(d) In Tanit II, the presence of as many as three children in a single urn supports the notion of sacrificial offerings linked to family units.

Analysis of the contents of the urns from the Tharros *tophet* suggests that from the beginning, in the seventh century BC, almost 50% of the urns contain the remains of a child and a small sheep or goat. As at Salammbô, this means that it was a matter of association rather than substitution. In general it was newborn babies or children under six that were sacrificed, at the end of the summer judging by the plant remains that have been analysed.

The votive stelae found in the *tophets* in the west, of which there are thousands, usually have an inscription with a formula referring to human blood sacrifice (*mlk'dm*) or the substitution of a sheep for the child (*mlk'mr* or *molchomor*). In every case there are offerings from individuals, intended as a gift, a promise or payment of a due to Baal Hammon in exchange for a favour received. The substitution would be basically hierarchical: the firstborn is a substitute for the king, the child for the firstborn and, lastly, the animal for the child.

In spite of everything, and to conclude, we must say that the exact meaning of the *molk* sacrifice in the west escapes us. We do not know how frequently the rite was practised and it is hard to accept that Phoenician families periodically sacrificed their children or their firstborn solely for the sake of tradition.

In Carthage and Tharros, the relatively high percentage of premature and newborn babies and foetuses indicates that, in many cases, the sacrifice was performed on sickly or stillborn babies, which would be logical up to a point in a period when infant mortality must have been fairly high. In Tharros, the evidence makes plain that it was not a question of a rigid and systematic practice but one that was performed at specified periods of the year. All this has fostered the idea, defended by some authors, that regular, institutionalized sacrifice did not exist and that the *tophet* was nothing more than a necropolis for infants.

However, both the written tradition and the archaeological record point in the opposite direction, that is to say to the existence of human sacrifice, practised in order to placate the wrath of the gods. In this sense, the hypothesis according to which ritual infanticide in Carthage was merely a mechanism for demographic control for economic and patrimonial ends carries little conviction. If that were the case, the victims would have had to be selected exclusively from among girls.

Social and political significance of the tophet

In the Phoenician colonies of the west, the *tophet* precinct began to be used barely a generation after the arrival of the first colonists on the site. The history of the Phoenician settlements thus appears to be very closely linked with that of the sacred precincts. Consequently it is logical that the *tophet* should appear to be a cornerstone in the reconstruction of the social, economic and ideological structure of the colonies.

The sacrifice of the firstborn or of the sons of the most illustrious families in Carthage had as its aim a periodic renewal of the energies of the state and this is stated explicitly by Diodorus (20:14) in connection with the collective holocaust of the year 310 BC. Judging by the epigraphy, the majority of the victims in the *tophet* at Carthage in the early days came from the families of rulers, generals, suffetes, magistrates and *rabs* or priests. Only from the fourth century BC on would human sacrifice be extended to other social strata, among which we encounter for the first time the children of artisans, freedmen, merchants, scribes and even slaves.

Originally, then, the *tophet* at Carthage seems to be reserved specially for the social class descended from the first contingent of colonists who arrived in the west with Elissa. The inscriptions on the stelae reveal genuine lineages and families whose genealogy goes back in some cases for as many as sixteen generations, all sacrificing in the *tophet*.

It may be inferred from all this that certain bonds of solidarity existed between groups of families who formed the basis of the civic and state structures, the great magistrates and princes of the city. Consequently, in Phoenician Carthage, the interests of the community as a whole, expressed through the medium of the *molk* sacrifice, were indistinguishable from those of the ruling class.

This does not appear to have been the case in Motya, where the expiatory offerings and the contents of the necropolis both reflect a less hierarchical society than at Carthage.

From all the information that has been collected to date, we can hazard an approximate interpretation of what the *tophet* represented in the west.

In the first place, human sacrifice appears to be identified with the concept of citizenship and bestows a kind of title legitimizing the rights of the citizenry and the community. The formula that appears in some of the votive inscriptions in Carthage, 'by decree of the people of Carthage', indicates the public and institutional nature of these sacred precincts, their strong conservatism and the clear intervention of the public authorities. *Tophets* were few in the west, because they were metropolitan sanctuaries in which only members of the colony in their own right made sacrifices. Only one category of citizens had access to the sacrifice.

Furthermore, the *tophet* was not for the use of the civic authorities of the colony alone but also for those of the territory under its immediate control. Thus, for example, the Phoenician establishment at Monte Sirai, built as an offshoot of Sulcis in the seventh century BC, did not possess its own *tophet* until the fourth to third centuries BC, that is to say, when it had been consolidated as an independent urban centre. Until then, the central *tophet* for all the secondary establishments in the interior would have been the one at Sulcis.

The organization of this type of sanctuary was thus conditioned by the category of the colony and its territory. In the west, the *tophet* appears as soon as there are signs of a qualitative and quantitative change in the socio-political structures of the Phoenician colonial enclave. In Carthage, for example, it only starts to function around 700 BC, in the centres of Sardinia even earlier. The *tophet* emerges at the same time as other structures and institutions: temples, fortifications and extensive necropolises. In other words, it only appears when a population increase and those features peculiar to an urban colony are recorded.

All this is undoubtedly exceedingly interesting when it comes to distinguishing between different categories of Phoenician settlement in the west. If we accept that the *tophet* is an entity expressing urban institutions, civic administration, community of sacrifice, family links and state intervention, we shall have to establish clear differences of category and function between the Phoenician establishments of the central Mediterranean and the more western group made up of Utica and the enclaves on the Iberian peninsula and in Atlantic Morocco, where not a single *tophet* has been recorded so far. They are precisely those Tyrian enclaves that in the written tradition appear initially to be most closely linked to a temple economy.

Conclusions

Except in the case of Malta and the earliest settlements in Sicily, before the founding of Motya all the Phoenician installations founded in the central Mediterranean show signs of permanence from the outset, which reflects a firm determination to develop into populous colonies. In some cases this determination is of a political nature (Carthage) or in others (Sulcis and perhaps Tharros as well) it is concerned with immediate territorial expansion into the interior, which sometimes finds expression in the building of sanctuaries or temples (Nora, Motya). In no case are there signs of a provisional attitude – absence of temples or of construction of warehouses for merchandise – such as we find for example in some of the territories in the far west of the Mediterranean or in transit zones like Malta.

Characteristic of the group of Phoenician colonies in the central Mediterranean is an early concentration of colonial population in a few agglomerations, which in 700 BC or even earlier already attain the rank of urban colonies. This qualitative leap finds expression in the appearance of centralized religious and cultural institutions, collective works and a whole series of civico–religious elements that stick to a central model: that of Carthage.

The most significant civico–religious institution was the *tophet*. As an institution for worship and sacrifice, it is easy to attribute its installation in the colonies of Sicily and Sardinia to the influence of Carthage. Although the antecedents of the *molk* sacrifice are encountered in the east, its definitive form and consolidation as a collective practice are of Carthaginian invention. The implanting of the *tophet* in Sicily and Sardinia linked those colonies of the central Mediterranean to the political interests of Carthage, insofar as it was political and social interests that may possibly have dictated the development and expansion of the *tophet* in the North African colony.

9

The colonies of the far west: Gadir and the silver trade

Classical historiography is unanimous in recognizing the silver trade as the objective of Phoenician expansion into the far west; and the procurement and production of silver on a large scale means Gadir and its immediate hinterland, Tartessos (Fig. 45). For once the archaeological record provides an abundance of elements corroborating this historical fact.

Diodorus tells us that the Phoenicians obtained so much silver in Iberia that, thanks to the profits made, they were in a position to found many colonies in Africa, Sardinia and Spain (Diodorus 5:35,5). Consequently Gadir was to be the origin not only of Tyre's wealth but also to a large extent of the Phoenician diaspora to the central and western Mediterranean.

Strabo states that, from very remote times, the Tyrians possessed the best lands in Iberia and Libya; and in the Iberian peninsula they occupied the whole of Turdetania (Andalusia), where Phoenician was still spoken during the first centuries BC and AD (Strabo 1:3,2; 3:2,13–14).

In order to give a more coherent account, we shall distinguish two large zones in the western Mediterranean, that of the commercial axis of Gadir and its huge sphere of economic influence (Tartessos, the Atlantic regions of Portugal and Morocco and the coastline of Oran), and that of the network of Phoenician establishments on the coast of Malaga, Granada and Almeria and of Ibiza.

For ancient Gadir, we can count on a host of written references concerning its history and general aspect but on very little archaeological evidence. Nevertheless we can establish its economic importance through its direct influence on Tartessian territory in the eighth to sixth centuries BC. For the history of the Phoenician colonies on the Mediterranean coast of Andalusia or of Ibiza, we must of necessity fall back on the archaeological remains, since the written sources are generally unaware of these territories before the Punic or Carthaginian period.

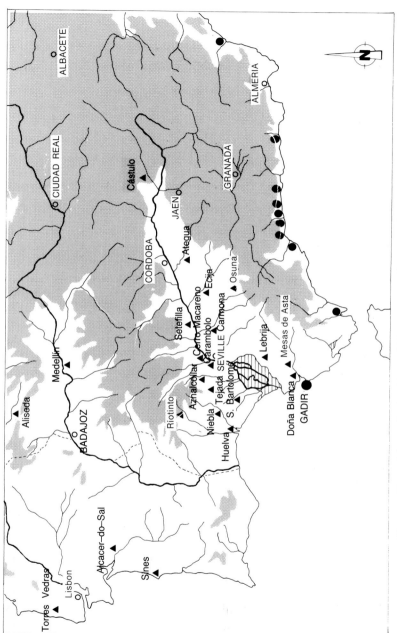

Fig. 45 Phoenician colonies (●) and Tartessian settlements (▲) in the south of Spain

As in previous chapters, we shall select those settlements or cultural elements that seem to us to be most significant for a reconstruction of the colonial process in the west, or that provide the most information about economic and commercial activities.

Introduction

In order to build up a rough picture of what Phoenician Cadiz was and signified, we are forced to rely on descriptions by Greek and Latin authors of the Hellenistic and Roman periods, and on the testimony of geographers and travellers who visited the city during the second century BC and collected from the Gaditanians tales and legends concerning its Phoenician origins. It is difficult to compare these tales, which are mostly passed on by Strabo, with archaeological evidence, since levels of human occupation have been superimposed on the ruins of the old Tyrian colony right down to the present day.

Reconstruction of Phoenician Gadir is an almost impossible undertaking nowadays. Nevertheless, items about the city and especially about its temple, reported by historians and geographers in antiquity, reveal, late as they are, information that we cannot overlook, given its particular interest. In fact, the classical authors are frequently describing a city and a form of worship that they do not understand, precisely because of the oriental features.

When the classical historians write about the origins of the Phoenician city, they are doing it under the influence of the grandeur and prosperity of Cadiz in the Hellenistic and Roman periods. Gades was then one of the most important cities in the Roman world and had the greatest population after Rome. It was renowned for its shipyards, its fishing and preserving industries, its export trade and its opulence – 'joyful and licentious city' (Martial 1:61,9; 5:78,26), and above all its famous Herakleion – the temple of Hercules, visited by illustrious politicians of the day. A city like that had to possess a grand and very remote past.

When the geographer Strabo described the city in the first century AD, on the basis of the account by three Greek travellers of the second century BC – Polibius, Posidonius and Artemidorus – the utmost confusion reigned on the subject of its origins. Gadir was confused with Tartessos, a kingdom that had already vanished, so that it is also said to be a river or a city (Strabo 3:1,6; 3:2,11; Herodotus 1:163;

4:152). The confusion arises because both had symbolized the same thing in the past, opulence and wealth from silver (Pliny, *Nat. Hist.* 4:22; Avienus, *O.M.* 85).

Be that as it may, there can be no doubt about the Phoenician origin of Cadiz. This is shown by the name Gadir, *gdr* in Phoenician, meaning 'wall', 'enclosed place' or 'fortified citadel' and alluding probably to the walled precinct around the colony in its early days.

The Greek authors hellenized the name, which always appears in the plural – *Gadeira, Gedeiroi* – and it became definitively latinized with the form of *Gades*, also plural. This is because Gadir was made up of various islands, nowadays a peninsula.

The myth of the foundation and historical chronology

The authors who have left us the most details about the origins of Gadir are Strabo and Velleius Paterculus, both from the first century AD, who collected accounts from other, more ancient historians and travellers.

Velleius belongs to that learned band who associate the Trojan War, the travels of Hercules and the Phoenicians in a single tale and so find themselves forced to push the chronology of the foundation back a long way. As will be remembered, this historian tells us that a Tyrian fleet had founded Gadir at the far end of the world eighty years after the Trojan war, when the Heraclides were returning to Greece and the monarchy in Athens fell (*Hist. Rom.* 1:2,3), which situates the event in the years 1104–1103 BC (Mela 3:6,46). We shall not repeat here the scant guarantees offered by these sources of information, and we refer you to Chapter 7.

More interesting is the information gathered by the Greek Posidonius, who heard the history told around 100 BC in Gadir itself. This is how Strabo (3:5,5) tells the story:

About the founding of Gadeira, this is what the Gaditanians say they remember: that an oracle ordered the Tyrians to found a settlement at the Columns of Hercules; those sent to explore arrived at the straits next to Calpe [Gibraltar] and thought that the promontories that form the straits were the boundaries of the inhabited earth and the end of Hercules' labours; then, supposing that these were the columns of which the oracle had spoken, they dropped anchor in a certain place very close to the Columns, where stood the city of the Exitani [Almuñécar]. But as they offered a sacrifice to the gods at that point on the coast and the victims were not propitious, they returned. Later the envoys passed through the straits, arriving at an island dedicated to Hercules that lies close to Onoba [Huelva], a city of Iberia and some one thousand five hundred stadia beyond the straits; as they thought that these were the Columns, they sacrificed once more to the gods; but again the victims were unfavourable and they returned to their country. On the third expedition, they founded Gadeira and erected the sanctuary in the eastern part of the island and the city in the western part.

So the Tyrian foundation of Gadir cost them three trial voyages before they found the most suitable place to settle. This is partly a reflection of the difficulties for shipping of going through the Straits of Gibraltar in adverse weather conditions (see Chapter 6).

Diodorus added a little to the account by Posidonius, stating that the Tyrians founded a city (*polis apoikos*) close to the Columns and called it Gadeira, on a peninsula on which they erected a sumptuous temple to Hercules (Melqart) and instituted magnificent sacrifices according to 'Phoenician usage' (25:10,1). He tells us too that they arrived driven before a storm and takes it for granted that their purpose was not colonization but trade (5:20,1–4). For Diodorus, the main Phoenician colony in the west was Gadir and not Carthage.

The interesting thing to emphasize here is not so much the chronology or the misadventures of the Tyrian fleet but, yet again, the politico-economic background to the founding of Gadir. As usual in the classical world, the founding of the colony is said to be due to chance, to a storm or to an oracle. Nevertheless, it is noted that Tyre had the firm intention of founding a settlement in a very specific zone and in the vicinity of a land rich in silver, gold and copper and the Tyrians must have had previous knowledge or intuition about the possibilities of exploiting these materials.

The Tyrian oracle is more significant because through it the god – no doubt Melqart – gives the explorers some very precise geographical directions. This reflects a fact of particular interest: that the commercial initiative for the founding of Gadir at the end of the known world is down to the temple in Tyre.

We do not know at what exact moment Melqart decided to organize this commercial enterprise. In any case, it could not have taken place in the twelfth century BC, since in Phoenicia and in Tyre the cult of Melqart does not pre-date the tenth to ninth centuries BC. In the final instance, it is the archaeological evidence from the territory close to Cadiz that has the last word. The indigenous Tartessian settlements on the bay of Gadir, some of them inhabited since the second millennium BC, did not receive their first Phoenician imports until the years 770–760. This fact seems to us to be a decisive argument to settle an interminable discussion about the historical value of the classical sources in the question of the origins of Cadiz.

Paleogeography and archaeology of the Cadiz Archipelago

The difficulties and risks presented by the bay of Cadiz to all sailing ships have been described in Chapter 6. The dangers involved in passing through the Straits of Gibraltar and the buffetings of the ocean made a colonial establishment in unknown waters very uncomfortable indeed for Mediterranean seamen. Only genuine economic rewards and the certainty of obtaining fat profits could justify the location of Phoenician Gadir.

In effect, Gadir was established close to the mouth of the Guadalete and not far from the valley of the Guadalquivir, so that it formed a bastion in the midst of the sea and guarded a bay that ensured direct access to the mineral wealth in the spurs of the Sierra Morena and the mountainous regions of the province of Huelva. Its island character made it safe from possible dangers from the sea or the mainland.

It is not easy to imagine what the bay of Cadiz looked like in antiquity, due to the major geomorphological transformations that have taken place there right down to our own days. This explains the controversy about the exact site of the colony and its sanctuaries, a controversy that was initiated in Roman times as a result of the changes experienced even then in the form and extent of the primitive archipelago.

The alluvial deposits from the river Guadalete in the eastern part of the bay have been reducing and filling up a bay that was much bigger in antiquity and they have finally joined the ancient archipelago to the coast (Fig. 46).

Moreover, erosion by the sea on the western flank of the bay, continuous since antiquity, has won 3 km of water for the sea in the last 2000 years, reducing the size of the islands and forming cliffs in the western and southern zones of the island of Cadiz.

To the transformation of the landscape must be added the confusion that reigned in the Roman period in descriptions of the topography of Cadiz. Pliny, for example, states in the year 77 AD that the Gaditanian archipelago was formed by three islands, but he confines his description to only two of them, a big island called Kotinoussa because it contained an abundance of olives or oleasters, and another, small one called Erytheia, where the *oppidum* of Gades was located and which the natives of the place also called Insula Iunonis (*Nat. Hist.* 4:22).

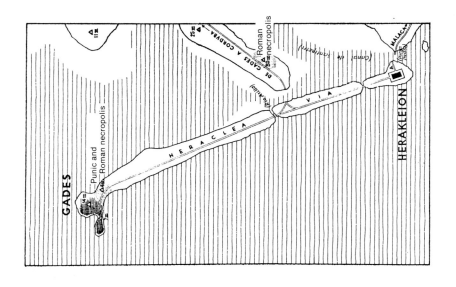

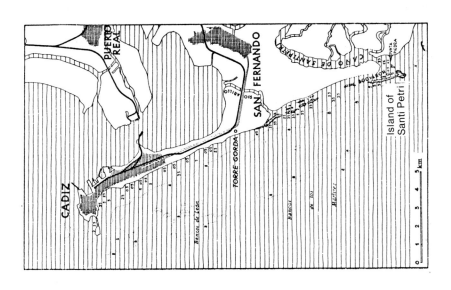

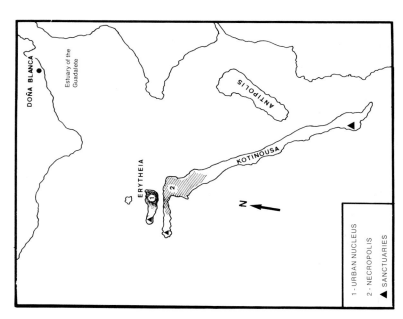

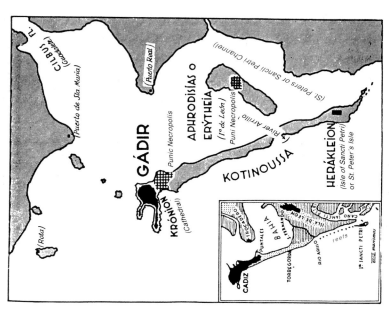

Fig. 46 The bay of Cadiz today and alternative models for a reconstruction of the ancient archipelago

According to the descriptions of other classical authors, the principal island was long and narrow and terminated in a promotory at each end; on the western promontory was the city and on the eastern, the famous temple of Melqart–Hercules (Mela 3:46), with a distance of 12 Roman miles, equivalent to 18 km, between the two (Strabo 3:5,5; Antonine Itinerary 408:3–4).

It is certain, likewise, that in the past Gadir constituted a fortress, also called *Arx gerontis* or the castle of Gerion, close to which was an island dedicated to Venus maritima (Astarte), with a temple and an oracle (Avienus, *Ora Maritima* vv. 85 and 267–270). The Phoenicio–Punic city was very small until, in the Roman period, Balbo, one of its citizens, built a new and very much bigger city nearby, which was called Didyme (twin or double) and constructed a harbour on the mainland, the Portus gaditanus, perhaps in Puerto Real (Strabo 3:5,3).

In short, from the descriptions in the classics we can infer the existence of an archipelago of three main islands, which would explain the plural form used to designate the area. In Erytheia, the smaller island, the Tyrian colony, called Aphrodisias or Insula Iunonis, was located. Kotinoussa, the larger island, housed the temple of Melqart at its eastern end; the location of the temple on the present-day islet of Sancti Petri has not presented too many difficulties. A third island, unnamed, used to be generally identified with the island of León (San Fernando). And yet the modern map of the bay shows only a long, narrow peninsula linked to the mainland in the place where Kotinoussa and Erytheia used to be (Fig. 47).

The ancient Tyrian colony is usually located on the site of the old centre of modern Cadiz and was shifted, for geological reasons, to the small island of San Sebastian, as Pemán and Schulten claimed formerly. Moreover, the existence of the Gaditanian necropolis of the Punic period in the Puertas de Tierra region invalidates the theory that the Phoenician city reached the area of the isthmus of the island of Cadiz.

Recent geological and archaeological work has settled the problem of the topography of the bay of Gadir, apparently for good. It has thus been possible to identify an ancient channel some 150 metres wide which split the island of Cadiz in two (Fig. 48). This channel, known as the channel of Bahia-Caleta, was deep and narrow and was probably originally an ancient course of the river Guadalete. So it marked the edge of a small islet some 1500 metres in diameter to the northwest of the island of Cadiz on a high point of which the nineteenth-century city was raised. The ancient acropolis of Gadir was probably located on the highest promontory of present-day Cadiz, in the so-called Torre de

Fig. 47 Aerial view of Cadiz

Tavira. The first island on which the Tyrian colony was set up – no doubt Erytheia – must have been very limited in extent and very similar to that of the old centre of the city of Cadiz, reckoned to be not more than 10 hectares.

The Punic necropolis of Gadir, then, was in the area outside the walls and separated from the colony by a channel of water. Consequently, Gadir reproduces a Phoenician settlement model which was to be common in the west. It was on the land occupied by the necropolis in Puertas de Tierra that Balbo was to build Roman Gades or Neapolis at a time when the ancient Bahia-Caleta channel had already been blocked.

The descriptions by the classical authors, and in particular that of Pliny, are consequently correct and show that the latter consulted very ancient sources of information, since the three islands no longer existed in his day. We can trace in general lines the following geographical and archaeological reconstruction of the bay of Cadiz in the Phoenician period.

There were effectively at least three islands in the bay and there is no reason to doubt that the most important was Erytheia, the smallest, lying to the north of the channel and housing the walled Tyrian colony

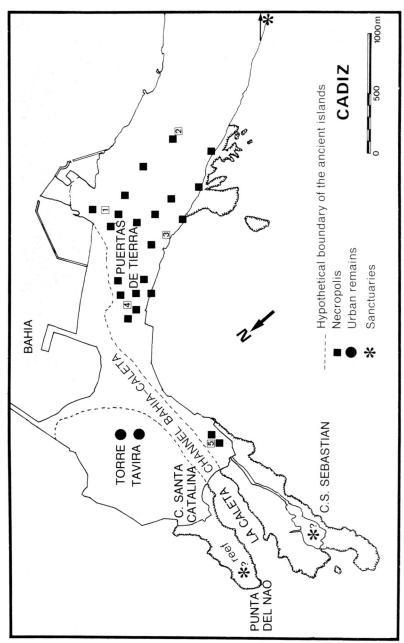

Fig. 48 Reconstruction of the island of Cadiz and position of the principal archaeological remains

Fig. 49 Proto-Aeolian capital from Cadiz

– the *Arx Gerontis* – on the small mound of Torre Tavira. It would correspond to the ancient centre of modern Cadiz and was also known as Aphrodisias or Insula Iunonis, possibly because a sanctuary of Astarte (Avienus' Venus maritima) had been raised there; the sanctuary may have been sited in the modern Punta del Nao. The little Tyrian colony possessed an excellent harbour in the south, in the channel of Bahia-Caleta, which almost constituted an enclosed harbour or *cothon*.

The second island, Kotinoussa, stretched from the present castle of San Sebastian to the islet of Sancti Petri. In the area close to the channel the Puertas de Tierra necropolis was built; it has been known since 1887 and so far no burials earlier than the fifth century BC have been located. On the small hill of the castle of San Sebastian, a second Gaditanian sanctuary may have been sited, the Kronion or temple to Cronos (Baal Hammon), mentioned by the classical authors (Strabo

3:5,3; Pliny, *Nat. Hist.* 4:120). In the sea close to the southern flank of the island of San Sebastian a limestone capital was discovered some time ago; it is 27 cm tall and in the proto-Aeolian style, which is dated to the eighth to seventh centuries BC. Its decoration of volutes and its form (Fig. 49) are related to architectonic elements from Megiddo, Jerusalem and Tyre and suggest that it might have embellished the entrance to an ancient temple. It is the only piece of monumental religious architecture that we know, so far, from the Phoenician colonies on the Iberian peninsula, which once again makes Cadiz different from the rest of the Tyrian establishments in its character as a central place of worship.

Both in this area and in the first island of Cadiz, some recently identified archaeological remains suggest that the place was already inhabited in the Chalcolithic. Nonetheless, when the Tyrians arrived the islands had long been uninhabited.

In the extreme southeast of the island of Kotinoussa, in Sancti Petri, the famous temple of Melqart was erected, exactly 18 km from Torre de Tavira, in the vicinity of which submerged monumental remains have also been identified.

The third island, León, now San Fernando, the original name of which is not known, appears to have been uninhabited until the Roman period.

But the Tyrian colony was not restricted to a couple of islands close to the mainland. Facing the mouth of the Guadalete, Gadir dominated an important inlet which provided it with easy access straight into the valley of the Guadalquivir, the main artery of communication for the whole of Lower Andalusia. Consequently the colony lay at the exit point for the riches from the interior of the country and of the coveted metals from the Tartessian region.

Only 4 km to the north of the Puerto de Santa Maria, the indigenous or Tartessian settlement of Castillo de Doña Blanca first made contact with Gadir around the years 770–750 BC, judging by the first Phoenician imports found on the site, and it was soon to be converted into an appendage of the Tyrian colony and its main port of embarkation on the mainland. The imports of Phoenician pottery dated to about 750 BC that appear in Tartessian settlements in the interior, such as Berrueco, Carambolo or Carmona (Fig. 50), suggest a relatively rapid extension of Gadir's trade towards the Guadalquivir valley.

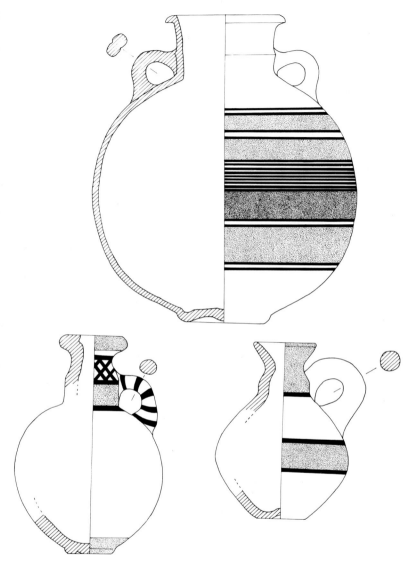

Fig. 50 Phoenician pottery from La Cruz del Negro, Carmona (seventh century BC)

The temple of Melqart, centre for the protection of trade

Until the end of the ancient world, the fame and prestige of the temple of Melqart in Cadiz were considerable. All this, combined with the fact that Roman emperors of Hispanic origin, like Trajan and Hadrian, raised the Gaditanian Heracles–Hercules to the status of an imperial cult and struck coins bearing the effigy of the god, undoubtedly increased its importance in the imagination of the classical writers.

The classical sources describe a Romano–Hellenistic sanctuary in Gadir, although the information they have passed on to us refers chiefly to a temple and a form of worship that preserved elements and traits of Semitic and eastern origin until a very late date. Thanks to these testimonies and to the information afforded by other known temples of Melqart in the Mediterranean, we are in a position to reconstruct a rough picture of the temple in Gadir and what it signified.

It should not be forgotten that, in the cases of Gadir and Lixus, the building of a sanctuary dedicated to the national god of Tyre preceded or coincided with the founding of the colony. In Cadiz it was in obedience to the command of an oracle or, if you like, of the political institutions of Tyre. In that way, Melqart sanctioned and legitimized a commercial initiative and from his position at the eastern end of Kotinoussa, only 800 metres from the mainland, exercised a tutelary function over the passage through the Cadiz channel.

The sanctuary and its worship

Many of the elements of worship in the temple in Gadir were foreign to Graeco–Roman religion and disconcerting to the classical authors, who singled out the temple's magnificence (Diodorus 5:20,2) and its architecture and rites of Phoenician origin (Arrianus, *Alex.* 2:16,4).

Like the temple in Tyre, it had three altars on which the priests preserved the eternal flame and sacrificed animals daily (Silius Italicus 3:29; Profirius 1:25). In addition there is mention of two springs of sweet water inside the temple which, by way of sacred basins, were used for worship (Strabo 3:5,7–8).

The absence of images or figured representations of the god is another Phoenician aspect of the worship and is in line with the Semitic religions, which prohibited representation of the deity. The strict banning of cult images in the *sancta sanctuorum* lasted until the first century AD in Gadir, and this never failed to surprise visitors (Silius Italicus 3:31–32). According to legend, the relics of Hercules, who died in Spain (Mela 3:46), were preserved in the Gaditanian temple, or else they had been transferred from Tyre to Gadir (Justinus 44:5,2).

Equally celebrated were the two bronze columns (Strabo 3:5,5–6) 8 cubits – a little over 3 metres – tall, which flanked the temple of Gadir, in the style of the two columns of the temple in Tyre. The story goes that the accounts of the expenses involved in building the Gaditanian temple had been engraved on them in a few enigmatic inscriptions that were already indecipherable in the days of Strabo (3:5,5; Philostratus, *v. Apoll. Tiana* 5:5). People have believed they saw an echo of these two famous Tyrian stelae in the Columns of Hercules. The term, whether it be geographical or architectural, may have been of Phoenician origin, which, when Hellenized from the fourth century BC on, had to be reinterpreted by the Greek historians on the basis of a religion and a god that were impersonal, devoid of ikons and mortal, totally different from their own. Be that as it may, in the Canaanite and Phoenician religions the presence of two columns, stelae or marker stones represents and at the same time expresses the deity itself.

The sanctuary at Cadiz sheltered, in addition, an oracle, administrative buildings and living quarters for the staff and the priests responsible for the worship. Access to the Gaditanian temple was reserved exclusively for the priests, who officiated before the altar with bare feet, shaven heads and wearing tunics of white linen (Silius Italicus 3:21 and 28). It follows that the tonsure conferred on them the status of genuine, professional priests. And, as in Tyre, they formed a hierarchical body with a high priest at the top (Porphyrius 1:25), whose power must have been considerable.

To judge by other known examples, we can imagine that we have here a priestly organization administered by a very few families, who handed the rites of worship down from generation to generation. This type of organization, based on an exclusive and engrossing service, ruled by the 'possessed of god' or the 'pure', is characteristic of the temples of Melqart in Tyre, Syria, Thasos and Ara Maxima.

In Gadir, as in Tyre, a festival commemorating the resurrection of Melqart was celebrated every year in the months of February and March. Access was prohibited to foreigners (Pausanias 10:4,6) and in Tyre, at least, a human victim was sacrificed by fire (Pliny, *Nat. Hist.* 36:39). Cicero is probably alluding to this when he refers to 'barbarous' sacrifices of human beings in Gades (Cicero, *Pro Balbo* 43; *Ad. Fam.* 10:32,3), the only known reference to human sacrifices in the Gadir area. In any case, this does not appear to be a matter of the *molk* sacrifice of the Carthaginian region. The immolation of a human

victim, whether in Gadir or in Tyre, may have been connected with the
actual worship of Melqart, a god who went annually through a process
of passion, death and resurrection and who, in his capacity as
redeemer of life (agriculture), died by fire (summer) every year.

The long survival of all these rites, customs and practices of oriental
worship in Roman Gades shows to what extent the cult of the Tyrian
Melqart had taken root in the region. The fact that the cult was still
celebrated in the Phoenician manner in the Roman period, perpetuat-
ing the strict observance of rites directed and controlled by a high
priest, is equally an indication of the conservative power of a priestly
caste, capable of preserving certain customs that were totally alien to
the classical world.

In support of the hypothesis of the Tyrian origin of the temple in
Gadir, we can instance other cultural features that usually appear in
association with the cult of Melqart in the eastern Mediterranean: the
regulation emphatically banning pigs, animals hateful to the god, and
women from entering the sanctuary (Silius Italicus 3:23–24; Diodorus
5:20; Apianus 1:2).

Contribution of the temple to the economy of Gadir

The temple at Cadiz was not used exclusively as a place of worship and
sacrifice. It must be remembered who Melqart of Tyre was in the
framework of Phoenician religion, a religion that constituted the best
instrument of their commercial and colonial policy. Melqart, the 'lord
of Tyre', represented the power of the monarchy insofar as he constituted the deified form or theological exaltation of the king of Tyre. In
distant places where he possessed a temple, his function was a very
concrete one: to ensure the tutelage of the temple of Tyre and the
monarchy over the commercial enterprise, thus converting the colony
into an extension of Tyre; and also to guarantee the right of asylum
and hospitality which, in distant lands, was equivalent to endorsing
contracts and commercial exchanges. In addition, the temple served as
a religious bond between the colony and the metropolis and created a
political and economic link in which the priests had an outstanding
part to play.

In ancient trade, the protection of visitors to the market or place of
exchange was guaranteed by a temple, built close by, which acted at
times as an efficient financial intermediary or bank. The sanctuaries in
antiquity were the first places for commercial transactions in a foreign
country. The first condition of any market or trading colony set up on
a frontier or in a distant land was to ensure that its visitors were not

molested or robbed. And, as a general rule, that security was offered by a god, under whose auspices and protection deals were verified. The name of the god was invoked in oaths sanctioning contracts.

Indeed, we know that sophisticated peoples negotiated covenants or commercial treaties, as did Hiram and Solomon. But between unequal or colonial societies, the only security offered lies in the recognized sovereignty of a god in his temple or sacred precinct. A supernatural or divine presence automatically converted any act of fraud or violence into sacrilege and destroyed the mutual confidence between the two parties, by virtue of the norms of hospitality and asylum. The Greeks called this guarantee *asyle*.

The quality of the merchandise, exchange equivalencies and weights were also under the protection of the god. This is why Hercules–Melqart was called *Hercules ponderum*. In its turn, the temple fulfilled the role of treasury and bank and could keep a register of transactions. In this way, yet again, the deity replaced the political authority.

In exchange for all this, the god received taxes and dues in the form of offerings, jewels and money, which were administered by the priests. There are reports, at a later date, of substantial treasure in the temple at Gadir (Livy 28:36,2). It is known, too, that Melqart of Gadir enjoyed the privilege of receiving legacies (Ulpianus 22:6). In every way, the building of the temple at Gadir proved a good investment.

It is possible that the first Tyrian colonies in the west, like Gadir, started just as sanctuaries administered by a priestly group directly linked to the interests of Tyre. Melqart not only extended his protection over the commercial undertakings but he also set himself up as protector of the colonists in a foreign land. Phoenician seafarers came to his temple to offer sacrifices to him once they had achieved their objectives in the region (Avienus, *O.M.* 358). This explains why, as patron of seafarers, he had a temple in the main ports of call on the route westwards: Cyprus, Malta, Nora, Gadir.

To enable a trading post to progress from a foundational stage of simple barter to regular exchange relations with the indigenous population, the most effective formula in ancient societies was to resort to the protection of a god who would be respected by the natives as well, since respect for the foreigner is dependent on the respect in which his gods are held. The native world knew nothing about duties or markets and the political authority of the colonists – in this case the king of Tyre – was ill-defined as far as his power in a foreign territory was concerned. Only the presence of Melqart made it possible to create a new market, by settling the necessary conditions, as a representative of the authority of Tyre, for initiating peaceful contacts with the natives. In addition, Phoenician polytheism and the perfect organization of the practices of worship in the temple at Gadir made it easier for the native population to assimilate the cult from Tyre.

In any case we can say that the building of the temple of Melqart in association with the founding of the colony took place in the framework of a precise political and economic strategy. Temple and colonial foundation merge into one because the political will existed to initiate regular, organized trade. And not only could the temple fulfil an economic function but, as the pivot and protector of the commercial diaspora, it was able to preserve the original cultural integrity of the colonists because, up to a point, it also exercised social control through religion.

A legend relates that Archaleus, a son of Phoinix, king of Tyre, and closely involved with metallurgy, was the founder of Gadir (Claudius Iolaus, *FGH* 788). Here we see that the mythical founder of Gadir is the actual son of the king of Tyre and, at the same time, Melqart in his hellenized form (Archaleus = Heracles). This legend brings together in a single myth the Tyrian monarchy, the god Melqart and metallurgical activity, just as in other minero-metallurgical regions of the Mediterranean controlled by the Phoenicians (cf. Herodotus 2:44). This is undoubtedly the key to the significance of the Phoenician foundation of Gadir: the political institutions of Tyre and the Tartessian silver market.

Silver extraction and the silver trade

The origin of the first Phoenician expeditions to the west seems to be generally related to the wealth of silver in the Iberian peninsula. And in the Iberian peninsula, silver is synonymous with Tartessos, the territory stretching along the lower valley of the Guadalquivir and Huelva in the Late Bronze and Early Iron Ages. The wealth of silver and other metals in Lower Andalusia and the Atlantic region is reflected in many myths, legends and place names alluding to a kind of Eldorado in the far west. Tyre was to be the first to exploit and make a profit from all this economic potential.

One of the earliest known mentions of the west was picked up by Estesicorus around the year 600 BC and, alluding specifically to silver, it describes the immense sources of silver-bearing ore on the Tartessos river (Strabo 3:2,11). Place names and the mythical names of native kings in the region contain the root *arg-* as a symbol of that wealth, for example the *Mons Argentarius,* possibly the Sierra Morena, and Argantonio. And we recall the voyage of the Samian Colaios to Tartessos, where he picked up a cargo of 60 talents of silver, equivalent to some 1000 to 2000 kg of ore (Herod. 4:152). The arrival of the Phoenicians in this area is evoked in connection with a gigantic forest fire, which is said to have led to the discovery of tons of silver ore (Diodorus 5:35,4–5):

Having spoken of Iberia, it seems appropriate to mention its silver mines since this is the richest country in that metal, which brings large incomes to the exploiters . . . As in [the Pyrenees] there were many leafy woods, the shepherds had set fire to them – it is said – a long time before, so that the woodlands had been burning throughout the sierra. After burning for many days, the fire also scorched the surface of the ground, which gave rise to the name Pyrenees, used to designate these mountains. Much silver trickled away from the fiery ground and, as they melted, the silver-bearing ores formed countless rivulets of pure silver. The natives did not know how to exploit it but once the Phoenicians heard of the affair, they bought the silver in exchange for objects of negligible value. The Phoenicians took the silver to Greece, to Asia and to all the other countries then known, thus obtaining great riches. It is said that such was the cupidity of the traders that they replaced the lead anchors of their ships with silver ones after there was no more room for silver in the vessels, and there was still a great quantity of the metal left over. This commercial traffic was long the source of a great increase in the power of the Phoenicians, who founded many colonies, some in Sicily and neighbouring islands and some in Libya, Sardinia and Iberia.

Although the etymology of the Pyrenees (pyr = fire) is incorrect and the report is undoubtedly referring to Tartessian silver, this text, ascribed to Timeus or Posidonius, has a special interest for us. In the first place, it makes clear that the main reason for the Phoenician expansion to the west was to obtain silver. In the second place, it is stated that the Phoenicians took advantage of the ignorance of the natives to acquire it in exchange for gewgaws. In the third place, the legend leaves no doubt that the prosperity of the Phoenicians, that is to say Tyre, was due to trading in Iberian silver, which they sold on to Greece and Asia. Be that as it may, the exploitation of Iberian silver seems to have been the prerogative of the state of Tyre and preceded the founding of the colonies in North Africa, Sicily, Sardinia and the Iberian peninsula itself.

Other classical authors tell the same story (Strabo 3:2,9; Atenaios 6:233) and emphasize the skill shown by the Phoenicians in appropriating huge cargoes of silver in exchange for oil and cheap goods (Pseudo-

Aristotle, *De Mirabilis auscult.* 135). So we are looking at an example of unfair exchange, characteristic of a colonial system.

For once, archaeology confirms this trafficking in the hinterland of Gadir and places such activity in a firm spatial and temporal frame: the mountainous country inland in the provinces of Huelva and Seville between approximately 750 and 570 BC.

In the period of Phoenician colonization, the mining region *par excellence* consisted of the province of Huelva and the western region of the province of Seville, with secondary centres in the Sierra Morena and Portugal. But it was the region of Huelva that contained the richest deposits of pyrites with an abundance of gold and silver ore. So, for example, in the area of the Rio Tinto mines, considered one of the main centres of metal production in antiquity – gold, silver, copper, lead, iron – a mining settlement was established in the seventh century BC – Cerro Salomón – devoted entirely to extracting silver, gold and copper. The extraction process was in native hands, as can be inferred from the archaeological record, and the population took charge not only of the digging of pits and galleries but also of smelting operations which attained industrial proportions as the seventh century BC progressed.

In the Cerro Salomón, clay lamps, miner's tools, bellows and crucibles have been discovered, and analyses carried out on samples of ore indicate that the workmen knew a great deal about silica fluxes and how to treat the ore by adding lead to collect the silver. So we are dealing with an advanced technology and a well-organized mining enterprise. It is not by chance that all this activity in Rio Tinto began at the same time as the first traces of a Phoenician presence appear in the region.

The metal was transported in the form of ingots or crude ore, down the Tinto to Huelva, a native or Tartessian settlement which, as a result of this trade, was transformed in the seventh century BC into a prosperous port, frequented by the Phoenicians. The change is mirrored to perfection in the burials of the Tartessian aristocracy of Huelva – La Joya necropolis – a sector visibly enriched thanks to the silver trade and which, in its way of life and funerary practices, adopted forms showing Phoenician and eastern influence; hence the term 'orientalizing', applied to this period in Tartessos.

Furnaces for smelting silver dating to the eighth to seventh centuries BC have been located right in the centre of the town of Huelva (Fig. 51), which indicates that genuine metallurgical activities with the aim of processing the silver from Rio Tinto took place both alongside the

Fig. 51   Silver smelting furnace (calle del Puerto)

mines – Cerro Salomón – and in the port – Huelva – depending perhaps on fuel requirements or the need to save transport costs.

In addition, a second silver route existed leading directly into Gadir. This is the road that starts at the Aznalcóllar mines in the province of Seville and, passing through native villages like Tejada la Vieja, ends at the mouth of the Guadalquivir (Fig. 45). A modest native village, San Bartolomé de Almonte, has been located along this road, some 40 km from the mines and devoted exclusively to metallurgical activity during the eighth and seventh centuries BC. So Gadir was situated astride the exit route for silver from Almonte and Aznalcóllar and the metal must have arrived at the colony smelted and in the form of bars or ingots.

The existence of two silver trade routes, one connected with a native centre (Huelva–Rio Tinto) and the other leading directly to Gadir (Aznalcóllar–Almonte) does not so much point to two competing commercial ventures, one in Tartessian hands and the other controlled by Gadir, as reveal the existence of two distinct ways of transporting the metal within a highly efficient commercial organization. Thus the silver from Rio Tinto, arriving in Huelva by river, considerably reduced the costs that would have been incurred had it been transported overland, which, by contrast, was what had to be done on the trade route leading from Aznalcóllar. This second route, in addition to

being much longer, could boast of staging posts and intermediate
metallurgical installations like San Bartolomé de Almonte, which
undoubtedly increased the costs of labour and transport. So the use of
this second route must have had some compensations of an economic
nature.

The technique used at Huelva and San Bartolomé de Almonte for
processing silver was based on fusion and cupellation, using basically
gossan ore, with a high gold, silver and lead content. The process
consisted in placing the crushed ore together with the flux and heating
it so as to obtain the slag and the regulus (lead, silver and gold), the
lead serving to capture the metals. After this first stage of fusion came
the cupellation proper; the regulus was placed in a cupel and fired; the
cupel absorbed the lead, releasing a second regulus (gold and silver)
and separating the lead from it.

All this reveals an excellent knowledge of metallurgy, particularly
significant if we bear in mind that the Tartessians had only been initiated into silver metallurgy on a large scale from the eighth century BC.
This fact makes abundantly clear the existence of a complex organization, capable of coordinating simultaneously a series of mining
centres (Cerro Salomón, Tejada), metallurgical centres (San Bartolomé,
Huelva) and embarkation points. This enterprise perforce involved the
presence of specialist personnel – technicians, miners, metallurgists,
transport workers – in charge of the various processes or stages of production, since we have already seen that the ore was not always
extracted in the place where it was smelted or put aboard ship. Probably
the metal was transported in the form of ingots or bars, previously
weighed and divided up, from the ports of Huelva or Gadir direct to
Tyre or Greece, and perhaps even to Pitecusas or other Mediterranean
centres where we have documentary evidence of the activity of silver-
and goldsmiths during the eighth to seventh centuries BC.

In any case, Gadir was the principal reception centre for Tartessian
silver, either through middlemen or directly, at least until the end of
the seventh century BC. It can be said on this score that the money
invested by Tyre in this remote enterprise was more than recovered in
full, because only high economic returns can explain the eccentric
location of Gadir, outside the normal Mediterranean shipping routes
of the ancient world. What is more, the traffic in silver ore that we
have just described implies, in addition to considerable economic
investment, a high degree of coordination between the mine and the
wharf, such as the existence of an authority to centralize and coord-
inate those services. Given that the chief beneficiary was Tyre, we are

bound to think, as the classical sources (Diodorus 5:35,5) insinuate, that Gadir was acting under orders from Tyre by way of powerful commercial agents installed in the west. Only so can we appreciate the meaning of Posidonius' observation that there were in Gadir great transport ships, commissioned by the rich traders of the place (Strabo 2:3,4) and operating in safety under the protection of Melqart. Thanks to them, Tyre was able to supply the great centres of the Aegean and Assyria with silver.

The silver trade was equally beneficial to a section of the Tartessian population of Huelva, its chiefs and local rulers, and for the first time, social differentiation reared its head within these indigenous communities which had been relatively egalitarian before the founding of Gadir. This change was particularly accentuated during the seventh century BC, to judge by the contents of the local burials (Fig. 52).

The direct intervention of Gadir in silver production and its monopoly of the trade in the Mediterranean increased throughout the seventh century BC, at times when the great demand for silver in the east was forcing Tyre to intensify her trading relations and to open up new markets in the west. This is the time when commercial exchanges with Andalusia, Estremadura and Portugal attained their greatest volume and these native populations received quantities of oil, wine, unguents and jewels in exchange for their raw materials.

Trade with the Tartessian hinterland – an example of unfair exchange

The Tartessian area is today one of the best-known territories archaeologically, thanks to the boost that field of investigation has experienced since the beginning of the decade of the seventies. Without going into considerations of its material culture and its historical or proto-historical development, which would require a separate volume to itself, it is interesting to stress here the incidence of Phoenician trade in the Guadalquivir valley and adjoining regions and the forms of exchange that Gadir developed in the region.

The Guadalquivir valley offers several possibilities for metallurgical exploitation which could effectively complement the production of silver in Huelva province. An examination of all the archaeological data demonstrates that Phoenician trade made its way into the valley during the eighth to seventh centuries and into the spurs of the Sierra Morena – Carambolo, Setefilla, Cástulo – where it could obtain silver, gold, siderite, copper and lead with relative ease.

Fig. 52   Bronze jug from the necropolis of La Joya, Huelva

As the mainland harbour of Gadir, Castillo de Doña Blanca gave easy access straight into the fertile valley of the Guadalquivir and to its mouth, which in antiquity was an enormous lake, peopled with indigenous coastal settlements like Asta Regia, Nabrissa, Onoba and Ossonoba. The majority of these villages, like the great Tartessian centres of the interior, Carmona, Carambolo and Setefilla, received Phoenician goods very early on, more than half of which consisted of transport amphorae and containers. This would confirm the observation of the Pseudo-Aristotle that we have already commented on, namely that, in the beginning, the Tartessians received oil and gewgaws in exchange for metals.

Gadir's radius of economic activity widened considerably during the seventh century BC. Thus its control over mineral-metallurgical resources very soon extended to a new metal, tin, which was clearly in short supply in the eastern Mediterranean. We are told that, from very remote times, the Tartessians, and the Phoenicians as well, sailed to the Oestrymnides islands in search of tin (Avienus, *O.M.* 113–116). And Strabo adds that the Gaditanians obtained tin and lead in the Cassiterite islands, in exchange for salt and bronze articles (Strabo 3:5,11).

Generally speaking, the Oestrymnides or Cassiterites ('tin islands') were located off the coasts of Galicia, in Brittany or even in the British Isles (Pliny *N.H.* 4:119). Be that as it may, the Tartessians of Huelva developed regular contacts by sea with the northwest of the peninsula during the Atlantic Late Bronze Age and traces of Phoenician shipping are to be seen along the Portuguese coast during the seventh century BC. Phoenician imports in Sines, Santa Olaia and Alcacer do Sol on the mouth of the Sado seem to demonstrate this and indicate the possibility of coastal shipping along these coasts en route for the Cassiterites.

Gadir also used an overland route to gain access to the tin of the northwest, passing through Aliseda and Medellín, through a territory – Estremadura – that possessed gold, copper and tin in abundance. The famous Aliseda treasure (Cáceres), undoubtedly the work of Phoenician goldsmiths, was found, not surprisingly, in the grave of an indigenous chief or prince who probably controlled one of the natural passes on the tin route to the northwest. The discovery probably bears witness to the practice of merchants from Gadir offering gifts to a native chief in exchange for an economic *quid pro quo*: free transit of merchandise through his territory.

In addition to metals, the Phoenicians could not have overlooked the

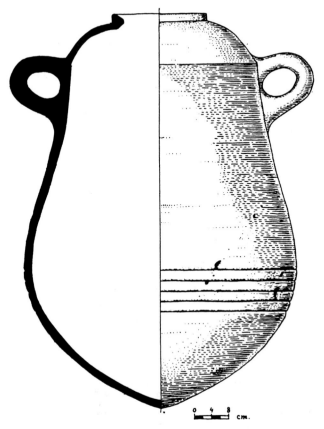

Fig. 53 Phoenician amphora from El Carambolo (seventh century BC)

agricultural and livestock potential afforded by the Guadalquivir valley. On this aspect, however, our information is minimal.

Another source of interest which would be difficult to verify archaeologically would be the slave trade, since it was considered to be one of the underlying reasons for Phoenician piracy in the Mediterranean and one of the pillars of Tyre's economy (Amos 1:9; Herodotus 2:54–55).

What did the natives get in exchange for all this? Assuredly oil and probably also wine, judging by the huge quantity of remains of Phoenician amphorae found in the Tartessian settlements in the provinces of Huelva, Cadiz and Seville (Fig. 53). The volume of oil imported into Tartessian territory argues for professional merchants, devoting them-

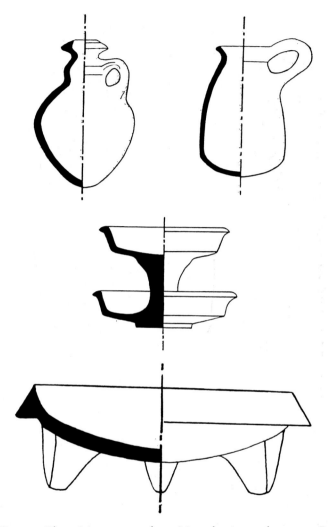

Fig. 54   Phoenician pottery from Mogador (seventh century BC)

selves to transporting amphorae from the great centres of oil production in the eighth to seventh centuries BC, such as Byblos and
Sarepta. During the seventh century BC, the Phoenicians transported
quality oil produced in Attica to the west, using small luxury amphorae
– the 'SOS' amphorae – also made in Attica.

Fig. 55   Astarte – bronze statuette, El Carambolo (eighth century BC)

The archaeological record likewise throws light on all kinds of merchandise and articles that the Phoenicians introduced into the territories of the interior, such as decorated pieces of ivory, imported from the east or made in workshops in Gadir, gold and silver jewellery, bronze jugs and, most of all, a great profusion of small receptacles – arryballoi, alabaster vases, bottles and flasks – which contained perfumed oils, essences, balms and cosmetics; there were also textiles, necklaces, glass beads and other trinkets (Fig. 54). In other words, a typically colonial system of trade existed: the production of genuine articles for 'export', such as the jars for unguents and perfumes which, to judge by their wide distribution in Andalusia, can be considered as one of the successes of Phoenician trade, in that they were able to create a demand for small luxury articles where there was none before.

A series of luxury and prestige objects such as jewels, ivories, bronze statuettes representing Astarte, cut glass and bronze jugs were destined for the Tartessian elite (Fig. 55). The concentration of luxury goods or prestige gifts in strategic areas like Huelva, Carmona, Carambolo, Setefilla, Aliseda and Cástulo, and forming part of princely grave goods, shows Gadir's interest in the peoples who controlled the main communication and access routes to the mineral and agricultural resources of the interior. The reciprocal exchange of gifts thus constituted one of the mechanisms used by Phoenician trade to attain its economic objectives. So one constant of trade in Lower Andalusia was the system of reciprocity, which appears to be restricted to the privileged sector of Tartessian society. And the exchange of silver, copper and tin for wine, oil and perfumes is an indication of unequal power and a typically colonial situation, rather than one of developed trade.

A situation in which exchange takes place between unequal societies can have only two consequences, also typically colonial: a social change within the indigenous society from the moment when certain sectors of the population are incorporated into the Phoenician trading circuit and take advantage of the situation, and a long-term frittering away of the resources of the territory.

The Atlantic trade: Lixus and Mogador

The classical sources mention that the Gaditanians sailed in big ships throughout the Mediterranean and the Atlantic Ocean and that, beyond the Straits of Gibraltar, there was a host of Tyrian colonies on the Moroccan coasts of the Atlantic, which subsequently became uninhabited and ruined (Strabo 3:1,8; 18:3,2; Avienus, O.M. 438–442 and 459–460). Indeed, it is known that the Phoenicians of Gadir used to sail beyond the Columns and in four days arrived at places abounding in shoals of tuna; they fished off the coasts of Mauritania as far as the river Lixus, with small boats known as *hippoi* because of the figurehead in the form of a horse on the prow (Pseudo-Aristotle, 136; Strabo 2:3,4). This is probably a reference to the Canary–Saharan shoals of fish, which even today are among the richest in the world.

The most important Phoenician installation in the area was Lixus, situated on a hill and dominating the fertile valley of the river Loukkos, close to its mouth (Fig. 56). Although this Phoenician settlement was thought to be very ancient (Pliny, *N.H.* 19:63), it has furnished very little archaeological documentation from the Phoenician period. It was an important Hellenistic and Roman city, with monumental temples which have so far yielded only a limited amount of ancient material from the seventh century BC as the sole evidence of the original Phoenician outpost, so we know very little about its extent and layout.

Nevertheless, what the Phoenicians were seeking was not just deep-sea fishing. The siting of Lixus on the mouth of the Loukkos

Fig. 56   View of the acropolis at Lixus

made the colony into a well-sheltered harbour at the entrance to one of the great navigable rivers of the Atlantic, an important consideration on an inhospitable coastline like that of Morocco, which was exceedingly dangerous to shipping and where, apart from Tangier, there were hardly any sheltered beaches or inlets.

In the hinterland of Lixus were powerful native kingdoms from which the Phoenicians were able to obtain ivory and gold. Lixus had access likewise to copper, iron and lead in the spurs of the Atlas mountains and deposits of salt in the Sahara and the Banasa region.

On the little island of Mogador, there was another Phoenician settlement, on the small side and of a temporary nature, used during the seventh century BC. Whalebone and fish remains indicate that this was a trading mart or shipping station devoted mainly to fishing.

Lixus and Mogador are of interest to us chiefly for their pottery – the best-known aspect of these Phoenician outposts on the Atlantic. This pottery, which includes a few Attic and Ionian amphorae, belongs in the same circuit of production and distribution as we find at the Castillo de Doña Blanca at the Puerto de Santa Maria. On the level of material culture, then, the Phoenician enclaves of Atlantic Morocco came within the orbit of Gadir and fitted into the Andalusian sphere of Phoenician hegemony, at least during the seventh century BC.

The name of Magón (*mgn*) is significant; it appears incised on Phoenician amphorae from Mogador and seems to be a seal of ownership. It is probably connected with a rich trader or seafarer from Gadir, belonging to the same social circles as the other Magón who was buried at Almuñécar with all his belongings and luxury possessions.

Overseas, the orbit of the commercial and fishing activity of Cadiz was not restricted to Lixus, Mogador or the Cassiterites. This can be inferred from the existence of two small settlements located at Rachgoun and Mersa Madakh in Oran, where the archaeological remains once more evoke the Gadir–Doña Blanca circuit in the seventh and sixth centuries BC. Probably these enclaves, devoted to commerce and fishing, acted as supply points for shipping making for Cadiz and the Straits of Gibraltar.

THE COLONIAL NETWORK ON THE EAST COAST OF ANDALUSIA AND IN IBIZA

The colonies of eastern Andalusia

Last of all we will set about analysing a coastal stretch lying roughly between Adra (Almeria) and the river Guadalhorce (Malaga) and occupied by Phoenician settlements, knowledge of which has provided one of the biggest surprises archaeology has been faced with in recent times. Indeed, this region, like Ibiza, was practically unknown to classical historiography and even erroneously linked by a few classical authors to Greek or Carthaginian colonization; yet today it constitutes one of the most spectacular and ancient archaeological clusters known in the western Mediterranean and its discovery has given an unexpected turn to the study of the Phoenicians in the west.

A historical reconstruction of the Phoenician enclaves on the Mediterranean coast of Andalusia rests exclusively on the archaeological evidence, which compensates to some extent for the lack of empirical data in Gadir itself, although it also involves risks. Thus the wealth of archaeological documentation recorded on sites like Toscanos, or the magnificence of the Phoenician necropolises at Trayamar or Almuñécar, has occasionally led to the importance of these Phoenician installations being distorted, because of the fascination exerted by Phoenician archaeology in the provinces of Malaga and Granada and because the cultural and economic weight of Gadir in western Andalusia and the Atlantic becomes forgotten. A few theories belong in this

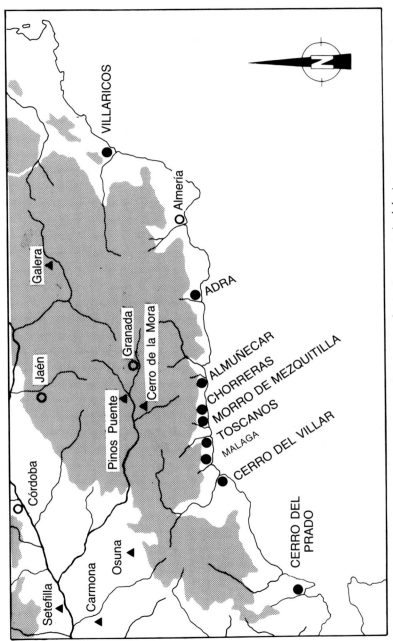

Fig. 57 The Phoenician colonies in eastern Andalusia

context, like those that argue that Gadir was a mere trading post whereas Toscanos and other Mediterranean enclaves would have been the genuine Tyrian colonies on the Iberian peninsula (Bunnens, 1985).

The classical historians prove very vague when describing this region, considered until a few years ago to have been colonized by the Carthaginians, and after 500 BC. Thus Strabo affirms that Malaka (Malaga), the city of the Saxitani (Sexi in Almuñécar) and Abdera (Adra) were Phoenician foundations (3:4,2–3), while other authors stress that this coastal region between Malaga and Almeria was crowded with Phoenicians in former times (Avienus, *O.M.* 440; 459–460). Since Malaka and Abdera were also called Libyo–Phoenician, that is, African Phoenician (Carthaginian), this territory was long considered to be a province of the Punic or Carthaginian period.

Nowadays, the first thing we notice in the coastal region between Malaga and Almeria is a great concentration of early Phoenician settlers, organized in small cities or ports that dominate the deltas of the main rivers in the provinces of Cadiz, Malaga, Granada and Almeria (Fig. 57). These eastern people settled down in the region for some 200 years (roughly between 770 and 550 BC), so we need have no hesitation in speaking of a genuine demographic explosion throughout the eighth century BC.

Some of these installations were hardly half an hour's walking distance apart and the distance between one centre and the next is, on average, some 800 metres to 4 km as the crow flies. Consequently it is not easy to determine the causes or significance of the presence of such a large colonial population in the region. Their relationship with Gadir is difficult to assess and their commercial function in relation to the metals of the interior is dubious. What is more, we have already seen in Chapter 6 how various maritime factors made it advisable for any vessel bound for Cadiz to anchor along that very stretch of coast in bad weather. But that alone does not justify the density of the stable and permanent Phoenician population in the region.

Settlement pattern

The topography and distribution of the settlements along the coast from Malaka to Abdera reflect a definite and very homogeneous settlement pattern. All have in common a location on a low coastal promontory at the mouth of a river.

There are no traces of Phoenician installations of this type either to the west of Cadiz or between Cadiz and the Straits of Gibraltar. Once

Fig. 58   View of Almuñécar

through the Straits, the first known Phoenician settlement is Cerro del Prado, in the bay of Algeciras and on the left bank of the mouth of the Guadarranque. Moving eastwards, this is followed by Cerro del Villar, in the mouth of the river Guadalhorce, the only known case in the region of a Phoenician island settlement. A few kilometres further on, the Phoenician enclave of Malaka dominated the river Guadalmedina at its mouth, and a little further on came Toscanos, on a hill dominating the then wide bay of the river Vélez, Morro de Mezquitilla and Chorreras on the river Algarrobo. Lastly, on the coast of Granada, Almuñécar, the ancient Sexi, was strikingly situated on the hill of San Miguel, dominating the delta of the rivers Verde and Seco (Fig. 58), and in the province of Almeria, Adra, the ancient Abdera, lay on the right bank of the Adra river.

The distances between one Phoenician establishment and another are surprisingly short. So, for example, between the settlement at Cerro del Villar on the Guadalhorce and the one at Malaka the distance as the crow flies is 4 km. Toscanos is 7 km away from Morro de Mezquitilla, and Chorreras is to be found 800 metres away from Morro de Mezquitilla. These distances cannot reflect the need for staging posts or bases for coastal shipping, so the reasons for such a concentration of early Phoenician population must be sought elsewhere. Obviously, for the strategic effectiveness of communications with the interior and coastal roads, visual links between one site and the next were highly desirable. So we should speak of compartmentalized control of the coastal territory.

The occupied area and the size of these establishments are fairly restricted by comparison with the big Phoenician colonies in Tunis or Sardinia. So for example, the area of Cerro del Prado and that of Cerro del Villar del Guadalhorce are estimated at one hectare each. Abdera and Morro de Mezquitilla each occupied some 2 ha, and Chorreras some 3 ha. Initially, Toscanos covered an area of 2.5 ha and only in the seventh century BC was it extended to cover 12 to 15 ha, including the surrounding defensive enclosure. It is obvious that these are small installations if we compare them with other Phoenician colonies like Gadir itself (some 10 ha) or Motya (some 40 ha), Kition (70 ha) or with Tyre (57 ha).

All the characteristics listed so far evoke the earliest model of Phoenician colonial settlement recorded in the west: the one described by Thucydides in pre-colonial Sicily, made up of a great number of enclaves set up on islands and coastal promontories for commercial purposes (Thucyd. 6:2,6).

Another feature to be stressed in the pattern of Phoenician settlement on the Mediterranean face of Iberia is the site chosen for the construction of the necropolis. Although we know only four early necropolises – the ones at Toscanos, Morro, Lagos and Almuñécar – they all follow the same geographic model: they are situated on the other bank of the river only a short distance from the area of occupation (Fig. 59). We are reminded of Gadir, where the necropolis is situated in the Puertas de Tierra region, on the other side of the Bahia-Caleta channel and facing the city.

The habit of siting the necropolis on the far side of a river bed or channel does not appear to have been a random occurrence, since we find it in Tyre as well. As will be remembered, the necropolis at Tyre must have been situated in Ushu or Paleotyre, on the mainland, just as happened in Delos, defined as a 'purified island' because it was devoid of tombs (Thucyd. 1:8). And Paleotyre was situated at the mouth of a river, the Ras el-Ain.

To conclude, let us remember that each and every one of the Phoenician establishments in eastern Andalusia combined all the right conditions for anchorages for shipping, located, as they were, on bays

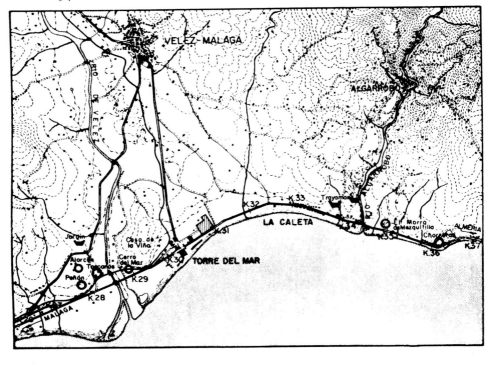

Fig. 59 The Phoenician colonies on the mouths of the Vélez and the Algarrobo

and inlets, well sheltered from winds and currents. The Phoenicians were familiar with the sea and knew where to site their permanent settlements.

The coast of Malaga, Granada and Almeria has changed considerably over the last 2000 years. River silts and changes in the basic river levels have filled up the ancient estuaries and moved the old Phoenician enclaves back from the coastline. Thus, for example, Toscanos, which today is a few kilometres from the sea, was originally a coastal port, as was Cerro del Prado, now 3 km from the sea. More striking is the example of Cerro del Villar, which today is a small mound some distance from the coast and which used to be an island in the middle of the estuary of the Guadalhorce (Fig. 60).

The advantage of an island settlement facing the mainland, like

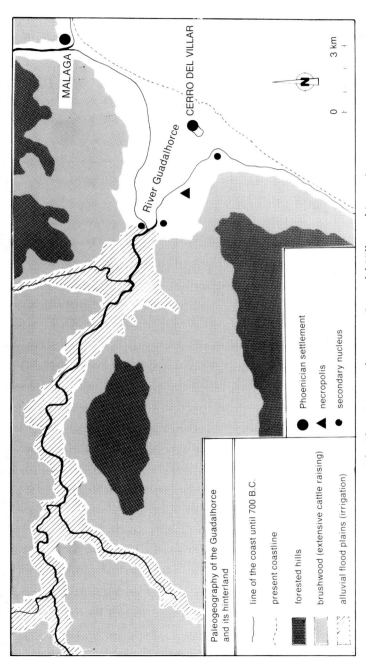

Paleogeography of the Guadalhorce
and its hinterland

——— line of the coast until 700 B.C.

- - - - present coastline

▓▓▓ forested hills

▒▒▒ brushwood (extensive cattle raising)

▒▒▒ alluvial flood plains (irrigation)

● Phoenician settlement

▲ necropolis

• secondary nucleus

MALAGA

River Guadalhorce

CERRO DEL VILLAR

N

0   3 km

Fig. 60   The Phoenician settlement at Cerro del Villar and its territory

Cerro del Villar, Gadir, Mogador, Sulcis or Motya, lay in the sureness
of its defence against possible dangers from the mainland or the sea.
Above all, it suggests wariness and prudence on the part of a few
colonists exposed to the rigours or threats of an unknown coast. In
general an island would constitute a bridgehead preparatory to a
subsequent occupation of the mainland. Moreover, by installing themselves on capes and promontories, they were guaranteed not only
natural defences but good visibility for shipping, a haven and a sheltered beach with facilities for loading and unloading.

We have already seen one constant factor apparently determining
the site of any early Phoenician outpost in the region: its position on a
river delta, which cannot have been accidental. Meanwhile, the situation on a river implies the possibility of following it upstream and, if
possible, as with the Vélez or the Guadalhorce, of sailing up it. A river
is, generally speaking, the ideal communication route insofar as by
simply following it upstream it is possible to gain access to the
resources of the interior and start trading with other groups. The
importance of rivers for ancient trade in general is only too well known
and is mirrored clearly in the Near East, where the term used for
market and trader – *kārum* – is the very one used to designate a
riverside wharf. Consequently a river means access to resources and a
favourable route for commercial penetration, facilities for the transport of merchandise and, in short, the economic autonomy of the
centre. But a river also means fertile lowlands and consequently the
possibility of irrigated crops.

Territory and resources

Between Adra and the Guadalhorce the coast lies relatively isolated
from the interior due to the Penibetic range of mountains, which runs
parallel with the shoreline at an average distance of only 20 km. The
range in turn forms a series of small, narrow alluvial valleys dominated
by a Phoenician post at the mouth, as has been seen. Several natural
ways through, like the river Guadalhorce itself or the course of the
Vélez through the gorge of Zafarraya, provide direct communication
between the coast and the plains of Antequera and the Vega de
Granada.

The region enjoys a warm, temperate climate, characterized by
short, mild winters, the mountains providing a barrier to the cold
winds from the north. The annual rainfall is some 300 to 400 mm with
five or six dry months in the year (May to October), which is reflected
in the flow of the rivers, such as the Vélez and the Algarrobo, com-

pletely dry in summer. This semi-arid climate, which produces a semi-steppe-like vegetation, has hardly changed in the last 3000 years, although we know that around 700 BC the humidity index was higher and extensive forests covered the mountains of the interior.

The intensive use of charcoal for smelting metals in ancient times and shipbuilding have been cited as probable causes of the deforestation. But, except at Villaricos (Almeria), where there are traces of the extraction of silver ore in the pre-historic and Carthaginian periods, the remaining territory is not exactly famous for spectacular metal deposits.

In reality, rich deposits of iron ore are known in the mountainous regions of Ronda, Archidona, Antequera, the upper Guadalhorce and Alpujarras, and mercury and lead are to be found in Adra and Granada. However, we have no proof that these were exploited in the Phoenician period. Moreover iron exploitation alone would not justify a Tyrian population staying in the same place for 200 years, since this metal is relatively accessible everywhere in the Mediterranean. We may take as an example Cerro del Villar, in the Guadalhorce, a Phoenician enclave a little more than 40 km away from the nearest iron mines in the Sierra Blanca de Marbella; it did not offer much in the way of facilities for processing iron. In the Malaga and Toscanos regions, the existence of copper and lead is documented 15 km from the coast, but there is no evidence that these very scarce metals were ever exploited.

The causes of deforestation such as has been observed in the mountains of the interior may have been quite different, cattle raising and intensive cropping perhaps. In order to reconstruct the economic activity of this type of Phoenician establishment, we must therefore of necessity resort to the archaeological record and to analyses of the fauna and other food resources.

Toscanos: an example of a commercial enclave

The archaeological record shows that considerable groups of Phoenician population gradually settled along the coast of Malaga, Granada and Almeria from the beginning of the eighth century BC. Around the years 580–550 BC, the majority of these centres were abandoned. The chronological sequence that has been established for Phoenician pottery – in particular the red burnished plates and jugs (Fig. 61) – fixes the time at which this commercial diaspora started at around the first decades of the eighth century BC, the time when the settlement of

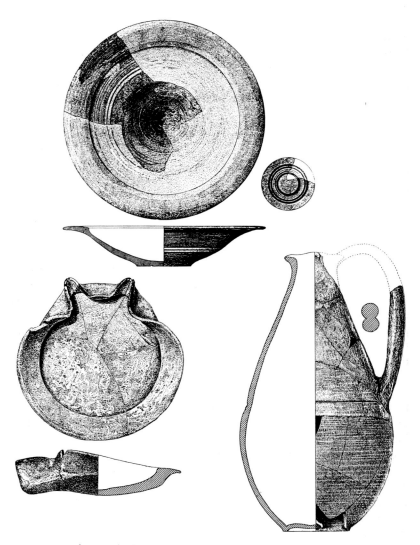

Fig. 61   Red varnished Phoenician pottery from Toscanos (eighth–seventh century BC)

Morro de Mezquitilla was founded on the banks of the Algarrobo. The majority of the Phoenician enclaves, however, appear to have emerged between the years 750 and 720 BC, as is the case for Toscanos, Chorreras or Almuñécar. Although differences and a certain hierarchical correlation between the settlements can be observed, an overall reconstruction of the process is possible on the basis of the history of Toscanos, the most extensively excavated of them all and the one about which we have the most information.

Toscanos was founded around the years 740–730 BC, judging by the chronology of the earliest pottery, all of which fits into the classic forms of Tyrian pottery of the eighth century BC (strata III and II at Tyre). Initially, a little band of Phoenicians occupied a small mound, the 'cortijo' or farm of Toscanos, dominating the plain of the river Vélez. There they built several large, isolated dwellings (building A), bounded by streets or paths similar to those of the contemporary Chorreras (Fig. 62). After this initial stage of occupation (Toscanos I) the settlement experienced considerable growth with new luxury dwellings being built (buildings H and K). During the second stage (Toscanos II), still dated to the eighth century, a tendency towards urban agglomeration is observed, possibly in response to a second wave of colonists, particularly notable being the construction of up-market houses, a phenomenon observed at the same date in Morro de Mezquitilla (phase B1) and Chorreras. In other words, the earliest architecture on these sites marks the arrival in the region of family groups or individuals of a fairly high economic level.

In the eighth century BC, an area of metal workshops was already being built in the settlement at Morro de Mezquitilla for the purposes of re-working and re-smelting iron locally. The appearance of this industrial zone on the edge of the housing area shows clearly the presence on the Algarrobo of a specialist population made up of qualified personnel, and once again does not fit in with the idea of an initial horizon of small trading posts for seafarers and modest merchants. At these same dates, at the end of the eighth century BC, the Phoenicians in Toscanos appear to have built a first fortification system surrounding the promontory, of which the corresponding ditch or trench cut in the rock has been preserved (Fig. 63).

Around the year 700 BC (Toscanos III), an important qualitative leap is observed in Toscanos which finally determines the economic character of the centre and is paralleled by similar changes taking place on the Algarrobo (Morro B2). An enormous building with three aisles and apparently two floors (building C) is erected in the centre of

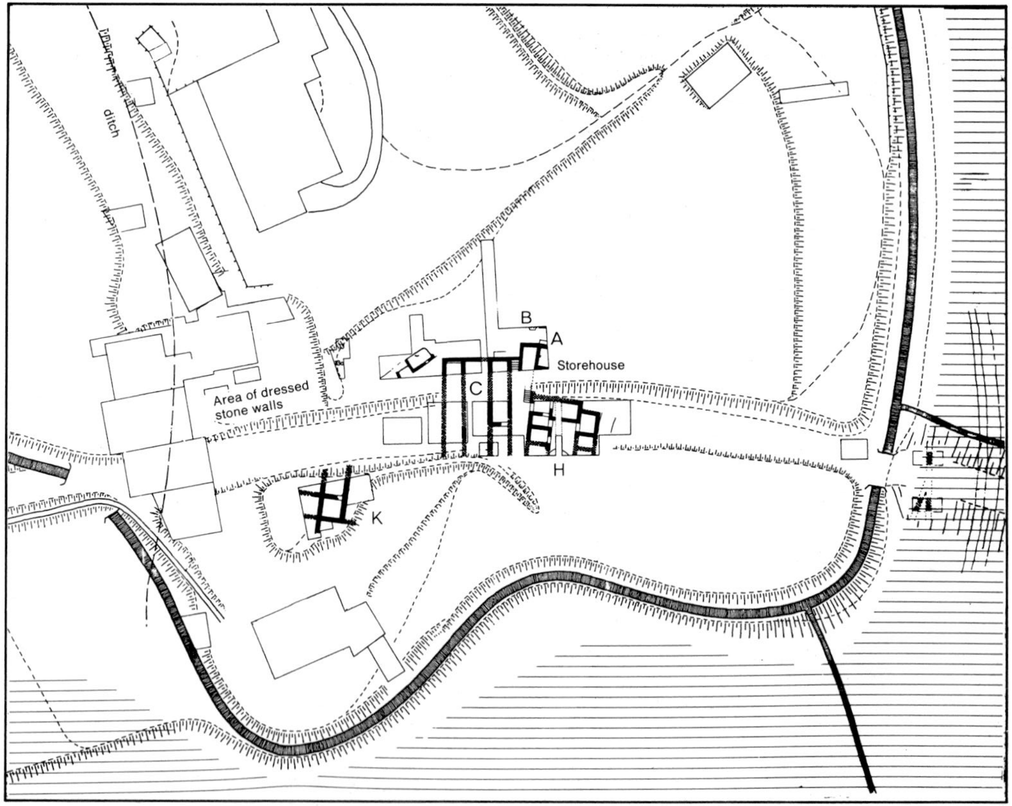

Fig. 62 Plan of Toscanos

Storehouse

A

B

C

H

K

Area of dressed
stone walls

ditch

Fig. 63   View of the triangular pit and ashlar wall, Toscanos

the hill at Toscanos and from then on it will act as a focus for all the economic activity on the site (Fig. 64). Its similarities to other structures in Motya and Hazor have allowed it to be classified as a warehouse or repository for merchandise. Inside it were found a great quantity of amphorae and vessels for storage and transport, confirming its function as a central installation for merchandise.

In the east a warehouse for merchandise, containing grain, oil or wine, was the characteristic structure of every marketing centre or geographical concentration of commercial transactions, and in general it was the forerunner of a market system. The marketplace was comparable to the modern suk and was generally an open-air site. Many of these early markets were converted later into cities like Carchemish, Kanesh or Hazor. In the Near East, the majority of these great repositories were of a private nature and in them great stocks of merchandise were stored for speculative purposes.

We do not know if this was the case with the warehouse in Toscanos. What is clear is that this building was of great architectural quality and occupied a central place in the life of the community. It is precisely at the time when the warehouse was being built that small dwellings or

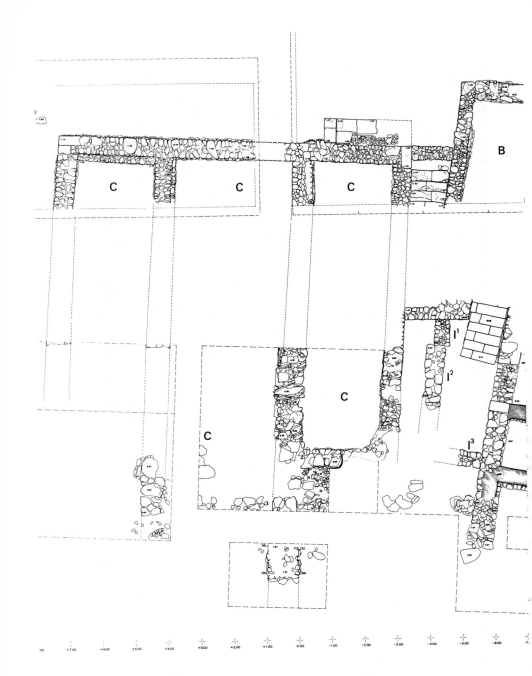

Fig. 64 Plan of the warehouse at Toscanos

Fig. 65 Bronze thymiaterion from Cerro del Peñón, Toscanos

huts appear for the first time in the vicinity of the edifice (houses E, F, G; not illustrated), probably intended for the staff of the warehouse and its services. And so the colonial population was organized and diversified socially.

The seventh century BC represents the period of maximum economic growth for all these coastal centres, except for the odd case, like that of Chorreras, where the place was abandoned. Toscanos at this time (phase IV) acquired an industrial district devoted to manufacturing articles of copper and iron for local use, and the settlement reached its maximum extent and invaded the hillsides around Peñón and Alarcon (Fig. 65). Around the years 640–630 BC, the population of

Toscanos reached some 1000 or 1500 inhabitants. At these dates a new walled precinct was erected. In the seventh century BC, Toscanos became a small cosmopolitan centre which, judging by the imports arriving in the Vélez region, maintained commercial contacts with Pitecusas, eastern Greece, Cyprus and the east.

Shortly after this commercial and urban highpoint, at the beginning of the sixth century BC (Toscanos V), the great central warehouse ceased to be used, the grand residences of the town centre were abandoned and the settlement was reorganized, to be finally abandoned around 550 BC. Something similar seems to have occurred in other nearby settlements. Some came into occupation again in the Punic period and others remained in ruins until the Roman period.

Economic activity

The Phoenician establishments on the coast of Malaga and Granada initiated very early commercial exchanges with the indigenous hinterland. This can be inferred from the presence of amphorae and imported articles from the second half of the eighth century BC in the native villages of the Vega de Granada and the interior of Almeria, such as Cerro de los Infantes, Pinos Puente, Cerro de la Mora and Peñón de la Reina. The presence of Phoenician amphorae in this region reflects the transport of oil or wine to the interior although we do not know what the economic rewards were. In any case, this was small-scale, local trafficking which never attained the volume of the trade in Gadir and the Lower Guadalquivir. These exchanges relied on excellent communications by river.

The presence of murex in Almuñécar, Toscanos and Morro de Mezquitilla indicates a purple cloth industry in the region, although the volume was not great. The Phoenicians also spent their time fishing for tuna, sturgeon, moray eels and other species, thus preparing the way for the famous industries based on fishing – salt fish, garum (a kind of fish sauce), preserves – which brought prosperity to this region during the Punic period in the fifth to first centuries BC, in particular to Sexi, Malaka and Abdera (Mela 2:94; Strabo 3:4,2).

All the industrial, commercial and fishing activity that these small Phoenician colonies developed appears to have been in response to a structure directed towards economic self-sufficiency. It is logical to think, therefore, that they needed sufficient arable land and pastures to feed a colony with a constantly growing population from the end of the eighth century BC. For this, the immediate territory offered them three alternatives: if it was occupied by an indigenous population, as was the case at Gadir, they could appropriate the land and extend their territorial sovereignty over irrigated areas and grazing land; a second possibility consisted in depending on the natives for a supply of meat and vegetable products. A third alternative was systematic occupation of the agricultural cattle-raising hinterland that was uninhabited or sparsely populated by indigenous groups.

The archaeological evidence seems to support the third alternative, that is, that the Phoenicians settled in a territory with an exceedingly sparse indigenous population scattered in small hamlets along the valleys and mountainsides. No doubt this facilitated the appropriation of a coastal territory rich in alluvial valleys and still today one of the most fertile in eastern Andalusia. Only intensive exploitation of the resources of the immediate territory could justify a prolonged stay by such a dense population from the east. Moreover, seen from this standpoint, the settlement pattern characteristic of this colonial network is more coherent – small, self-sufficient centres with their own territory and resources. It is the same pattern of land use that is prevalent today in the region, where we see substantial concentrations of people around the valleys, devoting themselves to intensive crop and animal husbandry. The real wealth of the coast of Malaga and Granada is rooted in the agriculture practised in its riverside lowlands, very fertile land and suitable for both irrigated and dry farming. What is more, only an economy of this nature practised since the Phoenician period, and not intensive metallurgy, could have degraded the countryside and the forest to this extent.

Furthermore, various archaeological, faunal and geomorphological studies of the territory reveal the following significant information.

In the first place they show that in the Phoenician period a mixed deciduous forest and open spaces with semi-steppe vegetation subsisted in the mountains close to the coast; the Phoenicians from Toscanos, Malaga and Cerro del Villar hunted deer, wild boar and wild cat there.

In the second place, we know that goats and sheep were raised in the environs of the Phoenician colonies, indicating a supply of wool, meat and milk at no great cost. Moreover, the high percentage of bovines in Toscanos, which had been increasing steadily from the beginning of the seventh century BC, indicates that cattle were used not only for meat but also for payment and as draught animals in the fields; this suggests indirectly that agriculture, for which native labour was probably used, was practised on the edges of the flood plain of the river Vélez: for example, Cerca Niebla and Vélez-Malaga (Fig. 59).

Lastly, in the estuary of the river Guadalhorce, the territorial conditions were ideal for high-yielding, irrigated agriculture. Archaeological finds at Cerro del Villar, such as stone querns, hint at cereal growing over an area of 18 km².

Consequently we have all the economic factors that could motivate the founding of this colonial network on the east coast of Andalusia: excellent harbour conditions and land communications for local traffic; abundant hunting and fishing in the region; availability of raw materials for internal industrial use; and territory with enormous agricultural potential, which could not only produce high yields per cultivated hectare but also in some cases cereal surpluses.

The necropolises and colonial society

Analysis of the necropolises is particularly important for a reconstruction of the social structure of a community. And the Phoenician necropolises situated along the coast of Malaga and Granada are doubly important because they are the only ones we know on the Iberian peninsula belonging to this early period.

In the west, we have a relative abundance of information about the period when the Phoenicians arrived at the Straits of Gibraltar, about their trading mechanisms, their economic objectives and even the institutional or ideological features underpinning this commercial enterprise. But we know almost nothing about those involved in it and their social origins; hence the importance of funerary archaeology in that the forms governing the funerary practices of a society are conditioned, in general, by the form and complexity of its social organization.

We have already seen that in Toscanos and other Phoenician centres on the coast, traders, metalworkers, storemen, stevedores, miners, fishermen, architects, craftsmen and potters were living, since a great deal of the Phoenician pottery was produced locally. This means that not all the population was involved in commerce.

The Phoenician population settled on the Mediterranean coast forms part of the cultural orbit of Gadir, Mogador, Lixus and, as we shall see, of Ibiza, an orbit defined by products of relatively uniform workmanship, the same settlement pattern and a few, very homogeneous trading circuits. In spite of several 'western' features, which reveal themselves in certain strange shapes of pottery – for example tripods, large lamps with two wicks, amphorae – this Phoenician society, probably dependent on Gadir, always maintained very close links with Tyre. In a way, the Phoenician material culture of the Iberian peninsula is more oriental or, if you like, Tyrian, than that of the groups in the central Mediterranean.

The Phoenicians who reached the shores of Andalusia or of Atlantic Morocco were not simple merchants, fishermen or sailors. The great central warehouse in Toscanos indicates that, from 700 BC onwards at least, a tendency for the settlements to specialize manifested itself in the region and they were distinguished one from another by their predominantly agricultural, mercantile or harbour activities. The storage capacity of the warehouse was undoubtedly greater than the needs of the population of Toscanos. The fortification of the place, too, and other urban elements denote a perfectly coordinated and to some extent centralized public and mercantile administrative organization. Lastly, the civic architecture of Chorreras, Toscanos and Morro de Mezquitilla suggests the presence in the region of a specialized and highly qualified mercantile 'bourgeoisie'. The form and content of their necropolises seems to point in the same direction.

So far, only four Phoenician necropolises are known on the coast of Malaga and Granada and even then only incompletely: the one for Toscanos, on the slopes of Cerro del Mar on the left bank of the Vélez, which has produced cremation tombs of the seventh century BC similar to those at Almuñécar; the one for Morro de Mezquitilla, at Trayamar, from the seventh century BC, on the right bank of the Algarrobo; the one for Lagos, near Chorreras; and, lastly, the one for Almuñécar, in Cerro de San Cristobal, the richest in numbers of burials from the eighth and seventh centuries BC.

One constant factor in all these necropolises is the absolute predominance of cremation, associated with a type of funerary offering that always follows the same model: two red-burnished jugs, intended perhaps to contain fragrant substances or water, plates for food, a lamp or censer placed next to the body and several amphorae and jewels placed in a recess or close to the burial (Fig. 66). The question of Phoenician cremation in the west is still an unknown quantity today; except in Carthage, it was much more common than inhumation until the sixth century BC. In ancient Carthage, cremation was sporadic and it was apparently very much a minority custom in Syria, where we note the first examples during the eleventh to ninth centuries BC in Hama, Tell Halaf and Carchemish, and in Phoenicia, where there are a few cremation burials from the eighth to seventh centuries BC in Tell Arqa, Khaldé and Tell er-Rechidieh, near Tyre (Appendix I).

In Andalusia, however, we must emphasize a significant feature: in

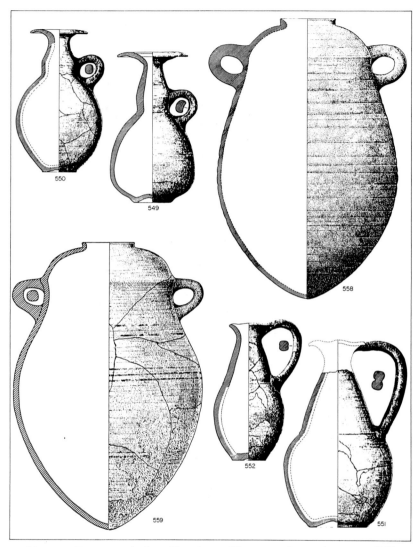

Fig. 66   Grave goods from Tomb 1 at Trayamar (seventh century BC)

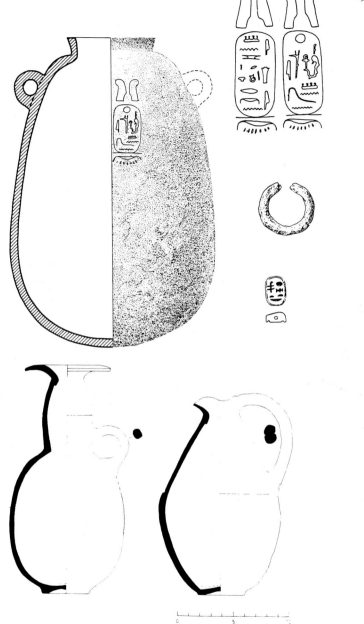

Fig. 67 Grave goods from Tomb 20 at Almuñécar (seventh century BC)

many of the cremation burials at Almuñécar, the ashes are placed in costly urns of alabaster or marble, made in Egypt (Fig. 67). In Trayamar or Toscanos, these alabaster urns could simply be imitations. The fact is that in Almuñécar some of them are adorned with inscriptions and emblems of the pharaohs of the Twenty-second Dynasty, such as Osorkon II, Takelot II and Sheshonq III, who governed Egypt between 874 and 773 BC.

These are undoubtedly exceptional pieces, proceeding from the sacking of royal Egyptian tombs or perhaps from gifts offered by the pharaohs to the king of Tyre–Sidon. These alabaster vases, which originally contained quality wine, have also been found in the royal palaces of Assur and Samaria, forming part of the booty of war or else gifts between royal houses.

We do not know under what circumstances they reached Spain, but the fact is that we have in Almuñécar one of the most spectacular collections of Egyptian royal pieces in the Mediterranean. The Phoenicians of Almuñécar elected to use them as cinerary urns which they deposited at the bottom of their grave pits, between 2 and 5 metres deep.

Furthermore, at Trayamar great hypogea built of ashlars and furnished with a wooden covering and an access corridor have been excavated (Fig. 68). The monumental architecture of these sepulchres reveals the presence in the Algarrobo and Morro de Mezquitilla region of eastern architects who used certain very standard techniques of rubblework in which stone and wood are combined, a technique known only in the east. The importance of these chambered tombs is that they were used for several generations all through the second half of the seventh century BC. So these great funerary chambers were periodically re-opened and several cremations were successively placed inside them, until the end of the seventh century when they were finally closed after the last burials had been deposited – this time, inhumations.

The chambered tombs of Trayamar were built in the vicinity of pit tombs similar to those at Toscanos and Almuñécar. Their great capacity, monumental architecture and re-use for one or two generations by members of a group or family suggest that we may be dealing with family hypogea or pantheons, intended to shelter the remains of a social group that clearly distanced itself from the rest of the population.

The family hypogeum can only mean a common funeral site for the members of a group that flaunts a permanent or exclusive burial area.

Fig. 68 Tomb 1 at Trayamar

This is only justifiable in the case of a kinship group which, in distant lands, maintains and ritually reinforces family bonds through continuing burial practices in the same funerary pantheon. A privileged sector of the eastern community is reproduced in the west through its monumental funerary architecture.

So the hypothesis that the burials in the chambered tombs of Trayamar were merchants, who died accidentally in the west on a journey or business trip, must be discarded. On the contrary, they are people who had decided to remain in the west and had invested time, money and energy in building their family sepulchres. The use of specialist architects and the costs in materials and dressed stone that the building of such hypogea would entail can only imply a high social status.

Both the tombs at Trayamar and those at Almuñécar and Toscanos confirm the presence in the Peninsula of specialist traders of high standing who dominated the economic and mercantile activity of this colonial network. The case of Trayamar suggests, moreover, the importance of the private firms or consortia that, in Phoenicia, were at the pinnacle of society. As you will recall, these trading companies, generally formed from families belonging to the merchant oligarchy, very close to the palace and so to the temple, were called *hibrum*, which means trading partnership or family unit. It is equally significant that in Akkadian the word for 'family' or 'house' (*bit. bitum*) also means 'firm' and that in Ugaritic the word for 'brother' or 'fraternity' means 'partner' or 'company' as well.

So the Phoenician necropolises and their contents mean that we can speak of commercial agents of some standing in the west and, above all, of the presence of elite family groups, permanently resident in the Straits of Gibraltar region and probably belonging to trading consortia with enough wealth and prestige to acquire luxury objects with a 'history', which, in the east, are pieces that belong in the circuits of reciprocal gifts exclusive to the royal houses of Tyre, Samaria and Assur.

Ibiza, a port of call on the shipping routes to the west

We have already described the importance of the island of Ibiza on the shipping routes to Gadir, in Chapter 6. Until a short while ago, Ibiza was considered to be a Carthaginian foundation: Carthage was thought to have founded the colony in the years 654/653 BC (Diodorus 5:16).

However, we know today that in Ibiza, as in the rest of the west, the Carthaginian element did not burst in until the sixth century BC, and prior to that the island was occupied by a Phoenician population very close, as regards material culture, to the group of Phoenician colonies on the Straits of Gibraltar and in Atlantic Morocco.

In the necropolis at Puig des Molins, cremation burials of the seventh and sixth centuries BC have recently been located. What is more, in the far south of Puig de Vila, where the old city of Ibiza is sited, the presence of early Phoenician pottery reveals the existence of a seventh century BC settlement in the style of the ones we know in eastern Andalusia. Lastly, on a small peninsula in the southwest of Ibiza, in La Caleta, another early colonial enclave of the seventh century BC was established.

The recent finds in Ibiza have given an unexpected turn to the study of the Phoenicians in the west by showing that they occupied a large part of the Mediterranean face of the peninsula at irregular intervals, but certainly from Ibiza–Alicante to the Straits of Gibraltar. The presence of Phoenician imports of the seventh century BC, for example, in the indigenous villages of Saladares and Peña Negra de Crevillente, both in the province of Alicante, points up the rapid commercial expansion that took place southeastwards from Phoenician Ibiza.

With all this, it is worthwhile reading Diodorus' text again. This historian from the first century BC is probably basing his account on

Timeus when he states that the island of Ibiza had a city, Ebesos or Ebusus (from the Phoenician Ibshim = island of pines), a Carthaginian colony that was inhabited by 'barbarians', mostly Phoenicians (5:16,2–3). On the other hand, Silius Italicus describes Ebusus as Phoenician (*Pun.* 3:362). So it is clear that when Carthage seized dominion in the island, it had already been occupied by Phoenicians.

Carthage occupied Ibiza for strategic reasons, as the Phoenicians had done before. From Ibiza as a bridgehead and with Gadir dominating the other extreme, the Phoenicians had absolute control over shipping to the western Mediterranean and the Atlantic.

THE CRISIS IN THE SIXTH CENTURY BC

The year 550 BC is usually considered to be the moment of transition from the Phoenician to the Punic phase in the west. This transition brought with it a major change in the geopolitical complexion of the western Mediterranean which took the form of a reorganization of the settlement pattern, economic and architectural changes, different pottery and transformations in the burial practices, with Punic inhumation replacing the old Phoenician cremation.

In the Iberian peninsula, the Punic period was accompanied by the very first appearance of traces of a cult and sanctuaries dedicated to Tanit, the principal deity of the Carthaginian pantheon, and by the presence of sober, functional pottery replacing the classic Phoenician red-burnished tableware. From the sixth century onwards, the first great urban centres like Ibiza appear; in them, the official religion of Carthage was imposed and the relatively peaceful trade of the eighth to seventh centuries gave way to a militarist policy that was to accompany the history of the west until Romanization. The old Phoenician settlements along the Mediterranean coast of Andalusia were abandoned, or were reorganized but always after a gap or generalized break.

In Gadir's sphere of influence, that is to say in the valley of the Guadalquivir and Huelva, all Phoenician activity and influence ceased in the years 600–580 BC. At those dates, Phocean trade bursts on the scene in Huelva and Greek merchandise and pottery reach the Tartessian port at that time. Probably the Greeks, who were then founding Massalia and Ampurias, momentarily took advantage of the trading vacuum left by the Phoenicians in Gadir. This event is picked up by Greek historiography through the well-known episode of the Phoceans and King Argantonio, who offered to let them settle in Tartessos

(Herod. 1:163). All this in turn prepared the way for the blossoming of the Iberian or Turdetanian world which grew out of the Tartessian cultural base but was more hellenized.

At the beginning of the sixth century BC, a profound economic crisis is observed in the Huelva region after the abandonment of silver extraction in Rio Tinto, which had been the basis of the wealth of Tartessos and was the reason for the founding of Gadir by Tyre. The silver had ceased to be profitable, although the mines had not been worked out, as is demonstrated by the renewal of extraction in the Roman period. This may constitute one of the reasons for the decline of Tartessos.

Other references show the complexity of the crisis. Thus, around 570 BC a Greek, Midocritos, journeyed to the Cassiterites in search of tin (Pliny, *N.H.* 7:1297), thanks probably to the relaxation of control of the Atlantic metal routes. Between 550 and 500 BC, an attempt was made on the part of the Turdetanian Iberians to storm Gadir from the sea (Macrobius, *Saturn.* 1:20,12). The city is thought to have been saved with help provided by Carthage (Justinus 44:5,2–4).

So in the middle of the sixth century BC the political balance in the western Mediterranean has been broken, and the change coincides with the beginning of the interventionist policy of Carthage in response to Greek expansionism. After sending military expeditions, Carthage seized Sicily and Sardinia at the end of the sixth century BC (Justinus 18:7,1–2).

It is not easy to determine the causes of such a complex and generalized crisis, in which the key appears to be the struggle between Carthage and the Greeks for dominion in the west. And it is not easy because all the indications are that Gadir managed to stay on the sidelines in the conflict and for a long time remained independent of the Carthaginian orbit. Furthermore, the crisis in the Phoenician colonies of eastern Andalusia does not appear to have occurred as a consequence of the Greek advance in the region but, on the contrary, the Phocean commercial incursion into Huelva and Andalusia in fact took advantage of a momentary trading vacuum.

The crisis of the Phoenician diaspora in the far west is probably due to problems that arose in the east since, from Gadir to Almuñécar, trade depended on a demand and on a few institutions that were basically eastern.

In the east, several circumstances converged in the politico-economic crisis through which Tyre was passing at the beginning of the sixth century BC. There can be no doubt that the fall of Tyre to

Nebuchadnezzar after thirteen years of siege (586–573 BC) must have had serious repercussions in the west, especially in the Iberian peninsula. But by then Gadir had already abandoned the silver trade and Toscanos had experienced the first symptoms of crisis. Moreover, as so often before, Tyre very quickly regained her power and prestige in the middle of the sixth century BC.

We must remember that the commercial network established around the orbit of Gadir was organized with the prime objective of obtaining silver, the demand for which came from Tyre and the trade in which was guaranteed as long as the Assyrian power existed in the interior. It was Iberian silver that allowed Tyre to recover economically and commercially and to keep her colonies in Spain; this was not the case with the colonies in Tunis, Sicily and Sardinia. The Phoenician colonies on the Iberian peninsula were directly dependent on Tyre through Melqart and his mercantile oligarchy, and they would only disappear insofar as the circumstances that gave rise to their creation disappeared in the east. And as will be remembered, all through the seventh century there was a declining demand for silver in Assyria, Tyre's prime customer, an inflationary situation as a result of the arrival of great quantities of silver, followed by a political crisis that culminated in the fall of the Assyrian empire in 612 BC into the hands of the Medes and Babylonians. The siege of Tyre came later and merely delivered the *coup de grâce* to an economic situation that made the presence of her commercial agents on the Straits of Gibraltar untenable.

To conclude, let us say that Gadir was undoubtedly the central axis of the Phoenician commercial diaspora to the western Mediterranean, the weight of which was felt in Tartessos during the eighth to seventh centuries BC through a process of social and economic change that we call 'orientalizing'.

There is no doubt that the Phoenicians generated wealth and prompted profound transformations within the indigenous societies of Andalusia and the Mediterranean seaboard. But this wealth was concentrated in minority sectors of the population, sectors known to us by their magnificent burials in Huelva, the Lower Guadalquivir and Estremadura.

But the Phoenicians also drained the resources of the west. If we add up the tons of silver taken from the mountains of Huelva and Seville, the ecological degradation and the deforestation following on the large-scale use of wood as fuel in the mining and metalworking, we must agree that the balance was a negative one for the Tartessian world.

On the east coast of Andalusia, intensive agriculture, the expansion of irrigation with the help of advanced technology, and animal husbandry, all prompted by the need to feed a considerable colonial population, involved a progressive move away from the areas devoted to pasture, a regression of the forested area, degradation of the environment and the transformation of large tracts of land into prairie and savannah. It is typical of the degradation of the countryside and of resources that occurs after a colonial period.

It has been suggested by one expert that the character of Phoenician society on the Iberian peninsula and the Atlantic coast of Morocco was an 'aberration' because it had no *tophets*. And yet, in all its cultural and religious manifestations, the most westerly group of colonies is closer to Tyre and its territory than the centres in the central Mediterranean. In Tyre and in Phoenicia the *tophet* is exceedingly rare, as we saw in the last chapter. And moreover, in Tyre as in Gadir, the god Melqart, the main focus and expression of the monarchy, coordinated the commercial activity and, in short, the economy.

10

Concluding thoughts

All through this volume, we have attempted to demonstrate that Tyre's commercial venture was far from being a uniform undertaking. Indeed, the expansion to the west, which constituted Tyre's last trading circuit and also her last monopoly, had arisen as a consequence of a situation marked by profound economic imbalances, with major deficits in, for example, metal and grain, but also with great surpluses – population, specialized production – which became more acute between the years 850 and 750 BC. The structural elements in this crisis must have influenced the orientation and development of the individual trading settlements of Tyre in the west, which were shaped primarily by the proposed objectives for, and the economic possibilities of, each territory. Thus, for example, the economic objectives pursued in the founding of Gadir could not have been the same as those that led to the founding of Carthage or Ibiza.

And yet there is a tendency to simplify the interpretation of the Phoenician settlement model in the west and to reduce the plan to two single possible alternatives – commercial expansion versus colonization. Similarly, it is customary to contrast two institutional models of long-distance trade – the state enterprise versus private initiative – as mutually exclusive mechanisms. But all these categories and terminologies, when used, have proved inadequate for assessing the complexity of the evolutionary process.

In effect, in order to reconstruct the forms of Phoenician expansion to the west, various categories of analysis are commonly proposed, based in general on the Greek colonial model – emporium, colony – or else on the substantivist theories of Polanyi's school – port of trade. A series of evolutionary stages in the west is also postulated, which would become a formula for compromise between different settlement patterns – the commercial emporium becomes a colony or city – by simply shuffling estimates of the area of occupation in the settlement or demographic theories.

The fact is that it is not easy to trace the boundaries between a colony and, for example, a commercial emporium since, in the last resort, very subjective criteria are in operation when it comes to an assessment of the different categories of colonial establishment. In general, Greek expansion to the west is thought to have been a fundamentally agrarian phenomenon with colonizing aims. As such, colonization would have been a movement of population aimed at acquiring new lands to farm, because of demographic and subsistence problems in the country of origin.

The term 'colonization', then, is economic and political in character insofar as it implies the emigration of groups of people to other territories where, by means of colonies or *apoikíai*, the residents maintain a 'feel' of their original community in matters of language, culture and political institutions. The essential characteristic of the Greek colony, or self-sufficient city-state, lies precisely in the fact that it had its own agricultural land, the *chora*, on the territorial organization of which depended the autonomy and sovereignty of the colonial structure.

This model is usually contrasted with the Phoenician overseas settlement, and it is asserted that the Tyrians were not seeking to occupy land but, basically, to obtain raw materials, if possible in places that offered harbour facilities and, in addition, would guarantee an indigenous clientele with whom to exchange merchandise. In this way, by stressing the exclusively commercial character of the Phoenician diaspora, its settlements in the west are reduced to the category of mere staging posts for shipping, trading marts and merchant ports, with no other purpose than trade. Only one Phoenician foundation in the west would have come into being with the rank of colony – Carthage – since its origins are connected with a phenomenon of political assimilation of territory.

Furthermore, a hierarchical scale is postulated in the ambit of the Phoenician establishments in the west, which goes from the lowest category of trading mart or temporary establishment in the form of a foreign branch, equivalent to the French *comptoir* and directed towards acquiring raw materials and engaging in industrial activity, to the highest category of commercial enclave, the *emporion* or centre for redistribution, equipped with warehouses for merchandise, inhabited by various kinds of merchant and organized around a temple. The best-known examples would be Al Mina, Naucratis, Pitecusas and Massalia. Only certain emporia would have attained the status of colony or city, as is the case with Naucratis, Pitecusas or Motya.

An eastern and substantivist version of the emporium would be the port of trade, administered by professional traders who act on behalf of the state and operate according to treaties and prices stipulated with the local or indigenous authorities. The fact is that, if we forget all its pre-mercantile and Polanyist connotations, the port of trade or merchant port is the closest to some of the Phoenician installations in the west, like Gadir itself.

As we have already stated in Chapter 4, the merchant port equipped with large warehouses, acted as a central site for the exploitation and distribution to the market of the natural resources of a territory and constituted the chief intermediate centre in long-distance trade. Its population was made up of professionals, high-ranking officials and guild organizations, who would usually settle in politically vulnerable regions, on the coast or the banks of a river, but with a hinterland that was rich in resources.

In western Asia, this institution was also called *kārum*, a centre administered by mercantile agents and consortia, whose activity was dependent on a central market (Assur, Tyre); in Phoenicia it developed under the aegis of the oligarchy. The merchant oligarchy was dependent on palace circles, although its activities did not exclude operations of a private nature.

Occasionally, these centres of international trade were no more than business areas, in the style of the Assyrian districts in Kanesh and Hattusas or the Phoenician districts in Damascus, Samaria and Memphis. An institution common to all of them was the temple, the protector of trade and the meeting place of merchants and natives; it represented the authority of Tyre or of Assur.

THE CONCEPT OF A 'COMMERCIAL DIASPORA'

Lastly, because of its importance, it is worth while drawing attention to a suprahistorical model of commercial expansion, which has been put forward recently by Curtin (1984) and which looks in particular at the dominant forms of interrelationship between trading communities with a common origin. This model, known as 'commercial diaspora', is defined by Curtin as a network of specialized communities, socially interdependent but spatially scattered, initiated by cultural minorities which, with time, tend to form a kind of monopoly over the indigenous or host society. According to this theory, the balance of political and social power would necessarily have been distorted in relation to the natives, in that the trader is a specialist and the native is not.

In any commercial diaspora, mercantile specialization and group solidarity would have dominated through various mechanisms ranging from what Curtin calls peaceful and neutral self-governing trading communities to commercial empires, run from a few colonial enclaves, genuine advance guards of the metropolis, in control of a broad territory and of exchange by coercion. The British and Dutch colonies in Asia in the sixteenth to eighteenth centuries would be an example of this.

As for the internal relations between the nodes of a diaspora, various degrees of formalism existed, ranging from a few minimal links, based on the solidarity afforded by a common religion, language and culture to colonies established as political entities controlled from a central colonial power – governor, viceroy – with the capital city, at least, in the country of origin, from where a powerful commercial firm would operate.

An example of the qualitative evolution of a commercial diaspora would be the Hanseatic League; its commercial network, initiated in the twelfth to thirteenth centuries by merchants in Cologne, gave rise to prosperous independent cities in North Germany and the Baltic in the fourteenth and fifteenth centuries.

In any case, ever since antiquity settlements arising from a commercial diaspora have been specialized and multi-functional centres, which came to form an independent network thriving on the different relationship of each settlement to its respective environment. This would logically have favoured a process of functional hierarchization and, in the long run, a phenomenon of political dependence by certain centres in relation to others. Something of this kind must have happened in the commercial network of Gadir or in the orbit of Carthage itself.

In spite of their relative autonomy, the centres of a commercial diaspora would have depended, in one way or another, still according to Curtin's model, on the metropolis. Therefore, the disappearance and decline of a commercial network of this kind was wont to occur when the trade ceased to be important for the metropolis.

THE WESTERN MODELS

We have already seen how certain categories of commercial or colonial settlement attributed to the Phoenicians do not match up to the empirical evidence in the west. So, for example, the model of the trading mart or merchant emporion does not fit the character of the establishments in eastern Andalusia, where the indigenous customers were very few or even non-existent.

By contrast, Gadir, which constituted the mercantile metropolis *par excellence* in the far west, is called *polis apoikos*, that is, colony, by Diodorus, after the author had assured us that Tyre's objective was not colonization but trade (Diodorus 25:10,1; 5:58,2–3; 5:74,1). So the contradictions are already arising in the Hellenistic and Roman period.

Elsewhere, it has been observed that the success of the Phoenicians in some areas of the west favoured the evolution of some of the bases or initial trading posts, like Ibiza or Motya, into genuine cities or colonies. From this point of view, the evolutionary process would have been the reverse of the Greek model: colonization would have succeeded trade and not trade agricultural colonization.

In the west, various models of Phoenician integration into the different occupied territories can be observed; their chief characteristics are determined by their own socio-political origins, their strategic function or their relationship with the territory being exploited economically. In this overall evaluation, we cannot leave aside an aspect that people often forget to mention when dealing with Phoenician expansion into the Mediterranean: that all through its history, the commercial policy of Tyre showed clear territorial and expansionist aspirations.

It is equally necessary to bear in mind that we are ignorant of the initial scope of the main colonies in the west. The evidence shows that the vast majority were founded throughout the eighth century BC, and that some of them, like the installations along the coastline of Malaga and Granada, brought in substantial contingents of oriental population from the start. In every case, it is between 720 and 700 BC that a spectacular growth of the western colonies is recorded, due, perhaps, to the arrival of a second wave of colonists or else to internal demographic growth, which is clearly going to coincide with their development and specialization. Around 700 BC the *tophet* at Carthage was established; Motya became a commercial and industrial centre of some standing and in Toscanos administrative buildings and mercantile installations arose, and so the functions of these colonies were diversified.

We shall go on to describe the main Phoenician settlement patterns recorded in the west. That will allow us, on the one hand, to review the whole discussion outlined in the course of the previous chapters and, on the other, to determine the mechanisms used by Tyre to consolidate her commercial empire. The models, which we propose to sum up in three large categories, are restricted to Carthage and Gadir, whose respective spheres of influence provide, in turn, various colonial models, aimed, to a greater or lesser extent, at making use of resources and raw materials.

The mercantile model of Gadir

Gadir was a mercantile metropolis, founded in response to the resources of Lower Andalusia – Tartessos – with which it established direct trade. This trade was centred to such an extent on the interests of supply and demand that in the end it generated a process of mutual dependence between the Phoenicians and the natives. As a projection of Tyrian society and its economy, the mercantile activity of the colony could have been controlled by powerful private traders and agents commissioned by the state, whose links with the political institutions of Tyre were established through the temple of Melqart. These 'merchant princes', in charge of important merchant fleets, operated as readily on their own account as on that of the king of Tyre, since, as we saw in chapter 4, in Tyre and other Phoenician cities the state and private spheres overlapped. In any case, the economy of Tyre depended on the success of its mercantile oligarchy abroad.

Gadir restricted itself to creating its own regions of mercantile exploitation – Atlantic Morocco, for example, and Oran – and gradually took control of the extraction of and trade in metals in the Lower Guadalquivir. The characteristics of Tartessian society, revolving around dense and relatively organized communities, determined the character and mercantile function of Gadir. In effect, Gadir did not control the Tartessian hinterland since that was already occupied by a developed population. For that reason, the only traces we know of Phoenician defensive systems or fortifications are limited to the city of Gadir itself.

Farming colonies

In eastern Andalusia we observe a genuine territorial strategy, aimed at controlling the agricultural hinterland from scattered farming units set up in a sparsely populated territory. The colonies of Toscanos, Morro de Mezquitilla and Almuñécar very soon developed a specialized production and formed small units in a single, vast territory devoted to crops and cattle raising.

The Phoenician tombs in Almuñécar or Trayamar denote the presence of a wealthy social class – a mixture of mercantile oligarchy and landowners – which specialized in managing trading expeditions and in the odd case was organized into family firms.

The construction of lines of fortifications in Toscanos, especially from the seventh century onwards, indicates the need to control and defend the territory at a late period in the history of this Phoenician colony.

A similar strategy is found in southwest Sardinia, where the main Phoenician colonies – Sulcis, Tharros – embark straightaway on a gradual control of the agricultural and mining lands, through a network of secondary establishments in the interior, which would later be transformed into fortifications for territorial control.

The aristocratic model of Carthage

In Carthage, rather than of a mercantile emporium, we must speak of an aristocratic colony, which very soon attained urban status and which, through its particularly puritanical and conservative civico-religious institutions, was to monopolize the economic and ideological activity of vast territories in the west.

Its ruling class, closely linked to the state and, especially from the sixth century BC onwards, with ownership of land, converted the North African metropolis into an aristocratic state, growing out of its own monarchic origins. The founding of Carthage was an institutional act, the work of Tyrian aristocrats who came into the possession of lands because of their status and who renewed and maintained firm links of friendship with Tyre until the Hellenistic period.

Tyre's western enterprise appears to us, then, to be somewhat multi-functional and fairly heterogeneous, a far cry from the theoretical assumptions that have so long predominated and that either reduce the Phoenician diaspora to a mere commercial adventure or else attempt to encapsulate it within a few predetermined plans.

With this book, on the contrary, we have sought to put forward a new reading of the subject, proposing a theoretical framework that incorporates new instruments of analysis and applies a whole body of new techniques and analytical methods, insofar as there are many questions that remain unanswered and extensive excavations in the Phoenician settlements are still rare. Among other things, we lack studies of settlement patterns which would tell us how the colonies evolved and what were the mechanisms of exchange with the occupied territory; we also lack studies of the geomorphology of the coastlines, analyses of anthracology and sedimentation and studies of fertility indices and land yields. Lacking, too, are quantitative analyses of the contents of the necropolises and *tophets* in the west, which could describe the social features objectively and clarify the arguments about the percentage of sacrifices and burials in the sanctuaries of Carthage, Sicily and Sardinia. Only by involving a range of analytical techniques and interdisciplinary studies shall we be able to go beyond simple inductive hypotheses based exclusively on the typology of artefacts.

Appendix I
Phoenician Iron Age archaeology

Archaeological information about the great Phoenician cities is almost non-existent, due to the uninterrupted occupation of the land right down to the present day. Nowadays, Beirut, Sidon and Tyre are still the chief cities of the Lebanon, which implies that Hellenistic, Roman, Byzantine and Islamic cities are superimposed. This makes any extended excavation impossible. A historical reconstruction of the Phoenician cities from the archaeological record has been feasible only in less major centres – Sarepta, Akhziv, Tell-Abu Hawam – or on the basis of stratigraphic *sondages* in urban nuclei like Tyre, with all the attendant negative implications, namely of a partial and restricted reading of the historical process.

Until a relatively short while ago, Phoenician material culture of the Iron Age was known to us in its principal manifestations – architecture, town planning, ceramics, gold work – basically through archaeological finds made in the west. The first reliable archaeological record was obtained in the colonies of the western Mediterranean. It is only a few years ago that the stratigraphic levels corresponding to Phoenician occupation in various sites on the Lebanese coast and in the Beqaa valley were reached. However, the majority of the systematic work undertaken since 1975 has been interrupted recently because of the war.

Hardly any archaeological remains from the Early Iron Age period in Phoenicia (1150–900 BC) are known. The greater part of the existing archaeological documentation is no earlier than Middle Iron I (900–725 BC) and comes chiefly from excavations of necropolises. Moreover it must be borne in mind that the earliest archaeological material recorded in the west and in the Iberian peninsula, particularly the pottery, corresponds without exception to the closing moments of that period in Phoenicia.

Let us now examine the main testimony provided by recent archaeology in Phoenician territory. For obvious reasons, we shall not concern ourselves here with the Late Iron Age period (600–300 BC) nor with later stages because these lie outside the limits of the present study.

A reading of the most significant data from Phoenician settlements will undoubtedly facilitate an analysis of the centres in the Iberian Peninsula and help us to make a correct diagnosis of the archaeological record. Without taking into account the archaeological evidence from the country of origin, it would be futile to claim to define the characteristic features of the western colonies from a broader, more global perspective.

The Middle Iron Age settlements (900–550 BC)

Of all the northern and central territory of Phoenicia, Byblos is undoubtedly the most intensively excavated so far. In spite of that, this port settlement has yielded only one indication concerning the levels of occupation in the first millennium BC. The same is true of Arvad, a city situated on an island unknown in terms of the archaeological record.

Tell Kazel and Tell Arqa

Only one northern site, that of Tell Kazel, lying to the north of Tripoli, has yielded interesting archaeological levels of the Early Iron Age. This settlement is commonly identified with the ancient city of Simyra or Sumur, mentioned in the Assyrian annals. In neighbouring Tell Arqa, the ancient Arqata, some Middle Iron Age necropolises have recently been located and we have become aware of the great development experienced by this city between the late ninth and early seventh centuries BC.

Al Mina and Tell Sukas

Lying, strictly speaking, outside the confines of northern Phoenicia, two port settlements, Al Mina and Tell Sukas, deserve special mention. Al Mina was established around 825 BC and was one of Syria's most important trading ports during the eighth century BC; thanks to its strategic position, in a very short time it came to dominate the great plain of Amuq and the trade routes to Cilicia, the Euphrates and Urartu. Al Mina was probably a key factor in the transmission of the Phoenician alphabet and other eastern elements to Greece. Other Greek enclaves, like Tell Sukas or Bassit, carried on, centuries later, the work initiated by the Euboeans of Al Mina at the end of the ninth century BC: the procurement of metals to supply the demands of the

Greek world and which the Phoenicians must already have been obtaining in the west. The archaeological evidence shows that at first in Al Mina, Greek traders and Phoenician residents from the south lived side by side. So the place must be defined as a neutral 'free port' in which the last Phoenician traders in Syria and the first Greek elements to settle in the Levant came together for a time.

An enclave with similar characteristics is Tell Sukas. In this port, situated on the Syrian coast a few kilometres south of Latakia, the Danish excavations of 1958–1963 discovered an Iron Age centre above rich levels of Late Bronze Age occupation. The commercial activity of this port seems to start around the tenth century BC, according to what can be inferred from one inscription. The original name of the city was Suksi, founded, apparently by Phoenicians. The colony was established in the centre of one of the most extensive and fertile plains of the Syrian coast, that of Djeble, on a hill lying between two excellent natural harbours.

In Tell Sukas, Early Iron Age necropolises have been excavated and also a *tophet*, situated to the south of the city and dated to the thirteenth to tenth centuries BC. Outstanding among the finds from the Middle Iron Age are an abundance of Greek–Cypriot pottery and a sanctuary of the seventh century BC of enormous proportions. From roughly 600 BC onwards, Sukas went on to become definitively a place of permanent residence for eastern Greeks until the destruction of the port in 550 BC. This change is inferred from the absolute predominance of Ionian and Rhodian pottery, the presence of Greek burials and, lastly, the progressive hellenization of the old Phoenician sanctuary.

Khaldé

In the north-central area of Phoenicia, the third city in importance after Arvad and Byblos was Beirut. The build-up of archaeological levels in the Lebanese capital makes access to the original Phoenician port of Berytos practically impossible. Nevertheless, in the years 1961–1966 an extensive necropolis, that of Khaldé (Fig. 69) was excavated in its territory, for the present the most important Iron Age funerary ensemble on the Phoenician coast. This necropolis has so far yielded more than 170 graves. The necropolis was used throughout two main periods: between the tenth and late ninth centuries BC (Khaldé IV) and between the late ninth and late eighth centuries BC (Khaldé III). During period IV, the rite of inhumation in a pit or cist predominated, while during the later period III, a few cremations appear, deposited in amphorae, alongside the inhumations, which are in the majority.

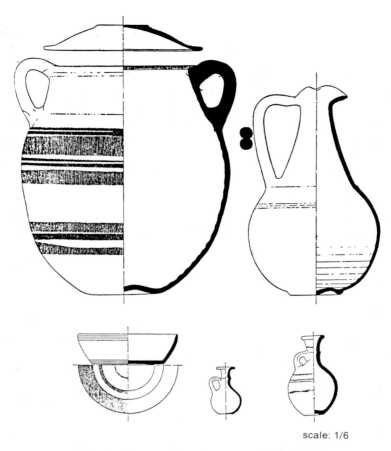

scale: 1/6

Fig. 69   Pottery from the necropolis at Khaldé

The importance of the Khaldé necropolis lies not so much in its size as in the data it has provided about Phoenician funeral practices, Middle Iron Age pottery styles and, in particular, Phoenician social organization. These data cannot possibly be inferred today from the urban settlements, given the current state of archaeological investigation in that field. Lastly, we should point out that the rite of inhumation associated with a funerary cist, such as appears in Khaldé, constitutes a funerary practice with a long tradition in Phoenicia, going back at least to the Late Bronze Age.

Sidon

In southern Phoenicia, Sidon is currently inaccessible to archaeological investigation. Nowadays Saida, the third city of modern Lebanon, is sitting on top of the famous Phoenician port. Nevertheless, in the territory situated inland from Sidon, the existence of two important necropolises situated at the foot of the hills dominating the city has been documented: the necropolises of Qraye and Tambourit. The distribution of the funerary nuclei around the Phoenician coastal cities and their position on slightly higher ground or at the foot of the mountains of the Lebanese pre-littoral corresponds to the characteristic topography of the whole southern zone of Phoenicia and we shall see this repeated again in the territory of Tyre.

In Tambourit, 6 km southeast of Sidon, a collective funeral cave was located a few years ago, with several cremation burials inside it. The presence of some Greek imports associated with the burials places the find between the years 850 and 775 BC.

In Dakermann, close to Sidon, another Phoenician necropolis, dated to around 600 BC, contained inhumation burials in cists.

Sarepta

In Sarafand, a place 10 km south of Sidon, is the site of ancient Sarepta, mentioned in the biblical texts because the prophet Elijah took refuge there in the ninth century BC. This city is described in Egyptian texts as early as the thirteenth century BC and for a long time was a satellite port of Sidon, although throughout the eleventh and eighth centuries BC it was incorporated into the territory of Tyre. Situated 100 metres above sea level and dominating a broad bay well suited to house a sheltered harbour, Sarepta combined all the necessary conditions to become the industrial port of neighbouring Sidon. In addition, it is the only Iron Age Phoenician city that it has been possible to excavate extensively, and it enables us to know the urban structure and layout of the inhabited area of a Phoenician city contemporary with the colonization of the west. Until Sarepta was excavated in 1969–1974, the stratigraphy of not a single Phoenician city of the Iron Age was known.

The place appears to have been inhabited for the first time during the Late Bronze Age and it has not been possible to recognize any level of destruction or violent break in its development to the Iron Age. Between the end of the ninth and the middle of the eighth centuries BC (stratum C), Sarepta entered its period of maximum activity and development, since a qualitative leap in all its cultural, industrial and architectural manifestations can be detected. The city becomes an important centre devoted to the manufacture and large-scale production of fine red-burnished ceramics – the 'classic' tableware that we shall see in the west and in the Hispanic enclaves.

In the industrial district of Sarepta, olive oil was produced in great stone presses, purple dye was made and bread was baked in countless circular ovens. From approximately the year 800 BC, in short, an increase in production at all levels is observed.

Among other interesting finds, that of the northern harbour with great blocks of worked stone and other structures for mooring ships is outstanding. Of note, lastly, is a sanctuary dedicated to Tanit–Astarte, which was in use during the eighth and seventh centuries BC. An inscription found in it contains a dedication to the goddess Tinnit or Tanit, a deity considered to be western and Carthaginian before the finds at Sarepta.

Tyre and its territory
A stratigraphic *sondage* of 150 square metres, directed by Bikai in the highest district of Tyre in 1973–1974 (Fig. 4), has been decisive for comparing data from written documentation with empirical or archaeological information. For the first time, an excavation in Tyre itself made it possible to record one of the few sequences of archaeological material so far obtained in Phoenicia. Moreover, the considerable volume of pottery found in the excavation has formed an invaluable instrument of analysis for revising Phoenician material coming from the Iberian peninsula and the west.

Bikai's excavation has made it clear that the island was in almost uninterrupted occupation from the Early Bronze Age. This has been one of the surprises furnished by the excavation since, up until then, it had been thought that Tyre had not flourished before the reign of Hiram I. The rich occupation levels from the Early Bronze Age (strata XXVII–XIX), dated to 2900–2500 BC, show considerable building activity and architecture comparable to that of other great Canaanite centres of the period.

Archaeology reports that the island of Tyre was abandoned all through the Middle Bronze Age, that is between approximately 2000 and 1600. Perhaps the population transferred to Ushu on the mainland during this period.

During the Late Bronze Age, between 1650 and 1050 BC, Tyre was inhabited again (strata XVIII–XIV). During this stage, a spectacular boom occurred in the purple cloth industry, judging by the find of hosts of shells of *Murex brandaris* and *Murex trunculus*. At the end of the Late Bronze Age (strata XV–XIV) symptoms of decline are observed and an interruption of industrial activities, but there is no evidence of the violent destruction seen in other cities of the period.

The occupation strata corresponding to the Iron Age (strata XIII–I) reflect extraordinary building activity and a thriving pottery industry, in particular in strata IX–VI of the excavation (850–800 BC). On top of this industrial district, in the years 760–740 BC (strata V–IV), great buildings of a monumental character were erected. After level I, dated to around 700 BC, the archaeological levels appear to have been destroyed by Roman constructions, which is why there is absolutely no documentation about Middle Iron Age II (725–550 BC) or the Late Iron Age (530–330 BC).

The most interesting levels, naturally enough, consist of strata IV–I and, in particular, the Tyre III–II horizon, dated to 740–700 BC, chiefly for their pottery, which is almost identical to that from the earliest levels of occupation in the Phoenician settlements of southern Spain. The most significant types of pottery from strata IV–I are the mushroom-lipped jugs, the trilobal-lipped jugs, the lamp with a single wick, the plates with a distinct rim, the tripods and the bowls (Fig. 70). They are the same shapes as we find, for example, in stratum I at Toscanos or Chorreras in Malaga. Neither in Carthage nor in the west in general are there at present any pottery finds earlier than the types characteristic of stratum IV in Tyre, dated to around 750 BC.

In addition, red-burnished, monochrome pottery – the kind documented in Andalusia – begins to predominate from the middle of the eighth century BC, the time when this type replaces the earlier bichrome material that we had noted in Khaldé and other funerary nuclei of Middle Iron I.

Among the finds made in the Tyre *sondage*, a protogeometric Greek vase, dated to the tenth century BC, and a Cycladic plate from stratum X and dated to 850 BC are outstandingly important for their chronology and its implications. The first constitutes one of the earliest Greek imports so far discovered in Phoenicia and would coincide with the beginning of Tyre's commercial expansion in the period of Hiram I.

On the mainland at Tyre, several necropolises from the beginning of the Middle Iron Age have been identified. Perhaps the most important of all is the one at Tell er-Rachidiyeh, lying 5 km to the south of Alexander's famous mole. Because of its position, then, it must be associated with the city of Ushu or Paleotyre. This necropolis has both

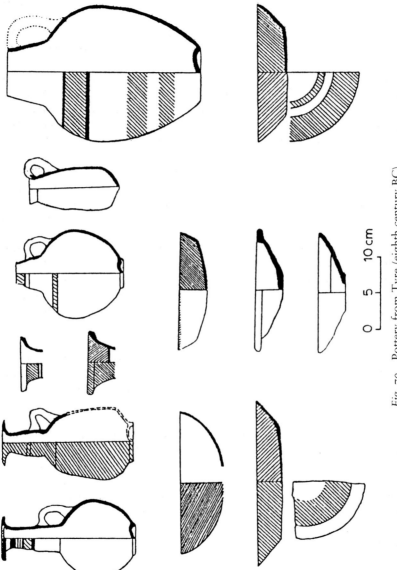

Fig. 70 Pottery from Tyre (eighth century BC)

0 5 10 cm

inhumations and cremations, although the latter predominate, especially during the eighth century BC.

The graves consist of a pit, square or circular in section, dug into the ground and approached by one or two steps. The pit ends in one of two hollows in which the cinerary urns and grave goods were deposited.

Other necropolises situated close to Tyre or in its hinterland are Qasmieh, Joya and Khirbet Silm. The last two contain equal numbers of inhumations and cremations; the one at Qasmieh has cremations exclusively. In these graves, the painted bichrome pottery stands out, with its decoration of painted red bands outlined in black; these outnumber the classic red-burnished ware.

Akhziv, Tell Abu Hawam and Tell Keisan

To conclude, we shall stress three important archaeological sites situated to the south of Tyre in Israeli territory. The first of these is Akhziv or Akhzib, mentioned in the Old Testament and situated between St John of Acre and Tyre. Akhziv was an important port enclave conquered by the Assyrians in 702 BC. On its outskirts, three Iron Age necropolises have been excavated; they differ from each other in their funeral rites and their chronology. The earliest necropolises date to the eleventh century BC and consist of inhumation burials. The southern necropolis, from the tenth to eighth centuries BC, is interesting: it is made up of two well-defined burial areas, one of large hypogeal chambers that contain collective burials, and the other containing exclusively cremations in urns deposited in open hollows in the ground. This area yielded many Phoenician funerary remains.

It has been deduced from this that two communities cohabited in Akhziv: the Israelite, which always rejected cremation of the corpse and individual inhumation, and the Phoenician, which burned its dead in accordance with the northern or Tyrian tradition. These dates also coincide with the period in which Tyre spread its territorial dominion down to Mount Carmel.

A little further south, in Tell Abu Hawam, there existed another Phoenician settlement, analogous with the one at Akhziv, situated on the bay of Akko or St John of Acre, between Mount Carmel and the river Quishon, where the city of Haifa stands today. It was a strategic enclave, from which Tyre dominated the plain of Asdralon and the road into the Jordan valley, Megiddo and Beth Shan.

The Phoenician enclave lay on top of Late Bronze Age levels (strata V–IV). The Phoenician levels (stratum III) date to between the beginning of the tenth century and 750 BC and contain pottery with a distinct Tyrian derivation.

The third Tyrian settlement in the Mount Carmel region is Tell Keisan (possibly ancient Ak-sa-pa), situated on a hill dominating the bay of Akko in Lower Galilee, the great alluvial plain of Asdralon, the mouth of the river Quishon and access to the great Palestinian centres of the interior like Megiddo. The excavations in Tell Keisan have shown uninterrupted Phoenician occupation from the tenth to the sixth centuries BC, with a climax in the eighth and seventh centuries. The archaeological finds clearly situate this enclave within the politico-cultural orbit of Tyre.

The extension of the frontiers of the kingdom of Tyre down to Mount Carmel during the tenth to eighth centuries BC is accompanied by considerable Phoenician influence over the territories of the interior of Palestine. The settling of Tyrian populations in Akhziv, Akko, Tell Abu Hawam and Tell Keisan coincides with the presence of Phoenician pottery of Middle Iron I in Hazor, Megiddo and Tell Qasile, among other Israelite cities.

Funeral rites

This set of archaeological finds raises the question of the duality of funeral rites existing in the Phoenician world during the Iron Age, which we shall see repeated in the colonies of the west, including the early Phoenician settlements on the Iberian peninsula, where the dominant funeral rite is again that of cremation.

In Syria–Palestine, cremation is documented for the first time in the eleventh century BC, in Carchemish, Hama, Tell Halaf, Hazor and at a few points in Cyprus. Attempts have been made on occasions to relate the introduction of this new burial rite to the invasion by the 'Sea Peoples' in the twelfth century BC. Whatever the reason for the origin of cremation in the region, one thing is certain, that from the middle of the ninth century BC this rite appears to take root in southern Lebanon chiefly, and in particular in the territory of Tyre and Sidon. Cremation is predominant in the Phoenician necropolises of the ninth to seventh centuries BC like Tambourit, Tell er-Rachidiyeh, Khirbet Silm, Joya, Qasmieh and Akhziv, although occasionally it coexists with a few inhumations. This contrasts with other territories in the north, where inhumation will continue to be absolutely dominant, as can be inferred from the finds in the Khaldé necropolis in Beirut.

The practice of inhumation in a pit or cist does not appear to have been totally abandoned in the south of Phoenicia. Moreover, a study of some late necropolises, like the ones in Sidon itself, makes a case for a return to the practices of inhumation from 600 BC onwards in southern Phoenicia.

Appendix II
The journey of Wen-Amon to Phoenicia*

YEAR V. IV MONTH OF THE III SEASON, DAY 16: the day on which Wen-Amon, Superior of the Forecourt of the House of Amon [Lord of the Thrones] of the Two Countries, left in search of timber for the great and august ship of Amon-Re, Sovereign of the Gods, who is in [the River called] 'User-het-Amon'. The day I arrived in Tanis, the place [where Ne-su-Ba-neb]-Ded and Ta-net-Amon were, I delivered the letters of Amon-Re, Sovereign of the Gods to them and they had (5) them read in their presence. And they said: 'I will do that which Amon-Re, Sovereign of the Gods, our [Lord] has said!' I SPENT THE IV MONTH OF THE III SEASON in Tanis. And Ne-su-Ba-neb-Ded and Ta-net-Amon despatched me with the captain of the ship, Menget-bet, and I embarked on the great Syrian sea IN THE I MONTH OF THE III SEASON, DAY I

I arrived at Dor, a city of the Tjekker, and Beder, its prince, made them send me 50 loaves, a jug of wine (10) and a leg of beef. And a man from my ship fled and stole a [vessel] of gold, [estimated] at 5 *deben*, four silver jugs, valued at 20 *deben*, and a bag of 11 silver *deben*. [The total of what] he [stole]: 5 *deben* of gold and 30 *deben* of silver.

I rose in the morning and went to the place in which the prince was, and I said to him: 'They have robbed me in your harbour. You are the prince of this land, and you are the investigator who should seek my silver. This silver belongs to Amon-Re (15), Sovereign of the Gods, lord of the countries; it belongs to Ne-su-Ba-neb-Ded; it belongs to Heri-Hor, my lord, and to other great personages in Egypt. It belongs to you; it belongs to Werret; it belongs to Mekmer; it belongs to Zakar Baal, the prince of Byblos.'

And he said to me: 'Though you be important and though you be eminent, take heed! I do not accept the accusation you present to me! Supposing it had been a thief from my land who went on board your ship and stole your silver, I should have compensated you from my

---

* Another English version of this text is available in J. B. Pritchard, *The Ancient Near East*, Princeton University Press, 1958, vol. I.

treasury until they had (20) found that thief of yours, whomsoever he may be. But the thief who robbed you belongs to you! He belongs to your ship! Remain as my guest a few days that he may be sought.'

I stayed nine days anchored [in] his harbour, and I went to call on him and I said to him: 'Hear me, you have not found my silver. [*Let*] me [*go*] with the ships' captains and those who go [to] sea.' But he said to me: 'Be silent! ...' ... I went out from Tyre at break of day ... Zakar Baal, the prince of Byblos ... (30) ship. I found 30 *deben* of silver in it and I took possession of it. [And I said to *the Tjekker: 'I have seized*] your silver, and it will remain with me [until you find my silver or the thief] who stole it! Although you may not *have stolen, it will remain with me. But as for you, ...' They went away and I relished my triumph in a tent [planted] on the shore of the [sea], [in] the harbour of Byblos. And [I hid] Amon-of-the-Road and placed his property inside him.*

And the [Prince] of Byblos sent me a warning, saying: 'Leave [my (35)] harbour!' And I replied to him, saying: 'Whither [*shall I go*]? ... If [*you have a ship*] that can transport me, send me back to Egypt.' Thus passed twenty nine days in his [harbour while] he [spent] the time sending to me daily and saying to me: 'Leave my harbour!'

THEN, WHILE HE WAS MAKING OFFERING to his gods, the god took hold of one of his young men and possessed him. And he said to him: 'Bring *[the] god*! Bring the messenger who brought him! (40) It is Amon who sent him! It is he who made him come!' And while the [young man] possessed spent that night in a frenzy, I had found a ship bound for Egypt and loaded all I had on to it. I was impatient for darkness, thinking that no sooner had it closed in than I would transfer the god on board also so that no other eye would see him, when the harbour master found me and said: 'Wait until morning, thus says the Prince.' And I said to him: 'Was it not you, by chance, who spent the time coming to me every day to say to me: "Get out [of] my harbour"? Tonight you say to me: "Wait (45) so that the ship that I have found will have sailed, and [then] you will come again [to] say to me: "Be off!"'?' At that, he went away and told it to the Prince. And the Prince sent orders to the captain of the ship, saying: 'Wait until morning, thus says the Prince.'

When MORNING ARRIVED, he sent for me and bade me go up, but the god stayed in the tent where he was, on the seashore. And I found him seated [in] his high room, with his back turned to a window, so that the waves of the great Syrian sea were breaking against the back (50) of his head.

And I said to him: 'May Amon *look favourably on you*!' But he said to me: 'How long is it now since you came from the place where Amon is?' So I said: 'Five months and one day till now.' And he said to me: 'You were truthful. It is well! Where is the letter from Amon that [you should have] in your hand? Where is the message from the high priest of Amon that [you should have] in your hand?' And I spoke thus: 'I gave them to Ne-su-Ba-neb-Ded and to Ta-net-Amon.' And he was much displeased and said to me: 'Let me see! You have neither letters nor messages in your hand! Where is the ship of cedar that Ne-su-Ba-neb-Ded gave you? Where (55) is its Syrian crew? Did he not deliver you to this foreign sea captain so that he should kill you and fling you into the sea? [And then] who would they have charged with seeking the god? And you also ... whom would they have charged with seeking you?' Thus he spoke to me.

BUT I SAID TO HIM: 'Was it an Egyptian ship or not? For indeed, the crews that sail under orders of Ne-su-Ba-neb-Ded are Egyptian! He has no Syrian crews.' And he said to me: 'Perhaps there are not twenty ships in my harbour that trade [hubŭr] with Ne-su-Ba-neb-Ded? As regards this Sidon (II 1), the other [place] through which you passed, are there not fifty more ships in it, that trade with Werket El, and are dependent on his house?' And at that I was silent for a very long time.

And he answered and said to me: 'What affairs bring you?' Thus I spoke to him: 'I came in search of timber for the great and august ship of Amon-Re, Sovereign of the gods. Your father did [it], (5) your grandfather did [it] and you also will do it!' Thus I spoke to him. But he said to me: 'Certainly they did it! And if you give me [something] for it, I shall do it. In truth, when my people fulfilled this charge, the pharaoh – life, prosperity, health! – sent six ships loaded with Egyptian merchandise and unloaded them in my storehouses. As for you, what do you bring me for your part?' And he bade them present the rolls of the annals of his fathers, and ordered them to be read in my presence, and they found a thousand *deben* of silver and all manner of things in his rolls.

(10) Therefore he said to me: 'If the ruler of Egypt were my lord, and I were his servant, he would not have sent silver and gold, saying: "Fulfil the charge of Amon!" They would not transport a royal gift, such as was the custom to do in the case of my father. As far as I am concerned, neither am I your servant! Nor do I serve him who sent you! If I shout to Lebanon, the heavens open and the logs lie at rest [on] the seashore! Give me (15) the sails that you carry to drive your ships, that will contain the logs for [Egypt]! Give me the ropes you

carry [*to fasten the*] logs [*of cedar*] that I must fell to build your . . . that I shall do for you [like] the sails of your ships, and the *spars* will be [too] heavy and will be broken, and you will die in the midst of the sea! Alas, Amon made thunder in the firmament when he placed Seth beside him! For indeed, Amon (20), when he established all the countries, on founding them, he set the land of Egypt, whence you come, before all; for the arts came out from her to reach the place in which I am. What are these stupid journeys that they oblige you to make?'

And I said to him: '[It is] not true! My errands "are" not stupid journeys! There is no boat in the River that does not belong to Amon! The sea is his, and Lebanon, of which you say "It is mine!" is his. It constitutes (25) the *nursery* of User-het-Amon, lord of [every] ship! Certainly he spoke – Amon-Re, Sovereign of the gods – and said to Heri-Hor, my lord: "Send me!" Therefore he bade me come, carrying this great god. But alas, you contrived that this great god should be anchored twenty nine days [in] your harbour, although you were unaware [of it]. Is he not here? Is he not the [same] as he was? You are stationed [here] to continue the trade of Lebanon with Amon, its lord. About what you say that the earlier kings sent silver and gold, suppose that they had had life and health; [then] they would not have had such things sent! (30) [But] they sent them to your fathers in place of life and health. Now, as regards Amon-Re, Sovereign of the gods, he is the lord of this life and of this health, and he was the lord of your fathers. They devoted their lives to making offerings to Amon. And you, also, are the servant of Amon! If you say "Amon: Yes, I will do (it)!" and you fulfil your charge, you will live, you will be prosperous, you will be healthy and you will be a cause of wellbeing to your whole land and your people. [But] may you not desire for yourself anything belonging to Amon-Re [Sovereign of] the gods. Why, a lion wants his own property. Have your secretary come so that (35) I may dispatch him to Ne-su-Ba-neb-Ded and Ta-net-Amon, *magistrates* whom Amon designated in the north of his land, and they will order that all kinds of things be sent. I will order him to say to them: "Let it be brought until I return again to the south, and I will [then] have occasion to pay every bit of the debt [owing to you].' Thus I spoke to him.

Therefore, I entrusted my letter to his messenger, and loaded the *keel*, the poop and the prow, with four other hewn logs besides – seven in all – and had them sent to Egypt. And in the first month of the second season, the messenger who had gone to Egypt returned to me in Syria. And Ne-su-Ba-neb-Ded and Ta-net-Amon sent: (40) 4 crocks and 1 *kak-men* of gold; 5 silver jugs, 10 garments of royal linen; 10

kherd of good linen from Upper Egypt; 500 rolls of finished papyrus, 500 cowhides; 500 ropes; 20 bags of lentils and 30 baskets of fish. And she handed to me [personally]: 5 garments of fine linen from Upper Egypt; 5 *kherd* of fine linen from Upper Egypt; one bag of lentils and 5 baskets of fish.

And the Prince rejoiced and he detailed three hundred men and three hundred beasts and appointed supervisors over them that they should fell the trees. Therefore they cut them down and they were there in the second season.

In the third month of the third season, they dragged them [to] the seashore and the Prince appeared and stopped beside them. And he ordered me to be called (45) saying: 'Come!' When I presented myself to him, the shadow of his lotus flower fell on me. And Pen-Amon, a majordomo belonging to him stopped me short, saying: 'The shadow of the pharaoh – life, prosperity, health! – your lord, has covered you.' But he was displeased with him and said: 'Leave him in peace!'

Therefore I approached him and he answered and said: 'Now, the charge that my fathers accomplished formerly, I have accomplished it [also], although you have not done for me what your fathers would have done and what you too [should have done]! Now, the last part of your timber has arrived and is [here]. Satisfy my desire and load it: perchance they will not give it to you? (50) Do not contemplate the terror of the sea! If you contemplate the terror of the sea, you will see mine [likewise]! In truth, I did not do with you what I did to the messengers of Ha-em-Waset, who spent seventeen years in this land: they died [where] they were!' And he said to his majordomo: 'Take him and show him the *tomb* in which they lie.'

But I said: 'Let it not be shown to me! As regards Ha-em-Waset, he sent you men as messengers, and he himself was a man. You do not have one of his messengers [in me], to whom you may say: "Go and see your companions!" Now then, you should rejoice (55) and order that a stele be raised for you, saying on it: "Amon-Re, Sovereign of the gods, sent me Amon of the Road, his messenger – life prosperity, health! – and Wen-Amon, his human messenger, in search of timber for the great and august ship of Amon-Re, Sovereign of the gods. I felled it. I transported it. I provided it with my ships and my crews. I ensured that they will arrive in Egypt, so as to beg Amon for fifty years of life for myself over and above my destiny." And it may happen that, in the fulness of time, a messenger may arrive from the land of Egypt, who knows writing and will read your name on the stele. And you will receive water [in] the West, like the gods who are (60) there!'

And he said to me: 'What you have said to me is a great testimony of words!' So I said to him: 'Concerning the many things you have said to me, if I reach the place where the high priest of Amon is and he sees how [you have performed this] charge, it will be [the performing of this] charge that *will obtain* something for you.'

And I went [to] the seashore, to the place where the timber was, and I espied eleven ships of the Tjekker coming in from the sea intending to say: 'Take him! Prevent his ship from [going] to the land of Egypt!' Then I sat down and wept. And the scribe of the Prince came to me (65) and said: 'What is the matter?' And I said to him: 'Have you not seen that the birds are descending on Egypt a second time? Look at them! How they travel to the fresh pools! [But] how long shall I be here! Do you not observe that they are coming again to take me?'

Therefore he went to refer the matter to the Prince. And the Prince started to weep because of the words that were spoken to him, because they were pitiful. And he sent me his scribe and he brought me two jugs of wine and a sheep. And he sent me Ta-net-not, an Egyptian songstress, who was with him, saying: 'Sing for him! Do not allow his heart to be distressed!' And he sent (70) to me to say: 'Eat and drink! Do not allow your heart to be distressed, for tomorrow you will hear what I have to say.'

The morning came, he called together his assembly, and he stood up in the midst of it and said to the Tjekker: '[Why] did you come?' And they said to him: 'We came to harass the *accursed* ships that you are sending to Egypt with our adversaries!' But he said to them: 'I cannot take the messenger of Amon into my land. Let him depart and then pursue him and capture him.'

Therefore I embarked and set out from the sea harbour. And the wind drove me to the land [of] Alashiya. And the men of the city came out to kill me, but *a way opened for me* between them to the place where Heteb, the princess of the city, was. I met her when she was leaving one of her houses and entering another.

And so, I saluted her and said to the people she had around her: 'Does nobody among you understand Egyptian?' And one of them said: 'I understand [it].' Therefore I said to him: 'Inform my lady that I heard, in distant Thebes, where Amon is found, that injustice is perpetrated in all cities, but, instead, in the country of Alashiya, justice is done. But, here injustices are committed daily!' And she said: 'What! What do you [mean] (80) by your words?' And I said: 'If the sea is stormy and the wind throws me on to your land, you should not consent that *they take* me to kill me, for I am a messenger of Amon.

Hear me, as for me, they will still seek me to assassinate me! As for this crew of the Prince of Byblos, whom they are preparing to kill, shall not their lord find ten of your crews, which he will kill?'

She summoned the people, who came together. And she said to me: 'Spend the night . . .'

(The papyrus breaks off at this point. It is permissible to conclude that Wen-Amon returned safely or successfully to Egypt, since the story is told in the first person.)

Appendix III
Oracles against Tyre

Isaiah

Oracle on Tyre

23 ¹ Oracle on Tyre:
　　Howl, ships of Tarshish,
　　for your fortress has been destroyed.
　　They learn the news
　　on their way from the land of Kittim.
　² Be struck dumb, you inhabitants of the coast,
　　you merchants of Sidon,
　　whose goods travelled over the sea,
　　over wide oceans.
　³ The grain of Nile, the harvest of the river,
　　formed her revenues,
　　as she marketed it throughout the world.
　⁴ Blush, Sidon,
　　for thus speaks the sea,
　　'I have not laboured nor given birth,
　　not reared young men
　　nor brought up young girls'.
　⁵ When the Egyptians learn the fate of Tyre,
　　they will be appalled.
　⁶ Take ship for Tarshish, howl,
　　you inhabitants of the coast.
　⁷ Is this your joyful city
　　founded far back in the past?
　　Whose footsteps led her abroad
　　to found her own colonies?
　⁸ Who took this decision
　　against imperial Tyre,
　　whose traders were princes,
　　whose merchants, the great ones of the world?
　⁹ Yahweh Sabaoth took this decision
　　to humble the pride of all her beauty
　　and humiliate the great ones of the world.

¹⁰ Till the soil, daughter of Tarshish,
the harbour is no more,
¹¹ He has stretched his hand over the sea
to overthrow its kingdoms;
Yahweh has ordained the destruction
of the fortresses of Canaan.
¹² He has said: Rejoice no more,
ravished one,
virgin daughter of Sidon.
Get up and take ship for Kittim;
no respite for you there, either.
¹³ Look at the land of Kittim . . .
They have set up towers.
They have demolished its bastions
and reduced it to ruins.
¹⁴ Howl, ships of Tarshish,
for your fortress has been destroyed.

The subjection of Tyre

¹⁵ That day, Tyre will be forgotten for seventy years. But in the reign of another king, at the end of the seventy years, Tyre will become like the whore in the song:

¹⁶ Take your lyre, walk the town
forgotten whore.
Play your sweetest, sing your songs again,
to make them remember you.

¹⁷ At the end of the seventy years Yahweh will visit Tyre. Once again she will begin to receive the pay for her whoring. She will play the whore with all the kingdoms on the surface of the earth. ¹⁸ But her profits and wages will be dedicated to Yahweh and not stored or hoarded. Her profits will go to buy abundant food and splendid clothes for those who live in the presence of Yahweh.

Ezekiel

Against Tyre

26 ¹ In the eleventh year, on the first of the month, the word of Yahweh was addressed to me as follows:
² 'Son of man, since Tyre has jeered at Jerusalem,
"Aha! It is shattered, that gate of nations;
it is opening to me; its wealth is ruined",

³ very well, the Lord Yahweh says this:
Now, Tyre, I set myself against you.
I mean to cause many nations to surge against you
like the sea and its waves.
⁴ They will destroy the walls of Tyre,
they will demolish her towers;
I will sweep away her dust
and leave her a naked rock.
⁵ She will be a drying-ground in mid-ocean for fishing nets.
For I have spoken – it is the Lord Yahweh who speaks –
she will be the prey of the nations.
⁶ As for her daughters on the mainland,
these will be put to the sword,
and everyone will learn that I am Yahweh.
⁷ For the Lord Yahweh says this.
From the North, I am sending Nebuchadnezzar,
king of Babylon, king of kings, against Tyre
with horses and chariots and horsemen,
a horde of many races.
⁸ He will put your daughters
on the mainland to the sword.
He will build siege-works against you,
cast up a mound against you,
raise a siege-tower against you;
⁹ he will break down your walls with his battering-rams,
and demolish your towers with his siege-engines.
¹⁰ His horses are so many their dust will hide you.
Noise of his horsemen and his chariots and wagons
will make your walls tremble as he rides through your gates
like a man entering a conquered city.
¹¹ His horses' hoofs will trample through your streets;
he will put your people to the sword,
and throw your massive pillars to the ground.
¹² Your wealth will be seized, your merchandise looted,
your walls razed, your luxurious houses shattered,
your stones, your timbers, your very dust, thrown into the sea.
¹³ I will stop your music and songs;
the sound of your harps will not be heard again.
¹⁴ I will reduce you to a naked rock
and make you into a drying-ground for fishing nets,
never to be rebuilt;
for I, Yahweh, have spoken
– it is the Lord Yahweh who speaks.

¹⁵ 'The Lord Yahweh says this to Tyre: When they hear of your fall,

the groans of your wounded and the havoc inside your walls, will not the island shake?

[16] 'The rulers of the sea will all get off their thrones, lay aside their cloaks and take off their embroidered robes. Dressed in terror they will sit on the ground unable to stop trembling, terrified at your fate.

[17] 'They will raise a dirge and say to you:

> "You are destroyed then, swept from the seas,
> city of pride,
> you who were mighty on the sea,
> you and your citizens,
> who used to terrorise
> the continent far and near.
> [18] Now the islands are trembling
> on the day of your fall;
> the islands of the sea are terrified by your end."

[19] 'For the Lord Yahweh says this:

'When I make you as desolate as any depopulated city, when I bring up the deep against you and the ocean covers you, [20] I will cast you down with those who go down to the pit, down to the men of old; I will make you live in the regions underground, in the eternal solitudes, with those who go down to the pit, so that you can never come back and be restored to the land of the living. [21] I will make you an object of terror; you will not exist. People will look for you and never find you again – it is the Lord Yahweh who speaks.'

A lamentation over the fall of Tyre

27 [1] The word of Yahweh was addressed to me as follows, [2] 'Son of man, raise the dirge over Tyre. [3] Say to Tyre, that city standing at the edge of the sea, doing business with the nations in innumerable islands, "The Lord Yahweh says this:

> Tyre, you used to say: I am a ship
> perfect in beauty.
> [4] Your frontiers stretched far out to sea;
> those who built you made you
> perfect in beauty.
> [5] Cypress from Senir they used
> for all your planking.
> They took a cedar from Lebanon
> to make you a mast.
> [6] From the tallest oaks of Bashan
> they made your oars.

They built you a deck of cedar inlaid with ivory
from the Kittim isles.
7 Embroidered linen of Egypt was used for your sail
and for your flag.
Purple and scarlet from the Elishah islands
formed your deck-tent.
8 Men from Sidon and from Arvad
were your oarsmen,
Your sages, Tyre, were aboard
serving as sailors.
9 The elders and craftsmen of Gebal were there
to caulk your seams.

All the ships of the sea and the sailors in them visited you to trade with you. 10 Men of Persia and Lud and Put served in your army and were your warriors. They hung up shield and helmet in you. They brought you glory. 11 The sons of Arvad and their army manned your walls all round and kept watch from your bastions. They hung their shields all round your walls and helped to make your beauty perfect. 12 Tarshish was your client, profiting from your abundant wealth. People paid you in silver and iron, tin and lead for your merchandise. 13 Javan, Tubal and Meshech traded with you. For your merchandise they bartered men and bronze implements. 14 The people of Beth-togarmah traded you horses, chargers, mules. 15 The sons of Dedan traded with you; many shores were your clients; you were paid in ivory tusks and ebony. 16 Edom was your client, because of the variety and quantity of your goods; she exchanged carbuncles, purple, embroideries, fine linen, coral and rubies against your goods. 17 Judah and the land of Israel also traded with you, supplying you with corn from Minnith, wax, honey, tallow and balm. 18 Damascus was your client, because of the plentifulness of your goods and the immensity of your wealth, furnishing you with wine from Helbon and wool from Zahar. 19 Dan and Javan, from Uzal onwards, supplied you with wrought iron, cassia and calamus in exchange for your goods. 20 Dedan traded with you in horse-cloths. 21 Arabia and even the sheikhs of Kedar were all your clients; they paid in lambs, rams and he-goats. 22 The merchants of Sheba and Raamah traded with you; they supplied you with the best quality spices, precious stones and gold against your goods. 23 Haran, Canneh and Eden, traders of Sheba, Asshur and Chilmad traded with you. 24 They traded rich clothes, embroidered and purple cloaks, multi-coloured materials and strong plaited cords in your markets. 25 The ships of Tarshish crossed the seas for your trade.

Then you were rich and glorious
surrounded by the seas.

[26] Out to the open sea
your oarsmen rowed you.
The east wind has shattered you,
surrounded by the seas.

[27] Your riches, your goods, your cargo,
your crew, your sailors,
your caulkers, your commercial agents,
all the soldiers
you carry with you the whole host
who are aboard:
all will sink surrounded by the seas
on the day of your shipwreck.

[28] When they hear the cries of your sailors
the coasts will tremble.

[29] Then the oarsmen will all desert
their ships.
The sailors and seafaring people
will stay ashore.

[30] They will raise their voices for you,
and weep bitterly.
They will throw dust on their heads,
and roll in ashes;

[31] they will shave their heads for you,
and put sackcloth round their waists.
They will raise a bitter dirge over you,
in their despair;

[32] They will raise a dirge and mourn for you,
they will bewail you:
Who could compare with haughty Tyre
surrounded by the seas?

[33] When you unloaded your goods
to satisfy so many peoples,
you made the kings of the earth rich
with your excess of wealth and goods.

[34] Now you are shattered by the waves,
surrounded by the seas.
Your cargo and all your crew
have foundered with you.

[35] All those who live in the distant islands
have been horrified at your fate.
Their kings have been panic-stricken,
their faces quite cast down.

³⁶ The traders of the nations
   have whistled at your fate,
   since you have become an object of dread,
   gone for ever."' '

Against the king of Tyre

28 ¹ The word of Yahweh was addressed to me as follows, ² 'Son of man, tell the ruler of Tyre, "The Lord Yahweh says this:

Being swollen with pride,
   you have said: I am a god;
   I am sitting on the throne of God,
   surrounded by the seas.
   Though you are a man and not a god,
   you consider yourself the equal of God.
³ You are wiser now than Daniel;
   there is no sage as wise as you.
⁴ By your wisdom and your intelligence
   you have amassed great wealth;
   you have piles of gold and silver
   inside your treasure-houses.
⁵ Such is your skill in trading,
   your wealth has continued to increase,
   and with this your heart has grown more arrogant.
⁶ And so, the Lord Yahweh says this:
   Since you consider yourself the equal of God,
⁷ very well, I am going to bring foreigners against you,
   the most barbarous of the nations.
   They will draw sword against your fine wisdom,
   they will defile your glory;
⁸ they will throw you down into the pit
   and you will die a violent death
   surrounded by the seas.
⁹ Are you still going to say: I am a god,
   when your murderers confront you?
   No, you are a man and not a god
   in the clutches of your murderers!
¹⁰ You will die like the uncircumcised
   at the hand of foreigners.
   For I have spoken – it is the Lord Yahweh who speaks."' '

The fall of the king of Tyre

28 ¹¹ The word of Yahweh was addressed to me as follows, ¹² 'Son of man, raise a dirge over the king of Tyre. Say to him, "The Lord Yahweh says this:

You were once an exemplar of perfection,
full of wisdom,
perfect in beauty;
¹³ you were in Eden, in the garden of God.
A thousand gems formed your mantle.
Sard, topaz, diamond, chrysolite, onyx,
jasper, sapphire, carbuncle, emerald,
the gold of which your flutes and tambourines are made,
all were prepared on the day of your creation.
¹⁴ I had provided you with a guardian cherub;
you were on the holy mountain of God;
you walked amid red-hot coals.
¹⁵ Your behaviour was exemplary from the day of your creation
until the day when evil was first found in you.
¹⁶ Your busy trading
has filled you with violence and sin.
I have thrown you down from the mountain of God,
and the guardian cherub has destroyed you from amid the coals.
¹⁷ Your heart has grown swollen with pride
on account of your beauty.
You have corrupted your wisdom
owing to your splendour.
I have thrown you to the ground;
I have made you a spectacle for other kings.
¹⁸ By the immense number of your sins,
by the dishonesty of your trading,
you have defiled your sanctuaries.
I have brought fire out of you to consume you.
I have made you ashes on the ground
before the eyes of all who saw you.
¹⁹ Of the nations, all who know you
are lost in amazement over you.
You are an object of terror;
gone for ever." '

(Taken from the Jerusalem Bible, published and copyright 1966, 1967, and 1968 by Darton Longman and Todd Ltd and Doubleday & Co. Inc., and is used by permission of the publishers.)

Appendix IV
The settlements of the central Mediterranean

Utica

This Phoenician colony, considered to be older than Carthage, was situated 40 km to the northwest of Carthage. From its position on a hill or small island, Utica controlled the mouth of the Bagradas and its fertile alluvial plains.

Of the ancient Phoenician colony, we know only its two necropolises, that of Ile (seventh to sixth centuries BC) and that of la Berge (seventh to fifth centuries BC). The most interesting fact to bear in mind regarding these necropolises, which so far have not furnished any material earlier than the eighth century BC, is their monumental funerary architecture, which is a reflection of a sophisticated and opulent Phoenician society, grown rich on maritime trade, to judge by the imports found in their tombs. In addition, this is a style of funerary architecture that is closer to that of the western Phoenician centres (Trayamar, in Malaga) than to that of Carthage itself.

As in Carthage, the ancient colony of Utica does not appear to have developed any relevant agricultural activity at first, nor to have started an immediate process of controlling the surrounding territory. Moreover, in the sixth century BC there is still no mention of Utica alongside Carthage in the outstanding political events of the day, such as the battle of Alalia. This suggests that until 540 BC Utica was still maintaining political and economic autonomy in relation to its powerful Carthaginian neighbour.

In spite of the scant documentation at our disposal about Phoenician Utica, there are three features we should remember here: its position on the mouth of a river, its ancient funerary architecture and, lastly, the absence of a *tophet* in the place, three features that place Utica close to the group of western colonies, rather than to the focal point of Carthage.

Panormo, Solunto and Malta

The Phoenician enclaves of Panormo and Solunto, situated on the island of Sicily, have not so far yielded any information on a par with that from neighbouring Motya.

All we know of Phoenician Panormo (the modern Palermo) are its necropolises, in use from the seventh century BC on. It seems that Panormo was a rich and opulent city under the sway of Carthage (eighth to sixth centuries BC), when a surge in population and building is recorded.

As for Phoenician Solunto, we still do not know its ancient site.

The small islands of Malta, Gozo and Pantelleria were also considered to be Phoenician colonies, destined to serve as a refuge or port of call on voyages to the west, because of their position and their excellent natural harbours (Diodorus 5:12, 3–4).

Although there are still no traces of permanent Phoenician enclaves, it is thought that the main centre in Malta could have been sited at Melita, the modern Medina–Rabat. There is evidence of the presence of Phoenicians in the Rabat region from the end of the eighth century BC, but they did not coalesce into great centres of population in the manner of Tunisia, Sicily or Sardinia. Malta is thus distanced from the settlement pattern defined in Carthage or Motya, which shows a marked tendency towards concentrating the population spatially. Malta, on the contrary, shows a scattered and limited population, as can be deduced from the distribution and volume of Phoenician tombs.

In spite of known graves from the late eighth century BC (Gajn Qajjet), the majority of the Phoenician burials correspond to the seventh century BC and are located in the interior and the west of the island, significantly the areas most populated by indigenous groups: Mtarfa, Rabat, Dingli. We should point out in this regard that the Phoenician pottery from Malta is morphologically more closely related to that of the more western centres – Andalusia, Oran, Lixus, Mogador – than to that of the central Mediterranean. A possible causal factor might be a separate origin for the Phoenician population in the west.

Undoubtedly the most important site in Malta is the sanctuary of Tas Silg, providing an opportunity to analyse the process of integration of the Phoenician colonists into the indigenous communities of the west. This is a sacred precinct used jointly by the Late Bronze Age indigenous population and the Phoenicians, who dedicated it to Astarte during the seventh century BC. All this lends weight to the view that Malta was used on the part of the Phoenicians as a support and transit base for shipping rather than as a colonial settlement.

As for the islands of Gozo and Pantelleria, the archaeological evidence still shows no traces before the fifth century BC.

Nora, Bithia and Tharros

We must omit Cagliari from the Phoenician establishments in Sardinia because of insufficient archaeological information concerning the early period.

As for Nora, its famous monumental inscription seems to suggest that the arrival of the Phoenicians coincided with the building of a temple to Pumay. It also states the tradition that Nora was the earliest Phoenician foundation in Sardinia. However, so far not a single archaeological trace earlier than the seventh century is known.

Ancient Nora was situated on the Capo di Pula, right on the gulf of Cagliari and 30 km distant from that city. The settlement, perched on the cape itself, was separated from the mainland by an isthmus to the north, on which stood the precinct of the *tophet*. The corresponding necropolis was situated on the mainland. Only in the sixth to fifth centuries BC was the city fortified and a temple built dominating the colony and the harbours, which provides a parallel with what has been observed at Motya.

Judging by the archaeological record, Nora does not seem to have developed a strategy of expansion into the interior in the early period, nor are there any traces of control of the hinterland, so characteristic elsewhere of the Phoenician centres in Sardinia.

Phoenician Bitia or Bithia was situated at the top of the promontory of Torre di Chia, beside the mouth of the river Chia and dominating two inlets suitable as natural harbours.

The archaeological record suggests that the Phoenician settlement was founded at the end of the eighth century BC and that it experienced rapid growth throughout the seventh and sixth centuries BC.

The early necropolis was situated to the north of the Chia promontory, on the mainland, following a model identical to the one we have seen in Nora. As in Sicily and the rest of the Phoenician enclaves in Sardinia, the characteristic funeral rite was cremation which, in the Punic period, was replaced by inhumation. The *tophet* of Bithia lies on the island of Su Cardulinu, to the northeast of the settlement.

As in Sulcis and Bithia, in Tharros, too, the presence of Phoenicians from the eighth century BC has been verified. Its topography also follows the usual settlement pattern in Sardinia: the early enclave is located on a cape, the Cape of San Marco, joined to the mainland by an isthmus. The settlement is situated right on the isthmus, to the east of Torre di San Giovanni and the corresponding necropolis lies to the south of the inhabited area and the northeast of the cape, in Punta Gabizza. In the Punic period, two other necropolises were set up, one in San Giovanni di Sinis, to the north, and the other in the far south of the settlement.

As in other Phoenician colonies, the *tophet* is situated on the periphery, to the north of the urban nucleus and close to the walls of the city. The elements characteristic of an urban centre consist not only of the *tophet* but also of a central sanctuary or templet, built in the eastern part of the cape of San Marco in the early period. Consequently, Tharros attained urban status, or at least equipped itself with civic institutions very quickly and perhaps as early as Sulcis.

There are no proofs, however, that Tharros exercised territorial sovereignty in the manner of Sulcis during the eighth to sixth centuries BC, although it seems likely that it very soon took control of the fertile agricultural valleys of the plain of the Sinis. On the other hand, there is clear evidence that it was a very active colony in the commercial sphere and that it developed a specialized production of luxury and gold articles for the rich Etruscan and Latin customers of mainland Italy.

Following the Carthaginian military intervention in all these territories in the middle of the sixth century BC, we observe for the first time in Sardinia an intensive exploitation of iron ore and a systematic occupation of all the agricultural regions of the interior of the island.

The Euboean connection

It is the general opinion that the massive arrival of the Greek element in the west was prejudicial in the long run to Phoenician trading interests in the Mediterranean, which meant that the Phoenicians found themselves obliged to change their strategy in the matter of exchanges and spheres of influence. There is also often talk of opposing interests, struggles for control of markets and an allocation of areas of competence and power. And yet the evidence seems to contradict this hypothesis of competitive spheres during the period of Phoenician expansion.

The earliest Greek colony in the west is Pitecusas or Pithecoussai (Ischia), founded by the Euboeans in the year 760 BC and consequently contemporary with the first Phoenician presence attested by the archaeological record: Carthage, the east coast of Andalusia and perhaps Sulcis. The settling of Phoenicians in western Sicily consequently comes after the settling of Greeks in Ischia and Cumas (around 750 BC).

As will be remembered, the absolute chronology of the Phoenician diaspora to the west was established mainly on the basis of Euboean–Cycladic pottery imports of Pitecusan provenance, reflecting, among other things, an exchange of products between Ischia, Carthage and Sulcis at the dawn of Tyrian expansion. On the strength of these imports in the central Mediterranean ambit, the Phoenician foundations of Carthage and Sardinia seem to pre-date those of Sicily and Malta.

The earliest pieces of late-geometric Greek pottery from the *tophet* in Carthage (around 760 BC) are identical with the ones we find in the earliest horizon of the colony of Pitecusas and it was undoubtedly that Greek colony or its offshoot, Cumas, that channelled these products to the Phoenician colonial establishments. Some of these pieces, indeed, were produced by a Pitecusan workshop, as is the case of the Euboean urn from the *tophet* at Sulcis and an imitation proto-Corinthian vase found in a Phoenician tomb at Almuñécar, from the mid seventh century BC.

Phoenician ceramics and inscriptions have, in turn, been found in Ischia, which suggests the presence of Semitic craftsmen or traders in the Greek colony at the end of the eighth century BC. What is more, the find of an occasional metal fibula in Pitecusas, combined with certain shapes of imported Phoenician pottery, give a glimpse of the existence of direct contacts between the Greek colony and southern Spain at the end of the eighth century BC. In any case, Phoenician expansion towards the west seems to be connected in some way with Euboean activity and there may well have been common interests and enterprises, at least in the years 760–700 BC.

This symbiosis between the Phoenician and the Euboean is no novelty to us since we had already noticed a similar phenomenon in the eastern Mediterranean. Indeed, at the end of the ninth century BC Phoenicians and Euboeans were developing joint trading activities in Al Mina and Tell Sukas.

Because of all this, it is difficult to see Euboean colonization in the west as a competitive undertaking, prejudicial to Phoenician trade. In both enterprises certain common features are noticeable, such as the quest for metals, the same settlement pattern – coastal promontories and small islands – piracy, and probably a certain private component from the start. What is more, the economic objectives, far from being conflicting, are complementary. Thus the main interest of the Greeks of Pitecusas and Cumas are centred on exploiting and acquiring tin, copper and iron ore from Tyrrhenian Etruria, whereas the initial objective of the Phoenician diaspora appears to have been directed towards Atlantic metals.

Like many Phoenician enclaves in the west, the colony of Pitecusas did not take long to become an industrial centre, devoted to working silver – coming, perhaps, from Gadir – and smelting and working iron, obtained from the island of Elba.

Bibliography

I WHO WERE THE PHOENICIANS?

The name

Baurain, C. 'Portées chronologiques et géographiques du terme "phénicien"', *Studia Phoenicia* IV, pp. 7–28 (Namur, 1986).

Bunnens, G. 'La distinction entre phéniciens et puniques chez les auteurs classiques', *Atti del I Congresso Internazionale di Studi Fenici e Punici*, pp. 233–238 (Roma, 1983).

Edwards, R. B. *Kadmos the Phoenician. A Study in Greek Legends and the Mycenean Age* (Amsterdam, 1979).

Garbini, G. 'Chi erano i fenici?' *Atti del I Congresso Internazionale di Studi Fenici e Punici*, pp. 27–33 (Roma, 1983).

Moscati, S. *Problematica della civiltá fenicia*, C.N.R. (Roma, 1974).

'Fenicio o punico o cartaginese', *Rivista di Studi Fenici* XVI (1988), pp. 3–13.

Muhly, J. D. 'Homer and the Phoenicians', *Berytus* 19 (1970), pp. 19–64.

Röllig, W. 'On the origin of the Phoenicians', *Berytus* XXXI (1983), pp. 79–93.

Tzavellas-Bonnet, C. '"Phoinix"', *Les Etudes Classiques*, LI, pp. 3–11 (Namur, 1983).

'La Légende de Phoinix à Tyr', *Studia Phoenicia*, I–II, pp. 113–123 (Leuven, 1983).

The territory and the forbears in the Bronze Age

Albright, W. F. *The Role of the Cananites in the History of Civilization, The Bible and the Ancient Near East*, pp. 328–362 (New York, 1961).

Baramki, D. *Phoenicia and the Phoenicians* (Beirut, 1961).

Dunnand, M. *Fouilles de Byblos*, Direction Générale des Antiquités de la République Libanaise (Paris, 1973).

Dussaud, R. 'Topographie historique de la Syrie antique et médiévale', *Bibliothèque Archéologique et Historique* IV, pp. 5–73 (Paris, 1927).

Garbini, G. 'Fenici in Palestina', *Annali dell' Instituto Orientale di Napoli* 39 (1979), pp. 325–330.

Gray, V. *The Canaanites* (London, 1964).

Hachmann, R. (ed.). *Frühe Phönizier im Libanon. 20 Jahre deutsche Ausgrabungen in Kamid el-Loz* (Mainz a. Rhein, 1983).

Jidejian, N. *Byblos through the Ages* (Beirut, 1968).

Liverani, M. *Storia di Ugarit nell'etá degli archivi politici* (Roma, 1962).

Montet, P. *Byblos et l'Egypte, Quatre campagnes de fouilles à Gebel, 1921–24* (Paris, 1928–29).

Pettinato, G. 'Le città fenicie e Byblos in particolare nella documentazione epigrafica di Ebla', *Atti del I Congresso Internazionale di Studi Fenici e Punici*, pp. 107–118 (Roma, 1983).

Saade, G. *Ougarit, Métropole cananéenne* (Beirut, 1979).

Saghieh, M. *Byblos in the Third Millennium B.C. A Reconstruction of the Stratigraphy and a Study of the Cultural Connections* (Warminster, 1983).

Saidah, R. 'Ougarit et Sidon', *Les Annales Archéologiques Arabes Syriennes*, vol. XXIX–XXX, 1977–1980, pp. 89–103.

Sandars, N. K. *The Sea Peoples* London (1978).

Swiggers, P. 'Byblos dans les lettres d'El Amarna: Lumières sur des relations obscures', *Studia Phoenicia* III, pp. 45–58 (Leuven, 1985).

Teixidor, J. 'L'inscription d'Ahiram à nouveau', *Syria* LXIV (1987), pp. 137–140.

2 PHOENICIA DURING THE IRON AGE

The literary sources

Attridge, H. W. and Oden, R. A. *Phylo of Byblos, "The Phoenician History"*, The Catholic Biblical Association of America (Washington, 1981).

Baumgarten, A. I. *The Phoenician History of Phylo of Byblos* (Leyden, 1981).

Garbini, G. 'Gli 'Annali di Tiro'' e la storiografia fenicia', *Oriental Studies Presented to B. S. J. Isserlin*, pp. 112–127 (Leiden, 1980).

Goedicke, H. *The Report of Wenamon* (Baltimore–London, 1975).

Mazza, F., Ribichini, S. and Xella, P. *Fonti-classiche per la civiltà fenicia e punica*, C.N.R. (Roma, 1988).

General works

Baramki, D. *Phoenicia and the Phoenicians* (Beirut, 1961).

Garbini, G. *I fenici. Storia e religione*. Isituto Universitario Orientale (Napoli, 1980).

Harden, D. *Los Fenicios* (Barcelona, 1967).

Jidejian, N. *Sidon through the Ages* (Beirut, 1971).

Moscati, S. *Il mondo dei fenici* (Milano, 1966).

The Iron Age

Albright, W. F. *Northeast Mediterranean Dark Ages and the Early Iron Age Art of Syria* Studies presented to H. Goldman, pp. 144–164 (New York, 1956).

'Syria, the Philistines and Phoenicia', *The Cambridge Ancient History*, II: 2, 1975, pp. 507–536.

Botto, M. Studi storici sullà Fenicia, l'VIII e il VII secolo a.c. (Pisa, 1990).

Röllig, W. 'Die Phönizier des Mutterlandes zur Zeit der Kolonisierung', in Niemeyer, H. G. (ed.), *Phönizier im Westen*, pp. 15–30 (Mainz, 1982).

Phoenician trade in Syria and Israel

Barnett, R. D. *Ancient Ivories in the Middle East*, Institute of Archaeology, The Hebrew University of Jerusalem (Jerusalem, 1982).

Bron, F. *Recherches sur les inscriptions phéniciennes de Karatepe*, Hautes Etudes Orientales 11 (Genève, 1979).

Fensahm, F. L. 'The Relationship between Phoenicia and Israel during the Reign of Ahab', *I Congresso Internazionale di Studi Fenici e Punici* (1979), pp. 589–594 (Roma, 1983).

Gubel, E., 'Phoenician Furniture', *Studia Phoenicia* VII (Leuven, 1987).

Kestemont, G. 'Les phéniciens en Syrie du Nord', *Studia Phoenicia* III, 1985, pp. 135–161.

Du Plat Taylor, J. 'The Cypriot and Syrian Pottery from Al Mina, Syria', *Iraq* 21, 1959, pp. 62–69.

Riis, P. J. 'La ville phénicienne de Soukas, de la fin de l'Age du Bronze à la conquête romaine', *I Congresso Internazionale di Studi Fenici e Punici* (1979), pp. 509–514 (Roma, 1983).

Stern, G. 'A Phoenician art center in post-exilic Samaria', *I Congresso Internazionale di Studi Fenici e Punici (1979)*, pp. 211–212 (Roma, 1983).

Winter, I. J. 'Phoenician and North Syrian Ivory Carving in Historical Context: Questions of Style and Distribution', *Iraq* 3, 1976, pp. 1–22.

'Is There a South Syrian Style of Ivory Carving in the Early First Millenium B.C.?' *Iraq* 43, 1981, pp. 101–130.

Yadin, Y. 'The "House of Baal" of Ahab and Jezebel in Samaria, and that of Athalia in Judah', *Archaeology in the Levant (Essays for K. Kenyon)*, pp. 127–134 (Warminster, 1978).

Phoenicia and the Assyrians

Elayi, J. 'Les cités phéniciennes et l'empire assyrien à l'époque d'Assurbanipal', *Revue d'Assyriologie et d'Archéologie Orientale*, LXXVII, 1, 1983, pp. 45–58.

Kestemont, G. 'Tyr et les assyriens', *Studia Phoenicia* III, 1985, pp. 53–78.

Oded, B. 'The Phoenician Cities and the Assyrian Empire in the Time of

Tiglath-pileser III', *Zeitschrift des Deutchen Palästina-Vereins*, 90, 1974, pp. 38–49.

Pettinato, G. 'I rapporti politici di Tiro con l'Assiria alla luce del trattato tra Asarhaddon e Baal', *Rivista di studi Fenici* III, 1975, pp. 145–160.

The Phoenicians in Cyprus and the Aegean

Barnett, R. D. 'Ancient oriental influence on archaic Greece, The Aegean and the Near East' (*Studies presented to H. Goldman*), pp. 212–238 (New York, 1956).

Bikai, P. M. 'The Phoenician Imports', in Karageorghis, V., *Excavations at Kition IV, The non-Cypriote Pottery*, pp. 23–35 (Nicosia, 1981).

The Phoenician Pottery of Cyprus (Nicosia, 1987).

Catling, M. W. *The Knossos Area 1974–76*, Archaeological Reports for 1976–77, British School of Athens, 1977, p. 3–24.

Coldstream, J. N. 'Greeks and Phoenicians in the Aegean', in Niemeyer, H. G. (ed.), *Phönizier im Westen*, pp. 261–272 (Mainz, 1982).

Gjerstad, E. 'Pottery Types, Cypro-geometric to Cypro-classical', *Opuscula Atheniensa* III, pp. 105–122 (Lund, 1960).

Karageorghis, V. 'Excavations at Kition', *Department of Antiquities, vol. I: The Tombs* (Nicosia, 1974).

Kition, Mycenean and Phoenician Discoveries in Cyprus (London, 1976).

Lipinski, E. 'La Carthage de Chypre', *Studia Phoenicia* I–II, pp. 209–233 (Leuven, 1983).

Sznycer, M. 'L'inscription phénicienne de Tekke, près de Knossos', *Kadmos* 18, 1979, pp. 89–93.

Vandenabeele, F., 'Quelques particularités de la civilisation d'Amathonte à l'époque du Chypro-géométrique', *Bulletin de Correspondance Hellénique* XCII, 1968, pp. 103–114.

3 THE BASES FOR THE EXPANSION IN THE MEDITERRANEAN

Territory, resources and population

Bintliff, J. L. 'Climatic Change, Archaeology and Quaternary Science in the Eastern Mediterranean Region', in Harding, A. F. (ed.), *Climate Change in Latter Prehistory* (Edinburgh, 1982).

Butzer, K. W. *Environment and Archaeology* (Chicago, 1972).

Crown, A. D. 'Towards a Reconstruction of the Climate of Palestine 8000 B.C.–O-B.C.', *Journal of Near Eastern Studies*, 31, 1972.

Hopkins, D. C. *The Highlands of Canaan. Agricultural Life in the Early Iron Age* (Sheffield, 1985).

Lamb, H. H. *Climate History and the Modern World* (London, 1982).

Marfoe, L. 'Between Qadesh and Kumidi: a History of Frontier Settlement and Land Use in the Biqa', Lebanon', PhD. Dissertation, Univ. Chicago, 1977.

Price-Williams, D. *Environmental Archaeology in the Western Neguev, Nature* (London, 1973).

Sapin, J. 'La géographie humaine de la Syrie–Palestine au deuxième millénaire avant J.-C. comme voie de recherche historique', *Journal of the Economic and Social History of the Orient*, XXV, 1982, pp. 1–49 and 113–186.

Vita-Finzi, C. and Copeland, S. 'Archaeological Dating of Geological Deposits in Jordan', *Levant* 10 (Jerusalem, 1978).

Phoenician economy and trade in western Asia

Albright, W. F. 'New Light on the Early History on Phoenician Colonization', *Bull. American Schools of Oriental Research, (BASOR)* 83, 1941, pp. 14–22.

Bondi, S. F. 'Note sull' economia fenicia', *Egitto e Vicino Oriente* 1, 1978, pp. 139–149.

Botto, M. 'L'attività economica dei fenici in Oriente tra il IX e la prima metà dell VIII sec.a.C.', *Egitto e Vicino Oriente* XI, pp. 117–154 (Pisa, 1988).

Bunnens, G. 'Commerce et diplomatie phéniciens au temps de Hiram l de Tyr', *Journal of the Economic and Social Hisotry of the Orient*, XIX, 1976, pp. 1–31.

'Considérations géographiques sur la place occupée par la Phénicie dans l'expansion de l'empire assyrien', *Studia Phoenicia* I–II, pp. 169–193 (Leuven, 1983).

L'expansion phénicienne en Mediterranée. Institut Historique Belge de Rome, t. XVIII, 1979.

'Le luxe phénicien d'après les inscriptions royales assyriennes', *Studia Phoen* III, pp. 121–133 (Leuven, 1985).

Diakonoff, I. M. 'Main Features of the Economy in the Monarchies of Ancient Western Asia', *3ème Conférence Internationale d'Histoire Economique (München 1965)*, vol. 3, pp. 13–32 (Paris, 1969).

Fensham, F. C. 'The Treaty between the Israelites and Tyrians', Supplement to *Vetus Testamentum* XVII, pp. 71–87 (Leiden, 1969).

Finley, M. I. Metals in the Ancient World', *J R S A* 118, 1970, pp. 597–607.

Frankenstein, S. 'The Phoenicians in the Far West: a Function of Neo-Assyrian Imperialism', in Larsen M. G. (ed.), *Power and Propaganda. A Symposium in Ancient Empires*, Mesopotamia, 7, pp. 263–294 (Copenhagen 1979).

Garelli, P. 'Remarques sur les rapports entre l'Assyrie et les cités phéniciennes', *I Congresso Internazionale di Studi Fenici e Punici (1979)*, pp. 61–66 (Roma, 1983).

Heltzer, M. 'The Metal Trade of Ugarit and The Problem of Transportation of Commercial Goods', *Iraq* 39, 1977, 203–211.

Jankowska, N. B. 'Some Problems of the Economy of the Assyrian Empire', in Diakonoff, I. M. (ed.), *Ancient Mesopotamia*, USSR Academy of Sciences, pp. 253–276 (Moscow, 1969).

Kestemont, G. 'Les Phéneciens en Syrie du Nord', *Studia Phoen.* III, pp. 135–161 (Leuven, 1985).

Leclant, J. 'Les relations entre l'Egipte et la Phénicie du voyage d'Ounamon à l'expédition d'Alexandre', in Ward, W. A. (ed.) *The Role of the Phoenicians in the Interaction of Mediterranean Civilizations*, pp. 9–22 (Beirut, 1968).

Lipinski, E. 'Les temples néo-assyriens et les origines du monnayage', in ID., *State and Temple Economy in the Ancient Near East*, vol. II, pp. 565–588 (Leuven, 1979).

Oded, B. *Mass deportations and deportees in the Neo-Assyrian Empire* (Wiesbaden, 1979).

Oppenheim, A. L. 'Essay on Overland Trade in the First Milleunium B.C.', *Journal of Cuneiform Studies* 21 (1967), 1969, pp. 236–254.

Postgate, J. N. 'The economic structure of the Assyrian Empire', in Larsen, M. T. (ed.), *Power and Propaganda, Mesopotamia* 7, pp. 193–221 (Copenhagen, 1979).

Renfrew, C. 'Trade as Action at a Distance: Questions of Intergration and Communication', in Sabloff, J. A. and Lamberg-Karlovsky, C. C. (eds.), *Ancient Civilization and Trade*, pp. 3–59 (Albuquerque, 1975).

Schoville, A. N. 'A note on the oracles of Amos against Gaza, Tyre and Edom', Supplement to *Vetus Testamentum*, XXVI, 1974, pp. 55–63.

Winter, I. J. *North Syria in the Early First Millennium B.C., with Special Reference to Ivory Carving* (Ann Arbor, Michigan, 1979).

Zaccagnini, C., 'Materiali per una discussione sulla "moneta primitiva": le coppe d'oro e d'argento nel vicino Oriente durante il II millennio', *Annali dell'Istituto Italiano di Numismatica* 26, 1979, 29–49.

4 PHOENICIAN TRADE: EXCHANGE MECHANISMS AND ORGANIZATION

General works

Barcelo, A. *Reproducción económica y modos de producción* (Barcelona, 1981).

Belshaw, C. S. *Comercio tradicional y mercados modernos* (Barcelona, 1973).

Curtain, Ph. D. *Cross-cultural Trade in World History* (Cambridge University Press, 1984).

Dalton, G. (ed.), *Primitive, Archaic and Modern Economics. Essays of Karl Polanyi* (New York, 1968).

Garnsey, P., Hopkins, K. and Whittaker, C. R. *Trade in the Ancient Economy* (London, 1983).

Godelier, M. (ed.), *Antropología y economía* (Barcelona, 1976).

Hodder, I. and Orton, E. *Spatial Analysis in Archaeology* (Oxford University Press, 1976).

Lamberg-Karlovsky, C. C. 'Trade mechanisms in Indus–mesopotamian Interrelations', *Journal of the American Oriental Society*, vol. 92, 1972, pp. 222–229.

McC. Adams, R. 'Anthropological Perspectives on Ancient Trade'. *Current Anthropology*, vol. 15, no. 3, 1974, pp. 239–258.

Meillassoux, C. M. (ed.), *The development of indigenous Trade and Markets in West Africa* (London University Press, 1971).

Polanyi, K., Arensberg, C. M. and Pearson, M. W. (eds.), *Comercio y mercado en los imperios antiguos* (Barcelona, 1976).

'Traders and Trade', in Sabloff, J. A. and Lamberg-Karlovsky, C. C. (eds.), *Ancient Civilization*, 1975, pp. 133–154.

Renfrew, C. 'Trade and Culture Process in European Prehistory', *Current Anthropology* vol. 10, nos. 2–3, 1969, pp. 151–169.

'Trade as Action at a Distance', in Sabloff, J. A. and Lamberg-Karlovsky, C. C. (eds.), *Ancient Civilization*, 1975, pp. 3–59.

Revere, R. B. '"Tierra de nadie": Los puertos comerciales del Mediterraneo', in Polanyi, K., Arensberg, C. M. and Pearson, M. W. (eds.), *Comercio y mercado*, 1976, pp. 87–108.

Sabloff, J. A. and Lamberg-Karlovsky, C. C. (eds.), *Ancient Civilization and Trade* (University of New Mexico Press, Albuquerque, 1975).

Silver, M. *Economic Structures of the Ancient Near East* (London–Sydney, 1985).

Various authors, *Trade and Politics in the Ancient World*. Deuxième Conférence Internationale d'Histoire Economique (1962). Mouton (Paris, 1965).

Trade in the Near East in the second millenium

Astour, M. 'The Merchant Class of Ugarit', in Edzard, D. O. (ed.), *Gesellschaftsklassen im Alten Zweiströmland und in angrenzenden Gebieten*, pp. 14–15 (Munich, 1972).

Beale, T. W. 'Early Trade in Highland Iran: a view from a Source Area'. *World Archaeology*, 5, 1975, pp. 133–148.

Diakonoff, I. M. (ed.), *Societies and Languages of the Ancient Near East* (Studies in Honour of I. M. Diakonoff) (Warminster, 1982).

Garelli, P. *Les assyriens en Cappadoce* (Paris, 1963).

Hahn, I. *Foreign Trade of the nuclear or extended Family in Oriental Antiquity*. Eighth International Economic History Congress, Budapest 1982, pp. 34–43.

Kestemont, G. *Diplomatique et droit international en Asie occidentale (1600–1200 Av.C)* (Louvain, 1974).

'Remarques sur les aspects juridiques du commerce dans le Proche Orient au XVIIe siècle avant notre ère', *Iraq* 39, 1977, pp. 191–201.

Larsen, M. T. 'Your Money or your Life! A Portrait of an Assyrian Businessman', in Diakonoff, I. M. (ed.), *Societies and Languages*, 1982, pp. 214–245.

Leemans, W. F. *The Old Babylonian Merchant. His business and his social position* (Leiden, 1950).

'Old Babylonian Letters and Economic History. A Review Article with Digression on Foreign Trade', *Journal of the Economic and Social History of the Orient*. XI, 1968, pp. 171–226.

Liverani, M. 'La dotazione dei mercanti di Ugarit'. *Ugarit-Forschungen* 11, 1979, pp. 495–503.

Nissen, H. J. and Renger, J. (eds.), *Mesopotamien und seine Nachbarn. Politische und Kulturelle Wechselbeziehungen im Alten Vorderasien vom 4. bis 1. Jahrtausend v. Chr.*, Berliner Beiträge zum Vorderen Orient, Band 1 (Berlin, 1982).

Oppenheim, A. L. *Ancient Mesopotamia, Portrait of a Dead Civilization* (The University of Chicago Press, 1964).

'La Historia económica mesopotamica a vista de pájaro', in Polanyi, K., Arensberg, C. M. and Pearson, H. W. (eds.), *Comercio y mercado*, 1976, pp. 77–86.

Polanyi, K. 'Intercambio sin mercado en tiempo de Hammurabi', in Polanyi, K. et al., (eds.), *Comercio y mercado*, 1976, pp. 61–75.

Renger, J. 'Patterns of non-institutional Trade and non-commercial Exchange in Ancient Mesopotamia at the beginnings of the second millennium B.C.', in Archi, A. (ed.), *Circulation of Goods in non-palatial Context in the Ancient Near East*, pp. 31–123 (Roma, 1984).

Veenhof, K. R. 'Aspects of Old Assyrian Trade and its Terminology', *Studia et Documenta*, vol. X (Leiden, 1972).

'The Old Assyrian Merchants and their relations with the Native Population of Anatolia', in Nissen, M. J. and Renger, J. (eds.), *Mesopotamien*, 1982, pp. 147–160.

Zaccagnini, C. 'Patterns of Mobility among ancient Near Eastern Craftsmen', *Journal of Near Eastern Studies*, 42, 1983, pp. 245–264.

The organization of Phoenician trade

Albright, W. F. 'The eastern Mediterranean about 1060 B.C.', *Studies presented to D. M. Robinson I*, St Louis, Missouri, 1951, pp. 223–231.

Barnett, R. D. *Ezekiel and Tyre, Eretz-Israel IX*, pp. 6–13 (Jerusalem, 1969).

Bunnens, G. 'Commerce et diplomatie phéniciens au temps de Hiram I de Tyr', *Journal of the Economic and Social History of the Orient*, XIX, 1976, pp. 1–31.

'La mission d'Ounamon en Phénicie. Point de vue d'un non-égyptologue'. *Rivista di Studi Fenici*, VI, 1978, pp. 1–16.

Bondi, S. F. 'Note sull'economia fenicia I: Impresa privata e ruolo dello Stato', *Egitto e Vicino Oriente*, 1, 1978, pp. 139–149.

Carpenter, R. 'Phoenicians in the West', *American Journal of Archeology*, 62, 1958, pp. 35–53.

Chiera, G. 'Is. 23: l'elegia su Tiro', *Rivista di Studi Fenici* XIV, 1986, pp. 3–19.

Dandamayev, M. A. 'The Neo-Babylonian Elders', in Diakonoff, I. M. (ed.), Societies and Language, 1982.

Garbini, G. 'Il comercio fenicio, en I fenici', Storia e Religione, pp. 65–69 (Napoli, 1980).

Katzenstein, M. J. 'The phoenician term hubūr in the Report of Wen-Amon', I Congresso Internazionale di Studi Fenici e Punici (1979), pp. 598–602 (Roma, 1983).

Leclant, J. 'Les relations entre l'Egypte et la Phénicie du Voyage d'Ounamon à l'expédition d'Alexandre', in Ward, W. A. (ed.), The Role of the Phoenicians in the Interaction of Mediterranean Civilizations, pp. 9–22 (Beirut, 1968).

Lepore, E. 'Osservazioni sul rapporto tra fatti economici e fatti di colonizzazione in Occidente', Dialoghi di Archaeologia, anno III, no. 1–2, 1969, pp. 175–188.

Lipinski, E. 'Products and brokers of Tyre according to Ezekiel 27', Studia Phoenicia III, pp. 213–220 (Leuven, 1985).

Oppenheim, A. L. 'Essay on Overland Trade in the First Millennium B.C.', Journal of Cuneiform Studies 21 (1967), 1969, pp. 236–254.

Pettinato, G. 'I Rapporti politici di Tiro con l'Assiria alle luce del trattato tra Asarhaddon e Baal', Rivista di Studi Fenici III, 1975, pp. 145–160.

Homer, reciprocity and the exchange of prestige goods

Ampolo, C. 'Il lusso nelle società antiche', Opus III, pp. 469–475 (Roma, 1984).

Austin, M. and Vidal-Naquet, P. Economía y Sociedad en la antigua Grecia, (Barcelona, 1986).

Coldstream, J. N. 'Gift Exchange in the Eighth Century B.C.', in Hagg, R. (ed.), The Greek Renaissance of the Eighth Century B.C., pp. 201–207 (Estocolmo, 1983).

Cristofani, M. 'Il "dono" nell'Etruria arcaica', La Parola del Passato, CLXI, 1975, pp. 132–152.

Cheal, D. The Gift Economy, (Routledge, London, 1988).

Finley, M. I. El mundo de Odiseo, Breviarios Fondo Cultura Económica, 2a, ed. (México–Madrid, 1984).

Fischer, F. 'Keimelia', Germania 51, 1973, pp. 436–459.

Gjerstad, E. 'Decorated metal bowls from Cyprus', Opuscula Archaeologica IV, pp. 1–18 (Lund, 1946).

Godelier, M. Racionalidad e irracionalidad en economía, Ed. siglo XXI (Madrid, 1967).

Gregory, C. A. Gifts and Commodities (Academic Press, London, 1982).

Levi-Strauss, C. El principio de la reciprocidad, en Las estructuras elementales del parentesco, pp. 91–108 (Paidos, México, 1983).

Liverani, M. 'Elementi "irrazionali" nel commercio amarniano', Oriens Antiquus XI, 1972, pp. 297–317.

'Dono, tributo, commercio: ideologia dello scambio nella tarda età del Bronzo', *Annali dell'Istituto Italiano di Numismatica* 26, pp. 9–28 (Roma, 1979).

Malinowski, B. *Los argonautas del Pacífico occidental*, (Península, Barcelona, 1973).

Markoe, G. *Phoenician Bronze and Silver Bowls from Cyprus and the Mediterranean* (University of California Press, 1985).

Mauss, M. 'Ensayo sobre los dones. Razón y forma del cambio en las sociedades primitivas', in *Sociología y Antropología, Tecnos*, pp. 155–263 (Madrid, 1971).

Mele, A. 'Il commercio greco arcaico. Prexis ed emporie', *Cahiers du Centre Jean Bérard* IV (Napoli, 1979).

Muhly, J. D. 'Homer and the Phoenicians'. *Berytus* 19, 1970, pp. 19–64.

Rathje, A. 'Silver relief bowls from Italy', *Analecta Romana Instituti Danici*, IX, Odense Univ. Press, 1980, pp. 7–46.

Sahlins, M. 'Sociología del intercambio primitivo', in *Economía de la Edad de Piedra*, pp. 203–296 (Madrid, 1977).

Stella, L. A. 'Importanza degli scavi di Ras Shamra per il problema fenicio dei poemi omerici', *Archeologia Classica* IV, 1952, pp. 72–76.

Wathelet, P. 'Les Phéniciens et la tradition homérique', *Studia Phoenicia* II, pp. 235–243 (Leuven, 1983).

Zaccagnini, C. *Lo scambio dei doni nel Vicino Oriente durante i secoli XV–XIII* (Roma, 1973).

'La circolazione dei beni di lusso nelle fonti neo-assire (IX–VII se. a.C.)', *Opus* III, 1984, 235–247.

Pre-monetary circulation

Dalton, G, 'Primitive Money', *American Anthropologist* 67, 1965, pp. 44–65.

Dayton, J. 'Money in the Near East before coinage', *Berytus* XXIII, 1974, pp. 41–52.

Freydank, H. 'Fernhandel und Warenpreise nach einer mittelassyrischen Urkunde des 12. Jahrhunderts v.u. Z., in Diakonoff, I. M. (ed.), *Societies and Languages of the Ancient Near East* (Warminster, 1982).

Lipinski, E. 'Les temples néo-assyriens et les origines du monnayage', in Lipinski, E. (ed.), *State and Temple Economy in the Ancient Near East*, II, pp. 565–588 (Leuven, 1979).

Lombardo, M. 'Elementi per una discussione sulle origini e funzioni della moneta coniata', *Annali dell'Istituto Italiano di Numismatica*, 26, 1979, pp. 75–121.

Muller, M. 'Gold, Silber und Blei als Wertmesser in Mesopotamien während der zweiten Hälfte des 2. Jahrtausends v.u.Z., in Diakonoff, I. M. (ed.), *Societies and Languages*, 1982, pp. 270–278.

Parise, N. F. 'Per uno studio del sistema ponderale ugaritico', *Dialoghi di Archeologia*, anno IV, no. 1, 1970–71, pp. 3–36.

'Per un'introduzione allo studio dei "segni premonetari" nella Grecia arcaica', *Annali dell'Istituto Italiano di Numismatica*, 26, 1979, pp. 51–71.

'Circuiti di "segni premonetari" nell'età dell' Orientalizzante', *Opus* III, pp. 277–279 (Roma, 1984).

'Fra Assiri e Greci. Dall'argento di Ishtar alla moneta', *Dialoghi di Archeologia*, Anno 5, no. 2, 1987, pp. 37–39.

Postgate, J. N. *Taxation and Conscription in the Assyrian Empire*, Studia Pohl, Series Maior 3, Biblical Institure (Roma, 1974).

Zaccagnini, C. 'Materiali per una discussione sulla "moneta primitiva": le coppe d'oro e d'argento nel Vicino Oriente durante il II millennio', *Annali dell'Istituto Italiano di Numismatica* 26, 1979, pp. 29–49.

5 THE GREAT POLITICAL INSTITUTIONS: THE PALACE AND THE TEMPLE

The Phoenician temple

Bonnet, C. 'Le culte de Melqart à Carthage: un cas de conservatisme religieux', *Studia Phoenicia* IV, pp. 209–222 (Namur, 1986).

Bonnet-Tzavellas, C. 'Le dieu Melqart en Phénicie et dans le bassin méditerranéen: culte national et officiel', *Studia Phoenicia* II, pp. 195–207 (Leuven, 1983).

Bonnet, C. 'Melqart. Cultes et mythes de l'Héraclès tyrien en méditerranée', *Studia Phoenicia* VIII (Leuven, 1988).

Bonnet, C., Lipiński, E. and Marchetti, P. (eds), 'Religio phoenicia', *Studia Phoenicia* IV (Namur, 1986).

Bunnens, G. 'Aspects religieux de l'expansion phénicienne', *Studia Phoenicia* IV, pp. 119–125 (Namur, 1986).

Dussaud, R. 'Melqart', *Syria* XXV, 1946–48, pp. 205–230.

Elayi, J. 'Le roi et la religion dans les cités phéniciennes à l'époque perse', *Studia Phoenicia* IV, 1986, pp. 249–261.

Picard, C., G. CH. 'Hercule et Melqart', *Hommages à Jean Bayet, Coll. Latomus* LXX, pp. 569–578 (Brussels–Berchem, 1964).

Piganiol, A. 'Les origines d'Hercule', *Hommages à A. Grenier, III*, pp. 1261–1264 (Brussels, 1962).

Rebuffat, R. 'Les phéniciens à Rome', *Mélanges d'Archéologie et d'Histoire de l'Ecole Française de Rome*, LXXVIII, 1966, pp. 7–48.

Van Berchem, D. 'Hercule-Melqart à l'Ara Maxima', *Rendiconti della Pontificia Accademia Romana di Archeologia*, Serie III, vol. XXXII, 1959–1960, pp. 61–68.

'Sanctuaires d'Hercule-Melqart. Contribution à l'étude de l'expansion phénicienne en Méditerranée', *Syria* XLIV, 1967, pp. 73–109 and pp. 307–336.

Xella, P. 'Le polythéisme phénicien', *Studia Phoenicia* IV, pp. 29–39 (Namur, 1986).

6 THE ROUTES OF PHOENICIAN EXPANSION INTO THE MEDITERRANEAN

General works

Bondi, S. F. 'Per una caratterizzazione dei centri occidentali nella più antica espansione fenicia', *Egitto e Vicino Oriente* VII, 1984, pp. 75–92.

'La Sicilia fenicio–punica: il quadro storico a la documentazione archeologica', *Bollettino d'Arte* 31–32, pp. 13–32 (Roma, 1985).

Bunnens, G. *L'expansion phénicienne en Méditerranée* (Brussels–Rome, 1979).

Cary, M., and Warmington, E. M. *The Ancient Explorers* (Harmondsworth, 1963).

Casson, L. *Los antiguos marinos. Navegantes y guerreros del mar en el Mediterráneo en la Antigüedad* (Buenos Aires, 1969).

Cintas, P. *Manuel d'Archéologie Punique, I* (Paris, 1970).

Mosse, C. *La colonisation dans l'Antiquité* (Paris, 1970).

Rouge, J. *La marine dans l'Antiquité* (Paris, 1975).

Shipping systems and routes

Allain, J. 'Topographie dinamique et courants géneraux dans le bassin occidental de la méditerranée au Nord du 42e. parallèle', *Revue des Travaux de l'Institut des Pêches Maritimes*, XXVII, 1960, pp. 127–135.

Alvar, J. 'Los medios de navegación de los colonizadores griegos', *Archivo Español de Arqueología* 52, 1979, pp. 67–83.

Bunnens, G. 'Tyr et la mer', *Studia Phoenicia* I, pp. 7–21 (Leuven, 1983).

Cintas, P. 'Fouilles puniques à Tipasa', *Revue Africaine* XCII, 1949, pp. 1–68.

Derrotero General del mediterráneo, I–II (Madrid, 1858, 1860, 1883).

Derrotero de las costas del mediterráneo, no. 3 (San Fernando, 1945).

Derrotero de las costas del mediterráneo (Instituto Hidrográfico de la Marina, Cádiz, 1956).

Harden, D. B. 'The Phoenicians on the West Coast of Africa', *Antiquity*, XXII, no. 87, 1948, pp. 141–150.

Isserlin, B. S. J. 'Did Carthaginian Mariners reach the Island of Corvo (Azores)?' *Rivista di Studi Fenici e Punici*, XII, 1984, pp. 31–46.

Mele, A. 'Il commercio greco arcaico', *Cahiers du Centre Jean Bérard*, IV (Napoli, 1979).

Michelot, E. *Portolano del mare mediterraneo ossia guide dei piloti costieri* (Marsella, 1806).

Moscati, S. 'L'espansione fenicia nel Mediterraneo occidentale', in Niemeyer, H. G. (ed.), *Phönizier im Westen*, pp. 5–12 (Mainz, 1982).

Pellicer, M., Menanteau, L. and Rouillard, P. 'Para una metodología de localización de colonias fenicias en las costas ibéricas: el Cerro del Prado', *Habis* 8, 1977, pp. 217–251.

Picard, C. 'Les navigations de Carthage vers l'Ouest. Carthage et le pays de Tarsis aux VIIIe.–VIe. siècles', in Niemeyer, H. G. (ed.), *Phönizier im Westen*, pp. 167–173 (Mainz, 1982).

Picard, G. Ch. 'Le Périple d'Hannon', in Niemeyer, H. G., (ed.), *Phönizier im Western*, 1982, pp. 175–180.

Ponsich, M. 'Territoires utiles du Maroc punique', in Niemeyer, H. G. (ed.), *Phönizier im Westen*, 1982, pp. 429–444.

Ruiz de Arbulo, J. 'Emporion puerto de escala, puerto de comercio', Tesis Licenciatura, Universidad de Barcelona, 1983.

Schüle, G. *Navegación primitiva y visibilidad de la tierra en el Mediterráneo*, IX Congreso Nacional de Arqueología, pp. 449–462 (Mérida, 1968).

Tofiño, V. *Derrotero de las costas de España en el Mediterráneo y su correspondiente de Africa, (1784)* (Madrid, 1832).

Phoenician ships and ports

Barnett, R. D. 'Early Shipping in the Near East', *Antiquity*, XXXII, no. 128, 1958, pp. 220–230.

Cederlund, C. O. (ed.), *Harbour Archaeology*. Proceedings of the first International Workshop to an International Symposium on Boat and Ship Archaeology in Stockholm in 1982, Swedish National Maritime Museum, (Estocolmo, 1985).

Debergh, J. 'Cartage: Archéologie et Histoire, Les ports–Byrsa', *Studia Phoenicia* II, pp. 151–157 (Leuven, 1983).

Frost, H. 'The Arwad Plans 1964. A Photogrammetric Survey of Marine Installations', *Annales Archéologiques Arabes Syriennes*, XVI, 1966, pp. 13–28.

'Recent observations on the submerged harbourworks at Tyre', *Bulletin du Musée de Beyrouth*, XXIV, 1971, pp. 103–111.

'The offshore Island Harbour at Sidon and other Phoenician Sites in the light of new dating evidence', *The International Journal of Nautical Archaeology*, II, 1973.

'The excavation and Reconstruction of the Marsala Punic Warship', *I Congresso Internazionale di Studi Fenici e Punici (1979)*, pp. 903–907 (Roma, 1983).

Frost, H., Culican, W. and Curtis, J. E. 'The Punic Wreck in Sicily', *The International Journal of Nautical Archaeology and Underwater Exploration*, 3:1, 1974, pp. 35–54.

Hurst, H. 'The War Harbour of Carthage', *I Congresso Internazionale di Studi Fenici e Punici (1979)*, pp. 603–610 (Roma, 1983).

Poidebard, A. *Un grand port disparu: Tyr. Recherches aériennes et sous-marines* (Paris, 1939).

Poidebard, A. and Lauffray, J. *Sidon. Aménagements antiques du port de Saida* (Beirut, 1951).

Rebuffat, R. 'Une bataille navale au VIIIe. siècle (Josèphe, "Antiquités Judaïques" IX, 14)', *Semitica* XXVI, pp. 71–79 (Paris, 1976).

7 THE PHOENICIANS IN THE WEST: CHRONOLOGY AND HISTORIOGRAPHY

General works

Beloch, K. J. *Griechische Geschichte, I:2* (Strassburg, 1913).
Bérard, V. *Les Phéniciens et l'Odysée, 2 vol.* (Paris, 1902–1903).
Bosch-Gimpera, P. 'Fragen der Chronologie der Phönizischen Kolonisation in Spanien', *Klio* XXII, 1928–29, pp. 345–388.
'Phéniciens et Grecs dans l'Extrême Occident', *La Nouvelle Clio* III, 1951, pp. 269–296.
Carpenter, R. 'Phoenicians in the West', *American Journal of Archaeology*, 62, 1958, pp. 35–53.
Culican, W. 'Aspects of the Phoenician Settlement in the West Mediterranean', *Abr-Nahrain* I, 1959–60, pp. 36–55.
Garbini, G. 'L'espansione fenicia nel Mediterraneo', *Cultura e Scuola*, II, 7, pp. 92–97 (Roma, 1963).
'I fenici in Occidente', *Studi Etruschi* 34, 1966, pp. 111–147.
Garcia Bellido, A. *Fenicios y cartagineses en Occidente* (Madrid, 1942).
'Una colonización mítica de España tras la guerra de Troya. El ciclo legendario de los "nóstoi"', *Cuadernos de Historia de España*, pp. 106–123 (Buenos Aires, 1947).
'Los más remotos nombres de España', *Arbor* 19 pp. 5–27 (Madrid 1947).
Gras, M., Rouillard, P. and Teixidor, J. *L'univers phénicien* (Paris, 1989).
Harden, D. B. 'The phoenicians on the West Coast of Africa', *Antiquity* XXII, 87, 1948, pp. 141–150.
Harden, D. *Los fenicios* (Barcelona, 1967).
Herrmann, J. O. *Die Erdkarte der Urhibel* (Braunschweig, 1931).
Moscati, S. 'L'espansione fenicia nel Mediterraneo occidentale', *in* Niemeyer, H. G. (ed.), *Phönizier im Westen*, 1982, pp. 5–12.
Moscati, S. (ed.) *I fenici* (Catalogo della Mostra a Venezia) (Milano, 1988).
Movers, F. C. *Die Phoenizier 4 vol.* (Bonn, 1841–1856).
Reinach, S. *Le mirage oriental* (Paris, 1893).

Phoenician 'pre-colonization'

Acquaro, E., Godart, L., Mazza, F. and Musti, D. (eds) *Momenti precoloniali nel Mediterraneo antico*, (C.N.R., Roma, 1988).
Bernabo Brea, L. 'Leggenda e archeologia nella protostoria siciliana', *Kokalos* 10–11, 1964–65, pp. 1–33.
Bisi, A. M. 'Fenici e Micenei in Sicilia nella seconda metà del II millennio a.C.', *I Congresso Internazionale di Micenologia*, pp. 1156–1168 (Roma, 1967).
'Le "Smiting God" dans les milieux phéniciens d'Occident', *Studia Phoenicia* IV, 1986, pp. 169–187.
Moscati, S. 'Precolonizzazione greca e precolonizzazione fenicia', *Rivista di Studi Fenici* XI, 1983, pp. 1–7.

'I fenici e il mondo mediterraneo al tempo di Omero', *Rivista di Studi Fenici* XIII, 1985, pp. 179–187.

Niemeyer, H. G. 'Anno octogesimo post Troiam captam ... Tyria classis Gadis condidit? Polemische Gedanken zum Gründungsdatum von Gades (Cádiz)', *Hamburger Beiträge zur Archäologie* VIII, 1981, 9–33.

'Die Phönizier und die Mittelmeerwelt im Zeitalter Homers', *Jahrbuch des Römisch Germanischen Zentralmuseums*, 31, 1984, pp. 3–94.

Ridgway, D. 'La "precolonizzazione"', *Magna Graecia* XXIV, 1989, pp. 1–7.

Tusa, V. 'La statuetta fenicia del Museo Nazionale di Palermo', *Rivista di Studi Fenici* I, 1973, pp. 173–179.

Tarshish–Tartessos

Alvar, J. 'Aportaciones al estudio del Tarshish bíblico', *Rivista di Studi Fenici* X, 1982, pp. 211–230.

Cintas, P. 'Tarsis, Tartessos–Gades', *Semitica* 16, 1966, pp. 1–37.

Galling, K. 'Der Weg der Phöniker nach Tarsis in literarischer und archäologischer Sicht', *Zeitschrift des Deutschen Palästina-Vereins* 88, 1972, pp. 1–18, pp. 140–181.

Garbini, G. 'Tarsis e Gen. 10,4', *Bibbia e Oriente* VIII, pp. 13–19 (Roma, 1965).

Gonzalez-Wagner, C. 'Tartessos y las tradiciones literarias', *Rivista di Studi Fenici* XIV, 1986, pp. 201–228.

Schulten, A. *Tartessos* (Barcelona, 1945).

Sola Sole, J. M. 'Tarshish y los comienzos de la colonización fenicia en Occidente', *Sefarad* XVII, 1957, pp. 23–35.

Täckholm, V. 'Tarsis, Tartessos und die Säulen des Herakles', *Opuscula Romana* V, pp. 143–200 (Lund, 1965).

'El concepto de Tarshish en el Antiguo Testamento', *V° Symposium Internacional de Prehistoria Peninsular*, pp. 79–90 (Barcelona, 1969).

'Neue Studien zum Tarsis–Tartessos Problem', *Opuscula Romana* X, 1974, pp. 41–57.

The Nora stele

Albright, W. F. 'New Light on the Early History of Phoenician Colonization', *Bulletin of the American Schools of Oriental Research* 83, 1941, pp. 14–22.

Amadasi, M. G. and Guzzo, P. G. 'Di Nora, di Eracle gaditano e della più antica navigazione fenicia', *Aula Orientalis* IV, 1986, pp. 58–71.

Delcor, M. 'Réflexions sur l'inscription phénicienne de Nora en Sardaigne', *Syria* XLV, 1968, pp. 323–352.

Dupont-Sommer, A. 'Nouvelle lecture d'une inscription phénicienne archaïque de Nora en Sardaigne', *Comptes Rendus de l'Académie des Inscriptions et Belles Lettres*, pp. 12–22 (Paris, 1948).

Röllig, W. 'Paläographische Beobachtungen zum ersten Auftreten der Phönizier in Sardinien', *Antidoron (Festschrift J. Thimme)*, pp. 125–130 (Karlsruhe, 1983).

The Iberian Peninsula

Almagro Gorbea, M. 'El Bronce Final y el Período Orientalizante en Extremadura', *Bibliotheca Praehistorica Hispana* XIV (Valencia, 1977).

Blanco, A. 'Los nuevos bronces de Sancti Petri', *Boletín de la Real Academia de la Historia*, CLXXXII, cuad. II 1985, pp. 207–216.

Coffyn, A. *Le Bronze Final Atlantique dans la Péninsule Ibérique* (Paris, 1985).

Freyer-Schauenburg, B. *Elfenbeine aus dem samischen Heraion* (Hamburg, 1966).

Gamer-Wallert, I. 'Zwei Statuetten syro-ägyptischer Gottheiten von der "Barra de Huelva"', *Madrider Mitteilungen* 23, 1982, pp. 46–61.

Karageorghis, V. and Lo Schiavo, F. 'A west Mediterranean obelos from Amathus', *Rivista di Studi fenici* XVII, 1989, pp. 15–30.

Schauer, I. 'Orient im Spätbronze–und früheisenzeitlichen Occident', *Jahrbuch des Römisch–Germanischen Zentralmuseums Mainz*, 30, 1983, pp. 175–194.

Lo Schiavo, F. *Nuragic Sardinia in its Mediterranean setting: some recent advances*, University of Edinburgh, Department of Archaeology, Occasional Paper 12, 1985.

8 THE PHOENICIAN COLONIES IN THE CENTRAL MEDITERRANEAN

Ancient Carthage

Benichou-Safar, H. 'Carte des nécropoles puniques de Carthage', *Karthago* XVII, 1976, pp. 5–35.

Les tombes puniques de Carthage (Paris, 1982).

Bisi, A. M. *Kypriaka. Contributi allo studio della componente cipriota della civiltà punica* (Roma, 1966).

Cintas, P. *Céramique punique* (Tunis, 1950).

Manuel d'Archéologie punique, 2 vols. (Paris, 1970–1976).

Chelbi, F. 'Carthage. Sépultures puniques découvertes à l'est du théâtre', *Revue des Etudes Phéniciennes–Puniques et des Antiquités Libyques* (REPPAL), I, pp. 79–94 (Tunis, 1985).

'Carthage. Découverte d'un tombeau archaïque à Junon', *REPPAL* I, 1985, pp. 95–119.

'Oenochoes "à bobèche" de Carthage. Typologie et chronologie', *REPPAL* II, 1986, pp. 173–255.

Forrer, E. O. 'Karthago wurde erst 773–663 v. chr. gegründet', *Festschrift F. Dornseiff*, pp. 85–93 (Leipzig, 1953).

Frezouls, E. 'Une nouvelle hypothèse sur la fondation de Carthage', *Bulletin de Correspondance Héllénique*, LXXIX, 1955, pp. 153–176.

Harden, D. B. 'Punic urns from the Precinct of Tanit at Carthage', *American Journal of Archaeology*, 31, 1927, pp. 297–310.

'The Pottery from the Precinct of Tanit at Salammbô, Carthage', *Iraq IV*, 1937, pp. 59–89.

Huss, W. *Geschichte der Karthager* (Munich, 1985).

Lancel, S. *Byrsa I–III. Mission archéologique française à Carthage* (Paris, 1979–1982).

'Fouilles françaises à Carthage. La Colline de Byrsa et l'occupation punique (VII siècle–146 a. J.C)', *Comptes Rendus de l'Académie des Inscriptions et Belles Lettres*, Paris, 1981, pp. 156–193.

Lipiński, E. (ed) 'Carthago', *Studia Phoenicia VI*, Leuven 1988.

Moscati, S. *Il mondo dei fenici* (Milán, 1966).

I fenici e Cartagine (Turín, 1972).

'Interazioni culturali nel mondo fenicio', *Rivista di Studi Fenici II*, 1974, pp. 1–9.

Niemeyer, H. G. *Das frühe Karthago und die phönizische Expansion in Mittelmeerraum* (Göttingen, 1989).

Picard, G. Ch. and C. *Vie et mort de Carthage* (Paris, 1970).

'Les navigations de Carthage vers l'Ouest', in Niemeyer, H. G. (ed.), *Phönizier im Westen*, pp. 166–173 (Mainz, 1982).

Rakob, F. 'Deutsche Ausgrabungen in Karthago. Die punische Befunde', *Römische Mitteilungen* 91, 1984, pp. 1–22.

'Carthage punique. Fouilles et prospections archéologiques de la Mission allemande', *REPPAL II*, 1986, pp. 133–156.

(ed.) *Karthago. Die deutschen Ausgrabungen in Karthago*, vol. I (Mainz a. Rhein, 1990).

Stager, L. E. 'Excavations at Carthage 1975. The Punic Project: First interim report', *Annual of the American Schools of Oriental Research*, 43, 1978, pp. 151–190.

'Carthage: A view from the Tophet', in Niemeyer, H. G. (ed.), *Phönizier im Westen*, 1982.

Sicily, Sardinia and Malta

Acquaro, F. 'La Sardegna fenicia e punica: fra storia e archeologia', *Bolletino d'Arte* 31–32, pp. 49–56 (Roma, 1985).

Barreca, F. *La Sardegna fenicia e punica* (Sassari, 1974).

'Le fortificazioni fenicio–puniche in Sardegna', *Atti del I Convegno Italiano sul Vicino Oriente Antico*, pp. 115–128 (Roma, 1978).

'Nuove scoperte sulla colonizzazione fenicio–punica in Sardegna', in Niemeyer, H. G. (ed.), *Phönizier im Westen*, 1982, pp. 181–184.

Bartoloni, P. *Studi sulla ceramica fenicia e punica di Sardegna* (C.N.R., Roma, 1983).

Bondi, S. 'Per una caratterizzazione dei centri occidentali nella più antica espansione fenicia', *Egitto e Vicino Oriente* VII, 1984, pp. 75–92.

'La Sicilia fenicio–punica: il quadro storico e la documentazione archeologica', *Bolletino d'Arte* 31–32, pp. 13–32 (Roma, 1985).

'Monte Sirai nel quadro della cultura fenicio–punica di Sardegna', *Egitto e Vicino Oriente*, VIII, 1985, pp. 73–90.

Ciasca, 'Note moziesi', *I Congresso Internazionale di Studi Fenici e Punici (1979)*, pp. 617–622 (Roma, 1983).

Isserlin, B. S. J., MacNamara, E., Coldstream, J. N., Pike, G., Du Plat Taylor, J. and Snodgrass, A. 'Motya, a phoenician–punic Site near Marsala, Sicily', *The Annual of Leeds University Oriental Society*, IV. (1962–63), 1964, pp. 84–131.

Isserlin, B. S. J. and Du Plat Taylor, J. *Motya. A Phoenician and Carthaginian city in Sicily* (Leiden, 1974).

Isserlin, B. S. J. 'Motya: Urban Features', in H. G. Niemeyer (ed.), *Phönizier im Westen* 1982, pp. 113–127.

'Phoenician and punic rural settlement and agriculture: some archaeological considerations', *I Congresso Internazionale di Studi Fenici e Punici (1970)*, 1983, pp. 157–163.

Moscati, S. *Italia punica* (Milán, 1986).

Pesce, G. *Sardegna punica* (Cagliari, 1961).

Tore, G. 'Notiziario archeologico (Pani Loriga)', *Studi Sardi* XXIII, 1973–74, pp. 3–17.

Tronchetti, C. *I sardi* (Milano, 1988).

Tusa, V. 'La presenza fenicio–punica in Sicilia', in H. G. Niemeyer (ed.), *Phönizier im Westen* 1982, pp. 95–108.

'La Sicilia fenicio–punica: stato attuale delle ricerche e degli studi e prospettive per il futuro', *I Congresso Internazionale di Studi Fenici e Punici (1979)*, 1983, pp. 187–197.

Various authors, 'Società e cultura in Sardegna nei periodi Orientalizzante e arcaico', *Atti del I Convegno di Studi 'Un millennio di relazioni tra la Sardegna e i Paesi del Mediterraneo'*, (1985), (Cagliari, 1986).

Whitaker, J. I. S. *Motya. A phoenician colony in Sicily* (London, 1921).

The 'tophet'

Amadasi Guzzo, M. G. 'La documentazione epigrafica del tofet de Mozia e il problema del sacrificio molk', *Studia Phoenicia* IV, 1986, pp. 189–206.

Acquaro, E. 'Tharros-V: Lo scavo del 1978', *Rivista di Studi Fenici* VII, 1979, pp. 48–59.

Barnett, R. D. *Passing children through the fire of Moloch, Illustrations of Old Testament History*, pp. 37–38 (London, 1968).

Benichou-Safar, H. 'A propos des ossements humains du tophet de Carthage', *Rivista di Studi Fenici* 9, 1981, pp. 5–9.

Bondi, S. F. 'Per una riconsiderazione del tofet', *Egitto e Vicino Oriente* II, 1979, pp. 139–150.

Day, J. *Molech. A god of human sacrifice in the Old Testament* (Cambridge University Press, Avon, 1989).

Eissfeldt, O. *Molk als Opferbegriff im Punischen und hebräichen und das Ende des Gottes Moloch* (Halle, 1935).

Fedele, G. 'Tharros: Anthropology of the tophet and Paleoecology of a punic Town', *I Congresso Internazionale di Studi Fenici e Punici (1979)*, 1983, pp. 637–649.

Green, A. R. W. *The Role of Human Sacrifice in the Ancient Near East* (The American Schools of Oriental Research, Missoula, Montana, 1975).

Grotanelli, G. 'Encore un regard sur les bûchers d'Amilcar et d'Elissa', *I Congresso Internazionale di Studi Fenici e Punici (1979)*, 1983, pp. 437–441.

Hennessy, J. B. 'Thirteenth Century B.C. Temple of human sacrifice at Amman', *Studia Phoenicia* III, 1985, pp. 85–104.

Moscati, S. 'Il sacrificio dei fanciulli', *Rendiconti della Pontificia Accademia Romana di Archeologia*, XXXVIII, 1965–66, pp. 1–8.

'Baitylos', *Rendic. Accademia Nazionale dei Lincei*, Serie VIII, vol. XXXVI, 1982, pp. 101–105.

'Il sacrificio punico dei fanciulli: realtà o invenzione?', *Accademia Nazionale dei Lincei*, Quaderno no. 261, pp. 3–15 (Roma, 1987).

Picard, G. Ch. *Les religions de l'Afrique antique* (París, 1954).

Picard, G. 'Les représentations du sacrifice Molk sur les ex-voto de Carthage', *Karthago* XVII, 1976, pp. 67–138.

'Les sacrifices d'enfants à Carthage', *Les Dossiers Archéologie* 69, 1982–83, pp. 18–27.

Simonetti, S. 'Sacrifici umani e uccisioni rituali nel mondo fenicio–punico. Il contributo della fonti litterarie classiche', *Rivista di Studi Fenici* XI, 1983, pp. 91–111.

Smith, M. 'A Note on Burning Babies', *Journal of the American Oriental Society*, 95, 1975, pp. 477–479.

Stager, L. G., Wolff, S. R. 'Child sacrifice at Carthage. Religious rite or population control?', *Biblical Archaeology Review* X, 1984, pp. 31–51.

De Vaux, R. *Les sacrifices de l'Ancien Testament* (París, 1964).

Weinfeld, M. 'The worship of Molech and of the Queen of Heaven and its Background', *Ugarit Forschungen* 4, 1972, pp. 133–154.

Xella, P. 'Un testo ugaritico recente e il sacrificio dei primi nati', *Rivista di Studi Fenici* VI, 1978, pp. 127–136.

9 THE COLONIES OF THE FAR WEST: GADIR AND THE SILVER TRADE

Gadir and its bay

Blanco Freijeiro, A. 'El capitel de Cádiz', *Zephyrus* 11, 1960, pp. 157–159.

Blanco, A. and Corzo R. 'Der neue anthropoide Sarkophag von Cádiz', *Madrider Mitteilungen* 22, 1981, pp. 236–243.

Bunnens, G. 'Le rôle de Gadès dans l'implantation phénicienne en Espagne', *Aulia Orientalis* 4, 1986, pp. 187–192.

Corzo, R. 'Paleotopografía de la bahía gaditana', *Gades* 5, 1980 pp. 5–14.

'Cadíz y la arqueología fenicia', *Anales de la Real Academia de Bellas Artes de Cádiz* 1, 1983, pp. 5–29.

'Panorama arqueológico de la ciudad de Cádiz', *Primeras Jornadas de Arqueología de las Ciudades Actuales*, pp. 75–79 (Zaragoza, 1983).

Escacena, J. L. 'Gadir', *Aula Orientalis* 3, 1985, pp. 39–58.

Gavala Laborde, J. *El origen de las islas gaditanas* (Cádiz, 1971).

Gamer-Wallert, I. 'Die Hieroglyphyeninschrift auf dem Alabastergefäss in Puerto de Santa María', *Habis*, 1976, pp. 223–228.

Garcia Bellido, A. *Fenicios y cartagineses en Occidente* (Madrid, 1942).

'Iocosae Gades', *Boletín de la Real Academia de la Historia*, CXXIX, 1951, pp. 73–122.

'Algunas novedades sobre la arquelogía púnico–tartessia', *Archivo Español de Arqueología* 43, 1970, pp. 3–49.

'El mundo de las colonizaciones', in Menendez Pidal, R. (ed.), *Historia de España I:* 2, (3a. ed.), pp. 281–680 (Madrid, 1975).

Lipinski, E. 'Vestiges phéniciens d'Andalousie', *Orientalia Lovaniensia Periodica* 15, pp. 81–132 (Leuven, 1984).

Menanteau, L. 'Les anciens étiers de la rive gauche des marismes du Guadalquivir', *Mélanges de la Casa de Vélazquez* 14, 1978, pp. 35–72.

Moscati, S. 'Tra Tiro e Cadice', *Studia Punica* 3 (Roma, 1989).

Pellicer, M. 'Yacimientos orientalizantes del Bajo Guadalquivir', *I Congresso Internazionale di Studi Fenici e Punici (1979)*, pp. 825–836 (Roma, 1983).

Peman, C. *El pasaje tartésico de Avieno*, Consejo Superior de Investigaciones Científicas (Madrid, 1941).

El capitel de tipo protojónico de Cádiz', *Archivo Español de Arqueología* 32. 1959, pp. 58–70.

Ponce Cordones, F. 'Consideraciones en torno a la ubicación del Cádiz fenicio', *Suplemento Diario de Cádiz*, 12 diciembre 1976.

Ramirez Delgado, J. R. *Los primitivos núcleos de asentamiento en la ciudad de Cádiz* (Cádiz, 1982).

Ruiz Mata, D. 'Las cerámics fenicias del Castillo de Doña Blanca (Puerto de Santa María, Cádiz)', *Aula Orientalis* 3, 1985, pp. 241–263.

'Castillo de Doña Blanca (Puerto de Santa María, Cádiz)', *Madrider Mitteilungen* 27, 1986, pp. 87–115.

The temple of Melqart

Blanco Freijeiro, A. 'Los nuevos bronces de Sancti Petri', *Boletín de la Real Academia de la Historia*, CLXXXII, 2, 1985, pp. 207–216.

Garcia Bellido, A. 'Hercules Gaditanus', *Archivo Español de Arqueología* 36, 1964, pp. 70–153.

Rebuffat. R. 'Les phéniciens à Rome', *Mélanges d'Archéologie et d'Histoire de l'Ecole Française de Rome*, LXXVIII, 1966, pp. 7–48.

Täckholm, U. 'Tarsis, Tartessos und die Säulen des Herakles', *Opuscula Romana* V, pp. 143–200 (Lund, 1965).

Tsirkin, J. B. 'The Labours, Death and Resurrection of Melqart as depicted on the Gates of the Gades Herakleion', *Rivista di Studi Fenici* IX, 1981, pp. 21–27.

Van Berchem, D. 'Hercule–Melqart à l'Ara Maxima', *Rendiconti della Pontificia Accademia Romana di Archeologia*, Serie III, vol. XXXII, 1959–60, pp. 61–68.

'Sanctuaires d'Hercules – Melqart. Contribution à l'étude de l'expansion phénicienne en Méditerranée', *Syria* XLIV, 1967, pp. 73–109 and 307–336.

Metallurgy and the silver trade

Barnett, R. D. 'Phoenician and Punic Arts and Handicrafts. Some reflections and notes', *I Congresso Internazionale di Studi Fenici e Punici (1979)*, 1983, pp. 19–26.

Blanco, A., Luzon, J. M. and Ruiz Mata, D. *Excavaciones arqueológicas en el Cerro Salomón (Ríotinto, Huelva)*, Universidad de Sevilla, 1970.

Blanco, A. and Rothenberg, B. *Exploración arqueometalúrgica de Huelva* (Barcelona, 1981).

Fernandez Jurado, J. 'Economía tartésica: minería metalurgia', *Huelva en su Historia*, Colegio Universitario de la Rábida, pp. 149–170 (Sevilla, 1986).

Ruiz Mata, D. 'El poblado metalúrgico de época tartésica de San Bartolomé (Almonte, Huelva)', *Madrider Mitteilungen* 22, 1981, pp. 150–170.

Ruiz Mata, D. and Fernandez Jurado, J. *El yacimiento metalúrgico de época tartésica de San Bartolomé de Almonte* (Huelva, 1986).

Snodgrass, A. M. 'Heavy freight in Archaic Greece', in Garnsey, P., Hopkins, K. and Whittaker C. R. (eds.), *Trade in Ancient Economy*, pp. 16–26 (London, 1983).

Wheeler, T. S., Muhly, J. D. and Haddin, R. 'Mediterranean Trade in Copper and Tin in the Late Bronze Age', *Annali dell'Istituto Italiano di Numismatica* 26, 1979, pp. 139–150.

Trade with Tartessos

Almagro Gorbea, M. *El Bronce Final y el período Orientalizante en Extremadura* (Madrid, 1977).

Aubet, M. E. 'Zur Problematik des orientalisierenden Horizontes auf der Iberischen Halbinsel', in Niemeyer, H. G. (ed.), *Phönizier im Westen*, pp. 309–335, (traducción castellana: *Pyrenae* 13–14, 1977–78, pp. 81–107) (Mainz, 1982).

La necrópolis de Setefilla, en Lora del Río (Sevilla), Consejo Superior de Investigaciones Científicas (Barcelona, 1975).

Marfiles fenicios del Bajo Guadalquivir (Valladolid, 1978–1980).

'La aristocracia tartésica durante el período Orientalizante', *Opus* III, pp. 445–468 (Roma, 1984).

(ed.), *Tartessos, Arquelogía protohistória del Bajo Guadalquivir* (Sabadell, Barcelona, 1989).

Barnett, R. D. 'Phoenicia and the Ivory Trade', *Archaeology* 9: 2, 1956, pp. 87–97.

Belen, M., Fernandez Miranda, M. and Garrido, J. P. 'Los origenes de Huelva', *Huelva Arqueológica* III, 1977.

Blanco Freijeiro, A. 'Orientalia', *Archivo Español de Arqueologia*, XXIX, 1956, pp. 3–51.

Blazquez, J. M. *Tartessos y los orígenes de la colonización fenicia en Occidente* (Salamanca, 1975).

Garrido, P. J. and Orta, E. M. *Excavaciones en la necrópolis de "La Joya"*, *Huelva*, Excavaciones Arqueológicas en España 96 (Madrid, 1978).

Maluquer, J. *Tartessos* (Barcelona, 1970).

Mata Carriazo, J. *Tartessos y el Carambolo* (Madrid, 1973).

Pellicer, M. 'Las cerámicas del mundo fenicio en el Bajo Guadalquivir: evolución y cronología según el Cerro Macareno (Sevilla)', in Niemeyer, H. G. (ed.). *Phönizier im Westen*, 1982, pp. 371–403.

Pellicer, M., Escacena, J. L. and Bendala, M. *El Cerro Macareno*, Excavaciones Arqueológicas en España 124, 1983.

Pellicer, M. and Amores, F. 'Protohistoria de Carmona', *Noticiario Arqueológico Hispánico* 22, 1985, pp. 57–185.

Ruiz Galvez, M. 'Navegación y comercio entre el Atlántico y el Mediterraneo a fines de la Edad del Bronce', *Trabajos de Prehistoria* 43, 1986, pp. 9–41.

Schulten, A. *Tartessos* (Madrid, 1945).

Shefton, B. J. *Greeks and Greek Imports in the South of the Iberian Peninsula*, in Niemeyer, H. G. (ed.), *Phönizier im Western*, 1982, pp. 337–368.

The Phoenicians in the Atlantic and on the coast of Oran

Aubet, M. E. 'Contactos culturales entre el Bajo Guadalquivir y el noroeste de Africa durante los siglos VII y VI a.C.', in *Gli interscambi culturali e socio-economici fra l'Africa settentrionale e l'Europa mediterranea (Amalfi, 1983)*, pp. 109–144 (Napoli, 1986).

Gamer-Wallert, I. 'Der neue Skarabäus aus Alcacer do Sal', *Madrider Mitteilungen* 23, 1982, pp. 96–100.

Jodin, A. *Mogador. Comptoir phénicien du Maroc atlantique* (Tanger, 1966).

Ponsich, M. *Nécropoles phéniciennes de la région de Tanger* (Tanger, 1967).

'Territoires utiles du Maroc punique', in Niemeyer, H. G. (ed.), *Phönizier im Westen*, 1982, pp. 429–444.

Tarradell, M. *Marruecos púnico* (Tetúan, 1960).

Vuillemot, G. 'Fouilles puniques à Mersa Madakh', *Libyca* II, 1954, pp. 299–342.

'La nécropole punique du phare dans l'Ile Rachgoun (Oran)', *Libyca* III, 1955, pp. 7–62.

'Reconaissances aux échelles puniques d'Oranie', (Paris, 1965).

The colonies of the southeast

THE SETTLEMENTS

Arribas, A. and Arateaga, O. *El yacimiento fenicio de la desembocadura del río Guadalhorce (Málaga)* (Granada, 1975).

Aubet, M. E. 'Excavaciones en las Chorreras (Mezquitilla, Málaga)', *Pyrenae* 10, 1974, pp. 79–108.

Aubet, M. E., Maass-Lindemann, G. and Schubart, H. 'Chorreras', *Noticiario Arqueológico Hispánico* 6, 1979, pp. 91–134.

Aubet, M. E. 'Los fenicios en España, estado de la cuestión y perspectivas', *Aula Orientalis* 3 1985, pp. 9–30.

Aubet, M. E. and Carulla, N. 'El asentamiento fenicio del Cerro del Villar: arqueología y paleogeografía del Guadalhorce y de su hinterland', *Anuario Arqueológico de Andalucía* (Sevilla, 1986), pp. 425–430.

Molina, Fajardo, F. (ed.) *Almuñécar, Arqueología e Historia, I–III* (Granada, 1983–1986).

Niemeyer, H. G. 'Die phönizische Niederlassung Toscanos: eine Zwischenbilanz', in Niemeyer, H. G. (ed.), *Phönizier im Westen*, 1982, pp. 185–204 (trad. castellana, in *Huelva Arqueológica* VI, 1982, pp. 101–121).

'Die Phönizer und die Mittelmeerwelt im Zeitaler Homers', *Jahrbruch der Römisch-Germanischen Zentralmuseums* 31, 1984, pp. 3–94.

'El yacimiento de Toscanos: urbanística y función', *Aula Orientalis* 3, 1985, pp. 109–126.

'A la búsqueda de Mainake', *Habis*, 10–11, 1979–80, pp. 279–302.

Pellicer, M., Menanteau, L. and Rouillard, P. 'Para una metodología de localización de colonias fenicias en las costas ibéricas: el Cerro del Prado', *Habis* 8, 1977, pp. 217–251.

Schubart, H. 'Phönizische Niederlassungen an der Iberischen Südküste', in Niemeyer, H. G. (ed.), *Phönizier im Westen*, 1982, pp. 207–231 (trad. castellana: *Huelva Arquelógica* VI, 1982, pp. 71–92).

'Morro de Mezquitilla 1976', *Noticiario Arqueológico Hispánico* 6 1979, pp. 177–217.

'Morro de Mezquitilla 1982', *Noticiario Arqueológico Hispánico* 23 1985, pp. 143–174.

'El asentamiento fenicio del siglo VIII a.C. en el Morro de Mezquitilla (Algarrobo, Málaga)', *Aula Orientalis* 3 1985, pp. 59–83.

'Endbronzezeitliche und phönizische Siedlungsfunde von der Guadiaro-Mündung (Cádiz)', *Madrider Mitteilungen* 29 1988, pp. 132–165.

Warning-Treumann, B. 'Mainake, originally a Phoenician Place Name?' *Historia* 39, 2, 1980, pp. 186–189.

Suarez, A., Aguayo, P. and Lopez Castro, J. L. 'Abdera', *Madrider Mitteilungen* 30, 1989, pp. 135–150.

THE NECROPOLISES

Aubet, M. E., Czarnetzki, A., Dominguez, C. and Trelliso, L. *Sepulturas fenicias en Lagos (Málaga)* (Sevilla, 1991).

Culican, W. 'Almuñécar, Assur and Phoenician Penetration of the Western Mediterranean', *Levant* II, 1970, pp. 28–36.

Debergh, J. 'La libation funéraire dans l'Occident punique', *I Congresso Internazionale di Studi Fenici e Punici (1979)*, 1983, pp. 757–762.

Gamer–Wallert. I' *Agyptische und ägyptisierende Funde von der Iberischen Halbinsel* (Wiesbaden, 1978).

Maass-Lindemann, G. 'Phönikische Grabformen des 7/6 Jahrhunderts v. Chr. im westlichen Mittelmeerraum', *Madrider Mitteilungen* 15, 1974, pp. 122–135.

'Toscanos 1971 und die importdatierte westphönikische Grabkeramik des 7/6 Jhs. v. Chr.', *Madrider Forschungen* 6:3, 1982.

Molina Fajardo, F. *Almuñécar en la antigüedad: la necrópolis fenicio–púnica de Puente de Noy*, 2 vols. (Granada, 1982–85).

Negueruela, I. 'Sobre la fecha de la necrópolis "Laurita" de Almuñécar', *Noticiario Arqueológico Hispánico* 22, 1985, pp. 193–210.

Pellicer, M., 'Excavaciones en la necrópolis púnica "Laurita" del Cerro de San Cristóbal (Almuñécar, Granada)', *Excavaciones Arqueológicas en España* (Madrid, 1962).

Schubart, M. and Niemeyer, H. G. 'Trayamar. Los hipogeos fenicios y el asentamiento en la desembocadura del río Algarrobo', *Excavaciones Arquelógicas en España* 90, 1976.

THE ECONOMY

Aubet, M. E. 'Note sull' economia degli insediamenti fenici del sud della Spagna', *Dialoghi di Archeologia*, 1987, in press.

Boessneck, J. (ed.) Tierknochenfunde von westphönizischen und phönizisch beeinflussten Ansiedlungen im südspanischen Küstengebiet, in *Studien über frühe Tierknochenfunde von der Iberischen Halbinsel* 4 (Munich, 1973).

Schüle, W. 'Los restos animales del poblado paleopúnico de Toscanos', in Schubart, H. Niemeyer, H. G. and Pellicer, M. *Toscanos 1964*, Excavaciones Arqueológicas en España 66, 1969, pp. 148–149.

Tsirkin, Y. B. 'Economy of the phoenician settlements in Spain', in Lipinski, E. (ed.), *State and Temple Economy in the Ancient Near East, II*, pp. 547–564 (Leuven, 1979).

Uerpmann, M. 'Archäologische Auswertung der Meeresmolluskenreste aus der westphönizischen Faktorei von Toscanos', *Madrider Mitteilungen* 13, 1972, pp. 164–171.

Von den Dreisch, A. and Boessneck, J. 'Osteologische Besonderheiten vom

Morro de Mezquitilla, Málaga', *Madrider Mitteilungen* 26, 1985, pp. 45–48.

Warning-Truemann, B. 'West-Phoenician Presence on the Iberian Peninsula', *The Ancient World* I: 1, pp. 15–32 (Chicago, 1978).

PHOENICIAN POTTERY

Culican, W. 'Quelques aperçus sur les ateliers phéniciens', *Syria* XLV, 1968, pp. 275–293.

'Phoenician oil bottles and tripod bowls', *Berytus* XIX, 1970, pp. 5–16.

'Sidonian bottles', Levant VII, 1975, pp. 145–150.

Bikai, P. M. 'The Late Phoenician Pottery Complex and Chronology', *Bulletin of the American Schools of Oriental Research*, 229, 1978, pp. 47–55.

Maass-Lindemann, G. 'Vasos fenicios de los siglos VIII–VI en España', *Aula Orientalis* 3, 1985, pp. 227–239.

Negueruela, I. 'Sobre le cerámica de engobe rojo en España', *Habis*, 1979–1980, pp. 335–359.

'Jarros de boca de seta y de boca trilobulada de cerámica de engobe rojo en la Península Ibérica,' *Homenaje a M. Almagro II*, pp. 259–279 (Madrid, 1983).

Ramon, J. 'Cuestiones de comercio fenicio: frascos fenicios de aceite perfumado en el Mediterráneo central y occidental', *Ampurias* 44, 1982, pp. 17–41.

Schubart, H. 'Westphönizische Teller?, *Rivista di studi Fenici* IV, 1976, pp. 179–196.

IBIZA AND THE SPANISH LEVANT

Arteaga, O. and Serna, M. R. 'Influjos fenicios en la región del Bajo Segura', *XIII Congresso Nacional de Arqueología*, pp. 737–750 (Zaragoza, 1975).

Fernandez, J. M., Gomez Bellard, C. and Gurrea, R. 'La première période de la colonisation punique à Ibiza', in Waldren, W. H., Chapman, R., Lenthwaite, J. and Kennard, R. C. (eds.) *Early Settlement in the Western Mediterranean Islands and the Peripheral Areas*, pp. 785–796 (Oxford, 1984).

Fernandez, J. M. 'Necrópolis del Puig del Molins (Ibiza): nuevas perspectivas', *Aula Orientalis* 3, 1985, pp. 149–175.

Gomez Bellard, C. *La colonización fenicia de Ibiza* (Madrid, 1990).

Gonzalez Prats, A. *Estudio arqueológico del poblamiento antiguo de la Sierra de Crevillente* (Alicante, 1983).

'Las importaciones fenicias en la Sierra de Crevillente (Alicante)', *Aula Orientalis* 4, 1986, pp. 279–302.

Ramon, J. 'Sobre els origens de la colonia fenicia d'Eivissa', *Rev. Eivissa* 12, 1981, pp. 24–31.

Tarradell, M. and Font, M. *Eivissa cartaginesa* (Barcelona, 1975).

The crisis in the sixth century BC

Aubet, M. E. 'La necrópolis de Villaricos en el ámbito del mundo púnico peninsular', *Homenaje a L. Siret*, pp. 612–624 (Sevilla, 1986).

Bosch Gimpera, P. 'Problemas de la historia fenicia en el extremo Occidente', *Zephyrus* III 1952, pp. 15–30.

Cabrera, P. and Olmos, R. 'Die Griechen in Huelva,' *Madrider Mitteilungen* 26, 1985, pp. 61–74.

Olmos, R. 'Los griegos en Tartesos: replanteamiento arquelógico-histórico del problema', *Homenaje a L. Siret*, pp. 584–600 (Sevilla, 1986).

Schubart, H. 'Jardín. Informe preliminar de 1976 en la necrópolis de los siglos VI–V a. C.', *Noticiario Arqueológico Hispánico* 6, 1979, pp. 153–157.

10 CONCLUDING THOUGHTS

Bisi, A. M. *L'espansione fenicia in Spagna, en "Fenici e arabi nel Mediterraneo"*, pp. 97–151 (Roma, 1983).

Bondi, S. F. 'Per una caratterizzazione dei centri occidentali nella più antica espansione fenicia', *Egitto e Vicino Oriente* VII, 1984, pp. 75–92.

Curtin, P. D. *Cross-cultural Trade in World History* (Cambridge, 1984).

Ferron, J. 'A propos de la civilisation phénicienne d'Occident', *Latomus* XXIX, 1970, pp. 1026–1037.

Frankenstein, S. 'The Phoenicians in the far West: a Function of Neo-Assyrian Imperialism', in Larsen, M. G. (ed.), *Power and Propaganda. A Symposium in Ancient Empires, Mesopotamia* 7, 1979, pp. 263–294.

Lepore, E. 'Problemi dell'organizzazione della chora coloniale', in Finley, M. (ed.), *Problèmes de la terre en Grèce ancienne*, pp. 15–147, (Paris, 1973).

Moscati, S. 'L'espansione fenicia nel Mediterraneo occidentale', in Neimeyer, H. G., (ed.), *Die Phönizier im Westen*, 1982, pp. 5–12.

'Tucidide e i fenici', *Rivista di Filogia e di Instruzione Classica*, 113, pp. 129–133 (Torino, 1985).

Niemeyer, H. G. 'Die Phönizier und die Mittelmeerwelt im Zeitalter Homers', *Jahrbuch des Römisch–Germanischen Zentralmuseums* 31, 1984, pp. 3–94.

Tsirkin, J. B. 'Carthage and the problem of "polis"', *Rivista di Studi Fenici*, XIV, 1986, pp. 129–141.

Whittaker, C. R. 'The Western Phoenicians: colonisation and assimilation', *Proceedings of the Cambridge Philological Society*, 200, N. S., XX, 1974, pp. 58–79.

APPENDIX I PHOENICIAN IRON AGE ARCHAEOLOGY

Amiran, R. *Ancient Pottery of the Holy Land* (New Jersey, 1969).

Balensi, J. and Herrera, M. D. 'Hawam 1983–84, Rapport préliminaire', *Revue Biblique* 92, 1985, pp. 82–128.

Bienkowski, P. A. 'Some remarks on the practice of cremation in the Levant', *Levant* XIV, 1982, pp. 80–89.

Bikai, P. M. 'The Late Phoenician Pottery Complex and Chronology', *Bulletin of the American Schools of Oriental Research* 229, 1978, pp. 47–55.

Briend, J. and, Humbert, J. B. (eds.), *Tell Keisan (1971–76). Une cité phénicienne en Galilée*, Editions Universitaires, Fribourg (Suisse), Orbis Biblicus et Orientalis, Série Archaeologica 1 (Fribourg–Göttingen, 1980).

Crowfoot, J. W., Crowfoot, G. M. and Kenyon, K. M. *Samaria–Sebaste III: The Objects from Samaria*, Palestine Exploration Fund (London, 1957).

Culican, W. 'Phoenician oil bottles and tripod bowls', *Berytus* XIX, 1970, pp. 5–16.

Chapman, S. V. 'A Catalogue of Iron Age Pottery from the cemeteries of Khirbet Silm, Joya, Qrayé and Qasmieh of South Lebanon', *Berytus* 21, 1972, pp. 55–194.

Chehab, M. 'Découvertes phéniciennes au Liban', *I Congresso Internazionale di Studi Fenici e Punici (1979)*, pp. 165–172 (Roma, 1983).

Loud, G. *Megiddo II. Seasons of 1935–39*, The University of Chicago Oriental Institute Publications, vol. LXII, University of Chicago Press, 1948.

Maisler, B. 'The Excavations at Tell Qâsile, Preliminary Report', *Israel Exploration Journal*, 1, 1950–51, pp. 61–76, 125–140 and 194–218.

Mazar, A. 'Excavations at Tell Qâsile: 1973–1974', *Israel Exploration Journal* 25, 1975, pp. 211–225.

Prausnitz, W. 'Achzib', *Revue Biblique* LXIX, 1962, pp. 404–405.

'Akhziv', *Revue Biblique* LXXII, 1965, pp. 544–d547.

'Die Nekropolen von Akhziv und die Entwicklung der Keramik vom 10, bis zum 7. Jahrhundert v. Chr. in Akhziv, Samaria und Ashdod', in Niemeyer, H. G. (ed.), *Die Phönizier im Westen*, pp. 31–44 (Mainz, 1982).

Pritchard, J. B. *Recovering Sarepta, a Phoenician City* (New Jersey, 1978).

Saidah, R. 'Fouilles de Khaldé', *Bulletin du Musée de Beyrouth* 19, 1966, pp. 51–90.

'Chronique', *Bulletin du Musée de Beyrouth* XX, 1967, pp. 155–180.

Thalmann, J. P. 'Tell Arqa (Liban Nord). Campagnes I–III (1972–1974)', *Syria* LV, 1978, pp. 1–144.

'Tell Arqa 1978–79. Rapport provisoire', *Bulletin du Musée de Beyrouth* XXX, 1978, pp. 61–75.

Tuffnell, O. *Lachisch III (Tell ed-Duweir). The Iron Age*, The Welcome-Marston Archaeological Research Expedition to the Near East, vol. III (Oxford, 1953).

Tyre

Barnett, R. D. 'Phoenicia and the Ivory Trade', *Archaeology* 9, 2, 1956, pp. 87–97.

Bikai, P. M. *The Pottery of Tyre* (Warminster, 1978).

Bunnens, G. 'Tyr et la mer', *Studia Phoenicia* I, pp. 7–21 (Leuven, 1983).

Doumet, C. 'Les tombes IV et V de Rachidieh', *Annales d'Histoire et d'Archéologie*, 1, Université Saint-Joseph, pp. 89–148 (Beirut, 1982).

Gubel, E. 'Art in Tyre during the first and second Iron Age', *Studia Phoenicia* I–II, pp. 23–45 (Leuven, 1983).

Jidejian, N. *Tyre through the Ages* (Beirut, 1960).

Katzenstein, H. J. *The History of Tyre* (Jerusalem, 1973).

APPENDIX IV THE SETTLEMENTS OF THE CENTRAL
MEDITERRANEAN

Uitca, Malta, Sicily and Sardinia

Acquaro, E. *Scavi al tophet di Tharros* (C.N.R., Roma, 1989).

Baldacchino, J. G. 'Punic rock-tombs near Pawla, Malta', *Papers of the British School at Rome*, XIX, 1951, pp. 1–22.

'Rock-tomb at Ghajn Qajjet, near Rabat, Malta', *Papers of the British School at Rome*, XXI, 1953, pp. 32–41.

Bartoloni, P. and Tronchetti, C. *La necropoli di Nora* (Roma, 1981).

Ciasca, A. 'Insediamenti e cultura dei Fenici a Malta', in Niemeyer, H. G. (ed.), *Die Phönizier im Westen*, pp. 133–151 (Mainz, 1982).

Cintas, P. 'Deux campagnes de fouilles à Utique', *Karthago*, II, 1951, pp. 5–79.

'Nouvelles recherches à Utique', *Karthago*, V, 1954, pp. 89–161.

Culican, W. 'The Repertoire of Phoenician Pottery', in Niemeyer, H. G. (ed.), *Phönizier im Westen*, 1982, pp. 45–82.

Chiera, G. *Testimonianze su Nora* (Roma, 1978).

Pesce, G. *Nora. Guida agli scavi* (Cagliari, 1972).

Tharros (Cagliari, 1966).

Tore, G. and Gras, M. 'Di alcuni reperti dall'antica Bithia', *Mélanges de l'Ecole Française de Rome* 88, 1976, pp. 51–90.

Pitecusas and the Phoenicians

Bisi, A. M. 'Importazioni e imitazioni greco-geometriche nella più antica ceramica fenicia d'Occidente', *I Congresso Internazionale di Studi Fenici e Punici (1979)*, 1983, pp. 693–715.

'Imports and borrowings of Greek geometric pottery in the west Phoenician world', *Proceedings of the International Vase Symposium Amsterdam ("Ancient Greek and related Pottery")*, 1984, pp. 202–203.

Buchner, G. 'Die Beziehungen zwischen der euböischen Kolonie Pithekoussai auf der Insel Ischia und dem nordwest-semitischen Mittelmeerraum in der zweiten Hälften des 8. Jhs. v. Chr., in Niemeyer, H. G. (ed.) *Phönizier im Westen* 1982, pp. 277–298.

Coldstream, J. N. *Greek Geometric Pottery* (London, 1968).

Ridgway, D. *L'alba della Magna Grecia* (Milan, 1984).

Index